Europe in the Reformation

Peter J. Klassen

California State University
Fresno

PRENTICE-HALL, INC.,
Englewood Cliffs, New Jersey 07632

Library of Congress Cataloging in Publication Data

KLASSEN, PETER JAMES (date).
 Europe in the Reformation.

 Includes bibliographies and index.
 1. Reformation. 2. Europe—History—1492-1648.
I. Title.
BR305.2.K57   274   78-11023
ISBN 0-13-292136-7

Editorial/production supervision and interior
  design by Kim McNeily and Dianne Poonarian
Cover design by Richard Lo Monaco
Manufacturing buyer: Gordon Osbourne

To: NANCY, KENTON, KEVIN, AND BRYAN

Printed in the United States of America

10 9 8 7 6 5 4

Prentice-Hall International, Inc., *London*
Prentice-Hall of Australia Pty. Limited, *Sydney*
Prentice-Hall of Canada, Ltd., *Toronto*
Prentice-Hall of India Private Limited, *New Delhi*
Prentice-Hall of Japan, Inc., *Tokyo*
Prentice-Hall of Southeast Asia Pte. Ltd., *Singapore*
Whitehall Books Limited, *Wellington, New Zealand*

Contents

Preface

Few centuries other than our own hold a greater fascination for the student of history than does the sixteenth. This era of Catholic and Protestant reformation, when societies were convulsed by movements which profoundly influenced European civilization, was characterized by titanic struggle and sweeping reorganization, so that during this period a new Europe came into being. By 1600, a militant, dynamic, resolute society had discarded much of the easygoing optimism which had found expression in Erasmus' confident prediction of a golden age of peace. An amazing cast of outsize actors performed on the European stage—Charles V, Martin Luther, John Calvin, Suleiman the Magnificent, Elizabeth I, Pope Paul IV, Philip II—and the list could be easily expanded.

This book seeks to capture some of the drama of that robust age, and is designed to help students sense the vitality and turbulence of the developments of that age. It is hoped that portrayal of events and people will allow readers to form their own interpretations. This history grows directly out of my teaching experiences with students at several colleges and universities both in the United States and in Canada. These students have served as participants and as spectators, and their responses have encouraged me to proceed with this effort.

An author soon discovers that he is largely dependent upon the work and assistance of others. Here, surely, "no man is an island, entire of itself." Indeed, one of the most refreshing aspects of preparing this book has been the warm and supportive response received from various sectors of the academic community. Librarians, archivists, curators, fellow historians—all have placed me in their debt. I wish to express my gratitude especially to Dr. Dieter Graf of the Kupferstichkabinett in the Kunstmuseum, Duesseldorf; the late Prof. D. Dr. Oskar Thulin and his successor, Dipl. Theol. Michael Krille of the Lutherhalle, Wittenberg; the helpful librarians and assistants in the Library of Congress and at the University of California, Berkeley. I also wish to thank my colleagues Prof. Stephen Benko and Dr. Leonard Bathurst for assistance in obtaining several rare illustrations.

Numerous scholars have given invaluable and much appreciated advice and encouragement. They have repeatedly demonstrated that a considerate, generous spirit is no stranger in the halls of academe. I am indebted to Prof. Franklin Littell, Temple University; Prof. Roland Bainton, Yale (now retired); the late Prof. Robert Friedmann; Prof. Heiko Oberman, Tuebingen University. For reading much of the manuscript and for making valuable suggestions, I wish to thank Prof. Robert Walton, Wayne State University; Prof. Abraham Friesen, University of California, Santa Barbara; and especially Prof. Charles M. Nielsen, Colgate-Rochester Divinity School.

I am also deeply grateful to my secretarial assistants whose constant concern and thoughtful support have demonstrated that what might have been an onerous task became a labor of love.

Fresno, California
    On the 460th anniversary of the   PJK
    posting of the Ninety-five Theses

MAP CREDITS

Pages 2–3, 25, 122, 168, 239, 266, adapted from Brinton, Christopher and Wolff, *Civilization in the West*, 3rd ed. © 1973. Reprinted by permission of Prentice-Hall, Inc.

Pages 97, 247, from A. G. Dickens, *The Age of Humanism and Reformation: Europe in the Fourteenth, Fifteenth and Sixteenth Centuries,* © 1972, pp. 154, 230. Reprinted by permission of Prentice-Hall, Inc.

Page 282, adapted from Solomon Modell, *A History of the Western World*, Vol. 2, © 1974. Reprinted by permission of Prentice-Hall, Inc.

1

Europe at the Beginning of the 16th Century

The opening of the sixteenth century found Europe alive with new ideas, seething discontent, demands for reform, and a growing fascination with distant lands and cultures. In the world of ideas, the often critical thought of numerous humanists, now given unprecedented currency by the development of printing by movable cast metal type, created an especially volatile situation. Increasing numbers of advocates of church reform ''in head and members'' trumpeted their demands throughout the land. Economic changes, as in commerce and nascent capitalism, heralded a new era that would witness the transformation of Europe. In many areas, kings and territorial princes were consolidating their control over the state. With centralized political authority came increased power, so that traditional religious and social structures often came under sharp attack. Adaptation or elimination were often the only alternatives faced by elements of the old order. The century was characterized by challenge and change met by a determined effort to preserve traditional practices and values.

INSTITUTIONS IN COLLISION

As a robust society gave rebirth to new movements and structures, tensions frequently developed, for entrenched interest groups were seldom ready to fade away. The pace of change was by no means uniform throughout Europe, nor were directions necessarily similar. Usually, economic change was most dramatic in those areas very closely tied to commercial expansion. On the other hand, some of the century's most violent social upheavals were generated by the peasantry.

Economic Effects on the Peasant and Laborer

Europeans were still largely bound to agricultural pursuits. While most of the peasants in western Europe were no longer serfs, they were still largely subject to the desires of the local lord who owned the land and exacted various services

1

Europe in 1500

········ Boundary of the Empire

0 ———————————— 500
Miles

Atlantic Ocean

North Sea

NORWAY

S W
Se

DENMARK
• Copenhagen

IRELAND
Dublin •

SCOTLAND
• Edinburgh

ENGLAND
Bosworth Field •
London •
Canterbury •
Calais •

Amsterdam •
Leyden •
NETHERLANDS
Antwerp •
Cleves •
Münster •
Bremen •

BRANDENBURG
Berlin •
Torgau •
Wittenberg •
Leipzig •
SAXONY

Elbe R.
Oder R.

SILE

BRITTANY
Nantes •

Ivry •
Paris •
Vervins •
Verdun •
Metz •
Toul •

LUXEMBOURG
HESSE
Marburg •

THE EMPIRE
Speyer •
Prague •

BOHEMIA
MORA

La Rochelle •

FRANCE
Cognac •

AUVERGNE

FRANCHE COMTÉ
Basel •
Zurich •
SWITZERLAND
Geneva •

WÜRTTEMBERG
Augsburg •
Constance •
BAVARIA

Danube R.

AUSTRIA
Vienna •

TYROL
Trent •

STYRIA
CARINTHIA
CARNIOLA

SAVOY
MILAN
Pavia •
Padua •
Bologna •
Venice •

VENETIAN REPUBLIC

Valladolid •
Tordesillas •
NAVARRE
BASQUE PROV.
Avignon •
(to the popacy)
PROVENCE
Genoa •

PORTUGAL
SPAIN
Madrid •
Toledo •
Lisbon •
CASTILE
Guadalquivir R.
Tagus R.
Palos •
Seville •
Cadiz •

ARAGON

TUSCANY
Rome •
PAPAL STATES

NAPLES
Naples •

Adriatic

CORSICA
(to Genoa)

BALEARIC IS.

SARDINIA

Mediterranean Sea

(Tributary to Ottoman Empire)

B A R B A R Y   S T A T E S

SICILY

MALTA

2

TEUTONIC
ORDER

RUSSIA

LITHUANIA

POLAND

Moscow

Oka R.

W. Dvina R.

Volga R.

R U S S I A

55

60

50

Ural R.

Don R.

Volga R.

55

45

Caspian Sea

40

50

Kiev
U K R A I N E

Dnieper R.

KHANATE
OF CRIMEA

Dniester R.

MOLDAVIA

TRANSYLVANIA

Belgrade

WALLACHIA

Danube R.

B l a c k   S e a

MONTE-
NEGRO

O T O M A N   E M P I R E

Constantinople

Salonika

Lepanto
Athens

Tigris R.

35

Euphrates R.

PELOPONNESUS
(to Venice)

RHODES

CRETE

CYPRUS
(to Venice)

25

30

35

40

45

from his tenants. During much of the century, a phenomenon often referred to as the Price Revolution brought a sharp increase in the price of agricultural products. This inflationary spiral, accelerated by unprecedented growth in population and stimulated by the influx of American gold and silver, was felt most keenly by the town laborer and the country peasant. Population increases tended to depress wages, while rack-renting kept profits in the hands of the landlords. During the century, grain prices in England, France, and Spain at least quadrupled. Some critics of society were not content merely to pronounce the times "out of joint"; they confidently identified culprits and demanded remedial action. Thus, the crusading bishop Hugh Latimer denounced the landlords as "rent-raisers" and "step-lords." Thomas Muentzer, the revolutionary peasant leader, blamed the nobility. Sometimes, parliamentary bodies such as the German diet, dominated by territorial princes, charged the great trading companies like the Fuggers with unsettling the economy. Whatever the cause of economic distress, peasant and laborer in particular could not escape its impact.

Not infrequently, as in England and Spain, enclosure movements stimulated by the demand for wool exacerbated an already serious agrarian problem. As the price of wool rose, landlords enclosed land used in common, and turned arable land into more lucrative pasture land for huge flocks of sheep. Whole villages were depopulated as tenant farmers went to the city to find work. Although the cities were developing new industry, they were often unprepared to accommodate the influx of labor. The traditional craft guilds attempted to protect their own position by regulating the number of apprentices admitted to a trade, and by supervising the quality and price of their products. During much of the sixteenth century, capitalist entrepreneurs attempted to counter these guild reactions by moving their spinning and weaving out of the towns and into the countryside where hard pressed peasants were ever ready to supplement their income by this domestic system. In the cities, the new commercial patriciates struggled with the guilds. These conflicts often produced sharp divisions in which the balance of power might be held by the citizenry, the territorial prince, or an influential religious reformer.

Empire, State, and Free City

In many cities, commercial expansion was accompanied by growing political independence. The Holy Roman Empire, characterized by a traditionally weak central government, contained large numbers of virtually autonomous cities. These imperial free cities, found chiefly in the south, owed allegiance only to a distant and weak emperor, not to the local territorial prince. Similarly, many northern cities, members of the Hanseatic League, followed a largely independent course. Various Italian city republics such as Venice and Florence were essentially independent states in which the city controlled the neighboring countryside.

On the other hand, states with strong central governments—such as Spain, France, and England—were experiencing significant commercial growth but only a modicum of local political autonomy. If towns pressed too vigorously for greater political power, strong monarchs might well move resolutely to crush such aspirations. One example is provided by the attempt of several Castilian cities to curb royal taxation powers. Known as the revolt of the *comuneros* (1520–1521), this movement was an attempt to regain traditional town prerogatives and powers which had been steadily eroded by an aggressive monarchy. In fact, the king was accused of impoverishing the realm and rewarding foreigners. Although the revolt was basically urban, it attracted substantial support from agricultural laborers as well as from the clergy. A fiery Dominican charged that the king, who had just secured the imperial crown, had "bought the Empire" and reduced Spain to poverty. Royal officials were denounced and soon rich nobles were similarly castigated. As this movement, which had begun as a protest against royal policies, assumed the dimensions of a social revolution against crown and aristocracy, the nobles rallied to their king. Confronted by such formidable foes, the comuneros collapsed. King and noble proved more than a match for merchant, artisan, and laborer. Centralized authority was stronger than ever.

Central Role of Landed Nobility

As wealth and power gravitated toward the cities, the old landed aristocracy was left with anachronistic privilege to which it clung tenaciously. By 1560, France was ready officially to adopt the principle of *dérogeance*. By its terms, nobles who engaged in trade were deprived of their special privileges. Such a policy was designed to prevent rural wealth from being siphoned off to urban commercial ventures, and to exclude the nobility from commerce. The comparatively rapid urban expansion and commercial development of western Europe intensified the clash between nobility and towns.

In central and eastern Europe, the nobility increasingly dominated the scene, so that large numbers of a once predominantly free peasantry were depressed into serfdom. Development of towns lagged far behind that in western Europe, where commercial interests in centers such as Lyon, Augsburg, and Antwerp engaged the support of central governments and successfully resisted pressures from the old aristocracy. Frequently, a defensive aristocracy precipitated social crises. In southwestern Germany, for example, harsh policies of princes and prince-bishops often led to explosive peasant protest. In eastern Germany and Poland, the sixteenth century witnessed substantial growth in the wealth and power of the landed nobility. Weak rulers, such as those in Poland, Prussia, and Brandenburg, were so financially dependent upon the aristocracy that no effort was made to safeguard the interests of the peasants. Economic production in central and eastern Europe remained essentially agrarian. There was no strong bourgeois class to check the aspirations of the aristocracy, while the peasantry lacked organization and effective means of defending its interests.

Throughout the century, commerce in most areas of Europe expanded, and towns tended to become more prosperous. Yet the increased wealth was for the few. Fully half the population of a town lived in abject poverty; most wages were at the subsistence level. Frequent bread riots in the towns presented a tempting opportunity for an ambitious demagogue. Sometimes religious enthusiasm was coupled with economic and social protest. Ordinarily, the town laborers had virtually no political rights; neither the patricians nor the skilled craftsmen in the guilds wished to share power with the masses.

Other Unsettling Factors

Political tensions were not the only factors contributing to the development of unstable and often volatile conditions. Bad harvests at the end of the fifteenth century, capped by a virtually total crop failure in the Empire in 1500, drove some peasants to seek violent protection of their interests. The revolutionary *Bundschuh* movement, which surfaced repeatedly before the great upheaval of 1524–1525, constituted a daring peasant challenge to the power structure. Frequently, incessant local wars encouraged marauding bands to pillage the countryside. For the first time in the history of most of Europe, paid policemen were an accepted part of the social order.

Shifts in the patterns of commerce were effecting other profound changes in the economic scene. By the beginning of the sixteenth century, overseas discoveries were making a substantial impact on trade. Portuguese and Spanish exploration meant that the Atlantic would gradually displace the Mediterranean as the center of European commerce. One of the immediate results was the rapid growth of trading centers such as Antwerp. Here the Portuguese brought their acquired spices and other wares, and in exchange received cloth, copper, and other goods from central Europe. Antwerp also provided a vital link in supplying Baltic grain to the Iberian peninsula. Soon the city was the most important commercial and financial center of Europe. The shift to the Atlantic brought new influence and prosperity to other cities in the Low Countries, and to England and France as well. The traditional commercial supremacy of the Mediterranean was broken.

POPULAR TENSIONS AND FEARS

Added to the uncertainties of economic dislocation, war, and famine, were rampant superstition and disease. In the first few years of the sixteenth century, the plague ravaged many areas of Europe and decimated the populations of innumerable villages and towns. It was at this time also that syphilis became a widespread problem in Europe. Ignorance of its cause only heightened the fear of

WOODCUT: FOUR HORSEMEN OF THE APOCALYPSE, by Albrecht Duerer

Impending doom was a common theme in the literature and art of the time. Here Duerer serves notice that even emperor and priest cannot hope to withstand the dread onslaught of the four horsemen—death, famine, war, and pestilence.

this disease that in the early years of the century reached epidemic proportions. Contemporary literature and graphic art reflected the concerns of people who constantly walked with death. Religious festivals and village celebrations, such as weddings, afforded at least some escape from the harshness of an uncertain life and from the obsession of an age whose leitmotiv in innumerable woodcuts and engravings is best described as the "dance of death."

Another phenomenon that profoundly shaped sixteenth-century life was the widespread belief in witchcraft. The devil and his cohorts were always likely suspects in a calamity or misunderstood event, and trials of witches were commonplace. In this atmosphere, anything that might ameliorate the pangs of purgatory was welcomed. The gaining of indulgences (remission of temporal penalties for sin) become a major concern of the faithful. Through good works, such as veneration of relics, donations to the church, and the making of pilgrimages, the

PAINTING: THE WEDDING DANCE, by Pieter Bruegel the Elder

The artist has captured the robust, lusty style of living that characterized the peasantry. Festive occasions such as weddings provided a welcome relief from the arduous life of most of the populace.

Detroit Institute of Arts

faithful were assured special rewards. By the sixteenth century, it had become common simply to buy indulgences, thus securing the blessing of the church in return for monetary support. Simultaneously, the traffic in relics assumed remarkable dimensions, as princes and ecclesiastics tried to surpass each other in the accumulation of various revered objects. Some observers among the humanists caustically commented on the "miraculous multiplication" of relics. Usually, however, the intensity of popular piety was such as to foster credulity, not skepticism.

Background of Religious Malaise

The late Middle Ages had been times of deep distress in Christendom. Eastern Orthodoxy had retreated before the onslaught of Islam, and the fall of Constantinople in 1453 was symbolic, not merely of the collapse of Byzantine power, but also of the decline of Greek Christianity. At the same time, in central and western Europe, there was overwhelming evidence that a profound malaise had engulfed the western church.

Few events so dramatically illustrated the religious disarray as did the schism of 1378–1417. A double election to the papal throne precipitated a bitter factional struggle in which the nations of Europe recognized either one of two—and later three—claimants to the papacy. The division spurred on a vigorous conciliar[1] movement that posed a direct threat to papal authority. In the early fifteenth century, church leaders in council, first at Constance, then at Basel, asserted their supremacy over the pope. The ensuing struggle did much to demoralize and weaken the church, but the pope emerged triumphant. By the end of the century he was so secure that he could be more concerned about diplomatic maneuvering and political power than about the spiritual condition of the church.

The ecclesiastical hierarchy's involvement in secular affairs provided a ready opportunity for prelates who were more interested in economic and political developments than in religious values. There was ample evidence of decay in the monastic orders and of widespread theological confusion, not only in remote outposts of Christianity, but in the very heart of western Christendom itself. Rome, that "sink of all iniquity," as Lorenzo de' Medici described it to his son, the future Pope Leo X, was the despair of many devoted and alarmed sons of the church.

The late fifteenth century produced a mountain of literature that deplored and condemned religious deterioration. The very abundance of such writings, however, attests to the fact that many of the faithful were determined to seek remedial action. Girolamo Savonarola (1452–1498), the fiery popular preacher of Florence, was only one of the most noted in a long array of champions of reform. Even when he denounced the clergy as "the cause of all this evil,"[2] he nonetheless confidently asserted that the church would be renewed. His death at the stake, however, demonstrated that serious reform would meet resolute opposition.

Despite the turmoil within the church, it remained a vigorous and influential institution. The strident voices of reform were not a new phenomenon on the ecclesiastical scene. The medieval church could boast a long tradition of critics of papal and other clerical abuses. Repeatedly, movements within the church had attempted to revitalize what was denounced as stagnant spirituality; now in the fifteenth century, the demands for reform became ever more widespread and insistent and assumed stronger apocalyptic overtones: God was about to break into history to punish the wicked and to establish his kingdom. Such emphases are readily apparent in the highly popular *Reformatio Sigismundi* (1439), a

---

[1]Advocates of conciliarism held that a church council, even if opposed by the pope, should act to end the schism.

[2]John C. Olin, *The Catholic Reformation: Savonarola to Ignatius Loyola* (New York: Harper & Row, 1969), p. 6.

PAINTING: DEATH OF SAVONAROLA, 1498 (unknown artist)

A fiery and charismatic champion of reform, Savonarola aroused strong political and ecclesiastical opposition. A contemporary chronicler lamented that "the wicked were more powerful than the good," and therefore Savonarola could be sent to the stake. His biographer contended that, had his warnings been heeded, the Protestant Reformation would probably never have come.

Museo di San Marco, Florence; Photo Alinari

treatise that envisioned radical transformation of social and religious patterns. Other writings, such as the apocalyptic sermons of the renowned Johann Geiler of Kaisersberg, warned the masses in Strasbourg of impending divine intervention; and the broad reception accorded his warnings indicates that many people took him seriously. Later, when Luther appeared on the scene, he declared that the time of waiting for God to end the corruption of the church had come to an end. The reformer was confident that he was the divinely chosen prophet through whom God would terminate centuries of corruption in the church.[3]

[3]Heiko A. Oberman, *Forerunners of the Reformation* (New York: Holt, Rinehart & Winston, 1966), p. 18.

THE CHALLENGE OF HUMANISM
AND MYSTICISM

Frequently, critics of society in general and the church in particular optimistically proclaimed that ills could be cured through the dissemination of learning and the fostering of piety. One of the remarkable phenomena of the early sixteenth century was the close relationship between humanism and mysticism, both of which had a lasting impact on the Reformation.[4] Humanism had long established itself as a powerful intellectual and artistic force in parts of Europe. In Italy, it had scored remarkable triumphs long before the sixteenth century. Characterized by a passionate interest in Greek and Latin classics, and by a rather optimistic view of man and his capacities, humanism in the Italian Renaissance also had a profoundly religious dimension. Study of the Scriptures and the writings of the early church Fathers is amply demonstrated by the work of Lorenzo Valla, Gianozzo Manetti, and Marsilio Ficino. Similarly, when Pico della Mirandola published his Genesis commentary (1489), he was expressing a growing conviction that scholars should return to the sources (*ad fontes*), and in them find the key to renewal of the church and thus of society. Humanist schools, such as those established by Vittorino da Feltre in Mantua, and Guarino of Verona in Ferrara, stimulated interest in careful study of ancient authorities.

In the Empire and the Netherlands, humanism was even more profoundly influenced by religious factors. Lay movements such as the Brothers of the Common Life, founded by Gerard Groote (1340–1384) of Deventer, emphasized spiritual and educational concerns, and demonstrated the devout concern of the laity. This *devotio moderna* (modern devotion), while critical of many abuses in society, mounted a special attack on corruption and secularism in the church. It called for a Christianity that stressed piety and communion with God. Some of the most persuasive advocates of this position, such as Thomas à Kempis, illustrated both a means whereby Christianity might be renewed and the passionate devotion of these mystics. Few, if any, religious movements of the fifteenth century received so enthusiastic and widespread a reception as did the *devotio moderna*.

The Brothers of the Common Life established numerous centers in the Netherlands and in Germany. As the influence of this brotherhood, and others like it, extended into ever broader areas of religion and education, ecclesiastical leaders attempted to gain control of this religious zeal. Church dignitaries could not sit idly by and allow lay leadership to threaten traditional patterns. Religious fervor, either uncontrolled or directed by the laity, was viewed with apprehension by high church officials such as Cardinal Nicholas of Cusa. An added cause for concern was the tendency of mystics to stress direct communion with God and thereby potentially undermine the position of the priests. Sacerdotalism was thus being challenged by some of the most devout members of the church. The

[4]See Steven Ozment, *Mysticism and Dissent* (New Haven: Yale University Press, 1973).

11

mystics, with their emphasis upon piety and learning, illustrated the quiet religious vitality of significant elements of western Christendom.

HUMANISM IN THE EMPIRE

The fact that humanism combined elements of piety and learning greatly affected the intellectual climate of the time. In the Empire, the humanism of Rudolf Agricola (1444–1485) established a pattern that would be often emulated. For him, religious renewal was inconceivable apart from a revitalization of learning. Passionately devoted to the church, he spent his later years studying biblical literature and languages. His career was a blend of Italian humanism and the *devotio moderna*, for like so many of his contemporaries his education, begun in a school of the Brothers of the Common Life, included studies at various northern and Italian universities. An admiring Erasmus commented that Agricola could have been "first in Italy, had he not preferred Germany."[5] Agricola also anticipated the humanists' assault upon scholasticism. Although he warmly defended much of the content of the writings of the schoolmen, he deplored their techniques. He viewed speculative philosophy with suspicion, and instead championed pragmatic studies to improve the quality of life.

Cautious calls for intellectual and religious reform, coupled with a sturdy defense of the institutions of the church, appeared in the writings of Jacob Wimpfeling (1450–1528). His formative influence on German humanism was considerably less than his substantial output would suggest, for his writings, including more than one hundred titles, were largely traditional and lacked originality. As a university professor and cathedral preacher, he urged reform of society by adopting educational methods that would place greater stress on Christian virtues. In 1480, Wimpfeling produced *Stylpho*, the first drama created by German humanists. This highly moralistic comedy was designed to portray the tragic consequences of ignorance. For Wimpfeling, as for other humanists, right learning was the panacea for the troubles of society. Unlike Agricola, however, Wimpfeling was firmly committed both to scholasticism and papal authority in the reform of church and society.

Nonetheless, such sentiments did not deter him from adopting a staunchly pro-German stance. In his *Germania*, for example, he did not hesitate to appeal to flimsy or even inaccurate evidence in support of an intense patriotism. Yet amidst an emotional defense of German interests and angered denunciation of Italian and French corruption, he refused to compromise his attachment to the papacy. When Emperor Maximilian indicated his intention of adopting an independent national religious policy, similar to that reflected in the French Pragma-

---

[5]Quoted in Lewis Spitz, *The Religious Renaissance of the German Humanists* (Cambridge, Mass.: Harvard University Press, 1963), p. 20.

tic Sanction of Bourges,[6] Wimpfeling strongly objected—for him the church took precedence over the fatherland.

Another vigorously pro-German but less cautious humanist was the poet Conrad Celtis (1459–1508). His lyrics, designed to emulate Horace, echoed the themes of Italian humanists, while his lectures and writings attempted to arouse a fierce pride in the heritage of his homeland. Celtis gained a short-lived fame as poet laureate of the Empire in 1487, but his works were soon overshadowed by greater artists.

Few of the German humanists delighted and infuriated so many contempories as did Sebastian Brant (1457–1521). The acid wit of such works as his *Ship of Fools* left no societal institutions unscathed. Again, however, the clergy was the chief target of his ridicule, for "St. Peter's Ship," the church, was in danger of floundering because of careless, selfish, and incompetent bishops and priests. When this poem was published in 1494, it quickly became a best seller. Depicting the clergy, and especially the monks, as immoral, corrupt, useless adjuncts of society, was coming to be the vogue. Certainly reformers such as Luther were no more severe in condemning clerical abuses. In fact, Luther emphatically asserted that his greatest quarrel was not with the conduct of the clergy, but rather with the doctrine of the church.

Other stars in the galaxy of German humanists included Conrad Mutian (1471–1526), Willibald Pirckheimer (1480–1530), and Johann Reuchlin (1455–1522). Mutian, a product of the Deventer school of the Brothers of the Common Life, and a champion of humanistic causes at the University of Erfurt, did not allow his criticism of abuses within the church to weaken his allegiance to it. He, too, was highly optimistic about the wholesome effects of pursuing the new learning. Pirckheimer, steeped in the wisdom of ancient literature, much of which he translated, ridiculed the defenders of the scholastic tradition. Their sophistries, he argued, had brought discredit to theology. For him, the humanist cry *ad fontes* expressed the hope for improving conditions in society, and especially the church. When Luther's movement seemed to carry out the logical implications of Pirckheimer's thought, many Germans were puzzled by the humanist's refusal to go along with the reformer. But for Pirckheimer, as for many of his humanist colleagues, reform and schism were worlds apart.

A similar view was shared by the erudite Reuchlin. One of the most educated men of the day, and a foremost champion of Hebraic studies, he was denounced for his avid admiration of Hebrew thought. Johann Pfefferkorn (1469–1522), a convert to Catholicism from Judaism, in his zeal to eradicate any vestiges of Judaism from Christianity, vigorously denounced Reuchlin's praise of Hebrew literature. The controversy gained notoriety throughout German humanist circles

---

[6]The Pragmatic Sanction of Bourges (1438) emphatically asserted royal, rather than papal, control over the church in France.

as an aroused Reuchlin published an unrestrained denunciation of his opponent's obscurantism. The vigorous pamphlet, *Augenspiegel*, elicited responses from numerous universities, and eventually brought papal intervention. In 1520 Pope Leo condemned Reuchlin's treatise, but by then the controversy had embroiled a wide array of literary warriors. To many of Reuchlin's contemporaries, his struggle personified the conflict between obscurantist scholasticism and humanist culture.

Foremost among the literary missives sent to defend Reuchlin and destroy the strongholds of ignorance and superstition was the *Letters of Obscure Men*. Created at least in part by a volatile humanist, Ulrich von Hutten (1488–1523), the literary work ridiculed Reuchlin's opponents by portraying them as buffoons and ignoramuses. Satire and invective, sarcasm and exaggeration were used to discredit those whom Hutten regarded as reactionary simpletons. Other writings also served to establish Hutten as a humanist of note. His stinging ridicule depicted the pope as a grasping, violent, false shepherd rapidly bringing Christendom to its ruin. Like many of his countrymen, he alleged that the papacy and corrupt clerics were largely responsible for the problems of the god-fearing Germans. Hutten's humanism took on a revolutionary guise, so that by 1520, in a letter denouncing Leo X, he urged his fellow countrymen to break the chains of papal servitude. Such iconoclastic outbursts caused many humanists to shrink back and call for moderation, for reform that led to heresy and schism was worse than no reform at all.

The English Humanists

In few countries was humanism as profoundly religious as in England. Here its greatest champions determined to use the new learning to make the old church better. Early champions of humanism were strongly influenced by intellectual currents in Italy and attempted to reform English education according to approaches then current in various Italian universities. Men such as William Grocyn (1446–1519) and Thomas Linacre (1460–1524) combined study at Oxford with study at Italian centers. When they returned to their homeland, they enthusiastically encouraged the study of classical languages and literature. Traditional scholastic methods were sharply attacked. The Venetian printer Aldus, having received some translations from the Greek by Linacre, delightedly noted that Britain had become the home of "learned eloquence."[7]

An even more powerful impact on English humanism was exerted by John Colet (1467–1519). While Colet was far more concerned with revitalizing Christianity than with encouraging strictly humanist endeavors, his efforts provided a powerful impetus for classical studies. The learned Erasmus of Rotterdam commented that when Colet spoke, it seemed as though Plato were alive again. Colet's studies in Italy were strongly influenced by Marsilio Ficino and Pico

---

[7]P. S. Allen, *The Age of Erasmus*(Oxford: Clarendon, 1914), p. 253.

della Mirandola. Upon his return to England, Colet rejected the traditional scholastic approach. His lectures stressed the necessity of mastering Greek and examining the sources of Christianity rather than analyzing commentaries. At Oxford, his lectures on St. Paul's letter to the Romans aroused great interest and attracted a large hearing, as he successfully combined historical and philological knowledge to illuminate the life of the early church. While using the approach of the Italian humanists, he deplored their frequent preoccupation with what he regarded as pagan antiquity.

Like many of his contemporaries, Colet was very optimistic about the potential results of education. In 1505, he was made dean of St. Paul's, and soon thereafter he devoted much of his own fortune to the founding of a school attached to the cathedral. As dean, and as a foremost educator, he was able to inspire others to share his ideals for education. Both Oxford and Cambridge felt the impact as new foundations were established to further the cause of humanistic learning. All the while, Colet championed rigorous reform in a church that he said had "become foul and deformed."[8] Various ills such as simony, greed of clerics, and persistent war brought his eloquent denunciation. Religious devotion and classical studies he regarded as natural allies; neither was adequate without the other.

The ideals of Colet found a vigorous champion in Thomas More (1478–1535). Unlike many of his humanist friends, More was a layman; nonetheless, he was greatly interested in religious issues. Reared in the household of Cardinal Morton in London, he studied Greek and Latin, then went to Oxford and the Inns of Court to prepare for the legal profession. In his travels and studies, he made the acquaintance of numerous humanists and formed an especially close friendship with Erasmus. He staunchly supported the new learning against the conservative scholastics who, as More charged, wasted their efforts in the discussion of "petty and meretricious questions."[9]

More's criticism of the shortcomings of his society included social problems as well. The *Utopia* outlined More's conception of a just society in which the common good took precedence over individual desires. More viewed his world as having been corrupted by pride and selfishness; to alleviate this problem, *Utopia* envisioned the creation of a community of people in which private property and an economy controlled by money were abolished. Social dislocation, caused by enclosure of lands previously used by the villagers, was strongly deplored. Similarly, More's literary masterpiece criticized the Draconian laws of the day, and decried the ready resort to violence, whether between nations or individual citizens. Like Colet, More believed that education, and especially humanistic learning, could help man rise above the problems of a corrupt society.

[8]Olin, *The Catholic Reformation,* p. 31. Colet made the statement at the convocation of the clergy of the archiepiscopal province of Canterbury in 1512.

[9]Myron P. Gilmore, *The World of Humanism* (New York: Harper & Row, A Harper Torchbook, 1962), p. 214.

French Humanism

At the beginning of the sixteenth century, France, like other European countries, was the scene of various efforts to combine humanistic scholarship and societal reform. Early humanists, such as the renowned classical scholar Guillaume Budé (1467–1540), drew much of their inspiration from the Italians. As a royal secretary and master of Greek and Latin, he persuaded Francis I to endow an academy that later became the Collège de France. Strong resentment from the University of Paris, still a stronghold of scholasticism, did not prevent royal support for humanistic studies in the new college. Budé, convinced that learning provided the key to reform of society, edited classical writings and urged his contemporaries to study the wisdom of the ancients. In his treatise *On the Education of a Prince*, he defended the view that an education in Greek and Latin was superb preparation for the duties of kingship.

France found an even more vigorous champion of reform and humanism in Jacques Lefèvre d'Étaples (1455–1536). After studying at the University of Paris, he continued his education in Italy, but soon returned to Paris and lectured on Aristotle. He edited and published some of the writings of Aristotle and other authors, but found that "divine" studies exuded "a perfume whose sweetness nothing on this earth could equal";[10] neglect of these studies, he insisted, had brought ruin to the monasteries, death to piety, and extinction to true religion. Lefèvre resolved to rectify this by concentrating on biblical studies. The church was to be reformed by abandoning arid scholasticism and embracing a theology drawn directly from the Scriptures. Anticipating some of the later emphases of Luther, Lefèvre declared, "We must affirm about God nothing except that which the Scriptures declare."[11] Similarly, he developed a doctrine of justification by faith. He advocated sweeping religious reform by the church, and hoped that his literary efforts, for example, his commentary on the letters of St. Paul, would help to effect such a reformation. Passionately devoted to the church and profoundly influenced by mystic religious experiences, Lefèvre never let his criticism of ecclesiastical abuse become rebellion. Indeed he regretted that some of his contemporary companions in criticism seemed not to share his devotion to the church. Lefèvre was not as optimistic in his evaluation of human nature as were many of his humanist friends. While he championed education, he also stressed the need for mystical, divine illumination.

The ideals of Lefèvre were staunchly supported by a group of humanist reformers who enjoyed the favor and support of Marguerite of Navarre, sister to King Francis I. Marguerite embodied the ideals of both Renaissance and reform; the bawdy tales in her *Heptameron* reflected the unrestrained enjoyment of pleasure at the French court, while her *Mirror of the Sinful Soul* revealed a

---

[10]H. Daniel-Rops, *The Protestant Reformation*, trans. A. Butler (New York: Image Books, 1963), p. 120.

[11]Gilmore, *The World of Humanism*, p. 217.

spiritual unease which called for reform. Marguerite's religious concerns found an avid champion in Guillaume Briçonnet (1470–1533), bishop of Meaux. As a leader in religious and humanistic studies, the bishop resolved to reform religious practices by encouraging education. Scriptural passages, in the vernacular, were distributed to the masses. Greater knowledge of the Scriptures, the bishop insisted, would raise the level of religious devotion. Numerous preachers, among them the bishop's friend and former teacher Lefèvre, were invited to urge reform throughout the diocese. Included among the reformers was Guillaume Farel, later to be Calvin's associate in Geneva.

Briçonnet's reform program coincided with disturbing events in Wittenberg, so it was not surprising that his efforts should be viewed with suspicion. In 1523, Lefèvre published his French translation of the New Testament. By then, he and his associates were under attack by the Sorbonne. The Meaux group was charged with holding to the Lutheran heresy. Lefèvre temporarily fled to Strasbourg, while the bishop took pains to eradicate anything that tended toward Lutheranism. Both protested their staunch allegiance to the church, and insisted that their goal was one of reform only. In the tense and uncertain atmosphere of the time, even this tentative move to revitalize the French church through the new learning, personal piety, and ecclesiastical reform was stymied. The specter of heresy and schism cast a numbing fear over the would-be reformers.

Humanism in Spain

The new learning gained vigorous and effective support in Spain. Here Cardinal Jimenes de Cisneros (1436–1517), archbishop of Toledo and confessor of Queen Isabella, guided humanist efforts so that they could become a powerful force in ecclesiastical reform. Later, as the rise of Protestantism rocked much of Europe, Spain remained a virtually impregnable bastion of Catholicism. In no small measure was this adherence to the traditional faith the result of the efforts of the indomitable cardinal.

As primate of Spain, Jimenes embarked upon a program designed to bring sweeping reform to the Spanish church. Religious houses were brought into strict conformity with the rules of their orders. As a Franciscan, Jimenes now championed the strict rule of the Observants and endeavored to impose the same standards on the later Conventuals. Other orders, such as the Dominicans and the Benedictines, were also reformed.

Jimenes was convinced that education was an indispensable tool in the renewal of the church. He established the University of Alcalá so that ecclesiastical leaders could be thoroughly trained in an institution that was sympathetic to his goals. The new university was from the first a center of humanism. The study of Latin, Greek, and Hebrew flourished under renowned scholars, one of whose most remarkable achievements was the Complutensian Polyglot. This multilingual version of the Scriptures presented Old and New Testaments in the original

languages as well as in the Latin translation of the Vulgate. The New Testament
was printed in 1514, although it did not receive papal approval for publication
until 1520; the Old Testament was completed in 1522. It should be noted that, for
all of his dedication to scholarship, Jimenes was concerned not with a critical
examination of the biblical text, but with the buttressing of the authority of the
Latin Vulgate. Education was to serve the church, not undermine it. Thus the
cardinal insisted that the parallel-column versions of the Old Testament should
have Latin holding the place of honor in the middle. It was flanked by the
Hebrew and the Septuagint (the Greek translation of the Old Testament), Jimenes
commented, ''like the position of Christ on the cross between two thieves.''[12]

In his determination to purify and strengthen the church, Jimenes left little to
chance. As grand inquisitor, he used the Inquisition to ensure the full implementation of his rigorous policies. This institution enabled him to scrutinize and
supervise the life of the whole Spanish church, and to use the authority of the
monarchy to compel conformity to his ideals.

ERASMUS

It was in the person of Desiderius Erasmus of Rotterdam that the attempt to
use the new learning for the enrichment and more complete recovery of Christian
tradition reached its zenith. His scholarship, admired throughout Europe, applied
historical and philological principles to accepted religious patterns and found
them woefully inadequate. Erudition and criticism combined to challenge an old
order that had too often become identified with obscurantism and irrelevance.
Contemporaries were not always sure that the renowned scholar's sarcasm and
massive learning were indeed urging reform rather than revolution, yet Erasmus
himself lamented schism when it came. His goal was to reform society through
education—and for him profitable study encompassed the wisdom of all the
illustrious men of the past. Christianity held no monopoly on the learning that
could ennoble man and transform society.

Erasmus, born probably in 1466 or 1469, was educated in the Netherlands at
the Deventer school of the Brothers of the Common Life. Subsequently, he
entered the Augustinian monastery at Steyn. Here he studied the works of various
humanists, and began to express his disgust with what he regarded as barbarous
monastic learning. By contrast, he professed his admiration for classical Latin
authors. He had begun an intellectual and literary battle that his pen would never
cease to wage.

Upon his ordination in 1492, Erasmus became a secretary to the bishop of
Cambrai. Three years later he began studies at the University of Paris, and
entered the College of Montaigu. Erasmus noted, however, that much of the
university was permeated by a stultifying emphasis upon the schoolmen. The
alert and observant student caustically commented that the theologians seemed

[12]*Ibid.*, p. 200.

WOODCUT: ERASMUS, by Albrecht Duerer

Many contemporaries shared Erasmus's belief that few weapons were as powerful as the pen. With his books at hand, the great humanist is portrayed as he gives substance to the Greek inscription: "His writings depict him better."

remarkably unaware of the new learning; instead they were content to expound at great length on obscure details of speculation. Impatient with his professors, Erasmus indulged his voracious appetite for reading and developed such a fondness for the ancients that he wondered if Seneca were not as good a Christian as St. Paul.

Erasmus soon resolved to continue his education by traveling and meeting various intellectual leaders. In 1499, he went to England and formed two especially important friendships. Both Colet and More left a deep impression on the sensitive Dutch scholar. Erasmus, for his part, was struck by the fact that two renowned scholars who shared his admiration of the ancient writers nonetheless retained their devotion to the church and its teachings.

Early in 1500, Erasmus was back in Paris. In the same year, he published his *Adages*, a collection of sayings from classical authors, together with his own comments. The work was immediately popular and went through numerous editions. Erasmus greatly expanded his first effort, and it became an important reference work. Despite this success, the rising scholar continued to be in financial straits, so that he was forced to engage in literary hackwork for wealthy clients. All the while, he continued his study of the Greek language, as well as the writings of classical authors. In 1503, he published his *Enchiridion militis Christiani*. This *Handbook of a Christian Soldier* discussed the qualities that constituted valid Christianity. Erasmus commented that it was more important to act in a spirit of love and concern than to observe fasts and penances. A simple, warm piety was declared to be far more significant than observance of formal ritual. This minimizing of outward observances came to have a profound influence on many who were attempting to restore the church to what they regarded as earlier purity. Some Erasmian admirers, such as the Spanish *illuminati*,[13] aroused suspicions of heresy with their emphasis on the inner character of Christianity.

Erasmus' deft pen was seldom so successful as when using satire to expose the foibles of the day. In *Praise of Folly*, written in 1509 but not published until 1511, the author was quickly established as a most engaging social critic whose telling gibes at vices and follies mirrored the sentiments of an age. Folly, personified as a naive and loquacious woman, serenely surveys the world about her and blithely expresses her evaluation of society. The satire, always clever, is sometimes so devastating and incisive that even artistic integrity suffers not a little. Erasmus reserves some of his sharpest barbs for those university professors who still debated questions no one was asking, and for ignorant, conceited monks who expected to merit entrance into heaven because they had been careful never to touch money unless they had on at least two pairs of gloves. Similarly, bishops, cardinals, and popes are subjected to scathing denunciation and depicted as the deadliest enemies of the church.

In his *Colloquies*, first published in 1522, Erasmus continued his analysis of societal problems. Intended at first for didactic instruction in Latin grammar, the work was repeatedly enlarged and revised until it became a vast commentary on the life of early sixteenth-century Europe. Once again, clergymen were the butt of ridicule and denunciation. Erasmus savagely denounced parental and ecclesiastical pressures to push children into monasteries, and deplored relic vendors who preyed on ignorant and superstitious masses. He noted with amazement the large supply of the Virgin's milk that had been preserved over the centuries, while he wryly commented that the relics of the cross would fill a ship. Some of the dialogues in the *Colloquies* heaped scorn on the much vaunted clerical celibacy; others depicted monks gathered as vultures around a deathbed, ready to derive maximal benefits from death. In contrast, Erasmus liked to depict the common folk as outwitting the clergy or the saints. One of the colloquies, the "Shipwreck," depicts a ship in danger of destruction, with the passengers outdoing each other in making vows to the saints. One bold soul promised a huge

---

[13]The *illuminati* emphasized a mystic, personal communion with God. They had little use for ceremonies and forms.

candle for St. Christopher, should his life be spared. When another passenger pointed out that such a vow would be beyond his means, the venturesome suppliant admitted his vow was a hoax to fool the saint. Once ashore, he would not give St. Christopher so much as a tallow candle.

The *Colloquies* repeatedly demonstrated Erasmus' sensitivity to social ills. For example, in one dialogue Erasmus deplored the practice of forcing women to marry against their will; in another, he called for higher standards for hygiene. A third dialogue restated a theme found in many of Erasmus' writings—the madness of war. The author caustically noted that each side always claimed to be on God's side. Few of the dialogues so vividly portray Erasmus as the devout, reforming humanist as the one in which occurs the remarkable request, "Holy Socrates, pray for us." For Erasmus, the noble heritage of classical civilization was in harmony with the ideals of Christianity.

Although some of his contemporaries were in doubt about his true intentions, Erasmus' designs were not to destroy the church, but to improve it, as well as the whole of society. With this objective in mind, he published in 1516 his Greek edition of the New Testament. Noting that the Vulgate Latin text had numerous textual errors, Erasmus set himself the task of producing as accurate an edition as possible. He used the best manuscripts available to him and produced a scholarly work that gained him wide acclaim, including a commendation from Pope Leo X. Significantly, this landmark of scholarship was greatly facilitated by the earlier work of men such as Lorenzo Valla. In the world of learning, Italian scholarship frequently provided the foundation which made northern achievements possible.

In his hope of using education to expand what he called the "philosophy of Christ," Erasmus prepared editions of the writings of the early church fathers, including Jerome, Cyprian, Augustine, Chrysostom, and Irenaeus. Erasmus was determined to use his erudition to divert theological interest from the medieval schoolmen to the works of these early divines.

Erasmus thus came to personify the aspirations of many of the northern humanists. He shared their enthusiasm for the culture of antiquity, especially Christian antiquity, and was optimistic about the effects of proper education. More importantly perhaps, he shared a growing dissatisfaction with many ecclesiastical practices. It was not surprising, therefore, that when Luther launched his attack on the papacy, many expected Erasmus to endorse the monk from Wittenberg. Indeed, Erasmus did at first show considerable sympathy for Luther's position. Even after Luther had been condemned, Erasmus declared that "should Luther go under, neither God nor man could longer endure the monks."[14] Yet, as the Lutheran revolt proceeded to divide western Christendom, Erasmus shrank back in dismay. He would have no part in "rending the seamless robe of Christ." Luther, for his part, denounced Erasmus as "an enemy of all

[14]Matthew Spinka, *Advocates of Reform* (Philadelphia: Westminster Press, 1953), p. 298.

religion, and especially an enemy and opponent of Christ.''[15] Erasmus, ever the champion of reform through education, could never accept reform through division. For him, corruption was preferable to schism.

Suggestions for Further Reading

Artz, F. B. *Renaissance Humanism, 1300–1550*. Kent, Ohio: Kent State University Press, 1966.

Bainton, Roland H. *Erasmus of Christendom*. New York: Scribner's, 1969.

Breen, Quirinus. *Christianity and Humanism*. Grand Rapids, Mich.: Eerdmans, 1967.

Bush, Douglas. *The Renaissance and English Humanism*. Toronto: University of Toronto Press, 1941.

Campbell, W. E. *Erasmus, Tyndale and More*. London: Eyre and Spottiswood, 1949.

Caspari, Fritz. *Humanism and the Social Order in Tudor England*. Chicago: University of Chicago Press, 1954.

*****Chambers, R. W.** *Thomas More*. Ann Arbor: University of Michigan Press, 1958.

Clark, James M. *The Great German Mystics*. Oxford: Blackwell, 1949.

Constello, W. T. *The Scholastic Curriculum at Early Seventeenth Century Cambridge*. Cambridge, Mass.: Harvard University Press, 1958.

Denieul-Cormier, Anne. *A Time of Glory: The Renaissance in France, 1488–1559*. Garden City, N.Y.: Doubleday, 1968.

Ferguson, Wallace K. *Europe in Transition*. Boston: Houghton Mifflin, 1962.

Gelder, Herman van. *The Two Reformations in the 16th Century: A Study of the Religious Aspects and Consequences of Renaissance and Humanism*. Translated by J. Finlay and A. Hanham. The Hague: M. Nijhoff, 1961.

Gilmore, Myron P. *The World of Humanism*. New York: Harper & Row, A Harper Torchbook, 1952.

Gilson, Etienne H. *History of Christian Philosophy in the Middle Ages*. New York: Random House, 1955.

Goldsmith, E. P. *The Printed Book of the Renaissance*. Cambridge, Mass.: Harvard University Press, 1950.

Grossman, Maria. *Humanism in Wittenberg 1485–1517*. Nieuwkoop: DeGraaf, 1975.

*****Harbison, E. Harris.** *The Christian Scholar in the Age of the Reformation*. New York: Scribner's, 1956.

Hay, Denys. *The Age of the Renaissance*. Englewood Cliffs, N. J.: Prentice-Hall, 1965.

---

[15]*Martin Luthers Werke, Tischreden* (Weimar: Hermann Boehlaus, 1921), VI: 252. Since 1883 almost 100 volumes have appeared in a critical edition of Luther's works. Hereafter this edition will be cited as *WA* (Weimarer Ausgabe).

*Indicates paperback edition.

*Holborn, Hajo, ed. *On the Eve of the Reformation:* "Letters of Obscure Men." Translated by F. G. Stokes. New York: Harper & Row, A Harper Torchbook, 1964.

*————. *Ulrich von Hutten and the German Reformation*. Translated by Roland Bainton. New York: Harper & Row, A Harper Torchbook, c. 1965.

Huizinga, Johan. *Erasmus of Rotterdam*. Translated by F. Hopman. London: Phaidon, 1953.

————. *The Waning of the Middle Ages*. Translated by F. Hopman. London: Edward Arnold, 1934.

Hyma, Albert. *The Brethren of the Common Life*. Grand Rapids, Mich.: Eerdmans, 1950.

Jayne, Sears R. *John Colet and Marsilio Ficino*. New York: Oxford University Press, 1963.

Kristeller, P. O. *The Classics and Renaissance Thought*. Cambridge, Mass.: Harvard University Press, 1955.

*Lortz, Joseph. *How the Reformation Came*. Translated by Otto Knab. New York: Herder and Herder, 1964.

MacFarlane, K. B. *John Wycliffe and the Beginnings of English Non-conformity*. London: English Universities Press, 1952.

Mattingly, Garrett. *Renaissance Diplomacy*. Boston: Houghton Mifflin, 1955.

Nieto, José C. *Juan de Valdés and the Origins of the Spanish and Italian Reformation*. Geneva: Droz, 1969.

Olin, John C., ed. *Luther, Erasmus, and the Reformation: A Catholic-Protestant Reappraisal*. New York: Fordham University Press, 1969.

————, ed. *Christian Humanism and the Reformation. Selected Writings of Erasmus*. New York: Fordham University Press, 1975.

Pastor, Ludwig von. *History of the Popes from the Close of the Middle Ages*. London: J. Hodges, 1891–1953.

Petry, Ray C. *Late Medieval Mysticism*. Philadelphia: Westminster Press, 1957.

*Phillips, M. *Erasmus and the Northern Renaissance*. New York: Collier Books, 1965.

Rice, E. F. *The Foundations of Early Modern Europe*. New York: Norton, 1970.

Ridolfi, Roberto. *The Life of Girolamo Savonarola*. Translated by Cecil Grayson. London: Routledge and Kegan Paul, 1959.

Spinka, Matthew. *Advocates of Reform, from Wyclif to Erasmus*. Philadelphia: Westminister Press, 1953.

Spitz, Lewis W. *Conrad Celtis, the German Arch-Humanist*. Cambridge, Mass.: Harvard University Press, 1957.

————. *The Religious Renaissance of the German Humanists*. Cambridge, Mass.: Harvard University Press, 1963.

Starkie, Walter F. *Grand Inquisitor, Being an Account of Cardinal Jimenes de Cisneros and His Times*. London: Hodder and Stoughton, 1940.

Weiss, Roberto. *Humanism in England During the Fifteenth Century*. 2d ed. Oxford: Blackwell, 1957.

2

Luther and Sola Fide

THE YOUNG LUTHER

For centuries, the voices of reform had reverberated throughout the church of Western Europe, and frequently powerful movements had arisen to carry out programs of reform. Yet the church had, in the end, always triumphed, sometimes by assimilating the new ideas, sometimes by crushing the proponents of drastic change. Council and crusade, inquisition and excommunication, reform and renewal, all had played their role in maintaining the church's position of inclusiveness and predominance. Now, early in the sixteenth century, the medieval pattern of containing reform was to be broken, for a personality of genius would attract so great a following that the traditional checks on reformers or heretics would prove unequal to the task. It was in Luther that a fortuitous set of external circumstances and a robust religious fervor coincided, and thus set in motion a revolution that broke the tradition of centuries.

Martin Luther was born on November 10, 1483, in the Saxon town of Eisleben, where, after having transformed the face of Europe and the character of much of Christianity, he would die on February 18, 1546. Luther's parents, Hans and Margaret, reared their son in an atmosphere of rigorous discipline, devout piety, and a generous dose of medieval superstition. In the year following Martin's birth, the family moved to Mansfeld in the heart of a copper-mining community. Here, the peasant-bred father became a member of a firm of copper miners, gradually emerging as a successful petty capitalist. The resulting association with bourgeois society would leave an indelible impression upon Martin, so that throughout his life, he tended to view society and its problems from the standpoint of the middle and upper classes. rather than from that of the peasantry. For him, social reform ought not to come from popular protest but from governmental paternalism. If there was to be a transformation of society, it would have to come through orderly and deliberate action, not through violence and destruction.

The Holy
Roman Empire

Seats of archbishops are underlined

DENMARK

POLAND

Vistula R.

Bremen

Elbe R.

BRANDENBURG

Warthe R.

Magdeburg

Weser R.

Rhine R.

G E R M A N Y

SAXONY

SILESIA

Cologne

NASSAU

Prague

BOHEMIA

Meuse R.

Mainz

PALATINATE

LUXEMBOURG

Trier

Moselle R.

Danube R.

AUSTRIA

FRANCE

STYRIA

HUNGARY

SWISS
CONFEDERATION

TYROL

CARINTHIA

Sava R.

Rhône R.

S A V O Y

M I L A N

VENETIAN REPUBLIC

Po R.

I T A L Y

0   100   200
Miles

Luther's father was determined that his son should have the best education available; accordingly, he willingly paid for Martin's early training at schools in Mansfeld, Magdeburg, and Eisenach. In 1501, Luther enrolled in what was then one of the most prestigious schools in Germany, the University of Erfurt, which had first opened its doors in 1392. Situated in the most important commercial center of Thuringia, the university proudly taught the *via moderna*, the Occamist response to Thomism. Here professors such as Trutvetter and Arnoldi ardently championed the anti-realist philosophy of William of Occam, the English Franciscan of the fourteenth century, and of his German disciple, Gabriel Biel. Luther was profoundly influenced by these attacks on the medieval schoolmen and came to recognize Occam as his "master." Thus, his later emphasis on the difference between faith and reason, and the fact that the truth of revelation must be accepted by faith alone, may be traced in part to these influences during his

25

formative years. His Erfurt experience also made him highly suspicious of the Thomistic attempt to achieve a delicate balancing of the roles of the human and the divine wills. In addition to pursuing his theological studies, Luther enjoyed reading Roman and Neo-Latin poets, and heard occasional special lectures on "the poets," although humanism did not gain a significant following in Erfurt until after Luther had completed his studies there.

In 1502, upon receiving the Bachelor of Arts degree, Luther became a teacher at the university. He began to instruct in grammar and logic, at the same time continuing his studies, so that in 1505 he was able to complete his examination for the Master of Arts degree. He ranked second in a class of seventeen, and for the occasion, the proud father presented Martin with an expensive edition of the *Corpus iuris civilis*, proof enough that parental ambition expected fulfillment in

ÆTERNA IPSA SVÆ MÆNTIS SIMVLACHRA LVTERVS
EXPRIMIT AT VVLTVS CERA LVCÆ OCCIDVOS
M. D. XXI.

ENGRAVING: LUTHER, by Hans Weiditz

Luther's fame was in no small measure promoted by numerous pamphlets and broadsides, usually embellished with a woodcut of the reformer. One of many artists to portray Luther was Hans Weiditz, who indicated his own feelings by attaching the inscription.

the legal profession. Luther dutifully registered as a student in the Faculty of Law, while the gratified father began to cast about for a suitable match for his promising son.

IN THE MONASTERY

Scarcely had Luther begun his study of law when his father was infuriated to learn that the son of hope and promise had decided to bury himself in a cloister. The immediate cause of this abrupt change of course was a terrifying experience in which Luther found himself overtaken by a thunderstorm. Lightning flashed about him, and Luther, his vivid imagination caught up with demons, hell, and the Last Judgment, was in mortal fear of death. In the terror of the moment, he implored his father's saint, the patroness of miners, "St. Anne, help me, and I will become a monk." Thus it was that in July, 1505, in response to what he believed to be a divine call, Luther entered the cloister of the Eremites of St. Augustine in Erfurt. The disappointed father remained bitterly unreconciled until the deaths of two other sons; he interpreted these as warnings of the danger of rebellion against God.

Of the twenty cloisters in Erfurt, the novice, in his zealous quest for peace with God and his fervent devotion to the church, selected one noted for its strict discipline and academic vigor. The Augustinian order of Eremites, founded in Italy in the thirteenth century, soon spread to Germany, where by the beginning of the sixteenth century it had more than 100 houses. Of these, some thirty had been brought together in 1477 by Andreas Proles, vicar-general of the Saxon-Thuringian province of the order, in an attempt to enforce a more rigorous observance of the rule than was characteristic of most of the order. These Observantines were, when Luther joined them, headed by Proles' successor, Johan von Staupitz, a man whose kindness and piety would exert a great influence upon Luther. The vicar-general frequently visited the monastery at Erfurt, and formed a close personal relationship with the zealous monk from Mansfeld.

The Augustinian cloister in Erfurt had close connections with the university, and so the Occamistic emphases of the university influenced the Augustinian students who sat in the university lectures. At the same time, the Occamist professors held that man could, by the exercise of his will, love and serve God so as to merit divine favor. For Luther, this meant diligent pursuit of the ideals of monasticism, so that he could assert later, without fear of contradiction, "I was a devout monk, and I kept the rule of my order so strictly that I may say that if ever a monk deserved to get to heaven by monkery it was I."[1]

The monastic life of renunciation and self-humiliation stressed man's dependence upon the sacraments as necessary means of grace, and the young Luther made every effort to assiduously follow the teachings of the church. In his attempt

---

[1]*Werke, WA,* XXXVIII:143.

to meet the highest standards, he became obsessed with the idea that his best efforts might not be good enough. The meticulous care with which he attempted to confess every sin—to the exasperation of his confessor—indicated not an unusually sinful disposition but rather an extraordinarily spiritually sensitive nature, passionately devoted to the *opus dei*.

When the novitiate was completed, Luther received what he would call his "monastic baptism." In September, 1506, he took the irrevocable vows that initiated him into the permanent ranks of the order. Already his sincerity and ability had gained the favorable attention of his superiors, who now called him to prepare himself for the priesthood. The young candidate progressed rapidly through the ranks of subdeacon and deacon, and in April, 1507, was ordained a priest.

TRIUMPH IN THE TOWER

A month later, Luther celebrated his first mass. His personal experiences at this time indicate again the overwhelming awe that he felt at the divine presence. On this solemn occasion, the new priest, overcome with terror at the realization of the great disparity between the righteousness of God and the unworthiness of man, would have fled, had not others prevented his doing so. Following the occasion, a banquet was held within the cloister walls. The elder Luther, who had come for the festivity and had not seen his son for two years, declared that he was not convinced that God had called Luther to enter the monastery. To the claim that Luther had been called in a heavenly vision, the skeptical Hans retorted that he hoped it had not been an illusion or a trick of the devil. Besides, did not the Scriptures teach, "Thou shalt honor thy father and thy mother?" Although Luther was convinced that his entry into the monastery had been in accordance with God's will, he could hardly fail to notice that his father had silenced him with a reference to biblical authority. The incident demonstrated the continuing tension between an imperious father and a zealous son.[2]

In 1508, Luther was appointed to the arts faculty in the newly established University of Wittenberg. Only six years earlier, the elector of Ernestine Saxony,[3] Frederick the Wise, had obtained from Emperor Maximilian I the necessary charter for founding the university. The Augustinian order held the professorship of the Bible as well as the lectureship in Aristotle's *Ethics*; the latter position now fell to Luther. Lecturing on philosophy, however, gave him little satisfaction. He much preferred theology, and accordingly continued his studies in this area. By the spring of 1509, he gained the degree of Bachelor of the Bible (*Baccalaureus biblicus*), so that he could now lecture on the Bible. Not long thereafter, he returned to Erfurt where, upon receiving the title of Senten-

---

[2] See Erik Erikson, *Young Man Luther* (New York: Norton, 1962).

[3] In 1485, Saxony had been divided between two brothers of the Wettin family. Ernest became elector of Saxony, while Albert retained the title of duke.

tiarius, he lectured on the *Sentences* of Peter Lombard. During this time, Luther's study of the various theological writers reveals that Augustine, who had stressed the role of divine grace and predestination, held a special attraction for him, as numerous marginal annotations attest.

While Luther was thus engaged in his lectures and studies, he was chosen to go to Rome on behalf of his order. Attempts were being made to unite the Observantine and Conventual branches of the Augustinians, and Luther, together with a fellow monk, was sent to Rome to oppose the union. In the Eternal City, the devout friar visited numerous churches and climbed the Scala Sancta on his knees, faithfully saying prayers to gain indulgences and to free his grandfather from purgatory. At the same time, the clerical professionalism, the secularism of the papacy, and the easy morality so shocked Luther's sensitivity that he would later complain, "Fool that I was, I also carried onions to Rome and brought back garlic."[4]

Luther returned to Erfurt and shortly thereafter was transferred to Wittenberg, where he would spend most of the remainder of his life. Here he was chosen sub-prior and, at the same time, was encouraged by Staupitz to prepare himself for the degree of Doctor of Theology. This he received in October, 1512, being only twenty-eight years of age—a fact that did not escape censorious notice by the professors at Erfurt. Shortly thereafter, Luther succeeded his friend and spiritual mentor, Staupitz, in the chair of biblical theology at the University of Wittenberg. He could now devote his energies largely to lecturing at the university, preaching to the townspeople, and studying.

In the pursuit of his new responsibilities, Luther became increasingly concerned about the spiritual problems that had long vexed him. How could he be certain that his sins had indeed been confessed and forgiven, that he was the recipient of divine grace? As the consciousness of his own sinfulness grew, the black despair of sleepless nights almost overwhelmed him. When he compared the magnitude of sin with the righteousness of God, the Wholly Other, hope of obtaining divine mercy seemed futile, for too wide a chasm separated God's standards from man's attainments. Repeatedly he turned to Staupitz, without whom Luther, in his own words, would have "sunk into hell." The vicar-general, a mystic, encouraged Luther to consider the merits of Christ rather than worry about his own inadequacies. Some consolation was found in this advice, as well as in the reading of other mystics, such as Eckhart, and in studying the *Theologia Germanica*; yet the nagging doubts persisted, so that "day and night there was nothing but horror and despair." Repeatedly, the troubled theologian was overcome by what for him was a persistent obsession—the righteousness of God, and its concomitant, divine judgment. In Luther's mind, the two were inseparable and inescapable, while their consequence was likely to be eternal perdition.

[4]*Werke, WA*, LI:20.

To better prepare himself as preacher and lecturer, Luther set himself the task of mastering the Bible. In 1513, he began lecturing on the Psalms, and in 1515 he undertook an exposition of St. Paul's letter to the Romans. His appointment as overseer of eleven monasteries followed in the same year, but it was the biblical lectures that continued to absorb Luther's interest and energy. In 1516, he began his analysis of the book of Galatians. In his study, situated in a tower of the monastery, he pondered these biblical statements, and reached the conclusion that the answer to his questions about salvation must be found in the person of Christ, not the teachings of the church. As the conviction grew, and as the Christ-intoxicated theologian became convinced that the human dilemma found its answer in man's identification with God, gnawing fear and uncertainty were superseded by robust faith.

Already in his lectures on the Psalms Luther had indicated that he was seeing rays of light breaking through an interminable darkness. He regarded the Psalter as a book foreshadowing the suffering and death of Christ, and the anguished cry in the twenty-second Psalm, "My God, My God, why hast thou forsaken me?" told Luther that his own despair had been experienced by Christ. The God of judgment was also the God of compassion, who too had known temptation and despair, and had identified himself with man. A new God was being unveiled. Then, when Luther turned to Romans and Galatians, he found his answer as to how God could be both just and merciful. St. Paul's assertion that "The just shall live by faith," told Luther that the requisite for justification was faith, not human achievement. As he pondered the meaning of justification by faith, he felt he was going "through open doors into paradise." The words *sola fide*—faith alone— would remain central to his theology.

A NEW FAITH

For Luther, the great interpreter of divine truth would be St. Paul. With the apostle, he surveyed the sweep of human endeavor and agreed that man was innately unrighteous, imperfect, and helpless. Man's efforts could never hope to meet the demands of a holy and just God; instead God himself imputed righteousness to those who believed. Salvation was the work not of man nor even the church, but solely of God. It was He who gave man the power to believe, so that faith did not proceed from any human merit; it was a divine gift. Convinced that salvation was determined by what God did for man, not by what man could do for God, Luther accepted St. Augustine's doctrine of divine predestination. This belief that divine mercy was not contingent upon human frailty turned interminable darkness into joyful assurance for Luther.

As Luther continued lecturing and writing, his emphases included, in addition to the writings of Paul, especially the Gospels, the first epistle of Peter, and the the first epistle of John. Luther became the first professor to devote all his lectures to biblical exposition. Soon he was contrasting "our theology" (the theology taught at Wittenberg) with the older scholastic learning. His colleague and dean, Andreas von Karlstadt, was at first scandalized. He admitted that, although he was a doctor of theology, he had never seen a Bible. Soon, however, he became a convert to the new teaching—and its passionate advocate. He did not hesitate to post 152 Latin theses challenging the scholastic veneration of Aristotle and defending the Augustinian view of grace and predestination, in accordance with Luther's interpretation. Luther reported joyously that at Wittenberg ''Aristotle is going down little by little, headed for oblivion.''[5] Meanwhile, he attempted unsuccessfully to convince his former teachers at Erfurt that he had found a better way. However he did strike at least one responsive chord in the Nuremberg humanist Christoph Scheurl, who provided an influential contact with intellectuals of the South.

As Luther began to reflect on the implications of his teachings of salvation by faith, he found himself increasingly perplexed by the role of all human effort. For him, the crucial error of the church was neither the corruption of the papacy, nor laxity of the priesthood, but rather the substitution of a righteousness based on works for salvation by faith alone. Luther would come to regard his task not as reforming corrupt practices but as restoring to the church the central doctrine of redemption through divine grace. This, he insisted, had been the message of the early church and had been admirably expressed in the writings of St. Augustine.

Such a view raised doubts about the whole matter of indulgences. According to church teachings, an indulgence was the remission of part or all of the temporal penalty imposed for sins already forgiven. Even though guilt could be freely forgiven a repentant sinner, the penalty remained to be discharged, either in this life or in purgatory. The church taught that there was a vast treasury of merits, won by Christ, the Virgin Mary, and the saints, all of whom had accumulated benefits that could be used for people who had failed to meet the divine standard. To the church had been entrusted the discretionary power of dispensing these merits to those who demonstrated particular devotion to the church. Thus, indulgences were granted for visiting relics of the saints, for going on a pilgrimage, or for making a financial contribution to the church. In 1476, Pope Sixtus IV had extended the efficacy of indulgences to souls in purgatory, so that the faithful might now shorten the time their departed loved ones need spend in torment. The traffic in indulgences proved a lucrative source of ecclesiastical revenue, especially as the unsophisticated common people came to regard indulgences simply as a means whereby they could be freed from the penalty and guilt of sins, even of those not yet committed. But how could indulgences be reconciled with salvation by faith?

On the eve of All Saint's Day, October 31, 1516, Luther devoted a sermon to the question of indulgences, although he did not yet attack the papal power to grant them; rather he emphasized the need of being genuinely penitent. By

---

[5]*Werke, Briefe, WA,* I:99.

February of the following year, he was warning that the indiscriminate issuing of indulgences might well be a license to commit sin with impunity. Luther noted that the elector was not pleased with any questioning of the value of indulgences. No doubt, Frederick the Wise found it difficult to see why a professor should attack a practice that was used to provide revenue for the university. Indeed substantial revenues were derived from the dispensing of indulgences, and Frederick was using these funds for such ventures as building a bridge over the Elbe and supporting the Castle Church. Luther's position, however, was not to be changed by the threat of economic loss. He had long before demonstrated that he would not permit economic or political factors to determine his religious stance.

Nor was he the first to question the theological basis of indulgences. Opposition to indulgences or their abuses had aroused earlier ill-fated protests. Several influential theologians of the late fifteenth century had incurred ecclesiastical wrath by voicing their disquieting opinions. When Pedro de Osma of Salamanca questioned the whole system of indulgences on the basis of predestination, he was brought before the inquisition and imprisoned. His contemporary, Wessel Gansfort, was more fortunate. Born in the Netherlands in 1419, educated in schools of the Brothers of the Common Life and at Cologne and Paris, he became a distinguished professor and theologian in the universities of Paris and Cologne. Later he returned to the Netherlands and launched a formidable assault on what he described as "the errors concerning indulgences which the Roman curia has conjured up and propagated like a plague."[6] Gansfort declared that no priest or pope could grant indulgences, yet when he died in Zwolle in 1489, he was still honored as a theologian and religious leader. Other clerics would not escape censure and punishment. A priest, Jean Laillier, maintained that the pope could not grant a plenary indulgence to the living, while an Observantine friar, Jean Vitrier, suggested that indulgences were of demonic origin. Ecclesiastical machinery silenced both critics. The work of some of the opponents of indulgences was known to Luther; he thus had little reason to expect anything but official opposition to his attack on indulgences. Personal considerations might well have suggested the strategy of retreat—but Luther was not to be deterred by personal considerations.

THE INDULGENCE CONTROVERSY

By the fall of 1517, the course of events drove Luther to take a public stand against indulgences. The immediate cause grew out of the policies of the house of Hohenzollern, which, in the person of Albert, brother of Elector Joachim of Brandenburg, was attempting to extend its measure of control over German civil and ecclesiastical life. In 1513, at the age of 23, Albert had become archbishop of Magdeburg and administrator of the see of Halberstadt. Although he was not yet old enough to hold such office, a costly papal dispensation had been secured

---

[6]Quoted in Oberman, *Forerunners,* p. 100.

on his behalf. Then, with the death of the archbishop of Mainz in the following year, Albert resolved to secure that archdiocese as well and thus become primate of Germany.

To realize his ambitions, and to secure papal permission to hold three sees simultaneously—a most unusual circumstance—Albert would have to make a very substantial payment to Rome. At the moment, Pope Leo was rebuilding St. Peter's and was badly in need of funds. His predecessor, Julius II, had begun the gigantic task and had proclaimed an indulgence in 1507, the proceeds of which were to be used for building the church in Rome. Leo X continued this policy which now provided the occasion for Luther's public opposition to the practice. Albert borrowed the necessary funds from the Fugger banking firm of Augsburg. To repay the debt, Albert was granted the privilege by the pope of dispensing an indulgence in his territories, with half of the income going to the building of St. Peter's, the other half to the Fuggers, who supervised the collection. The public, however, was not informed of this dual purpose, for the proclamation spoke only of the pious work of building the great church in Rome.

John Tetzel, a Dominican prior of Leipzig, was appointed subcommissioner for the sale of indulgences in Magdeburg and Halberstadt. The instructions that Archbishop Albert gave to his subcommissioners emphasized the vast benefits to be gained by those purchasing indulgences: "complete forgiveness of all sins" as well as "plenary remission of all sins to the souls in purgatory"[7] were offered to those who would make adequate financial contributions. Tetzel had earlier performed similar services for Frederick of Saxony, whose treasury of more than 18,000 relics was the marvel of Germany. Now, however, the elector closed his territories to Tetzel, for the practical Frederick had no intention of permitting the sale of any indulgences from which he himself would not benefit. Yet the resourceful vendor did come close enough to Wittenberg to permit Luther's parishioners to cross the border and secure the prized indulgences. Tetzel did not hesitate to appeal directly to the emotions of the faithful, assuring them that with a contribution they might release their loved ones from the pangs of torment, for:

> When the money in the coffer rings,
> The soul from purgatory springs.*

The excesses of Tetzel, which included such attractive features as remission of future sins, would later be repudiated, and he himself denounced by fellow Dominicans. Indeed, Archbishop Albert's instructions had specifically called for contrition and confession. The overly zealous Tetzel, however, conveniently overlooked these elements, while the people of Wittenberg gratefully bought their pardons, not hesitating to scorn Luther when he reprimanded them. For the professor of theology, who well remembered at what cost he had gained repose

---

[7]Quoted in Oskar Thulin, *A Life of Luther* (Philadelphia: Fortress Press, 1966), pp. 28, 29.
*Woodcut John Tetzel. (Lutherhalle, Wittenberg)

Johannes Tezelius Dominicaner Münch/mit sei-
nen Römischen Ablaßkram/welchen er im Jahr Christi 1517. in Deutschen-
landen zu marckt gebracht/wie er in der Kirchen zu Pirn in seinem
Vaterland abgemahlet ist.

O ihr deutschen mercket mich recht/
Des heiligen Vaters Papstes Knecht/
Bin ich/vnd br ing euch jtzt allein/
Zehn tausent vnd neun hundert carein/
Gnad vnd Ablaß von einer Sünd/
Vor euch/ewer Elter n/Weib vnd Kind/
Sol ein jeder gewehret sein
So viel jhr leg eins Kästelein/
So bald der Gülden im Becken klingt/
Im hup die Seel im himel springt/

WOODCUT: JOHN TETZEL, contemporary anonymous caricature

A savage caricature of John Tetzel, the indulgence peddlar. The jingle, ostensibly by him, advises the gullible listeners that:
> When the coin in the coffer rings
> At once the soul to heaven springs.

Courtesy Lutherhalle, Wittenberg

from the tempest within his soul, this flippant attitude toward sin, this "cheap grace," was intolerable; yet he knew that the reaction of the people reflected a profound theological problem, and it was to this that he now directed his attention.

On October 31, 1517, when Wittenberg was thronged with pilgrims who had come to view relics in the elector's shrine, Luther publicly took his stand. On a placard reputedly[8] posted on the door of the castle church, he listed ninety-five

---

[8]Some scholars have argued that Luther did not actually post the theses to the church door; instead, they claim he sent them to bishops and learned friends. Erwin Iserloh in *The Theses Were not Posted; Luther Between Reform and Reformation,* translated by Jared Wicks (Boston: Beacon, 1968), contends that Luther wanted to avoid an inflammatory appeal to a citizenry already seething with social discontent and anti-clericalism, and therefore avoided a public display of his attack on a widespread religious practice. The first known reference to the posting of the theses is a statement to that effect made by Philip Melanchthon in 1546, shortly after Luther's death. Kurt Aland, among others, has defended the traditional view.

theses for debate "out of love and zeal for truth and the desire to bring it to light."[9] He also sent a copy, together with a covering letter, to Archbishop Albert, and asked that Tetzel's traffic be suppressed. While the theses showed a deep respect for the sacraments and institutions of the church including the papacy, at the same time they indicated a strong distrust of the entire traffic in indulgences. Even the pope's power to grant indulgences was questioned, for if he were indeed empowered to free some souls from purgatory, why did he not release all its occupants? Again, how could papal love and justice be reconciled with the avarice of the indulgence vendors who did not hesitate to extract the last penny from those who lived in grinding poverty? Luther suggested that it would be better to let St. Peter's church collapse in ruins than to build it "with the skin, flesh and bones of his sheep." Indications of "our theology" were apparent when, in theses sixty-two and sixty-four, Luther warned that the "treasure of indulgences" should not be permitted to supplant "the true treasure of the church," the "holy Gospel of the glory and grace of God."

Although Luther had intended his theses for scholarly debate, he soon found that the printing press had turned them into watchwords of mass propaganda. The theses, quickly translated from Latin into German and published in many cities, everywhere aroused great interest, for more than one churchman had become the victim of ecclesiastical wrath by questioning established practices. Furthermore, the economic implications of Luther's challenge did not go unnoticed; here was a rallying point for the nameless masses. Both the letter and the spirit of the theses soon made Luther a household word.

In his letter to the archbishop, Luther had diplomatically suggested that the indulgence instructions had been issued without the prelate's "knowledge and consent." Albert, however, had no intention of taking advantage of this way out; instead he resolved to crush the "rash monk of Wittenberg." The University of Mainz was asked to respond to the theses, and a copy of Luther's assertions was sent to the pope, with the request that steps be taken to silence Luther. Tetzel, not to be outdone, responded to Luther's challenge by charging him with suspicion of heresy and by drafting his own series of theses supporting indulgences. He also gained the support of the Saxon chapter of the Dominicans, which, early in 1518, urged the papal curia to curb the actions of the incendiary Augustinian. Meanwhile, the controversy began to assume sinister overtones as participants reminded Luther that his position was not altogether different from that of the arch heretic, Jan Hus.[10] Tetzel confidently predicted that the fate of both would be identical. Cardinal Prierias, a Dominican and censor in Rome, issued a violent attack on Luther, accusing him of heresy and comparing him to the devil.

[9]Lewis W. Spitz, ed., *The Protestant Reformation* (Englewood Cliffs, N.J.: Prentice-Hall, 1966), p. 43.

[10]Jan Hus (1369–1415), the Bohemian reformer who was burned at the stake by the Council of Constance, defended the supremacy of the Scriptures and attacked papal authority. His position was complicated by the Great Schism (1378–1417), for the conflicting claims of several aspirants to the papal throne divided Europe into various camps.

Luther's reply was indicative of his future defense: He denounced the Commissioner of the Sacred Palace not because he had misinterpreted the pope and church council, but because "like an insidious devil," he had not hesitated to "pervert the Scriptures."

Luther's cause also attracted its supporters. When the Augustinian chapters met in Heidelberg in the spring of 1518 for their triennial convention, Luther's stand gained him a number of young admirers, including Martin Bucer, later to be a noted leader of reform in Strasbourg. Even before going to Heidelberg, Luther had secured an important ally in the Elector Frederick; George Spalatin, secretary and chaplain to Frederick, and friend of Luther, was instrumental in gaining court favor for the harassed professor. When the elector learned that Luther was going to the convention in Heidelberg, and that he might well be placed in dangerous circumstances, Frederick warned Staupitz to take protective measures. At the same time, the elector issued a letter of praise and safe-conduct for his embattled protégé.

In the earliest stages of the controversy, the pope had refused to become involved in what was dismissed as the "monks' quarrel," and Luther had repeatedly asserted his confident belief that if the full facts were known in Rome, the response would be a favorable one. Early in August, 1518, however, he was advised that he must appear in Rome within sixty days to answer charges against him. Convinced that a hearing in Rome would prejudice his case, and probably lead to prison or death, Luther requested the elector to use his influence to assure a hearing in Germany and, as far as possible, by impartial judges. Elector Frederick, then in Augsburg at the sessions of the imperial diet, agreed to the proposals, and suggested that Luther be heard in Augsburg. The elector was in a strong bargaining position, for the old emperor Maximilian was attempting to ensure the succession of his grandson, Charles I of Spain and Frederick's support would be a vital factor in defeating the hopes of Charles's rival Francis I of France. The pope also needed Frederick's support; he was anxious to enlist any and all military aid against the Turks, who were now pressing into the Austrian lands. Thus, neither pope nor emperor could afford to alienate Luther's protector. At the same time they did not wish to grant Luther a public forum.

Following a request to Rome, Cardinal Cajetan (1468–1534), general of the Dominican Order and papal legate to Germany, was duly empowered to hear the charges and to pronounce absolution or condemnation.

DEFENSE OF THE NEW FAITH

In October, less than a month after the sessions of the diet had been adjourned, Luther appeared before the scholarly cardinal, who himself had not hesitated to denounce ecclesiastical abuses. Cajetan hoped that the affair could quickly be settled in an amicable manner, but he was disappointed to note the distrust that Luther had reflected in his insistence that he be given an imperial safe-conduct. Many of Luther's friends, however, had warned him that his fate might be that of Hus, or that he might be killed enroute. Yet the fear of physical violence was hardly uppermost in his mind, for, as he wrote a friend, "I know that from the beginning the word of Christ has been such that whoever wants to present it to the world must necessarily, like the Apostles, renounce everything and expect death at every hour." More disturbing to Luther was the recurring doubt as he contemplated the magnitude of his repudiation of past teaching: "Are you alone wise?"[11] Could one man stand against the traditions of centuries?

The cardinal and the professor confronted each other in three interviews. Although the beginning was cordial enough, with Luther duly prostrating himself, Cajetan at once proceeded to set forth the purpose of the meeting, namely, to give Luther the opportunity of admitting his error by simply saying, "Revoco"—"I recant." Luther asked that he be shown where his teachings conflicted with Scripture rather than with papal decree. Pressed by his examiner, he admitted his belief that the pope could err, and that he was not above Scripture. Moreover, he rejected the efficacy of the treasury of merits, as defined in the bull *Unigenitus*, issued by Pope Clement VI in 1343. When no compromise could be reached, Luther suggested that the matter be referred to the universities, thus further antagonizing Cajetan. To his colleague Karlstadt he wrote that the cardinal was as suited to judge this case "as an ass to play the harp."

The last stalemated session ended when the exasperated cardinal declared that he would hear Luther no more until he was prepared to recant. But Luther was not content to rest his case with Cajetan. He addressed an appeal from "Leo badly informed to Leo better informed" and expressed hope that he might be heard before an impartial tribunal. Luther also wrote a conciliatory letter to Cajetan, but yielded nothing of substance. When the cardinal did not reply, Luther became uneasy. His friends advised him to leave at once, while rumors suggested that the cardinal had been empowered to arrest Luther. Under cover of night, and with the connivance of friends, he fled the city and returned to Wittenberg. Cajetan responded by asking Frederick to send Luther to Rome or drive him out of the country. On November 28, 1518, Luther appealed to the authority of a general church council, and requested that his case be heard by such a body, despite a previous papal ruling declaring such an appeal to be heretical.

Once again, Luther found aid at the electoral court. Frederick, although insisting on his absolute opposition to any heresy, addressed a letter to the Roman curia, stating that he had no intention of sending Luther to Rome; instead the professor should be heard impartially and not "condemned in advance." Pope Leo remained conciliatory, and sent the papal nuncio, Carl von Miltitz, to gain the support of Frederick. Miltitz was appropriately empowered to bestow on the elector the coveted prize, the Golden Rose of Virtue, given only to those who

---

[11]Roland Bainton, *Here I Stand* (New York: Mentor Books, 1962), p. 70.

had distinguished themselves in the service of the church. Papal bulls would also permit Frederick to reap even more substantial benefits from indulgences associated with his store of relics.

On January 5 and 6, 1519, Luther and Miltitz met in friendly discussion. At least for a time, there seemed to be some hope of reconciliation. Luther promised not to aggravate the situation by further attacks provided his opponents would do likewise. At the same time, he gave Miltitz a letter of humble submission to the pope which nonetheless contained a strong defense of actions which, he insisted, had been prompted by a desire to save the church from clerical abuses. The letter would never reach the pope; instead Miltitz sent a very optimistic report to Rome, which in turn moved Pope Leo to address a gentle letter to his "dearly beloved son" who was now experiencing "bitter anguish of heart." In September, Luther met the nuncio again, but by now Luther attached little significance to the emissary, regarding him as thoroughly unreliable.

The extent of Luther's estrangement from the official position of the church became apparent in his conflict with the professor of theology from the University of Ingolstadt, Johann Eck. This redoubtable scholar, a foremost disputant who had won wide acclaim, had attempted to bury Luther in a literary avalanche. But Luther could give in equal measure. While Luther was at the Heidelberg session of his order, his colleague Karlstadt, dean of the theological faculty at Wittenberg, also a noted scholar, attacked Eck with 405 *Apologetic Conclusions*. In these, he severely criticized the authority of the pope, emphasized the supremacy of the Scriptures, rejected freedom of the will, and championed freedom of conscience. Eck at once responded with his *Defense*, a systematic refutation of Karlstadt's position, and suggested that a conciliatory solution be found, perhaps by submitting the differences of opinion to several universities. Karlstadt's wordy reply indicated that he was not interested in reconciliation; accordingly, in typical scholastic fashion, the two professors agreed that they should meet in public disputation. At Eck's suggestion, and with the approval of Duke George of Saxony, the University of Leipzig was chosen as the scene of the encounter because the duke hoped to bring prestige to his university.

At first, only Eck and Karlstadt were expected to participate. Luther himself had agreed to such an arrangement, but before the debate began, it was apparent that Luther would be the center of the attack. After Eck published the twelve theses he proposed to defend, Luther countered with his own views on penance and forgiveness. At the same time, he included a radical new attack on the power of the pope, which he contended was only of recent origin. "That the Roman Church is superior to all others is shown by the impious decrees which the Roman popes have issued for four hundred years; against these are the historical evidence of fifteen hundred years, the text of divine Scriptures, and the decree of the Council of Nicaea, the most sacred of all."[12] Thus, another dangerous issue

---

[12]B. J. Kidd, *Documents Illustrative of the Continental Reformation* (Oxford: Clarendon, 1911), p. 46.

had been raised and Luther had strengthened suspicions of heresy, while privately he expressed his opinion that popes had often acted more like enemies of Christ than apostles.

Early in July, 1519, after proper pomp and colorful pageantry, the debate began. For the first four days, Karlstadt and Eck wrestled with the role played by grace and free will, with the astute Ingolstadt theologian confidently claiming that he had brought his opponent back to "the true Christian doctrine." When Luther entered the battle, the point of contention was the basis and extent of papal authority. He drew his arguments from Scripture and early church history, while Eck responded with references to scholastic theology, canon law, and conciliar pronouncements. When Eck cited various authorities, including the spurious Isidorian decrees, to support his position, Luther replied that Oriental and Greek church fathers, such as Basil the Great, had not recognized Roman primacy, yet they must be regarded as faithful Christians.

Luther's attack on the authority of the pope gave Eck the opportunity to associate such a view with that of noted heretics such as Wycliffe and Hus. To the assertion that some of the teachings of Hus were "plainly Christian," Eck retorted that the Council of Constance had not been of this opinion. Luther was now driven to the logical conclusion that councils might err, and indeed had done so, as he attempted to show by referring to a subsequent reversal of the claim by the council of Basel that a council is above a pope. Scripture must be the final authority. As Eck once again associated Luther with the Bohemian heretic, it was becoming apparent that reform had given way to heresy.

The later stages of the debate were anticlimactic. Old issues of purgatory and indulgences were reviewed, while Karlstadt again took up the matter of human depravity. Gradually, interest in the debate waned, and Duke George grew weary of the whole affair. In a spirit of bitterness, Luther and his associates returned to Wittenberg. Each side had maintained its position, and each side claimed victory. When the records of the debate were submitted for judgment to the theological faculties of several universities, Erfurt refused to render a verdict. Paris, after a long silence, issued a statement in April, 1521, avoiding reference to the Leipzig debate, but denouncing some of Luther's positions as heretical. The universities of Louvain and Cologne also issued statements condemning Luther's views. Luther replied that the universities had not even attempted to cite biblical evidence. For him, there could be no other basis for religious belief.

Luther's bold attacks on the power of Rome did not fail to gain widespread support among the German people. Princes and knights, merchants and peasants looked with approbation on the anticlerical pronouncements that had struck a responsive chord in the German heart. Numerous humanists agreed that the cause of reform and of free inquiry should be encouraged, while the renowned Erasmus insisted that Luther's views could hardly be heretical, for they reflected the position of such men as St. Augustine, Bernard of Clairvaux, and Nicholas of Cusa. For a while some powerful prelates, including the archbishop of Mainz, felt that the Wittenberg theologian was to be commended for some of his pro-

1ts, especially his denunciation of the financial oppression by the
. .. tne same time, colleagues at Wittenberg enthusiastically defended their
beleaguered hero and continued to assail Eck long after the debate ended. Bohemian Hussites also sent encouraging letters, hailing Luther as a worthy champion
of their great martyr. By February, 1520, Luther was prepared to admit the
similarity: "We are all Hussites without knowing it." A few months later, with
somber finality, he penned the ominous words, "Farewell, unhappy, hopeless,
blasphemous Rome! The wrath of God has come upon you . . . let us leave
her. . . ."[13]

EXPOSITION OF THE NEW FAITH

In the same year, Luther published perhaps his most famous polemical tract,
written in the stirring idiom of the common man. There was to be no indecision.
"The time to be silent is past and the time to speak has come," he declared in his
Address to the Christian Nobility of the German Nation. This revolutionary
pamphlet, which Luther compared to the trumpet blast that had brought down the
walls of Jericho, urged the church to return to its spiritual task. Since the clergy
was reluctant to take corrective measures, Luther called upon princes and magistrates to take the lead in reforming the church and in tearing down the walls that
the champions of papal supremacy had constructed for their own defense. The
walls Luther described as humanly inspired claims that spiritual authority could
judge temporal authority; that the pope alone could render a decisive interpretation of Scripture; and that the pope alone had the power to convoke councils.
Luther rejected these assertions with the explanation that "we are all consecrated
as priests by baptism, as St. Peter says, 'you are . . . a royal priesthood' ";
hence to claim spiritual supremacy was pointless. Furthermore, since all believers were priests, they possessed power "to test and judge what is correct or
incorrect in matters of faith." The third wall "falls of itself when the first two are
down."

Luther's proposed reforms were drastic. Temporal possessions and claims of
the papacy should be abandoned, so that proper attention might be given to
spiritual concerns. Apostolic simplicity should be enforced once again, while
annates[14] and other fees should be abolished. Mendicant orders should be reformed; ecclesiastical offenders who were Germans should be tried in Germany
by Germans. Here there was more than a hint of a national church. At least a
measure of religious toleration was suggested when the pamphlet urged that
heretics be "vanquished with books, not with burnings."

[13]*Werke, WA,* VI:329.
[14]Annates were the first year's income from an ecclesiastical office and were normally
paid to Rome.

Unlike the first of the polemical pamphlets, which had been written in German, the second, *The Babylonian Captivity of the Church*, appeared in Latin. It was designed for the scholar and theologian, but the far-reaching implications of Luther's statements assured immediate wide circulation. The slashing attack on the sacramental system was so violent that Erasmus sadly admitted, "the breach is irreparable." Luther substantially rejected five of seven sacraments, retaining only baptism and the Lord's Supper, since they alone had been directly instituted by Christ. Temporarily, he still attached some value to penance. The fateful consequences of such a position were readily apparent, for the church insisted that the sacraments were necessary channels of grace. To reject the sacraments was to reject the church, together with the prerogatives of the clergy. These prerogatives, institutionalized by the sacrament of ordination, Luther maintained, had created a false caste system, whereby the clergy established its "detestable tyranny over the laity." Ordination should be regarded as the "rite of choosing a preacher in the church." Luther had struck a blow for equality within the church; no longer would he accept the medieval notion that the clergy stood between God and the laity.

Most serious of all was Luther's radical transformation of the Lord's Supper. Transubstantiation[15] he rejected as an unbiblical remnant, although he affirmed Christ's real presence in the elements. Luther insisted that Christ was not sacrificed in the Mass, since he had been sacrificed once and for all on the cross. Moreover, only if the recipient had faith could he benefit from participation. Luther also contended that the cup should be given to all believers, and not reserved for the priest alone. Thus, Luther called for an end to practices that he contended had enabled the papacy to hold the church in captivity by altering the biblical teachings on sacraments and by reserving for priests alone the rights belonging to all believers.

This daring attack brought many conservatives as well as the less audacious to a parting of the ways with Luther. Among the responses to Luther's proposal was Henry VIII's defense of the sacraments, which won for him the title, "Defender of the Faith."

Luther's third important treatise of 1520 appeared late in the year. Entitled *The Freedom of the Christian Man*, it was conciliatory and prefaced with a commiserating letter to Pope Leo, a "Daniel among the lions." In the pamphlet, Luther stressed the joyful, responsive, and creative nature of Christian liberty, freely expressed in loving obedience to God. Instead of being overcome by the wickedness and helplessness of his own nature, man should devote himself to a life of joyous service, aware that, while he is justified freely by faith, he expresses such a faith by serving God and man.

[15]The doctrine of transubstantiation holds that when the priest consecrates the elements in the Lord's Supper, they are transformed into the actual body and blood of Christ, although they retain the outward appearance (accidents) of bread and wine.

Even while Luther's prodigious literary output continued, his case was being carefully studied in Rome. Early in 1520, numerous cardinals and theologians, including Cajetan and Eck, prepared a response. For a time, discussion revolved around the method that should be used to silence Luther. Some participants recommended a conciliatory policy, for part of Luther's attack had been directed against long recognized and deplored abuses, or against matters that were not yet official dogma, nor would they be expressly declared to be such until the sessions of the Council of Trent. The document that finally appeared specifically condemned forty-one of Luther's views as "heretical or scandalous or offensive to pious ears." This bull, *Exsurge domine*, with its stirring invocation of the apostles and saints, implored, "Arise, O Lord, and judge thy cause. A wild boar has invaded thy vineyard."[16] The bull went on to state that Luther would be given sixty days to recant. When no word of recantation came from Wittenberg, the pope issued the final bull of excommunication in January, 1521.

Exsurge domine was given a mixed reception throughout Germany. When Eck proudly published the bull in Leipzig, antagonism of the populace forced him to take cover in a cloister. Luther had quickly become a symbol of anticlericalism, even for those who did not understand him but knew only that he had defied ecclesiastical authority. In various other centers, among them Vienna, Erfurt, and even Ingolstadt, copies of the bull were torn to pieces, while the Bavarian dukes asked that it be suspended. Especially in North Germany, numerous bishops opposed its publication. Elector Frederick responded with his familiar demand that Luther be given a fair trial before learned and impartial judges.

A copy of the bull reached Luther in October and aroused a torrent of invective and anger. Luther's "anti-bull," *Against the Detestable Bull of Antichrist*, savagely denounced the author and cursed the bull "as sacrilege and blasphemy of Christ." At the same time, he expressed doubts that the bull was genuine; rather it seemed to him a fabrication of Eck, "the apostle of impiety." Luther lamented that the bull made no effort to refute his position but simply condemned it. On December 10, Luther made a dramatic response. Whereas the bull had ordered the heretic's books to be burned, Luther now did the same for his opponents. Students and colleagues gathered outside the wall of Wittenberg and lit a bonfire that sent smoke signals across Europe. Various works supporting papal power, treatises by Eck, and collections of canon law were burned. In a gesture of defiance, Luther flung the bull itself into the fire, with the words, "As you have vexed the Holy One of the Lord, may the eternal fire vex you." Luther had kindled a flame that was not soon to be extinguished. Simultaneously, in various cities, such as Cologne and Mainz, Luther's works were publicly burned. Zealots on both sides suggested that authors too should be consigned to the fire.

---

[16]Kidd, *Documents*, p. 75; quoted in Bainton, *Here I Stand*, p. 114.

ILLUSTRATION: LUTHER BURNS THE PAPAL BULL

Apparently Luther's supporters thoroughly enjoyed this public repudiation of papal authority. No one could know, however, how soon people might be taking the place of the books.

Bibliothèque Nationale

Suggestions for Further Reading

Aland, Kurt, ed. *Ninety-five Theses, with the Pertinent Documents from the History of the Reformation.* St. Louis: Concordia, 1967.

*__Atkinson, James.__ *Martin Luther and the Birth of Protestantism.* Baltimore, Md.: Penguin, 1968.

*__Bainton, Roland.__ *Here I Stand.* New York: Mentor Books, 1956.

*__Boehmer, Heinrich.__ *Martin Luther: Road to Reformation.* Translated by John W. Doberstein and Theodore Tappert. Cleveland: Meridian, 1967.

Bornkamm, Heinrich. *Luther's World of Thought.* St. Louis: Concordia, 1958.

————. *Thesen und Thesenanschlag Luthers.* Berlin: Toepelmann, 1967.

*__Chadwick, Owen.__ *The Reformation.* Baltimore, Md.: Penguin, 1964.

Dickens, A. G. *Reformation and Society in Sixteenth-Century Europe.* New York: Harcourt, Brace & World, 1966.

*————. *Martin Luther and the Reformation.* London: English Universities Press, 1967.

*__Dillenberger, John,__ ed. *Martin Luther: Selections.* Garden City, N. Y.: Anchor Books, 1961.

*Indicates paperback edition.

Ebeling, G. E. *Luther: An Introduction to His Thought.* Philadelphia: Fortress Press, 1970.

Edwards, M. V. *Luther and the False Brethren.* Stanford, Calif.: Stanford University Press, 1974.

Elton, G. R. ed. *The Reformation, 1520–1559,* Vol. II of *The New Cambridge Modern History.* Cambridge: Cambridge University Press, 1958.

*————. *Reformation Europe, 1517–1559.* New York: Harper & Row, A Harper Torchbook, 1963.

*****Erikson, Erik H.** *Young Man Luther: A Study in Psychoanalysis and History.* New York: Norton, 1958.

Fife, Robert H. *The Revolt of Martin Luther.* New York: Columbia University Press, 1957.

Friedenthal, Richard. *Luther: His Life and Times.* New York: Harcourt Brace Jovanovich, 1970.

Gerrish, Brian, ed. *Reformers in Profile.* Philadelphia: Fortress Press, 1967.

Grimm, Harold J. *The Reformation Era, 1500–1650,* rev. ed. New York: Macmillan, 1965.

Grisar, Hartmann. *Martin Luther: His Life and Work.* Westminister, Md.: Newman Press, 1950.

*****Harbison, E. Harris.** *The Age of Reformation.* Ithaca, N.Y.: Cornell University Press, 1955.

Hillerbrand, Hans J. *The Reformation: A Narrative History Related by Contemporary Observers and Participants.* New York: Harper & Row, 1964.

*————. *The Protestant Reformation.* New York: Harper & Row, A Harper Torchbook, 1968.

*————. *Men and Ideas in the Sixteenth Century.* Chicago: Rand McNally, 1969.

Holborn, Hajo. *The Reformation.* New York: Knopf, 1959.

*****Hurstfield, Joel,** ed. *The Reformation Crisis.* London: Edward Arnold, 1965.

*****Iserloh, Erwin.** *The Theses Were Not Posted: Luther Between Reform and Reformation.* Boston: Beacon Press, 1968.

Jensen, DeLamar. *Confrontation at Worms.* Provo, Utah: Brigham Young University Press, 1973.

Koenigsberger, H. G., and G. L. Mosse. *Europe in the Sixteenth Century.* New York: Holt, Rinehart & Winston, 1968.

Kohls, E. W. *Luthers Entscheidung zu Worms.* Stuttgart: Calwer, 1970.

Kooiman, W. F. *By Faith Alone: The Life of Martin Luther.* Translated by B. Woolf. New York: Philosophical Library, 1955.

Lau, Franz, and Ernst Bizer. *A History of the Reformation in Germany to 1555.* Translated by B. A. Hardy. London: Black, 1969.

Lortz, Joseph. *The Reformation in Germany,* 2 vols. Translated by R. Walls. New York: Herder and Herder, 1969.

Luther, Martin. *Luther's Works,* 56 vols. Edited by J. Pelikan and H. Lehmann. St. Louis and Philadelphia: Concordia and Muhlenberg, 1958–

*****Reid, Stanford, W., ed.** *The Reformation: Revival or Revolution?* New York: Holt, Rinehart & Winston, 1968.

Ritter, Gerhard. *Luther: His Life and Work.* Translated by John Riches. New York: Harper & Row, 1963.

***Rupp, Gordon.** *Luther's Progress to the Diet of Worms.* New York: Harper & Row, A Harper Torchbook, 1964.

Schwiebert, E. G. *Luther and His Times.* St. Louis: Concordia, 1950.

Simon, Edith. *Luther Alive: Martin Luther and the Making of the Reformation.* Garden City, N.Y.: Doubleday, 1968.

***Spitz, Lewis W.** *The Reformation: Material or Spiritual?* Boston: D. C. Heath, 1962.

*————, ed. *The Protestant Reformation.* Englewood Cliffs, N. J.: Prentice-Hall, Spectrum Books, 1966.

Thulin, Oskar. *A Life of Luther.* Translated by M. Dietrich. Philadelphia: Fortress Press, 1966.

————. ed. *Illustrated History of the Reformation.* Translated by J. Nopola et al. St. Louis: Concordia, 1967.

Tillmanns, Walter G. *The World and Men around Luther.* Minneapolis: Augsburg, 1959.

Todd, John M. *Martin Luther: A Biographical Study.* Westminister, Md.: Newman Press, 1964.

3

Imperial Opposition
and
Revolutionary Peril

THE EMPEROR AND THE DIET

Luther's open defiance posed an acute problem for secular rulers who admired his courage and shared his anti-papal stance, but who were not prepared to associate themselves with a heretical movement. Some, however, recognized his voice as that of an aroused German nationalism. Aleander, papal nuncio in Germany, complained that everywhere sentiment for Luther was apparent: "Nine tenths of Germany shouts for Luther; the other tenth . . . cries, 'Down with the Roman Court.' " Sometimes, the nuncio saw himself hanged in effigy, or even personally attacked. Elector Frederick, whom Aleander aptly described as that "German fox," offered no encouragement when the nuncio requested that Luther be silenced.[1] The nuncio was distressed to learn that his bribery was no match for national anger and anti-clerical sentiment.[2] Those who contended for the old faith could hope for decisive action only through the cooperation of the imperial estates and the newly elected emperor.

Events in Germany soon demonstrated that even an emperor's decision was ineffectual if it met with resistance from the imperial diet. The German princes and free cities had long been fiercely independent, a heritage they were not likely to jeopardize for the doubtful privilege of cooperating with His Imperial Majesty. During the latter part of the fifteenth century, some far-sighted German leaders attempted to bring about a greater measure of political unity, but particularism emerged triumphant again and again.

At the heart of imperial administrative problems was the structure and function of the diet, which was composed of three estates: the electors (the seven

[1]See Aleander's pessimistic account quoted in Oskar Thulin, *A Life of Luther* (Philadelphia: Fortress Press, 1966), pp. 53–71.

[2]Gordon Rupp, *Luther's Progress to the Diet of Worms* (New York: Harper & Row, A Harper Torchbook, 1964), p. 92.

princes, secular and ecclesiastical, who elected the emperor); the other princes and higher nobility; and the imperial free cities. The lower nobility, the knights, were not represented in the diet. Territorial princes were of course anxious to expand and strengthen their own jurisdiction, and tended to view the imperial cities as constant rivals. The cities in turn were determined to maintain their privileged position which freed them from obligations to local rulers and bound them only to a usually distant emperor. Frictions such as these tended to weaken the policy-making role of the estates, so that frequently questions of internal peace, foreign relations, and economic problems received only minimal consideration in the sessions of the diet.

Occasionally, princes whose vision extended beyond their particular borders urged a more effective means of approaching the problems confronting the Empire. In the last decade of the fifteenth century the archbishop of Mainz, Berthold of Henneberg, launched an ambitious reform movement. He contended that local autonomy must be subordinated to the welfare of the Empire. At his urging, an Imperial Cameral Tribunal (*Reichskammergericht*) was established in 1495. Composed of judges selected in part by the emperor but mostly by the estates, this court played a major role in ending the constant feuds among the smaller estates, although larger principalities were reluctant to surrender any jurisdiction to the imperial court. Further administrative consolidation was attempted with the setting up of an Imperial Governing Council (*Reichsregiment*) in 1500. This council, dominated by electors and princes, posed a potential threat to the administrative authority of the emperor, so that he accepted the scheme only with the greatest reluctance. The estates, for their part, remained hesitant to supply the necessary operational funds, so that in 1502 the council was dissolved. The Empire seemed destined to remain a loose federation in which effective power was exercised by territorial princes and cities. The estates, with their control over finances, were able to stop all attempts to strengthen the administrative position of the imperial court. Yet divisions among the estates, especially between the princes and the imperial cities, effectively curbed the influence of the diet. In effect, then, this malfunctioning system of checks and balances worked to thwart almost all imperial policies, except on those rare occasions when astute diplomacy reconciled differences between emperor and diet.

SECULAR FORCES
AND RELIGIOUS INNOVATION

In 1519, almost two years after Luther posted his ninety-five theses, the grandson of Emperor Maxmilian I and of Ferdinand and Isabella was elected emperor at Frankfurt am Main. From this time until his abdication almost forty years later, Charles V considered it his supreme duty to preserve the faith and to stamp out heresy.

Never before had western Christendom known a ruler with so vast an empire.

When his father Philip died in 1506, Charles inherited the ancestral lands of the Hapsburg dynasty; at sixteen he became Charles I, king of Spain and her possessions; at nineteen, when his paternal grandfather died, he aspired to the imperial crown. When his ambitions conflicted with those of Francis I of France and Henry VIII of England, and when the pope opposed his election, urging instead the election of Frederick of Saxony, Charles spent some 850,000 florins to secure the crown. Much of his money was borrowed from the Augsburg bankers, the Fuggers, who were now given important economic concessions, such as a lien on the port of Antwerp and control of Spanish mines. When the election was held on June 28, 1519, all seven electors cast their vote for the Hapsburg, now to be known as Charles V. In the following year, he went to Aachen to be crowned in the cathedral of the great Charlemagne. His grandiose list of titles reflected both imagined and real power: King of the Romans; Emperor-elect; semper Augustus; King of Spain, Sicily, Jerusalem, the Balearic Islands, the Canary Islands, the Indies and the mainland on the far side of the Atlantic; Archduke of Austria; Duke of Burgundy, Brabant, Styria, Carinthia, Carniola, Luxemburg, Limburg, Athens and Patras; Count of Hapsburg, Flanders, and Tyrol; Count Palatine of Burgundy, Hainault, Pfirt, Roussillon; Landgrave of Alsace; Count of Swabia; Lord of Asia and Africa.

His coronation oath promised that the rights and possessions of electors and princes would be guaranteed, whether from revolt within the Empire or attacks from without. Charles also promised to appoint only German-born imperial officials, to use only German or Latin in imperial documents, and neither to introduce foreign armies nor to summon any diet to meet beyond the borders of the Empire.[3] Similarly, Charles swore to uphold the faith and to protect the church, to govern justly and to revere the pope. The newly crowned king and elected emperor (he would be crowned emperor by the pope in 1530) now faced the task of fulfilling his vow amidst the ominous portents of dissension that continued to appear in Germany. In his *Address to the Christian Nobility*, Luther had expressed hope that the "young and noble ruler" would take the lead in reforming the church. Such hopes would soon be shattered, for Charles, while agreeing that the church needed to be reformed, readily acceded to the demand that Luther's books be burned. Unity of the church must be maintained as an essential part of the unity of the dynastic Empire. Any thought of a German national church, or of a united political Germany, would be completely contrary to Charles's chief purpose.

Yet the young emperor had heard the boisterous popular acclaim given Luther, and he wanted no precipitous action. While Aleander urged him to proceed against Luther without more ado, Charles carefully consulted Frederick of Saxony. The elector had been unable to attend the coronation, having been delayed in Cologne by the gout. Here Charles asked Erasmus what Luther's chief

[3]Karl Brandi, *The Emperor Charles V*, trans. C. V. Wedgwood (New York: Knopf, 1939), p. 123.

errors were. The renowned humanist responded with an epigram: "Two: he attacked the pope in his crown and the monks in their bellies." When Charles, after the coronation, paid a call on Frederick, he found the atmosphere cordial enough and agreed, to the dismay of Aleander, that Luther should not be condemned without a hearing.

A few weeks after the meeting, Charles wrote Frederick, requesting him to bring Luther to the next session of the diet, which would convene in Worms early in 1521. The emperor's concern that "no injustice be done" aroused strong ecclesiastical opposition, for to submit a theological dispute to a lay court would be to prejudice the authority of the Holy See. Aleander's persuasive arguments convinced the emperor to withdraw his invitation to bring Luther to the diet. Yet when the diet opened on January 27, 1521, the emperor found that any attempt to have the estates endorse an imperial ban on Luther would meet with strong opposition. Charles therefore decided once again to invite Luther. This time, the imperial herald was dispatched to "our noble, dear, and esteemed Martin Luther" to ask him to come to Worms, under safe-conduct.

THE DIET OF WORMS

Luther entertained no illusions about the danger of the situation. To Spalatin he confided his conviction that to go to Worms might well be to go to his martyrdom, yet when friends urged him to remain in Wittenberg, or to take refuge with a friendly knight, he replied that he would not be deterred, even if there were as many devils in Worms as tiles on the roofs. Once again, personal considerations of safety were dismissed, and the journey began—but more in the spirit of a triumphal procession than the humble trek of a heretic. Luther had fired the German imagination, and everywhere he was enthusiastically greeted. Luther's writings had preceded him, welding anti-Roman sentiment and anti-clericalism into a massive demonstration of support. The arrival in Worms on April 16 was announced with cheers and trumpets. Aleander bitterly complained that no doubt the Germans would soon say that Luther could work miracles. Then, when placards stamped with the *Bundschuh*, the clog that had become the symbol of peasant revolt, appeared throughout Worms, at least some of Luther's countrymen concluded that social and economic protest was masking itself in the guise of religious nonconformity. To change the religious fabric of the medieval world could well precipitate a total reformation.

On the evening of April 17, Luther made his first appearance before the diet. In accordance with prearranged procedure, he was asked simply if he admitted authorship of writings ascribed to him, and if he was prepared to recant all or part of them. Luther admitted his authorship, but requested time to ponder a reply to the demand that he recant. A delay was granted, and on the following evening Luther again appeared before the assembled diet. This time, the response would echo down the centuries, as Luther took a stand that enabled him to bestride

Germany like a colossus. When he was again asked if he was prepared to recant what he had written, he replied that his writings were of varied sorts and contained a number of different kinds of assertions. Some of them were simple expositions of matters of faith; to recant these would be to repudiate doctrinal truth accepted by the church. Other writings dealt with ecclesiastical abuses that had brought great suffering to the German people. To recant these statements would be to encourage tyranny. A third group of writings consisted of various polemical treatises directed against those who had attacked the gospel. Although he could not recant their substance, he was prepared to admit that his caustic language had not been becoming to a professor of theology. Nonetheless, if any charges of error could be supported on scriptural grounds, he would readily retract.

Charles and his papal advisors had no intention of turning a secular court into a theological debating forum. Luther's opinions had already been examined and condemned; therefore, the issue was simply a question of submission to the church. When pressed for a plain and candid response, Luther retorted, "Unless I am convinced by Scripture and plain reason—I do not accept the authority of popes and councils, for they have contradicted each other—my conscience is captive to the Word of God. I cannot and I will not recant anything, for to go against conscience is neither right nor safe. God help me. Amen."[4] The meeting ended when the angered emperor left the chamber. Luther, enroute to his quarters, heard the threatening hisses of the emperor's entourage: "Into the fire!"

On the following morning, the emperor again summoned the electors and princes to discuss procedures to be adopted against Luther. When they requested more time, he read them a statement in which he declared that, like his predecessors, he would defend "the holy Catholic faith and the honor of God," and he was determined to proceed against the "notorious heretic." A thousand years of tradition must surely be of more authority than the opinion of one monk. Yet the diet was in no rush to take disciplinary action; instead it busied itself with drawing up a list of grievances against the papacy and with appointing a commission to continue discussions with Luther. The resulting meetings, while cordial, served only to emphasize Luther's insistence on the finality of scriptural authority. Although he was prepared to refer differences to a future council, he was not prepared to submit unconditionally to its decisions. Meanwhile, *Bundschuh* placards appeared in Worms and warned that force would be used against any prince or bishop who threatened Luther. Intentionally or otherwise, Luther was emerging as the champion of the exploited. Failing to reach a compromise with imperial and ecclesiastical emissaries, Luther now resolved to return to Wittenberg. Enroute, he was "kidnapped" by horsemen in Thuringia and taken to the castle Wartburg, near Eisenach, where he would remain for the next ten months. An anxious Elector Frederick had decided that it would be safer to hide his embattled professor.

[4]Roland Bainton, *Here I Stand,* (New York: Mentor Books, 1962), p. 144.

PHOTOGRAPH: THE WARTBURG

From May 1521 until February 1522, Luther disguised as Knight George, was in seclusion here. He called it his "Patmos," and from here he anxiously watched the progress of his reforms.

Courtesy Deutsches Reisebüro

Luther had left Worms on April 26; one month later, the emperor affixed his signature to the Edict of Worms that condemned Luther as a "devil in the habit of a monk." He was accused of advocating policies that made for "rebellion, division, war, murder, robbery, arson, and the collapse of Christendom." As a "convicted heretic," he was to be cut off from society. Although the edict was issued in the name of the diet, many of the princes and electors, including Frederick and Louis of the Palatinate, had left earlier. Later, the estates favorable to Luther would question the legality of the edict.

PROGRESSIVE REFORM OR CHAOTIC REVOLUTION?

Meanwhile, in the castle retreat, Luther was seeking to calm his restless spirit with scholarly endeavor. His literary output indicated that his seclusion in his *Patmos* was anything but a vacation. From his pen came, in less than a year,

Gottes wort
bleibt ewig.

Biblia/das ist/die
gantze Heilige Sch=
rifft Deudsch.
Mart. Luth.
Wittemberg.
Begnadet mit Kür=
furstlicher zu Sachsen
freiheit.
Gedruckt durch Hans Lufft.

M. D. XXXIIII.

TITLE PAGE OF LUTHER'S TRANSLATION OF THE BIBLE, 1534

One of Luther's most influential efforts was his translation of the Bible into literary German.
His translation was a powerful force in shaping the Reformation and the German language.

treatises denouncing monastic vows, attacking auricular confession, castigating the doctrine of the mass, and rejecting violence in religious changes. At the same time, he wrote postils[5] expounding the faith he had embraced in terms of biblical thought rather than scholastic theology. His greatest achievement during his enforced exile, however, was the German translation of the New Testament. The first draft was completed in eleven weeks. This translation, destined to become a

[5]These were brief comments on biblical passages, and were designed for reading by the general public.

landmark in German literature and the spiritual reservoir of the German Reformation, was the first German translation to be based on the Greek text. In 1516, Erasmus' Greek New Testament had appeared, and Luther now used it rather than the Latin Vulgate of Jerome. Luther's translation, reflecting his mastery of the vernacular, appeared in September, 1522, and immediately swept Germany. Appropriately, the Reformation cry of *sola scriptura* had found, in its most ardent champion, its most concrete verification.

While the unhappy exile thus curbed his impatience with unending work, his colleagues in Wittenberg resolved to carry on the work of reform. Karlstadt, together with the professor of Greek, Philip Melanchthon, and an Augustinian, Gabriel Zwilling, assumed leadership. The scholarly Melanchthon wanted no part of radical and violent change, and his timid spirit was no match for the bombast and aroused holy indignation of his associates. Karlstadt and Zwilling were determined to usher in a new era; anyone who would not support them was their foe. Soon Wittenberg became the scene of startling changes and innovations. Communion, in keeping with Luther's assertion that the laity also be given wine, was served in both kinds; vestments were discarded, images destroyed, and fasting denounced. Marriage of priests, monks, and nuns was encouraged, and Karlstadt himself announced his betrothal to a young lady of about sixteen.[6]

As the pace of innovation quickened, Luther himself paid a clandestine visit to Wittenberg. The manuscripts he had forwarded to Spalatin, entitled *On Monastic Vows* and *On the Abolition of Private Masses*, had not been sent to the printer. Luther now convinced the hesitant Spalatin that they should immediately be published; at the same time, he approved the religious changes, although he warned against excesses and violence. His champions were encouraged to gain their victory through preaching and praying, not by fighting. Then, as quietly as he had come, he returned to the Wartburg, once more to drive himself on in his literary pursuits.

In Wittenberg the tempo of reform heightened as the emotions of the mobs were stirred. Turmoil threatened to disrupt normal life in the troubled town. Further confusion was injected when the *Zwickau prophets*, visionaries from the borders of Bohemia, arrived and confidently announced that they were receiving revelations directly from God. God was about to intervene in history, to punish the wicked, and to establish His kingdom, where social distinctions would be abolished. Some who heard the enthusiastic predictions of pending social revolution determined to take matters into their own hands. With the religious revolution in full swing and the specter of social revolt haunting Wittenberg, Melanchthon urged the return of Luther as the only man who could stem the threatening flood. Elector Frederick, smarting under the taunts from his rival, Duke George, insisted that order could not be sacrificed for reform. Karlstadt would have to stop preaching. The city council, without the elector's approval, invited Luther to return and restore sanity.

Again demonstrating total disregard for his personal safety, knowing that

---

[6]Gordon Rupp, *Patterns of Reformation* (Philadelphia: Fortress Press, 1969), p. 100.

ENGRAVING: KARLSTADT AND ICONOCLASM

In his zeal to reform the church, Karlstadt urged the populace to destroy images and other vestiges of the traditional faith. A wave of iconoclasm swept Wittenberg and alarmed both political and religious leaders. Luther, watching from the Wartburg, decided to return to restore order. In a series of public sermons which displayed remarkable oratorical skill, he regained control of his reform movement.

Courtesy Lutherhalle, Wittenberg

imperial ban and ecclesiastical excommunication had branded him a public enemy, and that the elector would assume no responsibility for what might happen, Luther resolved to return to Wittenberg. His cause, which he confidently asserted was that of the gospel, could not be allowed to suffer disrepute. Upon his return, Luther launched a vigorous and successful campaign—a campaign that drew its strength not from the official support of the authorities, although this was there, but from the persuasiveness of his preaching.[7] Religious reform was not to be a matter of iconoclasm, of outward austerity and puritanism, of anti-sacerdotalism, but of profound spiritual wrestling, of inner agony, of love and patience rather than violence and denunciation. "Without love," Luther declared, "faith is nothing."[8] Personal inspiration was not to supersede objective scriptural authority. As Luther continued to preach, tranquility returned, and

[7]The sermons Luther preached on this occasion appear in English translation in *Luther's Works* (St. Louis and Philadelphia: Concordia and Muhlenberg, 1955–   ), L1:69 ff. (Hereafter this edition is cited as *LW*.)

[8]*Ibid.*, p. 71.

those who saw their radicalism discredited left the town. Karlstadt, from his new pulpit in Orlamuende, denounced the new "pope" in Wittenberg. Zwilling moved to a pastorate in Altenburg. The discomfited "prophets," having failed to convince Luther of the reliability of their method of acquiring new truths, left Wittenberg to arouse dissension elsewhere. The splintering of the Reformation had begun.

THE KNIGHTS' WAR

But the threat of division was not restricted to religion. Some of the imperial knights, remnants of a medieval society, saw in Luther a possible remedy for their increasingly anachronistic position. They resolved to capitalize on the religious ferment and to exploit the church for their own ends. The knightly class, responsible only to the emperor, felt its position being steadily eroded as local princes extended their territorial claims, and as towns grew in commercial power. Changing economic and political patterns threatened the knights with extinction, and reduced them to the status of predators. Perhaps their wavering fortunes could find a godsend in the cause of Luther.

Foremost among those who fanned the smoldering discontent of the knights was the humanist and pamphleteer, Ulrich von Hutten. His disenchantment with clericalism, his distrust of foreign elements in Germany, his hope for restoration of the glories of the old German empire, led him to adopt an increasingly hostile attitude toward the papacy, and to devote his considerable literary skill to the firing of German nationalism. His rapier thrusts in *Letters of Obscure Men* gave way to a savage frontal assault in the *The Roman Triad*, a series of witty epigrams denouncing the ostentation and avarice of the papacy. Hutten, however, cared little for doctrinal subtleties; his philippics were designed solely to arouse a spirit of nationalism. When he saw that the Wittenberg movement, which he at first had scorned as the quarrel of hot-headed monks, might well become the ally of his own drive for liberty and independence, he responded enthusiastically. His notoriety was such that he was specifically denounced in the bull condemning Luther. Hutten's goals were readily endorsed by Franz von Sickingen—a powerful knight who from his castle, the Ebernburg, controlled part of the Rhine valley—and who was prepared to use his sword for "the cause of Luther" which he interpreted as the cause of Germany. Sickingen was not the only Knight who invited Luther to take asylum in the Ebernburg; Sylvester von Schaumberg was one of several who at the same time offered to bring one hundred knights to Luther's assistance.

In the summer of 1522, under the leadership of Hutten and Sickingen, a fraternal union of the nobility announced its intention of secularizing ecclesiastical lands. To the knights, the seizure of church properties seemed to fit in neatly with Luther's call for an end to the temporal power of the bishops. Victory here, Hutten boasted, would help to bring an end to "the reign of the devil."

The elector and archbishop of Trier, long a foe of Sickingen, was selected as a fitting victim. Sickingen, announcing his determination to "give the gospel an opening," led the attack, but the attempt to restore the prelate to his vows of apostolic poverty collapsed. When the archbishop, supported by forces from Hesse and the Palatinate, counter attacked, numerous knights' bastions were destroyed. Sickingen himself died in the war, carrying an era in German chivalry to the grave with him. Hutten fled to Switzerland, there soon to end his volatile career. Luther, who had been asked to associate himself with what was heralded as a movement to end tyranny and opposition in Germany, had opposed the appeal to violence, once again insisting that the solution of ills was not to be achieved with the sword.

THE PEASANTS' REVOLT

Luther demonstrated a rather ambivalent attitude toward the events surrounding the Peasants' Revolt. This massive uprising, the greatest in a series of social disturbances that convulsed Europe, was directly linked to religious innovation and imperial inaction.[9]

For more than a century, the German peasantry had been in ferment, but in the decade preceding Luther's emergence as a national figure, peasant uprisings had become especially violent and widespread. This came about as a result of the landlords' attempt to reimpose feudal rights that had fallen into disuse. In the aftermath of the Black Death, with a greatly lessened population, peasants and serfs were enjoying both higher wages and a heightened prosperity. At the same time, the position of the landlords deteriorated because of economic recession and rising prices. Peasants were determined to maintain their free use of commons and forests and to resist any new taxes and duties, such as indirect taxes on food. Nobles and peasants found it hard to reconcile their respective positions, especially since the German social pyramid lacked a strong middle level that could exert a moderating influence. Then, when Luther denounced ecclesiastical wealth and power and insisted that all were equal before God, social and economic grievance seemed to gain religious sanction.

The peasants, rallying around their symbol, the *Bundschuh*, believed that Luther's appeal to the Bible and his attack on clerical abuses would lend itself readily to support of their position. Alienation between prince and peasant increased in the years immediately following the Diet of Worms, as princes and bishops repeatedly asserted their determination to crush the new faith. In addition, despite a warning that his action would lead to riot and rebellion, Charles forbade the calling of a national church council as demanded by the diet in 1524. Then when various lords attempted to increase feudal dues on the restless peasants, the spark for conflagration had been supplied.

[9]Guenther Franz, *Der Deutsche Bauernkrieg* (Darmstadt: Hermann Gentner Verlag, 1952).

WOODCUT: MEMBERS OF THE BUNDSCHUH SURROUND A KNIGHT, by Hans Weiditz

The banner of the peasants boldly challenged the political, religious, and social order. Sometimes, unlike the discomfited knight in this woodcut, members of the lower nobility joined the revolt in the futile hope of improving their own position. One such adventurer was the celebrated Goetz von Berlichingen, "with the iron hand."

Staatliche Graphische Sammlung, Munich

Trouble broke out in Swabia and soon spread throughout southern and central Germany. Social, political, cultural, and economic conditions here were more conducive to revolution than conditions in the north. In the north, powerful secular and ecclesiastical lords had largely subordinated the lesser nobles, who in the south continued their despotic rule over the peasants. Serfdom was found chiefly in the southwest part of Germany, while areas along the lower Rhine had developed an economy in which state revenues came largely from commercial taxes rather than peasant dues. Also, the peasant village communities of the south, enjoying a significant measure of self-government, lent themselves more readily to organization for revolt than did the isolated farms of the north. Significantly, the largest south German state, Bavaria, remained largely untouched by the rebellion. Here, a strong central government had absorbed much of the power of local lords and prelates, thus restricting their capacity for despotism over the peasantry.

Champions of the revolt outlined their demands in various documents, most notably the *Twelve Articles* of Memmingen. On the surface, it was a remarkably restrained, conciliatory manifesto; the princes saw at once, however, that it posed a direct threat to their despotic power. The articles stipulated, among other things, that communities should have the right to appoint or depose their pastors; taxes should be reasonable and serfdom be abolished; the riches of nature should be available to all; and arbitrary laws and oppressive demands by lords would not be tolerated. Finally, in a deliberate attempt to tie their revolt to that of Luther, they asserted their willingness to withdraw any demand ''not in agreement with the word of God.'' The articles, with their clarion call for justice and liberty, were an unmistakable challenge to the old order whose very existence was predicated on privilege and exploitation.

The revolt soon spread beyond Swabia. Karlstadt, who had brought his iconoclastic ideas to Rothenburg, in Franconia, had encouraged peasant unrest and demands for political rights there. Although he attempted to mitigate revolutionary excesses, he failed to control the dissident elements. Disillusioned, he withdrew to Basel. But the revolt continued. In Frankfurt, the peasants' demands for religious, political, and social changes were expressed in the *Forty Two Articles*. In Thuringia, the incendiary Thomas Muentzer (1491–1525) exerted a strong influence.

This secular priest of considerable learning proclaimed the heavenly kingdom at hand. It was to be characterized by social equality and the extermination of all those who opposed drastic change and who wanted to continue the old order. Earlier, as pastor at Zwickau, Muentzer had developed radical ideas about a continuing divine revelation which superseded the written Word. Those who, like Luther, stressed the authority of the Scriptures he regarded as hopelessly enmeshed in the bonds of corrupt tradition. When he began to inveigh against those who refused to follow his lead, thus indicating that they were not of the ''elect,'' the town council opposed him. Having fled to Prague, he published his *Prague Manifesto*, an inflammatory appeal for support in the establishment of a new order, but again he failed.[10]

He withdrew, and became pastor in Allstedt, a town near Eisleben. Here his fiery preaching aroused such interest and consternation that John Frederick, nephew of Elector Frederick, complained of the ''Satan of Allstedt.'' Muentzer was asked to preach before Duke John and John Frederick, as well as other Saxon princes and officials.[11] He used the opportunity to make an audacious appeal for the extermination of the ''ungodly,'' for God was about to establish a new society. If the princes would hesitate to use the sword to wipe out the ''idolators,'' sure ruin would be the result. Muentzer soon realized that he had failed to recruit champions for his cause, and that flight would be the safest policy.

He came to Muehlhausen, where a spirit of unrest had gripped both peasants and townspeople; this social unrest coalesced with his apocalyptic design. A new

[10]Thomas Muentzer, *Schriften und Briefe*, ed. Guenther Franz (Guetersloh: Gerd Mohn, 1968), pp. 491–511.

[11]George H. Williams and Angel M. Mergal, eds., *Spiritual and Anabaptist Writers* (Philadelphia: Westminster Press, 1957), pp. 49–70.

political and social order was established. Ecclesiastical properties were secularized and class privileges terminated. Neighboring castles were destroyed, while nobles were either killed or compelled to join the revolutionary forces. Muentzer, exhorting the faithful not to let "the blood cool on your swords," was confident that the time of eschatological fulfillment had come. With a cry of "sword of the Lord and of Gideon," he aroused the mob into a frenzy. Social revolution had become a holy war.[12]

From Swabia and Franconia the movement swept down the Rhine to Cologne and Muenster. Sometimes knights, such as Goetz von Berlichingen and Florian Geyer, threw their lot in with the insurgents. More ominous was the fact that a number of towns joined the rebels. While most of the imperial free cities resisted cooperation with the peasants, a large number of territorial towns welcomed them. The free cities, anxious to preserve their commercial prosperity, were also concerned that they might lose their traditional domination over the surrounding peasants. However, where artisans wrested control from the city council, as in Rothenburg ob der Tauber, peasantry and townsmen were able to form a cautious alliance. Many of the territorial towns, usually small and dominated by an agricultural economy, found that common interests (and often a common enemy) provided the basis for strong cooperation with the peasants.[13] For a time, such a combination of forces proved strong enough to compel even powerful princes such as the electors of Mainz and of the Palatinate to accept the *Twelve Articles*.

But the revolutionaries would almost defeat themselves on account of internal dissension and confusion. Their lack of a central target, and of competent leadership, prevented their developing an effective force. Some of the peasant bands wanted a peasant-controlled government, others insisted on the abolition of all rulers except pope and emperor, while others wanted only moderate social and religious reforms. Nobles found their task greatly eased by the confusion of the exasperated peasants. At Frankenhausen, Philip, Landgrave of Hesse, offered to spare the peasants if they would hand over Muentzer. When they failed to do so, the landgrave's forces, combined with those of Duke George of Saxony, slaughtered the discomfited mob (May 15, 1525). Muentzer escaped only to be captured, tortured, and executed.[14]

The insurgents suffered a similar fate throughout the Empire. In Swabia and Franconia, the Swabian League, composed of princes and cities, drowned the revolt in a sea of blood, then imposed further restrictions on the hapless peasants. Count George Truchsess, his forces augmented by soldiers returning from the war with France, slaughtered, roasted alive, or barbarously maimed those who

[12]See Abraham Friesen, *Reformation and Utopia* (Wiesbaden: Franz Steiner Verlag, 1974), pp. 37–45.

[13]Peter Blickle, *Die Revolution von 1525* (Muenchen: Oldenbourg, 1975), pp. 156–174.

[14]In prison, he admitted and recanted his "errors," but the gruesome torture accompanying these assertions suggests that little significance can be attached to them (Rupp, *Patterns*, pp. 246).

dared to protest. The executioner of Truchsess boasted that he had personally beheaded 1200 rebels.[15] The lesson was further driven home when the bishop of Wuerzburg celebrated his restoration by a series of public executions, not only in Wuerzburg, but throughout his diocese. Equally harsh treatment was meted out to the peasants in western Germany, where the duke of Lorraine burned out the vestiges of dissent. Few princes agreed with Elector Frederick that secular and ecclesiastical oppression had given "the poor people cause for their revolt." His generosity of spirit might have softened the subsequent vengeance, but he died during the war. By late 1525, the conflagration in Germany had been quenched and the princes could breathe easier again, but the bitterness that the revolt had left in its wake continued to color the whole reformation movement. In the Austrian Tyrol, the revolt continued for another year. Here the radical Michael Gaismaier, demanding sweeping religious and social change, called for an end to economic inequality and for community ownership of mines and commerce. For a time he won a series of victories against the Hapsburg rulers but was eventually defeated. He fled to Venetian territory, where he was assassinated.

As we already intimated, peasant unrest seemed to coincide with Luther's call for reform of ecclesiastical abuses. Early in the revolt, the peasants appealed to Luther, and gained a sympathetic hearing. His *Admonition to Peace: A Reply to the Twelve Articles* urged the authorities to grant the just claims of the peasants. The princes were excoriated for having oppressed the poor and thus having driven them to desperate measures. At the same time, Luther warned that relief was not to be sought in armed insurrection against authority, nor was his call for a spiritual reformation to be used to justify demands in the secular realm. Attempting to bridge the gap between peasant and prince, he suggested that representatives of both groups meet to discuss grievances. When these warnings went unheeded, he visited the discontented areas, attempting to persuade the rebels to abandon their schemes. Now, at great personal risk, his voice often drowned in the hostile response of the masses, he once again set himself against a rising tide of disorder. While he was thus desperately but futilely engaged, word arrived that the dying elector Frederick wanted to see him. The message had come too late; the faithful elector had died amidst the trepidations and anxiety that were engulfing the land. As the torrent of tragedy continued to crest, Luther became convinced that unless order were restored all would be lost. He now published his savage pamphlet, *Against the Robbing and Murderous Peasant Gangs*, a virulent missive that encouraged the rulers to show no mercy in exterminating those who had become "like mad dogs." All restraint was gone: "Let him who can, smite, slay, and stab." The princes needed no goading in their grisly work.

The horror and tragedy of the peasants' uprising, and Luther's immoderate attack, would leave permanent effects on the struggle for religious change. Catholic princes blamed Luther for the conflagration, while some of the op-

[15]Adolph Waas, *Die Bauern* (Muenchen: G. Callwey, 1964), p. 236.

pressed masses bitterly denounced him as a traitor.[16] Fond hopes of associating social and economic change with religious reform seemed shattered. Many who had looked to a national hero now sullenly receded into the background. Although Luther attempted to heal the wounds of the war, and urged the victorious princes to be magnanimous, he remained suspicious of the common man. Fear of insurrection would continue to haunt him, so that even innocuous movements which he distrusted and misunderstood would arouse in him indignation and violent response. Hereafter, Luther insisted even more strongly that religious reform should filter down through the authorities, not up from the masses.

It is therefore all the more remarkable to note that Luther's sermons continued to be given to congregations that were largely peasant and artisan. His personal magnetism and persuasive power continued to attract and fascinate even those who were disappointed to see that he had so sharply separated secular from spiritual reform. Of course, many peasants had not been involved. In some areas, especially northern Germany, the religious reform movement continued to spread and attract the support of the lower classes, but in the regions where the revolt had been most severe, a strong reaction often set in.

Luther's actions during the convulsions of the war illustrated his theory of the two "realms,"[17] already enunciated in his *On Secular Authority: To What Extent It Should be Obeyed* (1523).[18] In this document, he asserted that the medieval church had been too concerned with political affairs. A better way, he insisted, was to recognize that both secular and ecclesiastical authority derived from God, and neither should dominate the other. Both the spiritual and the secular realms had their legitimate, divinely sanctioned spheres to control. Temporal authorities should be concerned with the maintenance of peace and justice, not with the definition of doctrine. Luther contended that "the soul is not under the authority of Caesar." Should a secular ruler command anything contrary to the Scriptures, he should be passively disobeyed, not violently opposed. Even a wicked ruler was entitled to obedience in matters relating to body and property. Violent revolution could never be condoned. As for bishops and priests, their rule was "not a matter of authority or power, but a service and an office." Their "authority" was "nothing more than the inculcating of God's Word."

LUTHER'S MARRIAGE

Amidst the tumult of war, Luther decided to marry. He had earlier helped other monks and nuns to overcome the pangs of conscience about breaking monastic vows, and assisted them in establishing their own homes. One such nun, Katherine von Bora, was not impressed with the mate that Luther selected

[16]Max Steinmetz, ed., *Der deutsche Bauernkrieg und Thomas Muentzer* (Leipzig: Karl-Marx Universitaet, 1976), pp. 79–84.

[17]Heinrich Bornkamm, *Luther's Doctrine of the Two Kingdoms in the Context of His Theology*, trans. Karl Hertz (Philadelphia: Fortress Press, 1966).

[18]*LW*, XLV: 83-117.

for her, although she indicated that he himself would meet with a different response. At first Luther, who insisted that he would soon die a martyr's death, refused to consider the idea. Eventually, with parental encouragement, he decided to marry so that, as he remarked, he might spite the devil and the pope and give testimony of his faith. Although the marriage began with little romance, a warm and genuine relationship developed. Luther never tired of singing the praises of Katherine, for whom he had such terms of endearment as "my lord" and "your grace." He ruefully admitted that he was paying more attention to her than to God. Six children were born to the marriage—and Luther's exuberance over his progeny eloquently testifies to thorough enjoyment of domestic life. Katherine, on her part, kept the home a cheerful place where her husband found release from his worries. The Luther household was a model of hospitality, for Luther gladly assisted poor students and travelers who had come to Wittenberg. It was not at all unusual to have a dozen guests. At least some measure of Luther's cordiality may be seen in his treatment of his old opponent Karlstadt. When, almost immediately after the wedding, Karlstadt, who was fleeing from the fury of the peasants' war, requested lodging, Luther did not refuse. Small wonder that his wife sometimes complained that he was always too ready to sacrifice himself for others, and was likely to bankrupt the household.

Suggestions for Further Reading

Althaus, Paul. *Luthers Haltung im Bauernkrieg.* Basel: B. Schwabe, 1953.

Bax, E. B. *The Peasants' War in Germany.* London: S. Sonnenschein, 1903.

Bensing, M., and S. Hoyer. *Der deutsche Bauernkrieg.* Berlin: Deutscher Militaerverlag, 1965.

Bornkamm, Heinrich. *Luther's Doctrine of the Two Kingdoms in the Context of his Theology.* Translated by K. H. Hertz. Philadelphia: Fortress Press, 1966.

Brandi, Karl. *The Emperor Charles V.* Translated by C. V. Wedgwood. New York: Knopf, 1939.

Brunner, Otto. *Adeliges Landleben und Europaeischer Geist.* Salzburg: Mueller, 1949.

Engels, Friedrich. *The German Revolutions: The Peasant War in Germany;* and *Germany: Revolution and Counter-Revolution.* Edited by Leonard Krieger. Chicago: University of Chicago Press, 1967.

Franz, Guenther. *Quellen zur Geschichte des Bauernkrieges.* Munich: Oldenbourg, 1963.

———. *Der deutsche Bauernkrieg.* 7th ed. Darmstadt: Hermann Gentner, 1965.

Friesen, Abraham. *Reformation and Utopia: The Marxist Interpretation of the Reformation and its Antecedents.* Wiesbaden: Steiner, 1974.

Gritsch, Eric W. *Reformer Without a Church.* Philadelphia: Fortress Press 1967.

Hitchcock, William R. *The Background of the Knights' Revolt.* Berkeley: University of California Press, 1958.

Muentzer, Thomas. *Schriften und Briefe.* Edited by. Guenther Franz. Guetersloh: Gerd Mohn, 1968.

Rischar, Klaus. *John Eck auf dem Reichstag zu Augsburg 1530.* Muenster: Aschendorffsche Verlagsbuchhandlung, 1968.

*****Sessions, Kyle C.,** ed. *Reformation and Authority: The Meaning of the Peasants' Revolt.* Lexington, Mass.: D. C. Heath, 1968.

Smirin, M. M. *Die Volksreformation des Thomas Muentzers.* Berlin: Ruetten & Loening, 1952.

*****Troeltsch, Ernst.** *The Social Teachings of the Christian Churches.* Translated by Olive Wyon. 2 vols. New York: Harper & Row, A Harper Torchbook, 1960.

Waas, Adolf. *Die Bauern im Kampf um Gerechtigkeit, 1300–1525.* Munich: Callwey, 1964.

*Indicates paperback edition.

4

Stalemate at Augsburg

GROWING POLITICAL PARTICULARISM
AND AUTONOMY

The peasants' war buttressed the opinion of many that Luther's ideas challenged not only the religious but the entire social order as well. Emperor Charles, unable to refashion society in his own mold, nonetheless resolved to exterminate what he regarded as pestilential heresy. For several decades, however, his plans against Luther were repeatedly sidetracked by pressures from the pope, the Turkish Empire, and the Valois dynasty. Shortly after the emperor left Worms in 1521, he was at war with France, spending much of his time in Spain. He would not return to the Empire until 1530. In the meantime, his brother Ferdinand acted as regent in the German possessions.

In the decade following the promulgation of the Edict of Worms, Ferdinand found his religious plans constantly thwarted by political demands of the German princes. Their insistence on a voice in government led to the establishment of a new imperial governing council. Reluctantly, Charles had agreed that such a council should function during his absence. But the council was more concerned with protecting the power of the estates than with enforcing the Edict of Worms. Internal dissension, fear of imperial encroachment on territorial rights, and popular clamor for religious and social reform prevented the council from actively pursuing uniformity in religion.

All three diets held in Nuremberg between 1522 and 1524 failed to produce a unified imperial religious policy. The first barely touched on religious issues, for the Turk was again threatening the Empire. When the second diet opened its sessions late in 1522, the papal nuncio, Francesco Chieregati, conveyed the pope's urgent desire for reform. Upon the death of Leo X in December, 1521, the former tutor of Charles, Adrian VI, had succeeded to the papal throne, and had immediately called for reform. Now at Nuremberg, the papal nuncio expressed official regret for ecclesiastical abuses and promised that reform measures would be undertaken. Meanwhile, however, he stressed that the internal threat of heresy, combined with external pressure from the Turkish invasion, demanded immediate enforcement of the Edict of Worms. The papal brief reminded the members of the exemplary punishment inflicted on Ananias and Sapphira, or Hus and Jerome. Luther was compared to Mohammed, whose continued activity periled the church. On his part, Adrian promised "to expend every effort to reform first this Curia, whence perhaps all this evil has come."[1] The response of the diet demonstrated the diversity of opinion relative to the Edict of Worms. While the pope was commended for promising reform, he was further requested to summon a church council to meet within a year in some convenient place in Germany. In 1522 the estates agreed to ask Elector Frederick to check Luther. Then, to impress upon the pope the urgency of reform, the estates drew up a list of *One Hundred Grievances of the German Nation* against the papacy. The papal confession had been found inadequate.

Economic concerns also figured prominently in the deliberations of the diet. The estates suggested that the payment of annates to the papal treasury was impoverishing Germany; the sums collected should be retained by the emperor for defense of the realm. There was also a clash between the nobles and the cities that manifested itself in the nobles' demand that growth of business monopolies be checked and that a tax be imposed on trade. To this, Augsburg, home of the Fuggers, vigorously replied that it would be wise to "let the merchant alone, and put no restrictions on his ability or capital." Siding with the emerging bourgeois class, the emperor saw to it that the restrictive measures against capitalism remained a dead letter. Once again, the diet failed to act with unity and power.

When the next diet met in Nuremberg in January, 1524, the papal cause would fare no better. The new pope, Clement VII, who had succeeded Adrian in 1523, directed Cardinal Lorenzo Campeggio to secure the suppression of heresy, but even prior to the legate's appearance before the diet, jeers and insults hurled by the mob along his way presaged futile effort. In an innocuous decision, the diet promised to carry out the Edict of Worms "as far as was possible." The real outcome of the diet was reflected in its call for a church council and its warning not to "root out the good with the bad." As an interim measure, the diet called for a general assembly of the German nation to precede the general church council. This attempt at compromise accomplished little and pleased none. While the diet expressed support of the Edict of Worms, it also admitted that the edict was unenforceable. Demands for a general council implied an infringement on papal authority, and the decision to call a special German assembly the following November asserted territorial independence, thus challenging imperial power.

[1]John C. Olin, *The Catholic Reformation: Savonarola to Ignatius Loyola* (New York: Harper & Row, 1969), p. 125.

Furthermore, as Campeggio observed, it was unthinkable that a German assembly should presume to settle problems that concerned the whole church.

GROWING RELIGIOUS DIVISION

In the aftermath of the diet, lack of leadership and unity again frustrated efforts at reform of the church and suppression of heresy. Charles vetoed the proposed assembly, and instead issued a decree demanding strict enforcement of the Edict of Worms. To Pope Clement he confided his uneasiness about delay in ecclesiastical reform, and suggested that the pope proceed with all due haste in summoning a general council of the church. Meanwhile, at the instigation of Campeggio, the Regensburg Union was formed for the express purpose of exterminating heresy and implementing a reform program. Its members, all staunch opponents of Luther, included Archduke Ferdinand, the two dukes of Bavaria, and several ecclesiastical leaders of southern Germany. In the following year, northern defenders of the old faith formed the League of Dessau, advising the emperor that the purpose was to combat the schemes of the supporters of Luther. Prominent members of the league included Duke George of Saxony, the electors of Brandenburg and Mainz, and Duke Henry of Brunswick. Also in 1525, a number of reforming princes, sympathetic to Luther, formed the League of Torgau. Its leaders, Elector John of Saxony, who had just succeeded his brother, and Landgrave Philip of Hesse, were joined by lesser nobles as well as several imperial cities which were determined to use the religious controversy to strengthen their independence. Germany was gradually being divided into two hostile camps.

With the decisive imperial victory over the French in the battle of Pavia in 1525, Charles appeared well-situated to demand submission to his will. Yet, before the diet met in Speyer in 1526, the tide had turned against him. Clement VII, fearful of too powerful an emperor, joined Francis I king of France, and several Italian princes, in the defensive League of Cognac. At the same time, the Turks were again threatening the Empire, and in 1526, gained a smashing victory over the Hungarians at Mohacs. Once again, Charles needed united German support against external threat; religious reform and suppression of heresy could not take precedence. It was against this background that Ferdinand presented to the estates in the summer of 1526, his brother's demands that the Edict of Worms be enforced. Several clerical members had refused to attend, for while the deliberations were being conducted, the emperor was at war with the pope. The most that could be extracted from the princes was a promise to conduct themselves in such a manner that they could answer to God and the emperor. This act, termed a recess, gave impetus to the establishment of a territorial ecclesiastical system and foreshadowed the formal acceptance of *cuius regio, eius religio* by the Peace of Augsburg, 1555.

THE CONSOLIDATION OF LUTHERANISM

Those estates sympathetic to Luther interpreted the recess as a mandate for religious reform according to their beliefs. Elector John, at the behest of Luther and his associates, appointed special visitation committees to examine, reform, and reorganize the life of the Saxon churches. These committees, composed of theologians, court representatives, and preachers, fostered the close association of secular and religious leaders and marked the beginning of a state church. The basic principles for reorganization were outlined in Melanchthon's "formula of doctrine and rites," his *Instruction of the Visitors to the Pastors* (1528). Luther, in his preface, noted that the visitation had been necessitated by the appalling ignorance of the clergy and the indolence of the bishops. He insisted that spiritual functions remained solely in the province of the church, and that the secular ruler should interfere only to prevent anarchy. Luther's views on the "two kingdoms,"[2] as developed in numerous treatises, stressed that church and state each had legitimate spheres of operation. The state should not define doctrine, nor should the church exercise political control. Both entities should supplement the other in building God's kingdom on earth.

The visitations eventually gave birth to the consistory. This instrument of church government, usually composed of lawyers and ecclesiastics, was appointed by the temporal ruler. It exercised discipline and, by its very structure, kept church authority centralized.

From his active participation in the visitations, Luther gained a close insight into the religious life of the people. What he saw sometimes horrified him. He found some priests scarcely able to read, others operating taverns or leading grossly immoral lives. The peasants, for their part, seemed to "learn nothing, know nothing, and abuse all their liberty." Luther resolved to try to ameliorate the problem by education. In 1529, he published the *Large Catechism*, a manual for pastors and teachers, and the *Small Catechism*, a simple, concise presentation of Christian doctrine, designed for use by laymen in the home. It was built around the Decalogue, the Apostles' Creed, the Lord's Prayer, and the sacraments of baptism and the Lord's Supper. This remarkable affirmation of faith and instrument of prayer would, next to Luther's translation of the Bible, become the most widely used and influential treatise in molding the character of what was already being called Lutheranism.

The Saxon system of visitation was similar to that followed in other areas sympathetic to Lutheran doctrine, although different patterns were sometimes suggested. In Hesse, at the diet of the Hessian estates in 1526, Francis Lambert, a former Franciscan friar from Avignon, presented a radically novel system for reorganization of the church. He proposed voluntary church membership and a

---

[2]See Heinrich Bornkamm, *Luther's Doctrine of the Two Kingdoms*, trans. K. H. Hertz (Philadelphia: Fortress Press, 1966).

democratic organization that would allow the congregation to elect its own pastor. Such congregations would then be organized into regional synods that would supervise the life of the church as a whole. When Landgrave Philip consulted Luther on the proposal, the reformer advised retaining the Saxon method of visitation. One suggestion that Philip did implement, however, was the founding of a university for the training of pastors and teachers. In 1527 the first Lutheran university came into being at Marburg, thanks to Lambert's foresight and the confiscation of monastic properties.

Elsewhere, the Saxon visitation became the model for the introduction or consolidation of Lutheran teaching. In 1525, Albert of Brandenburg (1490–1568), grand master of the Teutonic Knights, adopted Lutheranism, secularized his possessions as a duchy under the suzerainty of the Polish king, and, in 1526, introduced the visitation program. In Brunswick-Lueneburg, Schleswig, Holstein, Mansfeld, and Brunswick-Calenberg the visitation became the channel for reform. Numerous cities, such as Bremen, Hamburg, Luebeck, Brunswick, Goslar, Strasbourg, Augsburg, and Nuremberg, decreed reform according to the Lutheran pattern. Usually, the city council charged one of the clergy with the responsibility of reorganizing the religious life of the city. Monastic properties in states and cities were secularized, often to be used for education and poor relief; sometimes, unfortunately, the decision to adopt Lutheranism was prompted by the desire for personal enrichment. In most instances, however, the city council acted because of pressure from the "common man."[3] Frequently, members of a city council requested help from Johan Bugenhagen, a pastor at Wittenberg, in drawing up a constitution and outlining functions of religious and civic officials. Sometimes, if a council resisted too long, as in Memmingen, it was forced out of office.

This expansion of Lutheranism, especially in the towns, was often the result of popular pressure, but no simple formula can be applied to explain the acceptance or rejection of the Reformation teachings. In the imperial free city of Reutlingen, a Lutheran preacher, Matthew Alber, gained strong popular support. By early 1524, the city council, pressured by Archduke Ferdinand, the bishop of Constance, and the Swabian League, resolved to take action against Alber. A determined citizenry vowed to support him, and the city council was forced to reverse its position. In Ulm, a beleaguered city council referred the issue to its citizens, who overwhelmingly voted for the new teachings. A similar procedure in Rottweil, however, demonstrated that a majority of citizens there supported the traditional faith. Not infrequently, as in Schwaebisch-Gmuend, military intervention from outside preserved the old order against the wishes of the majority of the townsmen. Sometimes guilds, other organizations in the community, or newly formed citizens' committees became the vehicle for expressing support for

[3]Eberhard Naujoks, *Obrigkeitsgedanke, Zunftverfassung und Reformation* (Stuttgart: Kohlheimer, 1958), p. 57.

reform. Thus, in Goettingen the cloth makers successfully demanded that a reluctant city council decree a reformation (1529). Despite opposition from Erich von Calenberg, the territorial ruler to whom the city belonged, Goettingen became and remained Lutheran. In Brunswick, both the city council and Henry of Brunswick-Wolfenbuettel, the territorial prince, opposed the reformation, but popular demonstrations convinced the council to permit the introduction of Lutheranism. Continuing opposition by the prince did not prevent the establishment of the new faith. Similar procedures were followed in other German towns, including Hamburg, Rostock, Osnabrueck, Hannover, and Luebeck.[4] In each case, despite opposition from city councils, Lutheranism triumphed in the decade following the Peasants' Revolt. Often political struggles were associated with the demand for religious change, for the citizenry demanded a greater role in government. It is remarkable that, despite Luther's stance in the peasants' upheaval, the working classes in the cities often continued to espouse his reformation; the reformation was far greater than one man or one issue. Usually, Lutheran preachers would address the townsmen, gain a following, and eventually come to dominate some community organizations. Frequently, an avalanche of pamphlets and broadsides helped to galvanize public opinion. Eventually forces for change would become strong enough to compel the city council to support Lutheranism. The attitude of the citizenry in the towns was often of crucial significance. Despite the tragedy of the Peasants' Revolt, in many parts of Germany the Reformation continued as a folk movement.[5] As noted earlier, many peasants had not joined the revolt and large parts of Germany, especially in the North, had remained quiet during the upheaval.

Yet continued popular support of the Reformation was not unique to northern Germany. Repeatedly, imperial free cities in the south were moved to adopt the Reformation, not because the city councils wished it, but because the populace demanded it.[6] In centers such as Nuremberg, Memmingen, and Constance, wary councils decided that, rather than oppose the Reformation and face the wrath of the populace, it would be more prudent to accept the new faith and hope to control its expression.

At least in part, the role of the populace in shaping Reformation movements was a logical extension of Luther's teaching of the "priesthood of all believers," and the consequent removal of distinctions between clergy and laity. This was further buttressed by Luther's emphasis on the dignity of physical labor, asserting that the peasant and craftsman honored God as much with their "good

---

[4]The role of the populace in forcing religious change is graphically portrayed in a contemporary Luebeck chronicle (quoted in Helmar Junghans, *Die Reformation in Augenzeugenberichten* [Duesseldorf: Karl Rauch, 1967], pp. 383–387).

[5]Franz Lau, "Did Popular Reformation Really Stop with the Peasants' Revolt?" trans. Kyle Sessions, in *Reformation and Authority* (Boston: D. C. Heath, 1968), pp. 94–101.

[6]Bernd Moeller, *Reichsstadt und Reformation* (Guetersloh: Gerd Mohn, 1962).

works'' as did the cleric in his spiritual ministry, for the crucial test was not the type of work involved, but rather faithfulness to one's calling.

LUTHER'S IMPACT ON MUSIC AND OTHER ARTS

Religious reform profoundly altered worship and liturgy. Luther deplored the medieval emphasis upon sacrament at the expense of the proclamation of the Word, for "all the masses stacked together are worthless without the word of God." He therefore made the sermon central, insisting that "the principal purpose of any service of worship is the teaching and the preaching of the word of God." Nonetheless, he had a profound admiration for traditional liturgical forms. His *German Mass* demonstrated his willingness to retain those forms which did not negate his understanding of the Scriptures.

The role of the congregation in worship was also strikingly changed. In the medieval Catholic liturgy, the congregation had joined in only a few responses; now the congregation sang frequently. In 1524, the publication of three collections of hymns emphasized that the evangelical doctrines were to be propagated by a singing church. One of these hymn books, the *Enchiridion* of Erfurt, contained twenty-six hymns, most of them composed by Luther. Another collection, the *Gesangbuechlein*, was published by the composer and cantor, Johan Walther, with Luther writing the introduction and Lucas Cranach supplying the woodcuts. Other hymn writers, such as Paul Speratus, expressed Lutheran teaching by means of music. The popularity and effectiveness of congregational singing was soon recognized by Luther's opponents, who asserted that "the hymns of Luther killed more souls than his sermons." Luther's stirring "A Mighty Fortress Is Our God" would become the most widely translated hymn, fittingly described by the poet Heine as the "Marseillaise of the Reformation."

Luther's work also gained robust support in the popular music and drama of the day. Music guilds, known as the *Meistersaenger*, existed in most German towns. The most celebrated member of one of these groups was the Nuremberg cobbler, Hans Sachs (1494–1576). After a few years of formal schooling, this perpetual versifier became an apprentice, journeyman, and eventually a master in the shoemakers' guild. However, his vocation did not interfere with his writing some six thousand songs, poems, dialogues, and dramas. Characterized by humor, zest for life, and praise of the qualities of honesty, industry, love, and civic duty, Sachs's works dealt with many subjects, but one of his favorites was Luther, whom he hailed as the "nightingale of Wittenberg." He became an enthusiastic champion of the Reformation, and many of his poems and plays ridiculed abuses in monasticism and the papacy. Sometimes he addressed himself to scandals within the Lutheran movement. Usually, he was heavily didactic. He deplored the commercialism and immorality of the age, and urged instead a life of simple, happy piety in which the ideals of brotherhood would prevail. Al-

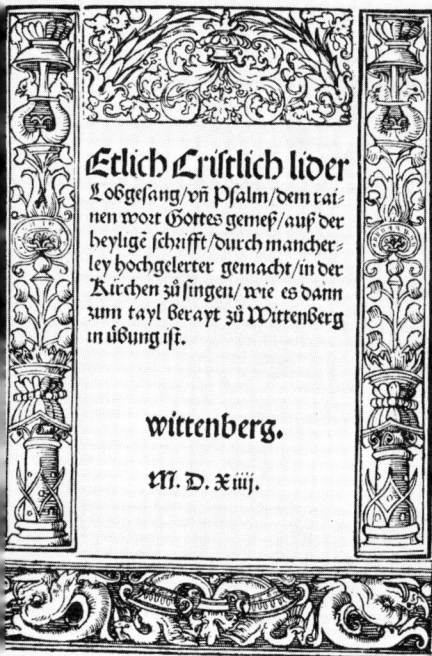

Ein Christenlichs lied Doctors
Martini Luthers/die vnausspechliche
gnaden Gottes vnd des rechten
Glaubens begreyffendt.

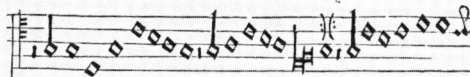

Etlich Cristlich lider
Lobgesang/vn psalm/dem rai-
nen wort Gottes gemeß/auff der
heylige schifft/durch mancher-
ley hochgelerter gemacht/in der
Kirchen zü singen/wie es dann
zum tayl berayt zü Wittenberg
in übung ist.

wittenberg.

M. D. Xiiij.

Nun frewt euch lieben christen gmeyn.

¶Nun frewt euch lieben Christen gmein/Vnd laßt vns frö-
lich springen/Das wir getrost vnd all in ein/Mit lust vnd
liebe singen/Was got an vns gewendet hat/Vnd seine süsse
wunder that/Gar theür hat ers erworben.

¶Dem Teüffel ich gefangen lag/Jm todt war ich verloren/
Mein sünd mich quellet nacht vn tag/Darinn ich war ge-
boren/Jch viel auch ymmer tieffer drein/Es war kain güts
am leben mein/Die sünd hat mich besessen.

¶Mein güte werck die golten nicht/Es war mit jn verdor-
ben/Der frey will hasset gots gericht/Er war zum güt er-
storben/Die angst mich zü verzweyffeln treyb/Das nichts
dann sterben bey mir bleyb/Zur hellen müst ich sincken.

TITLE PAGE: LUTHERAN HYMNAL

Congregational singing formed a vital part of the Lutheran Reformation. This is the first of several hymnals to which Luther contributed. For Luther, music was to be "praised as second only to the Word of God."

Courtesy Lutherhalle, Wittenberg

though Sachs cannot be regarded as a great artist, the role he played in populariz-
ing Reformation doctrines among these on whom theological subtleties would be
lost cannot be underestimated.

Other forms of art, such as woodcutting and engraving, also served as effective media for communication of Lutheran emphases. Albrecht Duerer, Peter
Vischer, and Hans Sebald Beham, with their woodcuts, etchings, and engravings, immortalized Reformation men and themes, while the painting of Lucas
Cranach the elder, and of Hans Holbein the younger, gave the Reformation some
of its most inspiring, as well as polemic, art.

THE EMERGENCE OF HOSTILE CAMPS

During this period of rapid expansion of the new faith, the tension between the
two religious camps was strained almost to the breaking point by the machina-
tions of Otto von Pack, a counselor at the court of Duke George of Saxony. This

Die Wittenbergisch Nachtigall
Die man yetz höret vberall.

Jch sage euch/wa dise schweygē/so werden die stein schreyē Luce.19.

TITLE PAGE: THE WITTENBERG NIGHTENGALE, by Hans Šachs

One of the numerous ballads composed by Hans Sachs praises Luther as a nightengale who had aroused a world from its slumber and lethargy.

Courtesy Lutherhalle, Wittenberg

adventurer persuaded Philip of Hesse that Archduke Ferdinand and other Catholic princes had secretly formed an alliance for the extermination of Lutheranism. To prove his case, Pack produced a fraudulent document which he promptly sold to the landgrave. Philip's response was to seek military allies, both in Germany and abroad. Elector John of Saxony agreed to take military action, but Luther refused to condone aggressive war, even if its purpose were to defend the Reformation. When the document was published, the Catholic princes immediately declared it a forgery. Duke George denounced Pack, who fled and was eventually executed as a traitor. Although full-scale war was avoided, the impulsive responses of Philip had increased mutual suspicion and embarrassed the reformers.

It was in this atmosphere of resentment and chagrin that the imperial diet convened in Speyer in 1529. Anti-Lutheran feeling was more truculent and

CARTOON AGAINST THE PAPACY

As the lines of division hardened, propagandists became increasingly harsh in their denunciation. Here the pope is depicted as a seven-headed monster advertising his wares: "For money, a sack full of indulgences." Further vilification of the papacy is intended by showing the devil emerging from the pope's indulgence chest, while the instruments of Christ's tormentors are used to buttress the papal power.

University of California Library, Berkeley

united than ever before. Thus, it was to be expected that the absent emperor's decree abolishing the recess of Speyer (1526) would be accepted.[7] The diet further stipulated that Lutheranism was not to be tolerated in Catholic territories, yet Catholics were to be accorded full rights in Lutheran lands. Further religious

[7]B. J. Kidd, *Documents Illustrative of the Continental Reformation* Oxford: Clarendon, pp. 240, 241.

73

innovations and secularization of church property were prohibited. Against this action, the Lutheran princes and cities issued a "protestation," from which the sobriquet "Protestant" would be derived.[8] These Protestants insisted that the recess of Speyer, having been adopted by both Catholics and Lutherans, could not thus be unilaterally abrogated. Furthermore, "in matters concerning God's honor and our soul's salvation everyone must stand before God and answer for himself." Thus, eight years after Luther had taken his stand at Worms, princes and representatives of the cities were making the same claim to liberty of conscience. Yet the demand for religious liberty was by no means absolute, for those making the protestation asserted their right to make the choice not only for themselves, but for their subjects as well. Members of society were to be bound by the decision of the rulers.

Charles refused to accept the protestation, and when it was proffered to him in Italy, he imprisoned the emissaries of the Protestant estates. He resolved to settle the religious dispute at the next session of the diet, to be held in Augsburg in 1530. This time the emperor attended in person.

THE DIET OF AUGSBURG

It was a triumphant Charles who came to Augsburg to restore harmony to the Empire. Another chapter in the Hapsburg-Valois rivalry had ended with the Peace of Cambrai (1529), while the struggle with the pope had apparently been resolved when Charles and Pope Clement signed an "eternal" alliance on June 29, 1529. Clement in turn crowned Charles in the cathedral in Bologna, in what was to be the last papal coronation of an emperor. On the eastern front, the troops of Sultan Suleiman were forced to lift the siege of Vienna. Charles thus had reason to expect victory at Augsburg. He could even afford to be magnanimous, which is reflected in his invitation to the Lutheran estates to present a statement outlining their position.[9]

In accordance with this summons, the Saxon elector instructed his theologians to draft a confession of faith for possible use at Augsburg. Upon arrival in the city, John secured the support of Lutheran princes and cities for the document that was essentially the work of Melanchthon. As a result, this Augsburg Confession was presented to the diet on June 25 by the Saxon chancellor Brueck. Melanchthon had attempted to be conciliatory and to emphasize respect for traditional Catholic forms and ideas; now he entered into discussions with the imperial confessor to work out further compromises. Luther, who was still under the ban of the Empire and remained at Coburg, fumed about all the "devils" who had come to the diet. He heard with dismay that Melanchthon was more bent on harmony than on doctrinal conviction. But Luther's fear of substantive doctrinal concession was unfounded. When he saw the final version of the Augsburg

[8]*Ibid.*, pp. 243–245.
[9]*Ibid.*, p. 258.

Confession, he fully endorsed it, admitting that its positive tone gave it added strength. The confession avoided a number of controversial issues, such as purgatory, transubstantiation, and the priesthood of all believers, but it vigorously asserted the doctrine of justification of faith, defended giving the cup to the laity, rejected obligatory celibacy of the clergy, and attacked the temporal power of ecclesiastics.

The emperor's response to the confession was resolute. His theologians drew up a reply, the *Confutation*, which flatly rejected the Lutheran document. Charles immediately endorsed this reply and demanded the Lutheran estates return to the traditional faith. Further negotiations failed to effect a reconciliation. Melanchthon's lengthy *Apology* offered only a momentary glimmer of hope, and when Charles expressed displeasure with the princes who attended Lutheran church services, the margrave of Brandenburg-Ansbach vowed that before he "would leave off the Word of God, I will kneel here on the spot and lose my head." At least for some of the Lutheran princes, matters of faith were as crucial as economic and political considerations.

The Augsburg Confession was only one of three Protestant doctrinal statements presented at the diet. From Switzerland came the reformer Huldrych Zwingli's *Ratio Fidei*, a frank assertion of belief in the orthodox doctrines of the Nicene and Athanasian Creeds, and at the same time a repudiation of purgatory and the corporal presence of Christ in the elements of communion. The document was contemptuously dismissed in Augsburg and never laid before the diet. Dr. Eck wrote a refutation, coupled with a personal attack on Zwingli. Another confession, the *Tetrapolitana*, was presented by the cities of Constance, Strasbourg, Lindau, and Memmingen. This statement, the first confession of what would come to be known as the Reformed Church in Germany, was prepared by Strasbourg theologians, Bucer and Capito. Like the Lutheran confession, it breathed a spirit of moderation, but was more emphatic in its insistence on biblical authority. Images were rejected, but the statement concerning the Lord's Supper was ambiguous. The *Tetrapolitana* was not read to the diet; instead, Eck and his associates prepared another refutation.

THE LEAGUE OF SCHMALKALD

Summoned in a spirit of confidence and hope, the diet of Augsburg broke up in disarray and discord. When it became apparent that there was to be no religious accord, the Protestant princes left. The final recess of the diet was thus a manifesto of the emperor and the Catholic estates, and constituted a sharp warning to those who had adopted Protestantism, in whatever form. Under threat of military coercion, dissenters were given until April 15, 1531, to return to the Catholic church. The Edict of Worms was to be enforced, while the Imperial Governing Council was to begin proceedings against those who had confiscated church property. At the same time, Charles agreed that a general council of the church be called to correct ecclesiastical abuses.

Confronted with this ultimatum, the Lutheran princes resolved to unite in the face of a common danger. Late in December, 1530, under the leadership of Elector John and Landgrave Philip, the League of Schmalkald was formed. By February, 1531, members included electoral Saxony, Hesse, Brunswick-Lueneburg, Anhalt, and Mansfeld, as well as the cities of Magdeburg, Bremen, Strasbourg, Constance, Ulm, Reutlingen, Luebeck, Memmingen, Isny, Lindau, and Biberach.[10] Largely through the efforts of Martin Bucer, adherents of the *Tetrapolitana* had joined the Lutherans in this defiance of imperial decree. If war should come, it would find many of the Protestant princes and cities united—and no one then could know that the dark clouds of war would, at least temporarily, be dissipated. Luther, in his *Warning to his dear Germans* (1531), confidently asserted: "If it should come to an outbreak of war, then my God and Lord Jesus Christ can save me and my people, just as he saved Lot at Sodom."

HUMANIST DISAFFECTION WITH LUTHER

Political uncertainties and hostilities were intensified by acrimonious debate and literary exchange. As the lines of religious division hardened, Luther found that many who had hailed his attacks on ecclesiastical abuses and papal authority now recoiled in dismay as they saw the church being divided. Humanists who themselves had criticized the church and had called for reform refused to support schism. Reuchlin, the Hebraist, who had denounced obscurantism in the church, now disowned his grandnephew Melanchthon. Pirckheimer, whose earlier support of Luther had brought excommunication, regretted that he had been "cruelly deceived."[11] Mutian, who had welcomed Luther as a "morning star," now alleged that the reformer was acting like a maniac.

These humanists deplored not only the schism that was developing; many of them were profoundly disillusioned by Luther's view of the nature of man. Whereas the humanists envisioned a rational Christianity evolving from man's basic goodness, Luther stressed man's total dependence upon God. For the humanist, the fundamental problem was human ignorance; for Luther, it was sin. While Luther shared the humanists' love for learning, and especially biblical studies, he had nothing but scorn for those who hoped to solve man's problems through education and reason. Luther's God-consciousness, his sense of divine majesty and holiness, so totally permeated his being that he could only express amazement at anyone who hoped to gain divine favor by human effort. Salvation could come only by the grace of God. For Luther, this conviction was a profound source of strength that freed him from dependence upon human frailty.

[10]*Ibid.*, p. 301.
[11]Ervin Panofsky, *Albrecht Duerer* (Princeton: Princeton University Press, 1948), I:233. According to Lewis Spitz, Pirkheimer remained unhappy with both Lutheranism and the Catholic church. See his *The Religious Renaissance of the German Humanists* (Cambridge, Mass.: Harvard University Press, 1963), p. 193.

Luther's emphasis upon the divine role in salvation elicited opposition from a number of sources. Catholics accused him of having stripped the sacraments of their efficacy, thus undermining the position of the church; humanists denounced him for degrading man by robbing him of his dignity and self-reliance. This crucial difference in point of view was epitomized by Luther's dialogue with Erasmus. Although the foremost humanist lamented that religious dissension had "rent the seamless robe of Christ," he squarely attacked Luther's basic ideology—his views on justification and free will. In his *Discourse on Free Will* (1524), Erasmus admitted that he did not fully understand the relationship between human choice and divine providence, but he insisted that Luther's doctrine of predestination reduced man to a helpless automaton and freed him of moral responsibility. Luther congratulated Erasmus for having gone "to the core" by centering the argument on the doctrine of man, then responded with sledgehammer blows in his *Bondage of the Will*. Reiterating his belief that man can be saved by grace alone, Luther stressed the omniscience and omnipotence of a transcendent and righteous God who mercifully grants salvation to human beings who alone can do nothing to merit divine favor. Thus, although Luther denied that good works were the basis of salvation, he emphatically asserted that faith entailed works of love. Man was saved by grace alone—but grace found expression in the believer's life. Between the scholar and the prophet, the breach was complete.

THE BELEAGUERED EMPEROR

From the Diet of Worms to the outbreak of war against the Protestants in 1546, the emperor's constant desire to end religious dissent was frustrated by challenges from numerous quarters. Repeatedly, when he felt he was ready to move against Luther and his associates, Charles would find his plans thwarted by another war with France, or a new invasion by the Turks, or another falling out with the papacy. And even if Charles gained a temporary victory against these enemies, they always showed a remarkable resilience. When Charles fielded superior Spanish and German infantry, Francis responded with superb cavalry and the finest Swiss mercenaries. And when the Turk once again moved into Hapsburg lands, Charles did not hesitate to call upon Protestant princes for aid. It was a time for concession and compromise, not for single-minded elimination of religious deviation.

HAPSBURG-VALOIS RIVALRY

The struggle between Charles and Francis was engaged virtually as soon as the emperor began his reign. For the French king, the election of Charles as emperor was a direct threat, for the Valois kingdom was now encircled by Hapsburg power. In 1520, the French attacked the Hapsburg Netherlands and soon afterwards extended the theater of conflict to the Italian peninsula. Here they were met by determined anti-French forces, spearheaded by emperor and pope, and were soundly defeated at Bicocca, near Milan, in 1522. Now virtually all of the peninsula was under imperial domination. Francis had scant reason to hope for allies. His effort to woo Henry VIII had brought a lavish display in what came to be known as the Field of the Cloth of Gold, but this elaborate exhibition near Calais merely indulged the vanity of the French and English kings; it led to no alliance. Instead Henry made an alliance with his nephew the emperor and signed the treaty of Windsor (1522) which called for an English invasion of France. Almost at the same time the constable of France, who was the duke of Bourbon and the wealthiest noble in the kingdom, decided to join the emperor. This act climaxed a testy relationship between an ambitious duke and a proud king. Francis confiscated Bourbon's possessions, while the duke became a leader in the imperial army.

Yet the very success of Charles provided a basis for his undoing. Pope Clement, who had ascended the papal throne in 1523, had no desire merely to see French influence supplanted by imperial. Determined to preserve the independence of the see of Rome, he reversed the papal position and joined an alliance of France, Venice, and Florence. Once again, imperial forces were compelled to retreat; once again French armies controlled much of unhappy Italy. Imperial power seemed about to collapse south of the Alps: The larger part of Charles's forces were besieged in Pavia, and Francis appeared on the verge of a decisive victory. But a combination of French miscalculations and foolhardy bravery altered everything. A frontal assault on the city and a resulting general melee ended with the flower of French chivalry lying strewn on the field of conflict. The battle of Pavia (February 24, 1525) had broken the power of France and left her king a prisoner.

Peace was made by the Treaty of Madrid (1526), Francis having been removed to Spain. By its terms, the proud Valois renounced his claims to Naples and Milan, as well as Burgundian territories, and promised to marry the emperor's sister. Other aspects of the treaty called for a united crusade against the Turks and the restoration of Bourbon lands. Henry VIII, who had contributed little to the war, asked for his share of the spoils: if not the crown of France, at least those French provinces which had been held by the Angevin kings. Charles, never willing to reward others for his own efforts, politely brushed aside all such demands. After all, the emperor could hardly be expected to welcome English expansion on the continent. Francis, solemnly swearing to uphold the agreement, and leaving two sons as hostages, returned to his realm—and as quickly began to plot revenge. Even the pope agreed that the treaty, signed under duress, was void. Before the end of the year, the League of Cognac, composed of France, the papacy, Venice, Florence, and the Sforza, confronted imperial ambitions. Pavia had been a hollow victory.

Nor was the new alliance the only portent of renewed trouble. To the south-east, the perennial Turkish threat loomed ever larger. At the battle of Mohacs (1526), Suleiman the Magnificent destroyed the Hungarian forces and their king Louis, last of the Jagiellon dynasty of Hungary and Bohemia. The Turks, masters of Hungary, were poised for a thrust into the European heartland, so that when the first Diet of Speyer was held in 1526, the beleaguered emperor found himself challenged on all sides. Added to the peril of military alliance and invasion was the perplexing task of finding a successor to King Louis. Ferdinand, brother of Charles and brother-in-law to the dead king, seemed a promising choice, especially to preserve Hapsburg interests. Nobles in Bohemia agreed, but in Hungary the nobility balked and selected instead John Zapolya, duke of Transylvania. Ferdinand's resolve to end the dispute by force of arms only encouraged the Hungarian aristocracy to cooperate with the Turks, who by 1529 had established Zapolya on his throne and driven to the very gates of Vienna.

THE SACK OF ROME

Charles's power seemed to be at an ebb when his troops of their own accord sacked the eternal city in 1527. Mutinous and disgruntled because of unpaid wages, and encouraged by anti-papal sentiments, especially among the German *Landsknechte*, the imperial forces subjected the city to a fury of plunder, rapine, rape, and violence that shocked even the calloused European conscience. Pope Clement found personal safety in the castle of Sant' Angelo, then at Orvieto, but he was helpless to defend the city, where treasuries, libraries, churches, and palaces were plundered. Much of what had once been a proud center of Renaissance art, inspiring beauty, and creative intellectual endeavor, lay in smoke and ashes. An era had ended.

Although Charles deplored the barbarous actions of his troops, he did not hesitate to take advantage of the weakened position of the papacy. Clement was reduced to the status of an unwilling protégé, while the emperor steadily pressed in on his remaining enemies. The battle of Landriano (1529) gave Charles his last and most decisive victory on Italian soil; Francis was ready to make peace. The resulting Peace of Cambrai (1529), actually negotiated largely by Margaret of Austria, the emperor's aunt, and Louise of Savoy, the mother of Francis, recognized Charles's supremacy in Italy, and in effect established imperial domination over the Holy See. Although the Sforza family was restored in Milan, the city remained under Spanish domination. Francis gained imperial recognition of his claims to Burgundy as well as the Bourbon lands—and finally agreed that the bitter rivalry between Hapsburg and Valois should be allowed to subside. Apparently the major threats confronting the emperor had been reduced to two: religious division and Turkish invasion.

Kayſers Karls Krönung zů Bononía.

CORONATION OF CHARLES IN BOLOGNA, from an old woodcut

A contemporary woodcut depicts Charles with his seven electors. He might well have wished their protestations of loyalty but by this time the harmonious scene shown here was far from reality. The imperial double eagle held uncertain sway over a bitterly-divided realm.

EMPEROR, POPE, AND SULTAN

The threat from the Turk and heretic seemed always to converge—to the great advantage of the Protestants. The formation of the League of Schmalkald gained in stature as a result of the recurring Turkish threat. At Augsburg in 1530 Charles issued an ultimatum to the recalcitrant Lutherans, but the deadline passed without notice, for from 1530 to 1532 King Francis and Zapolya were scheming to create an anti-Hapsburg alliance. In addition, by 1533, Pope Clement was able to demonstrate once again that he feared heresy less than imperial ambition, having concluded an alliance with Francis which stipulated that the Frence monarch would support the pope's refusal to call a general council as Charles was demanding. In return, Clement would assist Francis in regaining Milan and Genoa, and to seal the bargain, plans were made to marry Catherine de' Medici, Clement's niece, to the king's son Henry. A new state was to be set up in northern Italy for Henry.

By this time, the Turkish threat once again confronted Charles. Early in 1532, Suleiman resumed his push toward Vienna. Catholic estates dominated the Diet of Regensburg (April, 1532), but even in the face of impending peril, they refused to give the emperor the necessary military support. Forced to negotiate with the Protestants at Nuremberg, Charles secured military assistance in exchange for nullifying the Augsburg recess. Charles found himself at the head of an army of 80,000 men, but sultan and emperor were not to meet. Suleiman decided to withdraw from Hungary, leaving that embattled land to his client Zapolya. Charles, with little to show for his efforts, once again left Germany, not to return again for nine years.

LUTHERANISM ON THE OFFENSIVE

In the following decade, Lutheranism continued to expand. A major victory was scored in 1534 when the duchy of Wuerttemberg was added to the evangelical ranks. Duke Ulrich, who had been driven from his territory in 1519 by the Swabian League, had become a close friend of Philip of Hesse. The landgrave succeeded in expelling Ferdinand, archduke of Austria from the duchy and restoring Ulrich, who by now had embraced Lutheranism. Peace was made at

ILLUSTRATION OF THE TURKISH ADVANCE

A contemporary pamphleteer expresses some of the dread felt by a populace that had been warned to expect nothing but barbaric treatment at the hands of the invading Turkish forces. God is implored to give "gracious help against the horrible plundering of the bloodthirsty Turks." Propagandists conveniently overlooked the equally grisly atrocities carried out by the armies of the empire.

University of California Library, Berkeley

Cadan (1534). One of the by-products was an agreement that the Saxon elector would recognize Ferdinand as king of the Romans, and thus heir to the imperial crown. Philip's gains were substantial: Ulrich was restored and the triumph of the Reformation in Wuerttemberg assured, while the Swabian League was ordered dissolved. A legal agreement proved highly significant: Protestants were no longer to be compelled to submit religious disputes to the *Reichskammergericht*. This prevented Catholic powers from gaining indemnity or repossession when territories embraced the evangelical cause.

Philip's decisive intervention encouraged other territories and cities to introduce the Reformation and join the League of Schmalkald. A significant victory came in 1539, when Duke George of Saxony died, and was succeeded by his Protestant brother Henry. The duchy now became Lutheran. A triumphant Luther traveled to the scene of his debate with Eck twenty years earlier, and there, in the hall where he had aroused the ire of Duke George, he now preached the Reformation.

THE STRUGGLE FOR THE WESTERN MEDITERRANEAN

These events went for all purposes unnoticed by the harassed emperor, for his interests were more immediately threatened elsewhere. In the western Mediterranean, Turkish ships under the corsair Khair ad-Din Barbarossa were ruining Spanish commerce. Charles responded by seizing Tunis as well as Barbarossa's fleet. The corsair escaped and soon continued the struggle, this time with the assistance of the king of France. Francis once again resolved to turn Hapsburg discomfiture to Valois advantage. This third war with Charles (1535–1538) saw the French king allied with Suleiman and supporting Barbarossa. French forces challenged imperial interests in Italy and quickly seized Savoy and Piedmont. Francis was determined to press his claims to Milan, where the timely death of Francesco Sforza seemed to provide adequate excuse. Charles prevented the French intrusion into Milan by invading Provence; Francis, in turn, launched a rather successful attack on the Netherlands. The imperial cause was further weakened when Admiral Andrea Doria, commanding Venetian and Hapsburg forces, was defeated by a resurgent Barbarossa in the battle of Prevesa (1538). The victory assured a powerful Turkish presence in the western Mediterranean until the battle of Lepanto (1571).

During the course of the sporadic fighting, Charles challenged Francis to a duel, hoping to resolve the rivalries through personal combat. Francis, less confident of providential succor, demurred; then, in June, 1538, the Treaty of Nice terminated the conflict, with Pope Paul III (1534–1549) acting as mediator. France retained most of Piedmont and broke her Turkish alliance, while Charles retained control over Milan. The major contestants could take some comfort from the fact that both had gained, albeit at the expense of helpless weaker states. Once again, defense of small powers had been used as a cloak for aggrandizement.

Shortly after concluding the Treaty of Nice, Charles and Francis met at Aigues Mortes, blithely forgot their rivalries, and solemnly planned joint action against the enemies of the faith—the Lutherans, the Turks, and the English. Henry VIII, whose anti-papal policies had alienated Charles, now found his traditional enemy, Francis, an unlikely ally of the emperor.

ATTEMPTS TO CALL A CHURCH COUNCIL

Charles soon found that events in Germany precluded involvement in new adventure. Convinced that a resort to military force might still be avoided, he pressed for papal concession to Lutheran demands. Luther had appealed to a council of the German church; Charles pressed the pope to call a general, rather than a German, council. Luther had denounced corruption in the church; Charles urged sweeping religious reform. Pope Paul was responsive to both demands.

To prepare the way for a general council, which Paul had summoned for Mantua in 1537, Charles, in 1536, dispatched his inept vice-chancellor Matthew Held to the Lutheran princes. His mission was a failure. Elector John Frederick of Saxony refused to meet him, while Philip of Hesse roundly denounced him. Held could only threaten court action in the Imperial Supreme Court (contrary to the agreement of 1534). As a last resort, in 1538, he organized Catholic princes at Nuremberg to provide military enforcement of proposed court action. Even Ferdinand deplored Held's actions, and Protestant participation in a council seemed more remote than ever.

Nonetheless, the summoning of the council of Mantua forced Lutherans to reassess their position. Still regarding themselves as part of the Catholic church, Lutherans had often called for conciliar action to resolve the problems of the church. Thus members of the League of Schmalkald met in 1537 to plan a concerted strategy. Luther was asked to produce an appropriate response. The resulting *Schmalkaldic Articles*, published in 1538, categorically rejected compromise with Rome. Not only did Luther insist on his basic views, including justification solely by faith, denial of papal supremacy, and rejection of the Mass—he also defended the right to resist anyone, including the emperor, for the sake of the gospel. Although the articles were not officially adopted, they reflected the dominant mood of the league. While the Lutheran leaders did not reject a council outright, they insisted that it be free of papal control, that it be held in Germany, and that the Bible he recognized as final authority. Neither pope nor emperor could agree to such demands. Charles's hope of solving the religious question by means of a council seemed dim indeed, especially when Francis I also opposed the proposed council.

Charles, now allied with Francis and at peace with the Turks and the pope, still pressed for a nonmilitary solution to the religious schism. Held was replaced with the more conciliatory exiled archbishop of Lund, John of Weza, who now negotiated the Frankfurt Interim (April, 1539). This specified that Imperial court action against the Lutherans be halted and a religious settlement be delayed until a general council could be called. Meanwhile, a series of conferences was held between Catholic and Protestant theologians. At Regensburg, in 1541, the papal legate Gasparo Contarini made substantial concessions to the Lutherans, and there appeared to be some hope for a compromise. Papal repudiation of the concessions, however, once again underscored the irreconcilability of the two positions.

LANDGRAVE PHILIP'S BIGAMY

Internal difficulties within the imperial and Schmalkaldic camps complicated the issues. The Protestant alliance was badly shaken when its chief protagonist became involved in a bigamous relationship. Philip, who at nineteen had married the daughter of Duke George of Saxony, had had a series of mistresses before he embraced the Reformation. Now he declared his intention of restricting his affections—but not to his wife. Since divorce was forbidden, he requested—and finally obtained—the approval of the reformers in marrying Margaret von der Saal. Luther insisted that the bigamy be kept secret, even if this required that Philip should "tell a good strong lie for the sake and the good of the Christian Church." Attempts to conceal the arrangement failed completely, to the chagrin of the Protestant theologians and the embarrassment of the Schmalkaldic princes. Bigamy, according to the imperial law code, was a capital offense. Philip, disgraced and publicly berated by his allies, attempted to reach an understanding with the emperor. Charles was prepared to bargain: The imperial law would be suspended in exchange for recognition of Ferdinand as king of the Romans, submission to the emperor, and withdrawal of support from the anti-Hapsburg Duke of Cleves.

Given Schmalkaldic support, Cleves, with its ambitious Duke William, might well have become a powerful center of Lutheranism. Isolated through Philip's bigamy, it was in no position to flaunt imperial wishes. William, whose lands on the lower Rhine included Cleves as well as Juelich and Berg, successfully laid claim to Guelders when Charles of Egmont died without heir. Pressing his anti-Hapsburg policy, he explored closer ties with the League of Schmalkald, with France, and with England. In 1540, his sister Anne married Henry VIII. Emperor Charles could no longer ignore the threat to his position in the Netherlands. In 1543, Duke William was defeated and Guelders added to the Hapsburg possessions. The League of Schmalkald, compromised by Philip's capitulation to Charles, was helpless.

RENEWED IMPERIAL MILITARY PROBLEMS

Even so, the emperor had problems enough. In 1541, when Charles again resolved to punish the piratical Barbary corsairs, his fleet was destroyed in a storm off Algiers. In the same year, the Turks seized Buda and threatened the Empire. Hungarian nobles, disregarding an earlier treaty that had promised the throne to Ferdinand upon the death of Zapolya, instead crowned Zapolya's son John Sigismund and asked Suleiman to defend them against the outraged Hapsburgs. Once again, Charles asked for and received Lutheran support against the Turk. Joachim II of Brandenburg led the imperial army against Suleiman, but was routed. The Turk continued to advance and consolidate his position.

At this difficult juncture, Hapsburg-Valois rivalry again erupted into war. Francis, supported by Cleves, Sweden, Denmark, and Scotland, made common cause with Suleiman. Then, in 1542 French troops invaded the Netherlands, while the Franco-Turkish fleet sailed at will in the Mediterranean. Italian ports were ravaged, Nice was captured, and hundreds of defenseless Italians were seized as slaves.

But Charles once again slowly but inexorably pushed on to victory. He succeeded in forming an alliance with Henry VIII, and by the summer of 1543 English troops were threatening Boulogne. Charles, having crushed William of Cleves, crossed the Marne. When the imperial forces had advanced to within a few miles of Paris, the king once again decided to end the war. In the Peace of Crépy (September, 1544), Charles completely ignored his English ally, but his own interests were well-served: Francis renounced his claim to Naples, Flanders, and Artois, while Charles reciprocated by giving up Burgundy. In addition Francis blandly promised to aid Charles against the German heretic, Luther and the Turkish infidel. Consequently, when peace was concluded with the Turk in 1545, Charles at last appeared ready to concentrate on ending the religious schism.

Events in the 1540s had given urgency to Charles's resolution. In 1542, Duke Henry of Brunswick-Wolfenbuettel, one of the few remaining Catholic princes in northern Germany, seized the imperial cities of Goslar and Brunswick. Philip of Hesse, ostensibly defending imperial interests, and aided by Elector John Frederick, promptly expelled the duke and invited Bugenhagen to introduce the Reformation into the duchy. Meanwhile, Archbishop Albert of Mainz, hard pressed by reformers in his territories of Magdeburg and Halberstadt, allowed Lutheranism to spread in those areas. A special financial remuneration made the concession more palatable.

Ecclesiastical territories on the lower Rhine appeared in even greater danger. In 1542 the powerful electorate and archbishopric of Cologne seemed ready to go Protestant. Archbishop Hermann von Wied invited Melanchthon and Bucer to introduce Protestantism into the proud and influential territory. Bucer came to Cologne, while Melanchthon sent letters outlining procedures for reform. In neighboring Muenster, Bishop Francis of Waldeck similarly moved to introduce Protestantism, and in the Palatinate, Elector Frederick II invited Lutheran theologians to his territory and entered into negotiations with the League of Schmalkald.

DEFECTION FROM PROTESTANT RANKS

Charles recognized that the league represented the greatest obstacle to the triumph of his policies; accordingly, he carefully exploited its most vulnerable members. The Schmalkaldic allies suffered a staggering blow when Maurice, since 1541 duke of Saxony, agreed to support Charles in exchange for receiving the electoral title and gaining control over the sees of Magdeburg and Halberstadt. In addition, he was assured freedom in determining religious policies in his lands. Several other Protestant princes, such as Margrave John of Brandenburg-Kuestrin and Margrave Albert Alcibiades of Brandenburg-Culmbach, agreed not to oppose the emperor—in exchange for territorial concessions. Shrewd diplomacy and a sacrifice of lesser goals had set the stage for what Charles hoped would be the decisive act in eliminating the religious division.

Before moving his troops against a divided Schmalkaldic League, the emperor attempted to ensure neutrality on the part of former or potential enemies. At the Diet of Speyer in 1544, Catholic and Protestant estates were encouraged to maintain the status quo until there could be a "general, free and Christian Council." Protestants even agreed to assist the emperor in his war with France. When the pope denounced the diet's mild stand on the religious division, Protestants including Luther and Elector John Frederick staunchly defended Charles.

The emperor soon overcame the hostility of the pope. When Charles promised Piacenza and Parma to the Farnese family, of which Paul II was a member, the pope agreed to call a council and to send troops to aid the emperor against the Protestants. Charles, with France neutral, the Turks quiet, the Protestants disorganized, and the pope urging him to destroy "the enemies of God," finally was ready to go to war.

THE SCHMALKALDIC WAR

Amidst the lengthening shadows of war and despite personal illness, Luther had gone to Eisleben to help the counts of Mansfeld settle an inheritance dispute. Four days after a reconciliation had been effected (February 18, 1546), the reformer lay dead in the city of his birth. Friends who attended him at his death reported that in his last moments he had again professed his staunch adherence to the faith he had preached and lived.[12] His body was returned to Wittenberg and

[12]Christof Schubart, *Die Berichte ueber Luthers Tod und Begraebnis* (Weimar: Boehlaus 1917), p. 31. Quoted in Oskar Thulin, *A Life of Luther*, (Philadelphia: Fortress Press, 1966), p. 129.

1547.

HIC MAIESTATI *SESE* OFFERT CAESARIS HESSVS,
ANTE QVIDEM INDOMITVS, NVNC VEL MANSVETIOR AGNO.

ENGRAVING: PHILIP SUBMITS TO CHARLES, by Dirck Coornheert

Landgrave Philip, who had repeatedly taken the initiative in forming military alliances against the emperor, in 1547 found that Charles was in no mood to negotiate. Despite professions of loyalty and submission, Philip was imprisoned.

Staatliche Graphische Sammlung, Munich

buried in the castle church. Melanchthon, who delivered the funeral oration, expressed the profound conviction, not only of those who crowded into the church, but of innumerable distant admirers, when he paid tribute to Luther as the man "chosen of God for the reformation of the Church."[13]

Shortly before his death, Luther had warned that military action by the emperor was soon to be expected. He hoped he would not live to see the distress of war, and he died while Charles was concluding plans for moving his troops against the Lutherans. In July, 1546, both Elector John Frederick and Landgrave Philip were placed under the imperial ban. In the same year, Charles formally divested the elector of his title and gave it to Maurice, who proceeded to seize Ernestine territory. League forces temporarily checked Maurice, while Charles attempted to establish his authority along the Danube. By the spring of 1547, imperial forces had advanced into Saxony. There, at Muehlberg in April, John

[13]Quoted in Lewis W. Spitz, ed., *The Protestant Reformation* (Englewood Cliffs, N. J.: Prentice-Hall, 1966), p. 74.

Warhafftige Abcontrafactur Johans Friderichs
des alten/Hertzogen zu Sachsen etc. Wie er itzund
in seinem gefengnis vnd elend anzusehen ist. Gott tröst in
mit gnaden durch Christum vnsern Selig-
macher/ Amen.

1551

Zu Wittemberg bey Jörg Formschneider.

1551.

ENGRAVING: THE IMPRISONED JOHN FREDERICK

While imprisoned by the emperor, John Frederick continued to be championed by those who shared his religion.

University of California Library, Berkeley

Frederick was defeated, taken prisoner, and compelled to surrender his title and most of his lands to Maurice. Philip of Hesse, upon the pleas of his son-in-law Maurice, decided not to fight but rather hope for imperial leniency.[14] But the time for leniency was past. Philip was promptly imprisoned and destined to bear humiliation for five years as a prize exhibit of the emperor as he traveled across

[14]Philip had been misled to think that he would escape harsh punishment. See Karl Brandi, *The Emperor Charles V*, trans. C. V. Wedgwood (New York: Knopf, 1939), p. 123.

his lands. At last, Charles, could confidently survey a realm secure from both internal and external threats. A once proud League of Schmalkald was shattered; most Protestant cities of the Empire had been compelled to submit to the emperor, although the majority retained their Protestant faith; the elector of Cologne, now that Hermann von Wied had been expelled, was once again Catholic; and Francis I had died in March, 1547.

Charles's day of glory was destined to be short-lived. Now that the emperor seemed to be on the pinnacle of success, the pope and the Protestants once again became unintentional allies in thwarting Hapsburg ambition. Differences between the pope and the emperor once again surfaced as the Council of Trent, finally convened in December, 1545, continued its deliberations. Both Charles and Pope Paul were determined to use the council for their own purposes. When the pope suggested reconvening the council at Bologna in 1547, Charles was vigorously opposed, for the move would strengthen papal influence and alienate the Germans. Tension mounted when Pier Luigi Farnese, the pope's son, was murdered in Piacenza under circumstances that cast suspicion on Charles's Spanish officials in Milan. Nor was the situation alleviated when Charles hinted darkly at military action against Rome.

Despairing of the development of a joint imperial-papal policy, Charles resolved to settle the German problem on his own. At the Diet of Augsburg, in session from September, 1547, until May, 1548, Charles proposed to restructure the Empire along the lines of an imperial league which would function under his direction and would maintain a standing army. But the estates, fearing loss of territorial independence, rejected the plan and thus effectively terminated Hapsburg hopes to unite Germany politically. It was small consolation to Charles that he was granted authority to select judges for the Imperial Supreme Court and to strengthen his control over ecclesiastical litigation.

THE ILL-FATED INTERIM

Religious policies adopted at the diet proved unsuccessful. An attempt at compromise led to the *Augsburg Interim* (May, 1548). This document, asserting basic Catholic doctrine, offered some concessions to the Protestants: communion in both kinds, clerical marriage with papal permission, and an ambiguous statement on justification by faith. Clearly, such a compromise could only meet with severe disapproval from both the pope and the Protestant clergyman. Learned treatises by theologians such as Melanchthon, as well as innumerable fiery broadsides called upon Protestants to reject the perfidious scheme. A chagrined emperor could do nothing to halt the wave of popular indignation that swept Protestant Germany. In those Protestant areas where princes gave nominal consent to the Interim, resistance by the populace left Masses largely unattended, or encouraged the clergy to continue their preaching according to Protestant belief. In Saxony, where Maurice was now officially elector, public pressure moved him to attempt a further concession to Lutheranism. The resulting *Leipzig Interim*, worked out by Melanchthon and Bishop Pflug of Naumburg, was somewhat more Lutheran. Even so, since it contained several features supporting such Catholic practices as the use of Latin in church services and a recognition of the seven sacraments, most Lutheran clergymen refused to adopt it. Melanchthon in particular was subjected to scathing denunciation for having betrayed Luther. Magdeburg became a center for those who considered themselves genuine followers of Luther (Gnesio-Lutherans). Professors such as Matthias Flacius Illyricus and Nicolaus von Amsdorf left Wittenberg and came to Magdeburg to lead the literary battle for the preservation of the faith. A flood of pamphlets, broadsides, and songs proclaimed the Interim the work of the devil. Some more scholarly efforts resulted in the publication of the *Magdeburg Centuries*. In this history of the church, Flacius attempted to show how various forces, especially the papacy, had continuously corrupted original Christianity. Melanchthon, who asserted that he had compromised only in nonessential matters (*adiaphora*), was increasingly ostracized.

Charles was confident that the formal adoption of the *Augsburg Interim*, or its Leipzig modification, would substantially resolve the Catholic-Protestant schism, but public opposition proved too strong. Luther's views had left so profound an impression on his followers that a mere princely act was not enough to enforce religious uniformity. Lutheran leaders, both religious and secular, who had advocated compromise with Catholicism found themselves subjected to scathing abuse in pamphlets and sermons. A belated papal recognition of the *Augsburg Interim* shortly before Paul III's death did little to alter the German problem.

Charles's dynastic ambitions further weakened his diplomatic relations with the German princes. In his determination to preserve Hapsburg power, he urged that, after the death of his brother Ferdinand, who was already king of the Romans and thus heir-apparent, the imperial dignity should pass to the Spanish branch of the Hapsburg house. Thus, Charles hoped that his own son Philip, rather than Ferdinand's son Maximilian, would become emperor. This ambitious scheme not only antagonized the Austrian Hapsburgs but also aroused strong opposition from the electors. Eventually, Charles gained the reluctant cooperation of his brother, but the German princes remained adamant. Upon Ferdinand's death, the crown would go to Maximilian.

Imperial fortunes seemed to improve slightly with the election of Pope Julius III (1550–1555). The pope and emperor collaborated in reconvening the Council of Trent in 1551, this time with Catholic and Lutheran representatives from Germany. Again, Charles's frantic hopes for reconciliation proved only a chimera, for papal legates could not permit heretics to assist in defining dogma or prescribing reform. From his residence in Innsbruck, Charles carefully watched proceedings at Trent, only to see anxious hope give way to bitter disillusionment.

ENGRAVING: ELECTOR MAURICE OF SAXONY (from an old copy in the author's possession)

Previously bribed with lands and the electoral dignity, Maurice became disillusioned with the policies of the emperor. By turning on his former ally, he effectively shattered what hope Charles still had for the ending of religious schism.

COLLAPSE OF THE IMPERIAL POSITION

In this preoccupation with the council, the emperor remained aloof from his steadily-worsening German problems. By 1550, another anti-imperial German Protestant league had been formed. Margrave John of Kuestrin, allied with John Albert of Mecklenburg and Duke Albert of Prussia, stood ready to resist imperial and Catholic policies. This alliance was considerably strengthened when Elector Maurice, disenchanted with the continuing imprisonment of his father-in-law and suspicious of imperial designs, deserted Charles. The astute and unprincipled elector skillfully maneuvered until he gained control of the substantially enlarged League of Torgau (May, 1551), which was formed to gain freedom for Landgrave Philip and to ensure German liberties against "insufferable and everlasting

91

Spanish servitude." Then, in 1552 the league, in the Treaty of Chambord, formed an alliance with France. In return for money and troops, the League of Torgau calmly recognized Henry II as "imperial vicar" over the bishoprics of Metz, Toul, and Verdun. Although devoid of any legal right to give away imperial territory, the princes did not hesitate to sacrifice imperial territorial integrity in the interests of territorial particularism.

In March, 1552, the French renewed the war by seizing the three bishoprics, and a month later Elector Maurice led his troops into the Tyrol. Charles, barely escaping capture, fled across the Alps, while the Council of Trent, now threatened by military forces just north of the Brenner Pass, dispersed in haste.

With the council and imperial forces in disarray, and Ferdinand once again fighting the Turks, the League of Torgau seemed to have cause for optimism. Yet enmity to the pope and the emperor was no guarantee of German unity. Margrave Albert Alcibiades attempted to seize the opportunity to create his own personal principality, and ravaged Franconia as he tried to bring the bishoprics of Bamberg and Wuerzburg under his rule. In Lorraine, the expansionist policies of Henry II met strong resistance. Strasbourg held out fiercely, while various imperial cities, more fearful of the princes than of the emperor, aided Charles. Eventually, the desultory fighting between Charles and the German princes ended with the Peace of Passau (1552), which granted at least partial toleration to Lutherans in Germany. Both Landgrave Philip and former Elector John Frederick were released, but this act now had little significance.

Charles, ever resilient, once again dared to hope for victory against France. With the accession of Mary Tudor to the English throne, and the hope of marrying his son Philip to her, he might yet forge an alliance that would break France. Albert Alcibiades now became the emperor's ally. Metz was besieged, but the skillful generalship of Francis, duke of Guise, forced Charles to abandon the effort. An embittered, broken emperor once again left Germany. Alcibiades however, still spreading rapine and plunder, antagonized both Catholic and Lutheran princes and was confronted by a curious alliance of Elector Maurice and Archduke Ferdinand. At Sievershausen (June, 1553) the allies defeated Alcibiades, who temporarily continued the struggle, but in the following year he fled to France. Germany, sick of war and constant dissension, finally turned to peace-making.

THE PEACE OF AUGSBURG

At the sessions of the Diet of Augsburg (February to September, 1555), the German estates turned their attention to the creation of a lasting peace. Neither emperor nor papal representative was there, although Ferdinand came to salvage what he could of imperial, Hapsburg, and Catholic interests. Despite rather inauspicious beginnings—most of the German princes, including the electors, were absent—the agreements forged here would form the basis for imperial peace for the rest of the century.

In September, Ferdinand published the recess of the Diet—*cuius regio eius religio*—the principle of allowing each ruler to determine the religion of his territory. Although this phrase was actually a later invention, both Lutheran and Catholic acted to secure a jealously-guarded right. Both Lutheranism and Catholicism were to be tolerated, but any other form of Christianity was prohibited. Anyone dissatisfied with the religion of his prince was free to move elsewhere. Ecclesiastical territories gained by the Protestants prior to the Peace of Passau could be retained, but archbishops, bishops, or abbots who might adopt Lutheranism were to be replaced with Catholic clergy. The recess declared that

PROXIMVS·A·SVMMO·FERDNANDVS·CAESARE·CARLO
REX·ROMANORVM·SIC·TVLIT·ORA·GENAS
AET·SVAE·XXIX
ANN·M·D·XXXI

ENGRAVING: ARCHDUKE FERDINAND, by Heinrich Aldegrever

When Charles abdicated the imperial dignity, his brother Ferdinand inherited a wide array of unsolved problems. The new emperor abandoned attempts to restore German religious uniformity by means of military action. Instead, each territory was now permitted to adopt the faith of its ruler, provided that faith was either Catholic or Lutheran.

Kunstmuseum der Stadt Düsseldorf, Kupferstichkabinett

Lutheran princes, imperial knights, and imperial cities were to be granted the same rights as their Catholic counterparts, with both pledged to "eternal, unconditional peace." Altogether, the Peace of Augsburg demonstrated that, in both politics and religion, territorial independence had triumphed over imperial and Catholic solidarity. The power of the emperor had been further diminished; for centuries hereafter, the dominant factor would be not the Empire, nor even the German "nation," but rather the principality. Territorial princes had been the real victors in the struggle.

Suggestions for Further Reading

Babelon, Jean. *Charles Quint.* Paris: Société des éditions françaises et internationales, 1947.

Bornkamm, Heinrich. *Luther's World of Thought.* Translated by Martin H. Bertram. St. Louis: Concordia, 1958.

Cranz, F. Edward. *An Essay on the Development of Luther's Thought on Justice, Law, and Society.* Cambridge, Mass.: Harvard University Press, 1959.

Drion du Chapois, F. *Charles Quint et l'Europe.* Bruxelles: Brepols, 1962.

Eastwood, Cyril. *The Priesthood of All Believers.* Minneapolis: Augsburg, 1962.

Fischer-Galati, Stephen A. *Ottoman Imperialism and German Protestantism, 1521–1555.* Cambridge, Mass.: Harvard University Press, 1959.

Forell, George W. *Faith Active in Love.* New York: American Press, 1954.

Gerrish, Brian. *Grace and Reason: A Study in the Theology of Martin Luther.* Oxford: Clarendon, 1962.

Koenigsberger, H. G. *The Hapsburgs and Europe, 1516–1660.* Ithaca, N. Y.: Cornell University Press, 1971.

Koenneker, Barbara. *Hans Sachs.* Stuttgart, J. B. Metzler, 1971.

Manschreck, Clyde L. *Melanchthon, the Quiet Reformer.* New York: Abingdon Press, 1958.

Melanchthon, Philip. *Melanchthon: Selected Writings.* Translated by C. L. Hill. Edited by E. E. Flack and L. J. Satre. Minneapolis: Augsburg, 1962.

Meyer, Carl S. *Luther for an Ecumenical Age.* St. Louis: Concordia, 1967.

Moeller, Bernd. *Reichsstadt und Reformation.* Guetersloh: Verein fuer Reformationsgeschichte, 1959.

Mueller, William A. *Church and State in Luther and Calvin, A Comparative Study.* Nashville: Broadman Press, 1954.

Ozment, S. E. *The Reformation in the Cities.* New Haven: Yale University Press, 1975.

Pelikan, Jaroslav. *From Luther to Kierkegaard.* St. Louis: Concordia, 1950.

Prenter, Regin. *Spiritus Creator.* Translated by J. M. Jensen. Philadelphia: Muhlenberg, 1953.

Rassow, Peter. *Karl V: Der Kaiser und seine Zeit.* Cologne: Boehlau, 1960.

Stupperich, Robert. *Melanchthon.* Translated by R. H. Fischer. Philadelphia: Westminister Press, 1965.

Swanson, G. E. *Religion and Regime.* Ann Arbor: University of Michigan Press, 1967.

Urban, Georg. *Philip Melanchthon, 1497–1560.* Bretten: Melanchthonverein, 1960.

Watson, P. S. *Let God Be God!* London: Epworth, 1947.

5

The Growth of Zwinglianism

THE TRADITION OF SWISS INDEPENDENCE

When the Lutheran movement was spreading throughout Germany and other parts of Europe, there arose in the Swiss cantons a resolute drive for reform which ultimately produced a distinctive form of Christianity. Once again, economic and political factors aided religious nonconformity, for the long and fierce tradition of independence acted as a deterrent to any papal or imperial attempts to curb religious deviation.

Centuries of struggle had brought political self-determination. As early as 1291, the forest cantons of Uri, Schwyz, and Unterwalden formed a league to defend themselves against the Hapsburg emperor, Rudolf I. The defeat of the imperial armies, however, did not end the threat to the Swiss. As external pressures continued, the league expanded, so that when Charles the Bold of Burgundy launched an attack in 1476 and again in 1477, he faced a confederation that by then included, in addition to the original three cantons, Zurich and Bern, as well as Zug, Lucerne, and Glarus. In 1481, the cantons of Solothurn and Fribourg, as fearful of the ambitions of neighboring Swiss cities as of foreign threats, joined the confederation. The last Hapsburg attempt to assert suzerainty over the Swiss failed in 1499, and in the same year, the Peace of Basel in effect recognized the Swiss Confederation as an autonomous state within the Empire. Complete independence would be formally recognized in 1648.

The successful rejection of foreign control did not assure a closely knit national state. By 1513 the confederation consisted of thirteen cantons loosely allied with other cantons, cities, and ecclesiastical territories. Included in this conglomeration were the cantons of Grisons and Valais, the counties of Toggenburg and Neuenburg, the abbey of St. Gall, the cities of Biel, St. Gall, Rottweil, Muehlhausen, and, later, Geneva. The confederation also governed other districts, including Aargau and Thurgau.

The Swiss Confederation

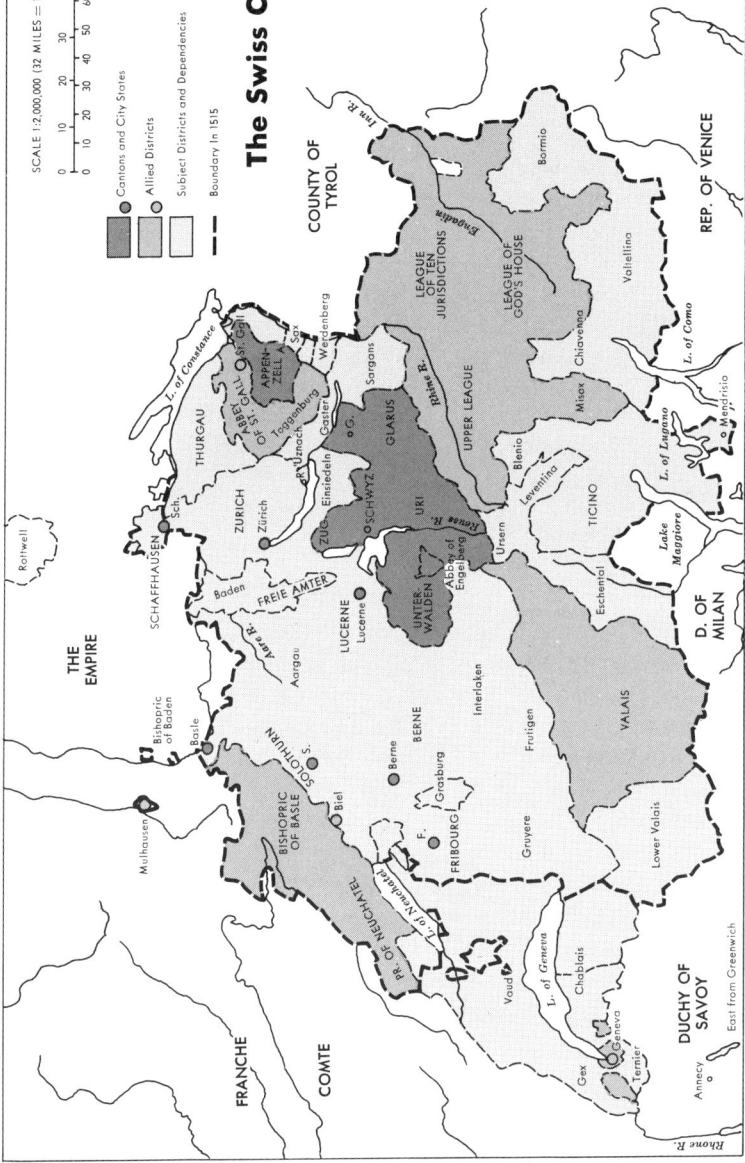

SCALE 1:2,000,000 (32 MILES = 1 INCH)

| 0 | 10 | 20 | 30 | 40 Miles |
| 0 | 10 20 | 30 | 40 | 50 | 60 Km |

- Cantons and City States
- Allied Districts
- Subject Districts and Dependencies
- Boundary in 1515

THE EMPIRE

FRANCHE COMTE

DUCHY OF SAVOY

COUNTY OF TYROL

REP. OF VENICE

D. OF MILAN

Rottweil

Mulhausen

Basle
Bishopric of Baden

BISHOPRIC OF BASLE

SOLOTHURN
S.
Biel

PR. OF NEUCHATEL
L. of Neuchatel

BERNE
Berne
Gratsburg

FRIBOURG
F.

Gruyere

Vaud

L. of Geneva

Gex

Geneva
Ternier

Annecy

Chablais

Lower Valais

VALAIS

Interlaken

Frutigen

Aargau

Aare R.

Baden

FREIE AMTER

LUCERNE
Lucerne

UNTER WALDEN

Abbey of Engelberg

URI

ZUG

SCHWYTZ

Ursen

Eschental

TICINO

Leventina

Blenio

Misox

Chiavenna

Valtellina

Bormio

LEAGUE OF GOD'S HOUSE

Engadin

LEAGUE OF TEN JURISDICTIONS

Inn R.

Rhine R.

UPPER LEAGUE

Sargans

Gaster

G.

GLARUS

Einsiedeln

Utznach

Wesen

Toggenburg

APPENZELL

ABBEY OF ST. GALL

CITY OF ST. GALL

Werdenberg

Sax

THURGAU

ZURICH
Zürich

Sch.

SCHAFFHAUSEN

L. of Constance

Reuss R.

Lake Maggiore

L. of Lugano

L. of Como

Mendrisio

East from Greenwich

Rhone R.

97

Emphasis upon local autonomy rather than central authority characterized political activities both in the cantons and the diet, the central governing body. Effective administrative machinery was lacking, so that although the confederation usually presented a united front in foreign affairs, each canton was permitted to negotiate its own trade agreements and so on. Economic difficulties often intensified independent tendencies. The poorer peasant cantons, among them Glarus, Lucerne, and Zug, as well as the forest cantons, were suspicious of the greater power and prosperity of Basel, Bern, and Zurich. At the same time, social ferment often challenged existing political and economic structures within the cantons. Peasants were still compelled to supply their lords, whether secular or spiritual, with the payment of tithes and the performance of services. Numerous peasant uprisings demonstrated the restless spirit of the rural communities, and their dissatisfaction with the local lords or city oligarchies that often controlled the cantons. The movement toward a greater measure of participation in government was also vigorously pushed by the smaller guilds, so that by the beginning of the sixteenth century the patrician class was hard-pressed to maintain its position. Not infrequently, an alliance of artisans and laborers gained significant political concessions and established artisan oligarchies. Since many of the cantons were governed by councils elected either directly or indirectly by the citizens, popular opinion often became a vital factor in shaping governmental policy. Charismatic preachers, in particular, could exploit such a situation.

ZWINGLI: HUMANIST, PATRIOT, AND REFORMER

Into this intensely independent atmosphere Huldrych Zwingli was to introduce what he believed to be the pure teaching of the gospel. This Swiss reformer was born of stout peasant stock in Wildhaus, a town in the Toggenburg Valley, on January 1, 1484, just a few weeks after Luther. His father as a member of the rural establishment, served as an *Amman* (bailiff). Zwingli was fortunate enough to be sent to schools in Basel and Bern, and later attended the universities of Vienna and Basel where, while pursuing his goal of the priesthood, he became an avid humanist and a critic of ecclesiastical corruption.

In 1506, at the age of twenty-two, Zwingli became the parish priest of Glarus. Here he continued his humanistic studies. He read widely, mastered Greek, established a small school, and fostered the growth of Swiss nationalism. On several occasions he had accompanied Swiss mercenaries called to defend papal interests in northern Italy. When he had seen the hardships these Swiss soldiers faced, he was struck by the meaninglessness of their dying for causes that did not concern them. He urged his countrymen to remain at home and let the foreign princes fight their own battles: "Keep away, Switzerland, from foreign powers,

PORTRAIT: HULDRYCH ZWINGLI, by Hans Asper

A man of driving energy and impressive ability, Zwingli vigorously and sometimes violently championed what he believed to be the best interests of his faith and his people. The inscription over the door of his home in Zurich records his departure for the battlefield at Cappel "where he died for his faith." Zwingli, at least, would have agreed with this verdict.
Kunstmuseum Winterthur

for they are leading you to ruin.'' In his political poem, *The Labyrinth*,[1] a Swiss adaptation of the myth of Theseus and the Minotaur, he attempted to convince his parishioners of the futility of involvement in foreign wars designed to build empires for others. He could not agree with the idea that the only way the poorer cantons could solve their problems of over-population was to hire their sons to foreign princes. He was especially opposed to efforts to bring Glarus under French influence. The Swiss should look to their own interests.

[1]Huldreich Zwingli, *Saemtliche Werke*, eds. E. Egli, G. Finsler et al. (Leipzig und Berlin: C.A. Schwetschae, 1905–1959), I:59.

99

In 1516, after he had aroused the enmity of prominent men who were paid to recruit mercenaries for the French, Zwingli was transferred to nearby Einsiedeln, in the canton of Schwyz, and here he engaged in a systematic study of the Greek New Testament just published by Erasmus. In the following year, he called for biblical supremacy in all matters of faith. Meanwhile, he did not hesitate to attack abuses in the church. When in 1518 the Franciscan Samson sold indulgences in Schwyz, Zwingli publicly denounced him and urged his parishioners to rely on the merits of Christ, not indulgences. Significantly, Zwingli's superior, the bishop of Constance, supported his priest.

On January 1, 1519, Zwingli was installed as parish priest in the Great-Minster, the principal church in Zurich; he was now in a strategic position to advocate reform. To the dismay of many of his associates, Zwingli parted with the traditional practices and began to deliver a series of sermons drawn directly from the Gospel of Matthew. Fully utilizing his humanistic learning, Zwingli explained the biblical text and discarded the usual commentaries. His powerful preaching electrified the city and attracted a large following. The popular priest combined his biblical expositions with a liberal sprinkling of criticism of various aspects of contemporary society. The poorer classes especially sensed his sympathy and concern, while the wealthier burghers were reminded of their social and moral responsibilities.

Zwingli's influence also became apparent in his relations with the city councils. Political power was vested in two bodies, the Council of Two Hundred and the Little Council. The former, composed of delegates from the guilds and a few nobles, could decide all important issues. However, in actual practice the Little Council whose members were drawn from the larger council made most major decisions and was responsible for administration. A burgomaster stood at the head of the political structure. Similar political systems characterized many other cantons. Zwingli recognized that support of the councils was crucial to the success of his program of religious reform for their dominant position might well make their attitude decisive.

Having already familiarized himself with some of Luther's writings, when the reports of the Leipzig debate reached Zurich, Zwingli was convinced that here was a kindred spirit. Even though the Swiss priest did not publicly take a stand defying the papacy, he now encouraged his parishioners to read Luther's writings. Then, in 1519, Zurich was decimated by the plague. Perhaps 2,500 people fell victim to it—more than one-fourth of the population. Zwingli himself, risking his life in aiding the sick, became dangerously ill, but gradually recovered. During his convalescence, he had more time to ponder the religious situation, and gradually became convinced of the necessity of reform. When he returned to the pulpit, he continued preaching directly from the Greek text of the New Testament, not following the prescribed excerpts for the Christian year. Whereas the Mass was central in Catholic worship, Zwingli made the sermon dominant. The priest was now primarily a teacher.

Zwingli's zeal for reform went far beyond religious considerations. He continued to oppose the use of Swiss mercenaries by foreign powers, and persuaded Zurich to reject a proposed alliance with Francis I. When he urged other cantons to adopt similar policies, he was subjected to numerous attacks but remained undeterred. When Cardinal Schinner continued to recruit mercenaries for papal forces, Zwingli bitterly charged that the cleric's red hat had been dyed by the blood of Swiss countrymen.

Meanwhile, Zwingli continued his biblical expositions, becoming more insistent that the Scriptures be the sole guide in matters of faith and practice. Soon he was questioning those religious observances not directly enjoined by the Word of God. He denounced monasticism and purgatory, and questioned the institution of the tithe, thereby bringing upon himself the wrath of local clerics. In 1522, he rejected compulsory Lenten abstinence, and was followed in this by some prominent citizens including the printer, Christopher Froschauer. When the bishop of Constance, Hugo von Hohenlandenberg, admonished Zwingli, the city council stoutly defended its priest, for the reformer had been careful to work in concert with the civil authorities. For Zwingli, the goal was a society reformed according to biblical principles, and realized through the constant cooperation of secular and spiritual authorities.[2] This diplomatic but firm approach to reform is reflected in his *Concerning the Choice and Free Use of Food*. Zwingli contended that Christians should be free to eat meat or to abstain from eating, for the gospel freed men from ecclesiastical legalism.[3] However he did maintain that no one should insist on this freedom without considering the reactions of others.

Other attacks on traditional religious practices soon followed. Rejecting prohibition of priestly marriages, and at the same time condemning clerical immorality, Zwingli quietly married the widow of a Zurich patrician in 1522. Further radical ideas were presented in *Archeteles*, in which he emphasized biblical authority and insisted that ecclesiastical tradition could not supersede Scripture. Accordingly, he attacked papal power, enforced celibacy, the authority of councils, indulgences, and compulsory fasting because they were all products of human innovation. In another treatise, *Of the Clarity and Certainty of the Word of God*, he declared that there was no need for a council or pope, for "the Word of God is a bright light and does not let people go astray in the darkness." He suggested that if readers found parts of Scripture obscure, they should concentrate on passages that were clear. A third publication, *Of Mary, the pure Mother of God*, showed that Zwingli was still moved by a warm, fervent devotion to the Virgin.

Zwingli's treatises and religious innovations were subjected to public scrutiny in a disputation before the Great Council of Zurich on January 29, 1523. For the occasion, attended by some six hundred people, including numerous religious

[2] Peter J. Klassen, "Zwingli and the Zurich Anabaptists," in *Gottesreich und Menschenreich* ed. Max Geiger (Basel: Helbing und Lichtenhahn, 1969).
[3] Zwingli, *Saemtliche Werke*, I:106.

and civic officials as well as other interested spectators, Zwingli drew up his *Sixty-seven Conclusions*. The first fifteen vigorously set forth evangelical doctrines about the deity and the church, while the sixteenth began a series of denunciations of teachings regarding such matters as saints, the Mass, the papacy, indulgences, penance, pilgrimages, purgatory, and monastic vows.

When the debate began, Zwingli repeatedly insisted that the Scriptures must provide the final answer, and he had come prepared with Hebrew, Greek, and Latin Scriptures. When his opponents, headed by Johann Faber, vicar-general of the bishopric of Constance, suggested that doctrinal disputes be referred to the universities, Zwingli replied that he would accept only the verdict of Holy Writ. At the conclusion of the discussion, the city council ruled that Zwingli had vindicated his position. He, and the other priests in the canton, were to continue preaching the gospel in accordance with the views that had been presented in the disputation.[4] Thus, Zurich declared its adherence to the evangelical doctrines, and at the same time established the principle that a community, through its government, could decide for itself what faith was right. A basic religious position had been taken without reference to episcopal or papal authority; local autonomy in religious matters had been emphatically asserted. The pattern set in this disputation would be followed in many Swiss communities, where emphasis upon the laity in resolving religious issues was especially suited to democratic or oligarchic governments. Gradually, as the clergy and laity came to share religious authority, the presbyterian form of church polity developed. Its structure, parallel with that of the cantonal governments, provided a natural bond between Zwinglian and republican or other non-autocratic states.

IN QUEST OF THE MIDDLE WAY

As reform continued, extreme elements began to surface. Zwingli, determined to keep religious change orderly and peaceful, urged caution. Another disputation was held on October 26, 1523; it failed to come to a decision on the question of the Mass and images. When the city council declined to move resolutely in the situation, Zwingli advised his followers to proceed cautiously and to avoid antagonizing the civil authorities. He did, however, give notice that he would oppose the council should it decree anything contrary to the word of God. He believed that reform could come gradually and peacefully through preaching, but he had no intention of sacrificing his basic principles.[5] The council appointed a commission, including Zwingli and his staunch supporter Leo Jud, to draft guidelines for peaceful reform in the canton. The outcome was

[4]Emil Egli, ed., *Actensammlung zur Geschichte der Zuercher Reformation* (Zurich, J. Schabelitz, 1879), p. 327.

[5]Zwingli's consistent adherence to his philosophy of reform is carefully examined and substantiated in Robert C. Walton, *Zwingli's Theocracy* (Toronto: University of Toronto Press, 1967).

Zwingli's *Short Christian Introduction*, prepared for distribution to the clergy. When the Catholic hierarchy and the diet of the confederation objected, the Zurich council ignored the protests. Zwingli and his associates were permitted to continue to urge their parishioners to accept more sweeping reforms. The reformer was becoming convinced that his preaching would persuade ever greater numbers to his way of thinking.

But not all were prepared to follow this policy of moderation. On the one hand some of Zwingli's most avid supporters accused him of subordinating the word of God to the magistracy, while others bitterly denounced him for bringing dissension into the church. Former humanist friends now withdrew support. Zwingli had long been an admirer of Erasmus, and had profited greatly from the ideas advanced by the great humanist: the emphasis on the Bible and the patristic literature; the sufficiency of Christ for salvation; the criticism of superstition and abuse in the church; the attack on papal absolutism; and the belief that infants who die without baptism would not be damned. But Erasmus could not bear to see a rupture in the church and warned Zwingli to be more conciliatory. The breach was widened when Zwingli, in 1523, befriended Ulrich von Hutten, now a penniless humanist who had written a scurrilous attack on Erasmus. The "prince of the humanists" let it be known that he did not wish to be associated with the views of the Zurich reformer, and when Zwingli fell on the battlefield in 1531, Erasmus did not hesitate to express his relief. The old master completely disowned his too enterprising disciple.

Zwingli was also denounced by those who grew impatient with his pace of reform. One of the radicals, Simon Stumpf, pastor in Hoengg, publicly disagreed with Zwingli, asserting that since the Word of God had already decided the issue, it was not necessary to wait for any decision of religious or secular council. His viewpoint met with support from a number of dissenters, who, disenchanted with their former leader, began to form their own group.

The opposition of the more radical elements forced Zwingli to adhere to a more conservative position. As the champions of more drastic measures rallied their forces around men such as Conrad Grebel, Balthasar Hubmaier, Felix Mantz, and Stumpf, Zwingli bound himself more closely to the civil authorities. He was convinced that the state and church must work in harmony to create a national church; otherwise, he insisted, there would be a hopeless multiplicity of religious bodies, as well as an undermining of secular authority. When radical elements insisted that the church be patterned after the New Testament model, and that infant baptism, which they held to be a later innovation, be abolished, Zwingli broke with his former supporters. In his *Of Baptism, Anabaptism, and Infant Baptism*, as well as in *Of Divine and Human Justice*, he called for a gradual transformation of society by cooperation between church and state. If pastors demonstrated their faith through responsibility to society, men in positions of secular power would come to agree that reforms should be introduced; then, when the appropriate decree was issued, the change could be made. For

Zwingli, there could be no question of going against the law of the state, especially when that state was proving responsive to the message he proclaimed.

The essence of Zwingli's theological position was outlined in perhaps his most important religious work, *The Commentary on True and False Religion*. Published in 1525, it was not only a statement of his beliefs, but also an appeal for French support for the ideals of his reformation. It was accordingly prefaced with a letter addressed to the king of France. In the document, Zwingli contrasted his own religion, which he characterized as one resting on solid biblical and historical foundations, with the prevalent religion of human ingenuity and endeavor. Central to Zwingli's faith was his conception of Christ as the bond between man and a just and merciful God. Zwingli retained only the sacraments of baptism and communion. Although he did not accept the view that Christ was corporeally present in the elements, he did assert that the Eucharist was to be the occasion of "profound, almost mystical contemplation"[6] of the death of Christ. For Zwingli, the spiritual presence of Christ made communion more than a bare memorial.[7] This is where he differed with Luther. Other parts of the treatise breathed a warmth and fervor that too often was overlooked because of the resolute manner in which Zwingli propagated and defended his beliefs.

Meanwhile, Zwingli continued to remove those outer trappings of devotion which he regarded as harmful to a faith based solely on the Scriptures. Although his earlier life was characterized by an intense love of music, Zwingli now concluded that it was a distracting element in the worship service. Choirs, he charged, tended to "perform their deeds to be seen by the world."[8] Moreover, since he found no biblical warrant for choral singing, he declared that it too should be eliminated. Art works on the walls of churches were destroyed or covered with whitewash; organs were removed; ecclesiastical vestments sold; relics, such as the bones of saints, were buried; crosses were no longer carried in procession.[9] Then, in 1525, Zwingli introduced the celebration of the Lord's Supper according to his understanding of the Scriptures. The Mass was discontinued, for Zwingli insisted that there could be no repetition of the sacrifice of Christ.

The work of reform was safeguarded as Zwingli developed a school for the training of theologians.[10] Biblical study, based upon Greek, Hebrew, and Latin

[6]B. A. Gerrish, ed., *Reformers in Profile* (Philadelphia: Fortress Press, 1967), p. 128.

[7]Cyril C. Richardson, *Zwingli and Cranmer on the Eucharist* (Evanston, Ill.: Seaburg-Western Theological Seminary 1949), p. 16.

[8]Quoted in Charles Garside, *Zwingli and the Arts* (New Haven: Yale University Press, 1966), p. 44. Garside presents a sensitive study of the conflict between Zwingli the artist and Zwingli the theologian.

[9]B. J. Kidd, *Documents Illustrative of the Continental Reformation* (Oxford: Clarendon, 1911), pp. 442–443.

[10]*Ibid.*, pp. 425–427. Zwingli's philosophy of education is outlined in his *Of the Education of Youth* reprinted in *Zwingli and Bullinger,* ed. G. W. Bromiley (Philadelphia: Westminster Press, 1953), pp. 102–118.

texts, formed the core of the curriculum. Not surprisingly, emphasis on the true interpretation of God's Word led to the publication in 1530 of the Zurich translation of the Bible, to which Zwingli contributed substantially, including some passages that reflected his own environment; for example, he translated the second verse of the twenty-third Psalm: "He makes me rest in lovely Alpine pastures."

Religious reform was paralleled by remedial action in the social arena. Through his intervention, serfdom was abolished and relief for the poor completely reorganized. State and church cooperated in bringing material assistance to the oppressed and impoverished. Begging was prohibited—instead the paupers received bread and soup from the secular authorities. Jurisdiction in civil affairs, as in matrimony, was given to the city council, which now also assumed the role of guardian of public morals. In this capacity, it did not hesitate to use coercive measures to eradicate unacceptable practices and ideas. Citizens who openly opposed the official religious policy might expect to find themselves sentenced to prison or to death. Obviously, Zwingli's new society had little room for dissent.

THE SPREAD OF ZWINGLIANISM

The events in Zurich were viewed with grave apprehension by most members of the Swiss Confederation. Although attempts had been made to have the Swiss diet take action to remedy some of the most glaring ecclesiastical abuses, most of the cantons opposed all innovation. To settle the whole problem, the diet agreed to call a disputation, to be held in the staunchly Catholic town of Baden. The debates lasted from May 21 to June 8, 1526. Johann Eck, who had earlier debated Luther, again appeared to defend the traditional position. His party included a number of bishops as well as foreign theologians. The evangelical cause was defended by only a small group; Zwingli himself had been prevented from attending because the Zurich council feared for his safety.[11]

Eck faced Zwingli's friend, Oecolampadius, a classical and Hebrew scholar from Basel, and Berchtold Haller of Bern. Issues discussed included the sacrifice of the Mass, the real presence, the invocation of the Virgin and of saints, purgatory, and original sin. As at Leipzig, the basis of authority was again the crucial issue. The evangelical party insisted that only the Scriptures could be admitted as authoritative in matters of faith, while Eck rejected such a limitation. The debate ended with a declaration of victory by the papal party. Zwingli was excommunicated, and Basel was asked to dismiss Oecolampadius from his pastoral office.

Nevertheless, the tide of Zwinglian reform was not to be stayed, for evangelical preaching soon elicited demands for popular reform—demands that, in ac-

---

[11]Several supporters of the Zwinglian position had been tortured and beheaded in Baden in 1524.

cordance with accepted political practices, needed to be given a public hearing. In Bern, the largest of the cantons and the seat of the political capital of the confederacy, a disputation lasting nineteen days began on January 7, 1528.[12] This time the reform party was represented by delegates from Zurich and other Swiss cities, as well as by Bucer and Capito from Strasbourg. Zwingli led the attack on the papal position, and the city council declared his party the winner. Bern now became a reformed city, with Zwingli and Haller providing a confessional statement that served as a doctrinal and ecclesiastical guide for the church. By edict of the council on February 7, 1528, Zwinglian doctrine was established, the jurisdiction of bishops terminated, and changes in worship and discipline implemented. Images were forbidden and monastic properties appropriated for public use. Once again, a school was established so that ministers of the new faith might be carefully trained.

A less peaceful course of events brought triumph to the reform movement in Basel. Here the impetus came from Oecolampadius, priest of St. Martin's Church and professor of theology at the university. His attacks on what he regarded as the idolatry of the Mass aroused the citizenry to destroy images, whitewash frescoes, and remove paintings. Erasmus, disgusted with the violence, left the city, although even now he could not refrain from his characteristic gibes at the expense of the church. He professed surprise that the desecration of the holy objects had not called forth a punitive miracle "seeing how many there always used to occur whenever the saints were even slightly offended."

For a time, champions of reform met determined opposition from the city council. This body, staunchly conservative, issued an edict in February, 1528, proclaiming that religious change be halted. However, by the end of the year, some three hundred members of guilds drew up a statement demanding an end to the Mass and the introduction of other religious reforms.[13] The council thus found itself confronted by ever greater popular pressure. In February, 1529, a crowd gathered at the marketplace and demanded religious changes and a more democratic form of government. When the council delayed, the crowd went on an iconoclastic rampage. Now the council acted; a doctrinal statement, strongly evangelical in tone, was adopted.[14] Church services in German with congregational singing and communion supplanted the Latin Mass. State and church again cooperated in watching over the moral life of the city. Unacceptable doctrinal views and social practices were made civil offenses, with the offenders "punished according to the measure of their guilt in body, life and property."

---

[12]John T. McNeill, *The History and Character of Calvinism* (New York: Oxford University Press, 1954), pp. 63–65.

[13]Gordon Rupp, *Patterns of Reformation* (Philadelphia: Fortress Press, 1969), pp. 35–36.

[14]Ernst Staehelin, *Das theologische Lebenswerk Johannes Oekolampads* (Leipzig: M. Heinsius Nachfolger, 1939), pp. 478–487.

PORTRAIT: JOHN OECOLAMPADIUS, by Hans Asper

As the reformer's biographer, Ernst Staehelin, has observed, the Reformation in the university and printing center of Basel had repercussions far beyond its boundaries. The scholarly Oecolampadius played a significant role in helping the city resolve its problems by resorting to the pen rather than the sword.

Oeffentliche Kunstsammlung Basel

Oecolampadius continued to dominate the religious scene, and to make Basel a stronghold of the Reformation. His work, however, was cut short by his death in 1531.

Meanwhile, other cantons, reacting to the religious unrest, either adopted the reform faith or reassessed their stand on Catholicism. In northeastern Switzerland, as in St. Gall, Schaffhausen, Appenzell, Thurgau, and Aargau, the reformed faith gained a substantial following. In St. Gall, the humanist Joachim Vadian and pastor Johann Kessler were largely responsible for the triumph of Zwingli's teachings. Vadian, who had been rector of the University of Vienna, convinced that the reformed doctrines were biblical, now became their enthusiastic supporter. In 1525, he was chosen burgomaster, and was thus strategically situated to press for the introduction of the new faith. Calmly and confidently, he adopted a middle course between proponents of drastic and violent change, and

107

the adherents of the old order.[15] By 1526, images were being removed from the churches, and in the following year an evangelical church order was established. Nonetheless the Catholics found a staunch champion in Blaurer, the abbot of St. Gall, who zealously mounted a counter attack against the followers of Zwinglianism.

In Schaffhausen, Sebastian Hofmeister, a Franciscan monk and professor of theology at Constance, led the attack on what he considered to be the abuses and errors of Rome. In 1529, the reformed doctrines were officially adopted, again introduced and maintained by the typical pattern of church-state cooperation. In Grisons, religion was determined at the local level. The civic community (*Dorfgemeinde*) and the ecclesiastical community (*Kirchgemeinde*) were usually identical. Here, Zwinglianism made inroads among all three ethnic groups— German, Romansh, and Italian; however, each congregation in the canton was permitted to choose its faith. About one-third of the population remained Catholic, and this diversity helped to ensure a large measure of religious toleration. Reformers such as John Comander ably defended Zwingli's views in a disputation in Ilanz in 1526, thus gaining civil support for the Reformation in this part of Grisons. Another reformer, Philip Gallicius, was especially influential in the Romansh areas. His translations of religious writings, including parts of the Bible, helped to establish a literary tradition for the Romansh language. This work would be carried on by Ulrich Campell who translated the Psalter, wrote hymns, and prepared a catechism.

Reform practices were also apparent in the Italian valleys of Grisons, where the former papal nuncio, Peter Vergerio, persuaded some of the villages to end the Mass and to discard images. This recent convert had earlier persecuted the Protestants, but in 1549 he set up a printing press and began to issue a number of diatribes against the papacy. Later, he moved to Germany, where he became a counsellor at the court of Duke Christoph of Wuerttemberg.

The canton of Glarus, where Zwingli had begun his public ministry, became largely Zwinglian, although each congregation maintained the right to choose its religion. One of the most prominent men of the city of Glarus, Aegidius Tschudi, a renowned Swiss historian and a Catholic, advocated broad toleration, and attempted to reconcile the different parties. His cousin, Valentin Tschudi, Zwingli's successor at Glarus, continued to minister to the spiritual needs of Catholics as well as evangelicals. His latitudinarianism did much to avoid open hostility. When Zwingli attempted to persuade him to preach only the Word of God, and to stop the Catholic services, Valentin replied that each side should tolerate the other, and join in the worship of the same God. Differences in external matters should not become the occasion for bitter dissension. This spirit of toleration continued to dominate religious interaction in Glarus, and spared that city the strife that so often embittered relations during the Reformation.

[15]Rupp, *Patterns*, p. 372.

THE REFORMATION IN STRASBOURG

Zwinglianism also gained some adherents in Germany, especially in the imperial free cities of the south. Usually, reform was promoted by the various guilds, which pressured the town council into accepting the new faith.[16] In Strasbourg, Martin Bucer (1491–1551) and Wolfgang Capito (1478–1541), with substantial popular support, spearheaded the Zwinglian movement. In Augsburg, Martin Cellarius became the champion of the Zurich reformer. Despite resistance from the city aristocracy, he gained the backing of the craft guilds and helped to carry through a reformation in this center of Hapsburg financial interests. Other leaders, such as Ambrosius Blaurer in Constance, Hermann in Reutlingen, and Somius in Ulm, attempted to introduce Zwinglianism as the dominant religious position.

In no other imperial free city did the Reformation play so significant a role as in Strasbourg. This Rhineland city, strategically located at a crossroads of Europe, was the center of attempts to unite the different branches of Protestantism. Leaders of the reform movement here, especially Capito and Bucer, held moderate theological positions, attempting to reconcile the differing views of Zwingli and Luther. Capito, formerly cathedral preacher and professor in Basel, had also served as chaplain and chancellor to Albert, archbishop of Mainz. When he came to Strasbourg in 1523, he found the work of reform already under way, led by a local priest, Matthew Zell.

Capito at once identified himself with the reform party, and was soon joined by Bucer, who had come to the city at almost the same time. Bucer established himself as an aggressive leader and became the soul of reform in the city. Under his leadership evangelical doctrines first received the sanction of civil officials. The smooth transition Strasbourg made to the reformed faith is due to this civil sanction and to the fact that reform measures were introduced gradually, with a minimum of violence, only after citizens had been carefully instructed by the preachers.[17] Images were abolished, new measures of discipline adopted, and education made more readily available. The noted academy of Johann Sturm was now established. In 1529, the Mass was abolished, and in 1534, an evangelical confession of faith was formally adopted.

Some of the Strasbourg religious and civil leaders were reluctant to use coercion in matters of faith. Not surprisingly, the city became a refuge for those fleeing persecution elsewhere. Whereas many other Protestant leaders were prepared to admit that the true church existed where there was the preaching of the Word, the celebration of the sacraments, and the exercise of discipline, Bucer

---

[16]Bernd Moeller, in his *Reichsstadt und Reformation* (Guetersloh: G. Mohn, 1962) convincingly refutes the widespread notion that a city's response to the Reformation was simply dependent upon the attitude of the political authorities.

[17]Miriam U. Chrisman, *Strasbourg and the Reform* (New Haven: Yale University Press, 1967), p. 173ff.

insisted that the practice of love, as expressed in good works, was also necessary. When a penniless refugee arrived in Strasbourg, he would be given material assistance, and when the Peasants' War brought desolation and destitution to thousands, Bucer and his associates provided relief for these masses.

Bucer, believing that there was room for honest differences, urged a distinction between essential and nonessential (*adiaphora*) matters of faith. Christians should permit limited individual freedom in the latter. However, if a particular position threatened the triumph of reform policies, Bucer could be thoroughly uncompromising. Thus, he did not hesitate to urge the city council to adopt rigorous measures against the Anabaptists. He warned that the church in Strasbourg faced ruin "because of the toleration which is being shown towards the sects."[18] Freedom to err was still a luxury that few leaders would permit.

Nonetheless, a quest for limited toleration became characteristic not only of Strasbourg, but also of other cities in southern Germany—even in centers that had earlier adopted a more rigid form of Lutheranism. While the position of Zwingli and Bucer did not allow for individual liberty, it did permit a larger measure of lay participation and recognized the desirability of allowing medieval corporatism to shape ecclesiastical and political policies. City governments, ever suspicious of autocratic rule, saw in Zwinglianism a natural ally.

THE MARBURG COLLOQUY

The rapid growth of Zwinglianism made an encounter with an equally dynamic Lutheranism inevitable. Despite his strong admiration for Luther, Zwingli resolutely insisted that his movement to reform the church resulted from his independent study of Scripture and analysis of the contemporary situation. Although the two reformers agreed on the major points of doctrine, their strong views did not permit them to reach agreement on all theological issues. Zwingli remained much more a humanist than did Luther. In the quest for truth, he was more willing than Luther to appeal to human reason, and for him philosophy remained the handmaiden of divine revelation. Both reformers agreed that Christ alone could give man saving grace, and both recognized the absolute sovereignty of God, which led both to adopt a belief in predestination of the elect. But Zwingli placed more emphasis on the objective, sovereign act of God, while Luther, equally insistent that faith was the gift of God, emphasized the grateful response of the sinner who had experienced the love of God. Zwingli also adopted a more rational approach to church reform, while Luther was prepared to allow more room for his emotions. At least to some extent, the two reformers may be thought of as on opposite ends of a reason–emotion continuum. Luther never attempted to divorce religion from aesthetics, and for him the beauty of art could enhance the meaning of worship. Zwingli, however, concerned that no-

---

[18]Manfred Krebs and H. G. Rott, *Quellen zur Geschichte der Taeufer, VIII, Elsass, II* (Guetersloh: G. Mohn, 1960), pp. 181, 182.

thing should detract from the centrality of Scripture, attempted to
biblical simplicity of worship that could be affirmed by referring to
alone. He tended to reject all church practices and embellishments for wꞓꞓ... ...
did not find specific Scriptural warrant.

Although both reformers shared similar views concerning most theological
issues, in the doctrine of the sacrament of the Eucharist, they differed sharply and
openly. In 1529, they met in the Marburg Colloquy, initiated by Philip of Hesse
in the hope of evolving a united Protestant front against the threat of imperial
military action. Zwingli was supported by Oecolampadius, Bucer, and Caspar
Hedio, while Luther was seconded by Melanchthon, Justus Jonas, Osiander,
Brenz, Agricola, Cruciger, Menius, Roerer, and Myconius. Agreement was
reached on fourteen doctrinal issues, but on the Eucharist, they remained divided. Both rejected the Catholic doctrine of transubstantiation and the view of
the Mass as a sacrifice, but they could not agree on the manner of Christ's
presence in the elements; the question of the Lord's Supper remained the open
sore of Protestantism. With both sides determined to show the error of the other,
the lack of compromise was hardly surprising. Luther insisted that the words,
"This is my body," could not be interpreted symbolically, whereas Zwingli,
quoting numerous passages of Scripture where a symbolical interpretation is
obviously required, countered with Christ's statement, "It is the spirit that
quickens; the flesh profits nothing." When Zwingli attempted to disprove
Luther's position, the German reformer replied that he would not be guided by
reason, but by faith. Whatever the Bible said, he would believe. Zwingli maintained that the sacraments of baptism and the Lord's Supper were outward signs
and strengthened faith, but were not necessarily means of grace, while Luther
insisted that the sacraments were indeed the means of grace, just as the spoken
Word of the gospel, conveying the same promise and the same remission of sins.

Both parties signed the Marburg Articles, which outlined the extensive area of
theological agreement, and also stated that, despite the differing views relative to
the real presence, both parties would "show Christian charity to the other." The
political alliance that Philip sought, however, remained unrealized, for Luther
insisted that there must be religious agreement if there was to be political and
military cooperation. Henceforth, the two chief bodies of continental Protestantism would continue along a divided road. At least in Switzerland, Lutheranism
would gain little support.

ZWINGLI THE MILITARIST

The reform movement in Switzerland reached a decisive turning point when
Zwingli resolved to speed the triumph of his cause by resorting to political,
economic, and military force. He supported an alliance of Constance, Bern,
Basel, St. Gall, Schaffhausen, Biel, and Muehlhausen with Zurich to counter the
alliance of the Catholic cantons—Uri, Schwyz, Unterwalden, Lucerne, and Zug.
When, in 1529, the latter body further strengthened its position by forming an

alliance with Austria, the traditional enemy of Swiss independence, the lines of battle were drawn. The confederation had split.

The tension reached a peak when Jacob Kaiser, an evangelical preacher, was burned at the stake in the town of Schwyz. Zwingli counselled war. To his Bernese friends he wrote, ''Let us be firm, and not fear to take up arms. This peace, which some desire so much, is not peace but war; while the war that we call for is not war, but peace.'' Zurich, supported by soldiers from reluctant allies, sent an army to Cappel, on the borders of the canton of Zurich, where a Catholic force confronted the Zwinglian alliance. Few leaders on either side shared Zwingli's determination to go to war. Bern announced that it would have no part of an offensive war, while other towns, such as Glarus, attempted to mediate. Meanwhile, the troops fraternized with their opponents, even sharing their food. Zwingli attempted to gain concessions from the Catholics before he would agree to peace. He demanded that evangelical preaching be permitted throughout the confederacy, and he was prepared to grant Catholics the same rights. The sale of mercenaries (so crucial for the surplus population of the forest cantons) was to be terminated, while foreign pensions were to be abolished. Furthermore, he wanted the Catholic cantons to pay the cost of war preparation. Schwyz was also to pay an indemnity to the family of Jacob Kaiser.

Negotiations led to the First Peace of Cappel in June, 1529. By its terms, both sides were to practice religious tolerance. The Catholic cantons also agreed to abandon their Austrian alliance, pay for the war preparations, and give financial assistance to Kaiser's family. For the moment, moderation had prevailed.

Neither side was satisfied with the provisions of the peace. Catholic cantons resumed their alliance with Austria, while Zwinglians resorted to force to gain control of the lands of the monastery of St. Gall, and reformed Thurgau and Rheintal without waiting for majority action. Zurich made an alliance with Philip of Hesse, although overtures to other foreign powers were unsuccessful.

Zwingli, convinced that war was inevitable, urged his allies to take the offensive, but they demurred. Finally, Bern imposed an economic blockade on the forest cantons, hoping to deprive them of grain, salt, wine, iron, and steel. Provisions could still be brought from the south, although this was much more difficult and costly. Thus pressured, the Waldstaetters (those living in the forest cantons) responded by sending their troops against Zurich. The opposing armies met, again at Cappel, only this time there was little opportunity for conciliation. Zwingli, as a chaplain, accompanied the Zurich army, but the poorly led force of two thousand was soon routed by the eight thousand of the forest cantons. Among the dead was Zwingli himself, whose body was now quartered and burned, while his ashes, mixed with the ashes of swine, were scattered to the winds.

Hostilities were terminated by the Second Peace of Cappel, signed in Zug on November 20, 1531. Its provisions essentially retained the status quo—Catholic and Zwinglian were to tolerate each other, and both were to give up foreign alliances. The monastery of St. Gall, with its lands, was to be restored to the Catholic church.

Zwinglianism now entered a less militaristic phase. Heinrich Bullinger (1504–1575), successor of Zwingli, soon established himself as a consummate diplomat and politician. His forceful, persuasive writing gained him a reputation far beyond the borders of his native land, while his vast correspondence bore convincing testimony to the regard shown him by friend and opponent throughout Europe. His pen helped to shape the Protestant churches of many countries, including Hungary and Austria. It was surely no small recognition of the stature of the man when the English government, upon the excommunication of Queen Elizabeth, asked him to write a defense of their monarch. Bullinger also played a central part in bringing unity to Protestantism in Switzerland. When the coming of John Calvin to Geneva established that city as the major center of Swiss Protestantism, Bullinger worked for closer ties between Zurich and Geneva. He played a central role in bringing Zwinglianism and Calvinism together in the Second Helvetic Confession (1566), thus laying the foundation for a united Swiss Reformed Church.

Suggestions for Further Reading

Bornkamm, Heinrich. *Martin Bucers Bedeutung.* Guetersloh: Bertelsmann, 1952.

Bromiley, G. W. *Zwingli and Bullinger.* Philadelphia: Westminister Press, 1953.

Chrisman, Miriam. *Strasbourg and the Reform.* New Haven: Yale University Press, 1967.

*****Courvoisier, Jacques.** *Zwingli: A Reformed Theologian.* Richmond, Va.: John Knox Press, 1963.

Eells, Hastings. *Martin Bucer.* New Haven: Yale University Press, 1931.

Farner, Oskar. *Huldrych Zwingli,* 4 vols. Zurich: Zwingli-Verlag, 1943–1960.

———. *Zwingli the Reformer.* Translated by D. G. Sear. New York: Philosophical Library, 1952.

*****Fast, Heinhold.** *Heinrich Bullinger und die Taeufer.* Weierhof, Pfalz: Mennonitischer Geschichtsverein, 1959.

Garside, Charles. *Zwingli and the Fine Arts.* New Haven: Yale University Press, 1966.

Hopf, C. *Martin Bucer and the English Reformation.* Oxford: Blackwell, 1946.

Kittelson, James M. *Wolfgang Capito: From Humanist to Reformer.* Leiden: Brill, 1975.

Koehler, Walther. *Huldrych Zwingli,* 2d ed. Leipzig: Koehler und Amelang, 1954.

Locher, Gottfried. *Die Theologie Huldrych Zwinglis im Lichte seiner Christologie.* Zurich: Zwingli-Verlag, 1952.

Pauck, Wilhelm. *Melanchthon and Bucer.* Philadelphia: Westminister Press, 1969.

*Indicates paperback edition.

Pollet, J. V. *Huldrych Zwingli et la Réforme en Suisse.* Paris: Presses universitaires de France, 1963.

Richardson, C. C. *Zwingli and Cranmer on the Eucharist.* Evanston, Ill.: Seabury-Western Theological Seminary, 1949.

Rilliet, Jean. *Zwingli: Third Man of the Reformation.* Translated by Harold Knight. Philadelphia: Westminister Press, 1964.

Rupp, E. Gordon. *Patterns of Reformation: Oecolampadius, Karlstadt, Muentzer.* Philadelphia: Fortress Press, 1969.

*Schmidt-Clausing, Fritz.** *Zwingli.* Berlin: de Gruyter, 1965.

Staehelin, Ernst. *Das Theologische Lebenswerk Johannes Oecolampads.* Leipzig: M. Heinsius Nachfolger, 1939.

Staehelin, Rudolf. *Huldreich Zwingli: Sein Leben und Wirken,* 2 vols. Basel: B. Schwabe, 1895–97.

Walton, Robert C. *Zwingli's Theocracy.* Toronto: University of Toronto Press, 1967.

6

The Radical Wing
of the Reformation

As the Reformation movement spread, European society witnessed a wide variety of revolutionary upheavals. The old order found itself under attack, and the shape of the new one was not immediately clear. At the same time, there was much in the Lutheran and Zwinglian movements that was basically conservative, for traditional social, economic, and political patterns were not the objects of attack. For both Luther and Zwingli, the frontal assault on the old faith was essentially a religious protest. Neither intended to upset the balance of long-established institutions and relationships within society. In fact, both shared the ideal of the *corpus christianum*—the belief that church and state formed an essential unity and that membership in both was identical. Thus, while religious doctrines might change, the political and ecclesiastical authorities were still envisioned as supporting one another. This was the rule rather than the exception among Protestant leaders. While many reformers became spokesmen for greater social and economic justice, they did not find it necessary to uproot the foundations of society.

Yet there were those who called for changes so drastic that, at least to their sixteenth-century counterparts, they seemed revolutionaries, not simply reformers. In previous centuries, the close collaboration of secular and spiritual powers had successfully contained such challenges; now, with the Reformation in full swing, the usual forces of restraint could not readily be brought into action. The turmoil in the Empire and the religious changes in Switzerland and elsewhere afforded a unique opportunity for radical forms of dissent, even revolution. These forms of dissent were varied in their goals and methods. Some called for a frankly new society, such as the one envisioned by Muentzer. Those who shared this apocalyptic dream confidently expected God to break into history, destroy the godless, and establish the millennium on earth. Other radicals called for the elimination of traditional church-state ties, a change that would alter the entire fabric of society. These visionaries supported the idea of a totally voluntary

115

religious community independent of any external coercive power, for to them faith under duress was a contradiction of the very nature of faith.

Some free spirits called for the elimination of all external ecclesiastical practices, including the administration of the sacraments, and set forth instead an essentially mystical conception of the church, with each person free to follow the dictates of his conscience, even apart from the Scriptures and the organized church or its sacraments. Others, such as some of the anti-trinitarians, launched an attack on the doctrines of the church and called instead for a religion measured in ethical, not dogmatic, terms.

In this seething ferment, it was not surprising that some bold spirits called for the abolition of private property or for the total repudiation of existing economic and social interests. Some expressions of discontent seemed frankly anarchistic; others proclaimed a new order in accordance with mystical visions. Altogether, it was a time which, at least to many, seemed strangely out of joint. Defenders of the old order, whether Catholic or Protestant, were determined to crush a dangerous radicalism. Little distinction was made between those who peacefully challenged traditional values and relationships, and those who, with whatever means at their disposal, tried to destroy age-old systems and institutions. Like the medieval crusader, preservers of the old order were quick to enjoin: "Slay them all. God will know his own." Many years of burning heretics and witches had inured Europe to the spectacle of torturing and executing new varieties of dissenters.

ANABAPTISM

Rise of the Movement

One of the new forms of dissent found its genesis in the Zwinglian upheaval. As the Swiss Reformation gained strength, abolishing many of the established religious practices and teachings, Zwingli found himself increasingly pressed by the advocates of sweeping reform. His insistence on gradual change, always with the support of the city government, led the radicals to denounce him as a creature of expediency rather than a leader of spiritual principle. Zwingli's position in Zurich was now not unlike that of Luther in Wittenberg after his return from the Wartburg. As Karlstadt and his associates had denounced Luther for his reluctance to move rapidly, now an impatient element around Zwingli urged him not to wait for approval by the city council. Indeed, the Zurich radicals may well have been influenced by nonconformists and iconoclasts such as Karlstadt and Muentzer. The latter was highly praised by the Zurich group in 1524, although his violent methods were firmly denounced.[1] Dissatisfaction with Zwingli's pace

[1]George H. Williams and Angel M. Mergal, eds., *Spiritual and Anabaptist Writers* (Philadelphia: Westminster Press, 1957), pp. 71–85.

and extent of reform centered around Conrad Grebel, humanist, patrician, and intellectual of Zurich. Earlier he had been a staunch supporter of his fellow humanist, Zwingli; now the bonds of friendship were severely strained as the Grebel circle proclaimed its refusal to accept anything less than a restitution of the early church.

By 1523, the lines of division between Zwingli and the champions of radical reform were hardening. When, in the disputation held in October of that year, Zwingli warned against the dangers of precipitate change, Grebel, Hubmaier, Ludwig Haetzer, and Felix Mantz became disillusioned with their former hero. Grebel asserted that Zwingli, who had previously insisted on biblical authority, had now rejected his own standard.

As the rift widened and the radicals continued their studies of the Scriptures, they went beyond those principles earlier suggested by Zwingli. They concluded that the biblical church was composed only of believers who had deliberately chosen to associate themselves with a movement that was separate from the civic order. Similarly, they concluded that baptism, the sign of membership in this voluntary community, had validity only when performed in response to deliberate choice. Thus, Grebel's group not only rejected infant baptism but also called for an end to a state church and urged the formation of a church composed only of those who wished to join. Further biblical studies convinced these dissenters that, like the early Christians, anyone who seriously took the challenge to follow Christ must identify himself with the suffering of the cross. Gradually, there emerged the conviction that the essence of Christianity was *Nachfolge*—a deliberate and costly following of Christ, offered to all but forced upon none. Such a church should expect not popular support, but constant persecution.

Although Zwingli himself showed a temporary vacillation on the question of infant baptism,[2] his initial hesitation was soon overcome. To reject infant baptism would, in his opinion, undermine the state church and indeed threaten the whole of society. Following a public debate between Zwingli and the radicals on January 17, 1525, the city council declared that the position of the Zwinglians had been vindicated. The council further ordered that all parents, upon pain of banishment, must have their infants baptized. Shortly hereafter, the champions of a voluntary church met secretly and resolved to maintain their position. On January 21, 1525, at a gathering for Bible study in the home of Felix Mantz in Zurich, a new movement was initiated, as Grebel baptized Georg Blaurock, one of the most vociferous opponents of Zwingli; Blaurock then baptized others.[3] This act of rebaptism led opponents to castigate the radicals as Anabaptists (from a Greek word meaning "rebaptizer"), although the members insisted that the epithet was inappropriate, since they refused to recognize their earlier infant

[2]Huldreich Zwingli, *Saemtliche Werke,* eds. E. Egli, G. Finsler et al. (Leipzig und Berlin, 1905–1959), IV:228.
[3]Williams and Mergal, *Spiritual and Anabaptist Writers,* p. 44.

baptism as valid. They called themselves simply Christians, or brothers. As opposition to the new movement increased, its advocates withdrew to the nearby village of Zollikon and there established the first Anabaptist congregation.

As the Anabaptists vigorously proclaimed their faith, it was inevitable that they would arouse the wrath of conservative reformers. Within a few days, Felix Mantz, Blaurock, and twenty-five others were arrested and imprisoned. Zwingli attempted to convince them of error but failed. Most of those who had been imprisoned were released shortly, but warned not to continue disseminating their beliefs. As the pressures of religious and civic opposition mounted, many Anabaptists fled to other areas, their missionary zeal intensified by persecution.

In Zurich, the Anabaptist movement continued to gain strength and, largely because of popular pressure, the city authorities permitted the radicals to participate in a number of disputations. After one such confrontation in November, 1525, Grebel, Mantz, and Blaurock were tried and imprisoned. Then, in March, 1526, the council decreed the death penalty for all who would practice rebaptism. Two weeks later, the Anabaptists escaped and continued their proselytizing missions. The council resolved to adopt sterner measures, and on November 19, 1526, made attendance at Anabaptist meetings a capital offense.

In Zurich, the conflict between radicalism and conservatism was soon to be measured in terms of civil power and martyrdom. In December, 1526, several Anabaptists, including Mantz and Blaurock, were captured and tried. Both were found guilty of having violated the laws forbidding Anabaptist activities. Since Mantz had actually performed a rebaptism, he was condemned to death. On January 5, 1527, he was thrown into the Limmat River, a stick thrust between his tied, doubled up legs and arms, thus becoming the first Protestant religious martyr to die at the hand of other Protestants. Blaurock, who had not been convicted of performing an actual rebaptism, and who also was not a citizen of Zurich, was stripped to the waist, publicly flogged, then driven from the city. The chief leader of the Anabaptists had been removed earlier, for in the summer of 1526, Conrad Grebel was struck down by the plague.

As the Anabaptists carried their teachings throughout Switzerland into Austria and southwestern Germany, then down the Rhine, they encountered ever more determined opposition. Many authorities believed that here was a continuation of that spirit of revolt which had convulsed much of Europe in the peasant upheaval. Indeed, some who had been a part of the ill-fated rebellion now joined the Anabaptist cause, even though most of the Anabaptist leaders deplored any appeal to violence. By 1528, an imperial edict prescribed the death penalty for Anabaptists. Then, in 1529, Catholic and Lutheran estates at the diet of Speyer, citing the Justinian Code, resolved to proceed vigorously against the rebaptizers. The aroused estates of the Empire determined to unite in the extermination of a movement they regarded as a threat to the social and political order. When Charles issued his mandate on April 23, 1529, it advised the estates that every Anabaptist "shall be condemned and brought from natural life into death by fire, sword, and the like . . . without proceeding to the inquisition of the spiritual judges.''

Peril and Consolidation

With the secular authorities thus ranged against them, the Anabaptists became all the more convinced that theirs was the cause of God, of the true church. Theirs was the challenge of being the bearers of history, of doing spiritual battle for the Lord. And the conviction grew as the persecution became more widespread. At the same time, religious devotion and missionary emphasis also served to swell the ranks of the radicals. Sometimes, recruits to the movement were motivated by social and economic considerations; often they were attracted by the practical Christianity, the avowedly biblical faith, and the remarkable courage of those who were not afraid to oppose secular and religious authority. Zwingli himself was forced to admit that the life of the Anabaptists was exemplary.

As communities of radicalism sprang up in numerous parts of Switzerland, cities such as St. Gall, Bern, and Basel passed laws to combat the new teaching. Offenders were subjected to confiscation of property, exile, or death. In the face of this opposition, Anabaptist leaders attempted to maintain a unity of belief and avoid doctrinal vagaries. A synod was held in Schleitheim in the canton of Schaffhausen in February, 1527. Michael Sattler, a former Benedictine prior, presided at the sessions and was largely responsible for the content of the first Anabaptist articles of faith. This Schleitheim Confession,[4] originally entitled *The Brotherly Union*, denounced antinomian excesses, called for baptism of believers only, stipulated that the ban (exclusion from the congregation) be used to discipline those who ''fall into error and sin,'' and rejected the use of violence and oaths. The articles further defined mutual responsibilities of pastor and congregation, noting that the physical necessities of the pastor should be supplied by the congregation. Although the confession was not intended to be a full statement of beliefs, and dealt only with issues of immediate concern, it would have a strong influence in shaping that part of Anabaptism which sought reform by peaceful means and flatly denied the right to employ physical force in defense of faith.

While Sattler[5] was returning from the synod to Horb on the Neckar, scene of his most recent missionary activities, he was apprehended by Austrian authorities. Prolonged grisly tortures failed to bring a retraction, and on May 21, 1527, he was burned at the stake. The occasion prompted Bucer in Strasbourg to defend Sattler as a ''true friend of God'' and to issue another plea for moderation in dealing with religious nonconformists. But neither secular nor religious pow-

[4]Hans J. Hillerbrand, ed., *The Protestant Reformation* (New York: Harper & Row, A Harper Torchbook, 1968), pp. 129–36.

[5]His writings, together with a brief sketch of his life, are found in John H. Yoder, *The Legacy of Michael Sattler* (Scottdale, Pa.: Herald, 1973).

Eenige die se niet gantfch richten wilden, hebben fy aen het lijf geftraft, eenige de vingers afgehouwen, enige kruycen aende voorhoofden laten branden, en veel moetwils met hen aengegaen. So dat ook de gemelde Burggraef felve fprak: Wat fal ik doen? hoe ik 'er meer laet richten, hoe fy meerder worden.

Gen. i, 22.

Defe Dietrig Burggraef, die fich veel aen fulk ontfchuldig bloed befondigt hadde, is fchrickelijk (toen hy eenmael van de tafel en eten opgeftaen is) een haeftige dood geftorven.

In de Chronijk van den Onderg. der Tyrannen, editie 1617. op 't Jaer 1529. pag. 1029. col. 1. uyt de oude hift. der Doopfg. Martelaren, lib. 1. &c.

Philips van Langenlonsheym.
Anno 1529.

E En van de laerfte Broeders die fy tot Creitze in de Stad richteden/ was een met name Philips van Langenlonsheym, als hem de Scherpreehter het hooft affloeg/ foo

tot afgevallen/ alfoo plaegde en beforht hem God/ om dat ontfchuldig bloed/ waer mede Job. 6.17. hy fich niet weynig bevlekt hadde: en God gaf daer door opentlijk en merckelijk te kennen/ hun overlaft aen de bronnen bedreven. De Palsgraef wiert ook door 't een en 't ander fodanig verfchrikt/ en beweegt/ dat hy hier na geen luft meer hadde om fijn handen in fulken bloed te waffchen; en veel daerom gegeven foude hebben dat 'er niet gefchied ware.

Juriaen Bouman. 1529.

O Ntrent defe tijd is een Broeder met name Juriaen Bouman, tot Baufchler in 't Land te Wirtenberg gevangen geworden/ om des Geloofs en Gods Woords wille/ en de Jonker daer hy onder was/ heeft hem eenen tijd in de Gevankenis gehouden/ hem ook grouwelijk laten recken en prijnigen/ en foo veel aen hem gedaen/ met gevankenis/ marter en prijn/ ook alderley toefegging/ dat fe hem berededen en bewil-

---

ENGRAVING: ANABAPTIST MARTYRS, by Jan Luyken from the *Martyrs' Mirror*

Bitterly divided over religious issues, Protestants and Catholics nonetheless united in their determination to root out the radical Anabaptists. Few leaders, secular or spiritual, shared Philip of Hesse's view that no person should be put to death because of his religion.

ers were prepared to permit anyone to hold views that seemed heretical and seditious.

Elsewhere, Anabaptism was accorded a similar fate. Since the movement stressed an ethic of love, and expressed concern for those in economic distress, it was frequently popular among the masses but encountered implacable hostility from those in authority. From the Swiss cantons, the new teachings were carried into Austria. In Waldshut, just inside the Austrian border, Hubmaier, the parish priest, convinced that only believers should be baptized, submitted to rebaptism, as did more than three hundred of his parishioners. When he resigned his clerical office, the congregation immediately elected him minister. The act was of historical significance, for it demonstrated the principle of local church autonomy. Soon hereafter, Austrian troops dispersed the group, but Hubmaier escaped to continue his missionary activities and become the leader of a flourishing Anabaptist community in the Moravian town of Nicolsburg. Unlike many other Anabaptists, Hubmaier strongly championed the right of the state to use the sword to punish evil and defend its citizens. While church and state were to be separate, and there was to be no coercion in matters of belief, Hubmaier rejected pacifism, for Christian magistrate and Christian subject should support each other. Participation in a just war, or in any of the necessary coercive activities of the state, Hubmaier argued, constituted a valid aspect of the citizen's responsibility to his state. Hubmaier propagated his views by writing, debating, and preaching, but in 1528, his aggressive missionary endeavors ended with imprisonment and subsequent death at the stake. A few days later, his wife, with a stone tied to her neck, was thrown into the Danube.

The Anabaptist Movement in Southern Germany   Meanwhile, in southern Germany, Anabaptism spread rapidly, with Augsburg and Strasbourg becoming centers of the movement. Here leaders such as the scholarly Hans Denck, master of Latin, Greek, and Hebrew, and the equally learned Ludwig Haetzer were joined by Hans Hut, Pilgram Marpeck, and Michael Sattler in building conventicles for those who advocated a radical transformation of the church and of society in general. Anabaptist teachings were vigorously propagated, whether by itinerant missionaries or by writings of various sorts. Among the most noted publications of the time was the translation of the Old Testament prophets into German by Denck and Haetzer. This work, appearing in Worms in 1527, was widely read and circulated until it was superseded by the publication of Luther's translation in 1534.

Doctrinal problems and eschatological urgency led to the convening of the Martyrs' Synod in Augsburg in August, 1527. Many of the Anabaptist leaders were convinced that the establishment of the heavenly kingdom was imminent, and that the propagation of Anabaptist teachings should be intensified. A cooperative missionary program was developed, and each participant assigned a specific area in the surrounding lands. Secular authorities responded with even more vigorous persecution, so that within a few years most of the participants in the synod had been martyred.

The Spread of the Radical Reformation

Major areas of radical activity, especially Anabaptists

Important centers of the Radical Reformation are underlined

Baltic Sea

Elbe R.

BRANDENBURG

Oder R.

Danzig

Ebing

Bremen

Amsterdam

Leyden

Münster

Berlin

Wittenberg

Antwerp

Cleves

Torgau

NETHERLANDS

Rhine R.

Wartburg

Muehlhausan

Leipzig

HESSE

SAXONY

Zwickau

SILESIA

THE EMPIRE

LUXEMBOURG

Prague

BOHEMIA

Verdun

Metz

Worms

Speyer

MORAVIA

Toul

Strasbourg

WÜRTTEMBERG

Nikolsburg

Danube R.

AUSTRIA

Schleitheim

Waldshut

Augsburg

Vienna

Basel

Constance

BAVARIA

Zurich

STYRIA

Bern

Innsbruck

SWITZERLAND

TYROL

Geneva

CARINTHIA

HUNGARY

Trent

BURGUNDY

SAVOY

MILAN

CARNIOLA

Rhône R.

Pavia

Po R.

Padua

Venice

Bologna

In part, the hostile reception given Anabaptism in south Germany stemmed from the fear of radical teachings that had earlier been propagated by Thomas Muentzer and Andreas Karlstadt. Convinced that the peaceful Anabaptists did not differ in any practical respect from the incendiary leader of the Peasants' War, authorities resolved to stamp out the new faith. Although the association between Muentzer and the Anabaptists would long be taken for granted, the two had basic differences. Muentzer neither taught nor practiced rebaptism, although he eventually denounced infant baptism. He did not accept the Anabaptist separation of church and state nor the predominant ethic of love and nonresistance. When Muentzer began to preach his appeal to violence, contending that the "elect" should now establish God's kingdom, Grebel and his friends expressed their complete disagreement with such methods, and drafted a long letter of warning. According to the Anabaptists, in matters of faith there could be no physical coercion, and the Christian could not take up the sword. Nonetheless, both Muentzer and the Anabaptists attacked existing political, social, and ecclesiastical structures. Authorities rightly concluded that both peasant revolutionary and Anabaptist nonconformist called for a radical transformation of existing society.

Anabaptist Communitarianism Continued persecution drove some of the Anabaptists to adopt the practice of economic equalitarianism. The first systematic program of Anabaptist communism was adopted near the town of Nicolsburg. What began as a falling-out between Hubmaier, pastor of a thriving Anabaptist congregation and staunch supporter of the war against the Turks, and other Anabaptist leaders, such as the pacifist Hans Hut, led eventually to the emigration to Austerlitz in central Moravia of a splinter group under Jacob Wiedemann. Enroute, Christian communism was introduced as the group, composed of some two hundred members in addition to children, resolved to pool their resources. A contemporary chronicler recorded that leaders of the group spread a "cloak before the people, and every man laid his possessions down upon it, with a willing heart and without constraint, for the sustenance of those in need."[6] In Austerlitz, local lords, anxious to secure industrious and peaceful settlers, welcomed the refugees and granted them extensive liberties, including exemption from services and taxes for six years. A *Bruderhof* (community of brothers) was now established and Christian communitarianism was established on a carefully regulated basis. The colony at Austerlitz attracted refugees from Tyrol and elsewhere, and soon similar settlements were established on the lands of tolerant lords.

The rapid influx of oppressed Anabaptists and the formation of various communistic societies brought with it a great discord. However, under the aggressive leadership of Jacob Hutter, who was elected chief bishop, or *Vorsteher*, of the Moravian communities in 1533, communitarian Anabaptism in Moravia became a cohesive, well-disciplined movement. Particular stress was placed on the concept of *Gelassenheit*—joyful abandonment to God that entails complete submission to His will and service to man. Personal abilities and possessions were to be surrendered to the well-being of the community, for all demonstrations of selfishness, including the holding of private property, were regarded as the essence of evil. Hutter's influence would be so profound that the movement would soon come to be known by his name.

In 1535, because King Ferdinand compelled the Moravian nobles to take harsh measures against the communitarian Anabaptists, many of the flourishing colonies perished. Hutter himself was publicly burned on February 25, 1536. Forced to hide in woods and valleys, the hounded Hutterian Brethren were

---

[6]A. J. F. Zieglschmid, ed., *Die aelteste Chronik der Hutterischen Brueder* (Philadelphia: Carl Schurz Memorial Foundation, 1943), p. 49.

nonetheless able to survive, often because the nobles were reluctant to lose the services of their trusted artisans and farmers. Persecution gradually became more sporadic, and by the 1560s, this variety of Anabaptism would flourish again. From 1565 to 1578, Peter Walpot led the Anabaptist Community in what would later be known as the Golden Age, when colonies, scattered throughout Moravia, could boast of an adult membership of approximately 30,000. Not until the ravages of the Thirty Years' War would the group again be threatened with extinction.

Anabaptism Elsewhere in Europe   In other parts of central Europe, Anabaptism was chiefly noncommunistic. Congregations that stressed mutual aid, but not common means of production and distribution, arose in Thuringia, Saxony, Hesse, and other areas. In most instances, Anabaptists could expect exile or death, as recognized leaders of the Protestant Reformation joined with Catholic opponents in advising civil authorities to root out these dissident elements. Luther maintained that to tolerate Anabaptism would be to encourage sedition and blasphemy—and both offenses should be punishable by death.[7] In Hesse, however, the Anabaptists found rare respite, for Landgrave Philip, despite warnings from the Wittenberg theologians, permitted no execution of opponents of the state religion. Rather, he encouraged discussions between the Anabaptists and the theologians of the state church. The tolerant practices were largely successful, for Hesse was one of the few places where significant numbers of Anabaptists returned to the state church.

Most European rulers, however, disagreed with Philip and were convinced that Anabaptism must be exterminated. Sometimes, the constant pressure on the hounded Anabaptists elicited extreme and violent response. One such outburst, occurring in the Westphalian town of Muenster, would stigmatize Anabaptism as a movement of fanatic excesses.

The Revolution in Muenster

The Stage is Set   Political, social, and economic conditions in northwest Germany in the early sixteenth century seemed especially propitious for the growth of revolutionary and visionary ideas. The area was composed chiefly of ecclesiastical states, each with its own prince-bishop. Government was in the hands of a few aristocratic clergymen who chose one of their number as bishop. In the bishopric of Muenster, there were some thirty ecclesiastical centers, frequently with lucrative trading rights and virtual exemption from taxation. Financial burdens thus rested on the peasants and the townsmen. In return for paying taxes, the town of Muenster had been granted a large measure of self-government, but this concession did not satisfy the members of the guilds who resented economic competition from the monks. The latter enjoyed a great ad-

[7]Philip Melanchthon. *Corpus Reformatorum,* ed. C. G. Bretschneider (Halle: C. A. Schwetscke, 1834–1860), IV: 738–740.

vantage, for they were exempt from taxation, military service, family responsibilities, and guild regulations.

Relations between the guilds and the ecclesiastical establishments were usually strained. In the tense atmosphere of the Peasants' War, the Muenster guilds demanded and received financial concessions from the clergy, only to lose them in the aftermath of reaction and repression. Crop failure and the Black Death in 1529 and special taxes in 1530 to meet the Turkish threat brought further economic deterioration to the situation in Westphalia. Muenster seemed ready for a demagogue who would be able to direct the emotions of the populace and champion their aspirations.

In 1531, the restive masses found their charismatic leader in Bernard Rothmann, a university trained clergyman who deplored the economic oppression of the poor. By early 1532, Rothmann was openly espousing Lutheran doctrine and calling for a reformation of the city. The town council, despite the opposition of the bishop, appointed the popular preacher as pastor of the church of St. Lambert. Lutheran preachers were similarly appointed to the other five parishes of the town. Bernard Knipperdolling, a prominent merchant and patrician, ardently supported the reform movement, and now the guilds, aided by the other townsmen, gained control of the town government. The bishop, unable to resist the storm of public resentment, accepted a treaty establishing Lutheranism in the town. Muenster appeared to have made a relatively quiet transition.

The Takeover by Fanatics The first phase of the Reformation was soon superseded by a flood of fanaticism as Anabaptist visionaries from the Netherlands attempted to gain control of the town. Their inspiration was Melchior Hofmann, a zealous prophet of doom who had gained a wide following in Friesland and the surrounding areas. Proclaiming himself the returned Elijah, he confidently announced the imminent end of the world and the establishment of God's kingdom on earth. Although he spent his last ten years in a Strasbourg prison, dying in 1543, his ideas continued to gain adherents. Among the followers was the baker Jan Mathijs of Haarlem. Whereas Hofmann had insisted that believers should quietly and peacefully await divine intervention in history, Mathijs urged the extermination of the godless as a prerequisite to the second coming of Christ. It was this violent aberration that would triumph in Muenster.

Although the town had earlier been visited by more peaceful Anabaptists, in 1533 preachers of extreme chiliasm gained a foothold. Both Rothmann and Knipperdolling embraced the new radicalism. When Rothmann began to teach that economic possessions should be used for the common good, he gained a ready audience, not only in Muenster, but also in its environs. The town now became a haven for the propertyless, the discontented, and the persecuted, and protests by the town council were ineffective. Then, early in 1534, even more unbalanced spirits visited Muenster and began to lead the frenzied mob over the precipice of disaster.

Foremost among the newly arrived fanatics was Jan Beukels of Leyden, avid disciple of Mathijs, who would soon be followed by his mentor. Knipperdolling, leader of the guilds, gave the two self-proclaimed prophets his support. As the strength of the zealots grew, religious toleration was proclaimed by a city council that now had in its membership those who sympathized with Beukels and Mathijs. Knipperdolling was elected burgomaster, thus assuring official support of the radical policies by many of the prosperous and religiously conservative elements. Civil leaders, dominated by Mathijs, proceeded to give official sanction to ever more revolutionary measures. Catholic and Lutheran religious institutions and practices were forbidden, and rebaptism was made the test of acceptability in what was coming to be proclaimed the "New Jerusalem." Those who refused to submit were expelled and their possessions confiscated.

Meanwhile, the bishop, who had been busily raising an army of mercenaries, proceeded to besiege the town. Leaders within the walls responded by establishing rigid control over military, economic, and social affairs. During the ensuing siege, military exigency and religious teaching led to the adoption of communism. Then, confident in his divine mission, Mathijs led a small group against the besiegers and was defeated.

Now, with Mathijs dead, Jan Beukels assumed control of the town. The council was dissolved and replaced by twelve elders who were given supervision of all affairs, whether secular or spiritual, public or private. All forms of opposition were cruelly suppressed. Then as the casualties of war mounted, Beukels announced that polygamy was to be established. He himself was anointed king of the "New Zion." Meanwhile, the Muensterites confidently expected assistance from other Anabaptists, and perhaps from secular princes as well. Thus, in the summer of 1534, after Charles V had unsuccessfully attempted to persuade the bishop of Muenster to become his vassal, he sent an agent to negotiate with the leaders in Muenster, although the mission accomplished nothing. A few envoys from Muenster attempted to arouse popular support throughout the Netherlands, but the few parties formed to rescue the besieged saints were quickly dispersed.

The siege dragged on until June, 1535. At that time, two disillusioned Anabaptists deserted and betrayed a town gate to the forces of the bishop. In the ensuing bloody battle, most of the inhabitants were slaughtered. Three of the radical leaders, including Beukels and Knipperdolling, were captured, publicly paraded, then tortured with red-hot tongs. At the conclusion of the grisly spectacle, the mutilated bodies were suspended in iron cages from the tower of St. Lambert's. For many, Anabaptism had become a term synonymous not only with heretical beliefs, but also with sedition and revolution. This view was scarcely mitigated by Anabaptist leaders, both before and after the debacle of Muenster, who vigorously opposed all appeals to violence as well as attempts to establish an earthly kingdom. Thus, while most Anabaptists deplored the violent tactics, of the Muensterites, most political and religious leaders, whether Catholic or Protestant, warned that toleration of Anabaptism would pose a threat to social stability.

ETCHING: MENNO SIMONS, by Jan Luyken

After the tragedy of Muenster, he gave vigorous leadership to the Anabaptist movement in the Netherlands and North Germany. It was the work of men such as Menno that prompted the historian De Hoop Scheffer to write that from 1530 until 1566, the history of the Reformation in the Netherlands was essentially the history of Anabaptism.

Mennonite Library and Archives, North Newton

Menno Simons

After the debacle of Muenster, Anabaptism in the Netherlands was fortunate in that its greatest leader, Menno Simons, gathered the scattered remnants and formed a dynamic, largely cohesive group. Menno had been ordained a priest in

1524, but by the next year he was already questioning the doctrine of transubstantiation. He was encouraged by the example of Luther, but could not accept all of the reformer's views. As Anabaptism became known in the Netherlands, the courage of the martyrs impressed Menno and aroused his interest in their teachings. By the early 1530s, he had rejected infant baptism, although he still retained his post as pastor in Witmarsum. The Muenster fiasco prompted him to write a tract denouncing the excesses of Jan Beukels, but Menno was convinced that the atrocities of Muenster should not be allowed to discredit Anabaptism. Soon he began to preach the evangelical doctrines of the movement that was being branded seditious and heretical, and in 1536 he resigned his priestly office to shepherd the scattered and persecuted Anabaptists. Two brothers, Obbe and Dirk Philips, proved especially helpful to him as he tried to build congregations in northern Europe from the Netherlands to Danzig. By 1542, his fame was such that an imperial edict placed a price on his head. Menno became an itinerant minister, writing and preaching as he went from village to village. By 1545, Menno's preponderant influence was becoming increasingly apparent, for in the Netherlands the term "Anabaptist" was coming to be replaced by "Menist" or "Mennonite."

As Menno attempted to mold the Anabaptist movement, he set forth in writing those beliefs and practices that had largely characterized the movement from its inception. His *Foundation of Christian Doctrine* indicated that on many dogmatic issues, Anabaptism was similar to other Protestant persuasions. In some areas, however, such as church discipline, membership, and mutual obligations, there were significant differences. Great stress was placed on practical godliness, on loving one's enemies, and on helping those in need. A selfish use of material goods was considered adequate cause for expulsion from the group. At the same time, precautionary measures were taken to prevent anyone from taking unfair advantage of the generosity of others. Constantly harassed, frequently dispossessed, often threatened with the stake, Anabaptists nonetheless usually retained their ethic of love and nonviolence. Their "theology of martyrdom" taught them that the faithful disciple of Christ must expect suffering and rejection.

Persecution on the continent drove some Anabaptists to seek refuge in England. North Sea ships engaged in the wool and textile trade provided convenient means of escape, although the climate in England proved little more hospitable. Henry VIII promptly ordered that the "detestable sect" be eradicated, and as early as June 4, 1535, fourteen Anabaptists were sent to the stake. Doctrinal statements issued during the course of the English Reformation, such as the *Ten Articles* of 1536 and the *Six Articles* of 1539, denounced Anabaptism. Henry decreed that all rebaptized persons should leave the realm, and, in the course of his struggle with the papacy in 1540 when he issued a general pardon for heretics, he specifically excluded the Anabaptists. Throughout the sixteenth century, English Anabaptism encountered strong opposition. By the end of the century, it had virtually disappeared from the scene, and had been absorbed into the Brownist and Barrowist movements, precursors of English Congregational and Baptist churches.

SPIRITUALISM

Another element of the radical Reformation, related to Anabaptism in its rejection of the union of church and state, was the reform movement known as spiritualism, which stressed the role of the Spirit and rejected external religious practices and organizations. One of the chief proponents of this movement was Caspar Schwenckfeld, a wealthy knight of the Teutonic Order. He was privy counselor to the Duke of Silesia, and in 1518 had embraced the teachings of Luther.

Schwenckfeld supported reform in Silesia, but unlike Luther, he developed a spiritual interpretation of the sacraments. Whereas Luther emphasized the doctrine of justification by faith, Schwenckfeld emphasized spiritual experience and lofty ethics. He was convinced that organized Christianity placed altogether too much emphasis upon sacraments, rituals, and creeds. He called for freedom of conscience, the end of institutionalized religion, and the eventual abolition of the sacraments. He held that the believer might feed spiritually upon the body of Christ; therefore, no external sacrament was necessary.

Schwenckfeld believed that the way to reform was through tolerant discussion as in the "brotherhoods," or weekday conventicles where the sincere seekers of truth might meet to study, pray, and admonish each other. To foster this community of dialogue, he helped to found the short-lived University of Liegnitz. As persecution intensified in Silesia, Schwenckfeld moved to Strasbourg, where he hoped that the relatively tolerant attitudes would permit him to express his beliefs freely. He had no desire to found a new church, but rather to help believers find in spiritualism a bond which would unite them all. In his numerous writings, he entered into detailed theological arguments with various reformers, but even in Strasbourg his emphasis on the inner rather than the written Word was strongly opposed, and in 1534 he again took up his wanderings. Thereafter, his efforts were largely devoted to a literary battle with his opponents.

His views found a strong champion in Sebastian Franck, a south German priest who converted to Lutheranism but soon began to criticize what he believed to be the inadequacies of this faith. He contended that the *solafide* [ist][8] emphases of the state-supported reformers had failed to bring an adequate moral and spiritual change. In one of his earlier writings, the *Tuerkenchronik*, he asserted that different groups in Christianity, such as the Lutherans, Zwinglians, and Anabaptists, had failed; they should now be succeeded by a movement that would stress the spiritualist nature of the church. Outer means and forms were

---

[8]The belief that justification before God depends solely upon faith and is not dependent upon good works.

inconsequential, for God as a spirit communicated directly with the spirit of man. Other reformers had become bound to the "paper pope," the Scriptures, and had failed to experience the God behind the written Word.

In 1529, Franck came to Strasbourg and two years later published his *Chronica*, in which he again catalogued the erroneous views held not only in the past, but also by the heretics of the contemporary scene. His list of heretics included Erasmus, as well as many other contemporaries. Opposition to Franck led to confiscation of the *Chronica* and imprisonment of the author. Upon his release he was expelled from Strasbourg, eventually to find refuge in Basel, where he died in 1542. Just two years earlier, he had been roundly condemned by Zwinglian and Lutheran theologians of central and southwest Germany. Among them were Bucer and Melanchthon, whose statement, denounced by Schwenckfeld as a "new bull of excommunication," insisted that the Holy Spirit worked through the literal and preached word, not the inner Word. Defenders of the state church contended that the spiritualists had adopted a dangerous individualistic relativism which threatened to erode the authority of Scripture and church alike, and which encouraged religious vagabondage.

Indiscriminate contemporaries sometimes condemned the spiritualists as Anabaptists, although both groups insisted that numerous and fundamental differences divided them. Belief in direct divine illumination seldom characterized the Anabaptist position. Unlike the Spiritualists, the Anabaptists emphasized the authority of the Bible, and especially of the New Testament. Anabaptists also retained the sacraments of baptism and the Lord's Supper. In contrast to the Anabaptists on the issue of secular governments, spiritualists maintained that civil authority was fully compatible with Christian principles. At the same time, both spiritualists and Anabaptists generally rejected Luther's concept of original sin; both denied the necessity of baptism for salvation; both deplored coercion in matters of faith; and both stressed a faith that was profoundly existential.

EVANGELICAL RATIONALISM

Not least among the fruits of humanism were the frequent expressions of rationalism, such as anti-trinitarianism, with its rejection of traditional doctrines of the Trinity and the atonement. Often characterized by an emphasis on learning and ethical Christianity, the advocates of these heretical views drew their inspiration from textual criticism of the Scriptures, the climate of theological change and uncertainty, the revival of Neoplatonism, the renewal of the study of patristics, and the entire range of humanistic values.

Among the iconoclastic theologians of the sixteenth century, few gained more contemporary notoriety, yet brought sharper posthumous censure on his opponents than the gifted Spanish scholar, Michael Servetus. This anti-trinitarian declared the Nicene formulation of the Trinity to be contrary to both Scripture and the writings of early church fathers. His Christology contended that the Logos, or Christ, had combined with the human Jesus to form the Son of God.

According to Servetus, the Son of God had a beginning and was not eternally begotten. His unorthodox views were expressed in works such as *On the Errors of the Trinity* (1531) and *Dialogues on the Trinity* (1532).

Some reformers, such as Oecolampadius in Basel, had earlier befriended Servetus; however, with the publication of these heretical views, the radical found himself condemned by Zwinglian, Lutheran, and Catholic. For a time, he was able to live in anonymity in France, studying, writing, and eking out a bare existence. His discovery of the pulmonary circulation of the blood demonstrated his scientific ability, while his biblical writings and editorial work established him as a serious and critical scholar. He rejected Luther's *solafide*, as well as infant baptism. For him, baptism was the rite whereby man could become a son of God, and gain "deification," but such an act required spiritual maturity.

In 1553, he published the mature product of his theological studies, the *Restitution of Christianity*. He was now tried and condemned by the Inquisition. When he escaped, he was burned in effigy. He hoped to flee to Italy and join other radical elements there, but enroute he stopped in Geneva. Here he was apprehended and sentenced to death because of his views on baptism and the Trinity. In 1553, he was burned at the stake in the city of Calvin, his dying prayer directed to "Jesus, the Son of the Eternal God," not to the eternal Son of God.

Despite bitter and widespread opposition, unorthodox views continued to spread. In 1550, an anti-trinitarian synod held in Venice rejected the deity of Christ and repudiated traditional belief in hell and the devil. Such unorthodox views were given impetus by a number of Italian rationalists, especially the Sozzini. Laelius Socinus (1525–1562) challenged reformers such as Bullinger and Calvin to abandon doctrines that seemed contrary to reason. Faustus Socinus (1539–1604), nephew of Laelius, was forced to flee Switzerland when he continued to attack the Nicene interpretation of the Trinity. His reception was relatively tolerant in Transylvania and Poland, where weak central government made extermination of heresy dependent upon local lords. The city of Krakow became one of a number of centers of anti-trinitarian doctrines. Here, Francis Stancaro, appointed to the chair of Hebrew at the University of Krakow in 1549, attacked Nicene views of the Trinity until opposition from the bishop brought his dismissal. He secured another appointment at the University of Koenigsberg, but here too his radicalism would make his position untenable.

The persistence of unorthodox views in eastern Europe eventually led to the formation of a separate church. Under the leadership of men such as Gregory Paul, a pastor in Krakow; George Schomann, a pastor in Lublin; John Lutomirski, castellan of Sieradz; and Nicholas Sienicki, speaker of the Polish Chamber of Deputies, radicals in Poland and Lithuania formed an anti-trinitarian "Minor Church." Opponents denounced them as Arians, although they described themselves simply as "brethren who have rejected the Trinity." Late in the sixteenth century, Faustus Socinus molded the various anti-trinitarian views within the Minor Church into the enduring form of Socinianism, precursor of modern Unitarianism.

Suggestions for Further Reading

Armour, Rollin S. *Anabaptist Baptism: A Representative Study.* Scottdale, Pa.: Herald, 1966.

Bauman, Clarence. *Gewaltlosigkeit im Taeufertum.* Leiden: Brill, 1968.

Bender, Harold S. *The Life and Letters of Conrad Grebel.* Goshen, Ind.: Mennonite Historical Society, 1950.

Bergsten, Torsten. *Balthasar Hubmaier: Seine Stellung zu Reformation und Taeufertum.* Kassel: J. G. Oncken, 1961.

*Blanke, Fritz.** *Brothers in Christ: The History of the Oldest Anabaptist Congregation, Zollikon near Zurich.* Scottdale, Pa.: Herald, 1961.

*Cohn, Norman.** *The Pursuit of the Millennium.* New York: Harper & Row, A Harper Torchbook, 1957.

Davis, Kenneth R. *Anabaptism and Asceticism.* Scottdale, Pa.: Herald, 1974.

Durnbaugh, D. F. *Every Need Supplied.* Philadelphia: Temple University Press, 1974.

Dyck, Cornelius, J., ed. *A Legacy of Faith: The Heritage of Menno Simons.* Newton, Kansas: Faith and Life Press, 1962.

Estep, W. R. *The Anabaptist Story.* Grand Rapids, Mich.: Eerdmans, 1975.

———, ed. *Anabaptist Beginnings (1523–1533): A Source Book.* Nieuwkoop: de-Graaf, 1976.

Fast, Heinold, ed. *Der linke Fluegel der Reformation: Glaubenszeugnisse der Taeufer, Spiritualisten, Schwaermer, und Antitrinitarier.* Bremen: Schuenemann, 1962.

Friedmann, Robert. *Hutterite Studies.* Goshen, Ind.: Mennonite Historical Society, 1961.

Gratz, Delbert. *Bernese Anabaptists.* Scottdale, Pa.: Herald, 1953.

Hershberger, Guy F., ed. *The Recovery of the Anabaptist Vision.* Scottdale, Pa.: Herald, 1957.

Hillerbrand, Hans J. *A Bibliography of Anabaptism (c. 1520–1630).* Elkhart, Ind.: Institute of Mennonite Studies, 1962.

———. *A Fellowship of Discontent.* New York: Harper & Row, 1967.

Keeney, William. *The Development of Dutch Anabaptist Thought and Practice, 1539–1564.* Nieuwkoop: de Graaf, 1968.

Klassen, Peter J. *The Economics of Anabaptism, 1525–1560.* The Hague: Mouton, 1964.

Klassen, William. *Covenant and Community.* Grand Rapids Mich.: Eerdmans, 1968.

Kot, Stanislaw. *Socinianism in Poland: The Social and Political Ideas of the Polish Antitrinitarians.* Translated by E. M. Wilbur. Boston: Starr King, 1957.

Krahn, Cornelius. *Dutch Anabaptism: Origin, Spread, Life, and Thought, 1450–1600.* The Hague: Nijhoff, 1968.

Littell, Franklin H. *The Anabaptist View of the Church,* 2d ed., rev. Boston: Starr King, 1957.

Maier, Paul L. *Caspar Schwenkfeld on the Person and Work of Christ.* Assen: Van Gorcum, 1959.

*Indicates paperback edition.

McLelland, Joseph C. *The Visible Words of God: An Exposition of the Sacramental Theology of Peter Martyr Vermigli.* Grand Rapids Mich.: Eerdmans, 1957.

Oyer, John S. *Lutheran Reformers Against Anabaptists.* The Hague: Nijhoff, 1964.

Ozment, Steven E. *Mysticism and Dissent. Religious Ideology and Social Protest in the Sixteenth Century.* New Haven: Yale University Press, 1973.

Peachey, Paul. *Die soziale Herkunft der Schweizer Taeufer in der Reformationszeit.* Weierhof, Pfalz: Mennonitischer Geschichtsverein, 1954.

Sider, Ronald J. *Andreas Bodenstein von Karlstadt.* Leiden: Brill, 1974.

Simons, Menno. *Complete Writings.* Translated from the Dutch by Leonard Verduin. edited by John C. Wenger, with a biography by Harold S. Bender. Scottdale, Pa.: Herald, 1956.

Smithson, R. J. *The Anabaptists.* London: Clarke, 1935.

Stayer, James M. *Anabaptists and the Sword.* Lawrence, Kansas: Coronado, 1972.

Vedder, H. C. *Balthasar Hubmaier: The Leader of Anabaptists.* New York: Putnam's 1905.

Verduin, Leonard. *The Reformers and Their Stepchildren.* Grand Rapids, Mich.: Eerdmans, 1964.

Wenger, J. C. *Conrad Grebel's Programmatic Letters of 1524.* Scottdale, Pa.: Herald, 1969.

Wilbur, Earl Morse. *A History of Unitarianism*, 2 vols. Cambridge, Mass.: Harvard University Press, 1946, 1952.

Williams, George H. *The Radical Reformation.* Philadelphia: Westminister Press, 1962.

————, **and Angel M. Mergal,** eds. *Spiritual and Anabaptist Writers.* Philadelphia: Westminister Press, 1957.

Yoder, J. H. *Taeufertum und Reformation im Gespraech.* Zurich: EVZ-Verlag, 1968.

————, ed. *The Legacy of Michael Sattler.* Scottdale, Pa.: Herald, 1973.

Zschaebitz, Gerhard. *Zur mitteldeutschen Wiedertaeuferbewegung nach dem grossen Bauernkrieg.* Berlin: Ruetten und Loening, 1958.

Zuck, Lowell P. *Christianity and Revolution. Radical Christian Testimonies, 1520–1650.* Philadelphia: Temple University Press, 1975.

7

Calvinism

FRANCE IN THE SIXTEENTH CENTURY

By about 1550, a new, dynamic, aggressive force—Calvinism—had replaced Lutheranism as the major continental challenge to traditional Catholicism. During the second half of the century, this vigorous religious movement, with profoundly significant political, economic, and social overtones, attracted substantial bodies of adherents in France, the Low Countries, the Empire, Scotland, England, and eastern Europe. Eventually it found a broad base of support that surpassed in its scope the earlier Lutheran assault.

This force of renewal and change drew its inspiration from one of France's most illustrious sons, John Calvin (1509–1564). Calvin in turn was a product of a society which was alive with new ideas, economic vitality, political and military power, and cultural brilliance.

The strength of the French monarchy reflected the vibrancy of France herself. The nation was relatively prosperous, and had a population twice that of Spain and five times that of England. Although Germany had a population equal to that of France, it was a loose confederation of principalities and cities; France, on the other hand, was a model of centralized authority. A productive and prosperous peasantry, and a thriving trade in both the Mediterranean and the Atlantic gave the French monarchy a strength and vigor which was the envy of the courts of Europe. Paris, next to Constantinople, Europe's largest city, was the center of a vast administrative and judicial system. The extravagance of the king, his foreign adventures, and numerous other costly projects demanded that money flow continuously into the royal coffers; the power of the monarch was such that he could tax and legislate almost at will. The Estates-General, unlike Parliament, its English counterpart, was merely a rubber stamp; even the provinces were administered by governors appointed by the king. The *Parlement*, composed of both secular and ecclesiastical members, functioned as a supreme court and also registered royal decrees. A smoothly functioning bureaucracy directed by the king's ministers carried out the affairs of government. This left the monarch, Francis I, free to devote much of his time to dealing with foreign ventures, visiting his many splendid chateaux, establishing a reputation for the variety of his amours, and engaging artists at court.

Even at the beginning of the century, royal authority was felt in all aspects of the French realm. More centralized than any other European country, France was well on the way toward the absolutism associated with later monarchs. Relationships between state and church reflected many of the characteristics established by the Pragmatic Sanction of Bourges; the church in France was essentially a state church. The concordat that Francis I made with Leo X in 1516 further solidified this position: the king was now empowered to nominate archbishops, bishops, and abbés. Gallicanism had triumphed, although it expressed itself not in an independent church, but rather in a church subordinate to the king. Clearly, under such circumstances, it was in the royal interest to avoid changes in the ecclesiastical structure, for a strong, unified church was a powerful bulwark of a strong monarchy.

Francis embarked upon a number of unfortunate foreign adventures, but the strong central government survived these events. The king's ambitions involved him in costly campaigns in northern Italy that brought him into conflict with both the pope and emperor. Captured by Emperor Charles in 1525, he was taken to Spain, where his sister Marguerite had to negotiate to obtain his release. But the territorial concessions that Francis made to Charles by the Treaty of Madrid apparently served only to whet his appetite for future conflict. He promptly joined a new alliance against the emperor, and the long struggle between the Hapsburgs and the Valois resumed. Meanwhile, reformation ideas continued to spread throughout his realm. France and the Empire, through extensive trade with each other, had commercial ties that could easily serve as vehicles for the introduction of Luther's writings. Translated into French, they were printed in such commercial centers as Strasbourg, Antwerp, or Basel, then smuggled into France. Luther's works were soon bought and read in Paris, and printed clandestinely in Lyons.

The introduction of these writings soon forced pro-reform elements in France to take a definite position relative to the Reformation in Germany. Lefèvre and his circle had long called for sweeping reform in the church—indeed the bishop of Meaux urged his priests to "return to the Gospel"—but when Luther was condemned as a heretic, the bishop warned his subordinates to remain loyal to the church. Then, as iconoclasm erupted in several French cities, the king became increasingly determined to crush any movement which threatened the tranquillity of the realm. By 1526, dissenters were being sent to the stake for offenses such as "blasphemy," denying the intercessory power of the saints, or smashing statues. Most French humanists and champions of reform agreed with their king—the French national church, with its close ties to state authorities, could not be jeopardized; it must remain Catholic. This position would be subjected to a frontal assault by forces which eventually became strong enough to plunge the nation into civil war.

THE YOUNG CALVIN

The movement for theological and political change in France would draw its inspiration from John Calvin. Born at Noyon in Picardy, an urban and humanist environment, and separated from Luther by a full generation, Calvin grew up in a world where religious schism was already reality and where theological options had to be considered. His father, secretary to the bishop of Noyon and notary for the cathedral chapter, was able to gain ecclesiastical support for the education of a very promising son. Accordingly, in 1523, the young Calvin, intent upon entering the priesthood, enrolled in Montaigu College at the University of Paris. Supported by a benefice attached to the cathedral chapter in Noyon, he studied theology and received his Master of Arts degree. Upon the request of his father, who was a lawyer, in 1528 Calvin changed from theology to law, and pursued legal studies at Orleans and Bourges. Here he studied under humanists, and also encountered Lutheran views. His admiration of humanism was reflected in his first published book, a commentary on Seneca's *De Clementia* (1532).

In 1531, shortly before the death of his father, Calvin returned to Paris. He now abandoned his study of law and indulged in his humanist interests. Paris was ideally suited to such purposes, for under the vigorous stimulus of Francis I, the city had become a center of humanist learning. Elsewhere in the kingdom, too, the spirit of the Renaissance found a strong patron in the French monarch—until the king discovered that unchecked intellectual expression was inimical to his own political views.

Calvin developed close ties with several prominent humanist circles. The king's sister, Marguerite of Navarre (1492–1549), maintained a court that for a time attracted men like Rabelais. However, when she wrote the *Mirror of a Sinful Soul* and commissioned a French translation of the Psalms, it was evident that her interest had shifted to more strictly religious and mystic themes. A predisposition toward humanism was also evident at Meaux, where Lefèvre d'Étaples was championing humanist reform. His biblical expositions suggested more than a trace of belief in justification by faith. Theologians at the Sorbonne raised charges of heresy, so that Lefèvre and his associates were forced to take refuge at the court of Marguerite.

Sometime during 1533 Calvin experienced what he later described as a "sudden conversion."[1] He apparently suffered none of the anguish of soul that had

[1] In his preface to the *Commentary on the Psalms* (1557), he wrote "Since I was too obstinately devoted to the superstitions of popery to be easily extricated from so profound an abyss of mire, God by a sudden conversion subdued and brought my mind to a teachable frame." John Calvin, *Commentary on the Psalms.* Translated by James Anderson. (Grand Rapids, Michigan: Eerdmans, 1948)I:xl.

PROMPTE ET SINCERE ·

IOHANNES · CALVINVS ·
ANNO · ÆTATIS · 53 ·
· B ·

ENGRAVING OF CALVIN, by René Boivin, from an old print

Frequently remembered because of his severe theology and his insistence upon man's responsibility to engage in self-denying labor for the glory of God, Calvin left a legacy that shaped the thought of the Reformed churches. His contemporaries were impressed by his pioneering work in encouraging public education and in asserting that the state was responsible for the economic welfare of its citizens. Tradition has tended to minimize his concern for the poor and his support of representative forms of government. When he died, Geneva mourned a man who, despite his powerful influence and often harsh attitudes, was profoundly respected and loved. In accordance with his own wish, "the theologian," as Melanchthon called him, was buried in an unmarked grave.

tormented Luther; rather he became utterly convinced of the sovereignty and grandeur of God. Calvin believed himself chosen by God to carry out a divine program of reform; he never doubted his calling in helping to build God's kingdom on earth in accordance with his understanding of the divine purpose.

Even as Calvin was developing his own set of theological beliefs, he was forced to go into hiding. His friend Nicolas Cop, rector of the Sorbonne, delivered an address (1533) that championed justification by faith and appealed for greater toleration of those who held unorthodox theological views. Charges of heresy were brought against Cop, who went into hiding, and Calvin, suspected of complicity in the preparation of the speech, fled to Saintonge near Angoulême, where he was befriended by Marguerite. Here he visited Lefèvre and worked on the first draft of the *Institutes*.

THE INSTITUTES

In the fall of 1534, King Francis decided to move resolutely against the advocates of reform. When a number of placards attacking the Mass appeared on the streets of Paris and in various other cities, and even in the royal palace at Amboise,[2] the king resolved to crush any movement which threatened the church and his control over it. To allow attacks on the church might endanger the monarchy, so Francis moved swiftly to destroy radicalism. Those suspected of heresy were savagely hounded; some, like the man who had printed Marguerite's *Mirror of a Sinful Soul*, were burned alive. Public processions were held to demonstrate royal contrition for having delayed the suppression of heresy. The royal wrath came down with vengeance; some of the intended victims, including Calvin, Cop, and Lefèvre, were fortunate enough to escape by fleeing the country or going into hiding. Calvin's journey took him to more congenial places, such as the reformed court of Duchess Renée of Ferrara, or to Strasbourg, where Bucer was reforming the city. Most important, however, was the stay in Basel, for here in 1536, he published the first edition of the *Institutes of the Christian Religion*.

From the first appearance of this work until its final version in 1559, Calvin constantly revised and expanded it. Although the first edition contained most of the basic ideas of Calvinist theology, the final product was five times as voluminous. Written in Latin and prefaced by a lengthy letter to King Francis, it consisted of a brief catechism organized into six chapters that demonstrated a remarkable breadth of patristic and biblical learning, as well as a thorough understanding of scholastic theology and Christian humanism.

Following traditional religious teaching patterns, Calvin devoted the first four chapters to an analysis of the Ten Commandments, the Apostles' Creed, the Lord's Prayer, and the two sacraments he recognized—baptism and the Lord's Supper. The concluding two chapters presented an attack upon the five "false sacraments" and a defense of Christian liberty.

Calvin's Stand on Predestination and the Means of Redemption

On most crucial doctrines, Calvin stood very close to Luther. He described justification by faith as the "principle of the religion"; like Luther, Calvin also asserted that original sin left man guilty before God and man, unable to earn

[2]Régine Pernoud et al., *François Ier* (Paris: Hachette, 1967), p. 184.

salvation by his own efforts, was completely dependent upon divine mercy. Those to whom God extended his mercy were the "elect"—those who had been predestined to salvation. The rest of mankind, by virtue of what Calvin himself called a "dread (horrible) decree," was predestined to destruction. In his *Institutes* he wrote, "We call predestination God's eternal decree, by which he determined with himself what he willed to become of each man. For all are not created in equal condition; rather, eternal life is foreordained for some, eternal damnation for others."[3] In this belief, Calvin followed St. Augustine as well as Luther, although predestination never occupied so prominent a position in the theology of Wittenberg as it did in Geneva. Calvin held that belief in an omnipotent and omniscient God logically required belief in the salvation of those whom God had chosen; it was inconceivable that divine will should be thwarted. Calvin urged his readers to focus their attention on the grace and love of God, rather than on the status of their election: The Christian should live in hope, not in fear. While Calvin taught that the elect would live morally, he did not suggest that moral rectitude was proof of election. Nor did he ever contend that material prosperity was proof of divine favor. Subsequently, some Calvinists, and especially some interpreters of Calvin, would equate material success with proof of election, but such a view was foreign to Calvin.

While Calvin stressed the God-centered nature of redemption, he carefully outlined the function of external means—Scriptures, church, and sacraments—in bringing man into fellowship with God. The written Word was regarded as the final authority in all matters of spiritual truth. The church, as a community of Christians, should be freed from hierarchical control, and should be zealous in its exercise of discipline, teaching of the Word, and administration of the sacraments. Calvin's understanding of the Lord's Supper led him to reject transubstantiation and the sacrifice of the Mass; similarly, he rejected Luther's doctrine of the bodily presence as well as Zwingli's tendency toward a symbolic interpretation. Instead he held that Christ was indeed "efficaciously" present in the elements, in a real but spiritual manner. For Calvin, the sacrament of communion was not simply a memorial, but a seal of God's promised grace. The sacrament of baptism, signifying remission of sins, was also regarded as an evidence of faith and a mark of the covenant between God and man.

The *Institutes* at once established Calvin as a foremost spokesman of Protestantism. In 1541 the first French edition appeared. Translated by Calvin from the Latin edition published in Strasbourg in 1539, it placed its author in the company of Rabelais as a preeminent figure in shaping French literature.

Shortly before the first edition of the *Institutes* was published, Calvin left Basel for Ferrara. Duchess Renée (1510–1575), daughter of Louis XII, had been a warm admirer of Lefèvre and welcomed Calvin. She became his devoted follower and, following the death of her husband, returned to France to join the

[3]John Calvin, *Institutes of the Christian Religion,* ed. J. T. McNeill and F. L. Battles (Philadelphia: Westminster Press, 1960), II:926.

French Calvinists, the Huguenots. Calvin remained in Ferrara until opposition from the duke, who was a son of Lucrezia Borgia, forced those sympathetic to reform to disperse. Calvin returned briefly to Paris to settle the family inheritance. Then, determined to continue his scholarly pursuits, he left Paris for Strasbourg. Because of war between Francis I and Charles V, Calvin took a fateful detour to Geneva. What followed would make Calvin and Geneva inseparable in the annals of the Reformation.

THE CONTINUING SWISS REFORMATION

Geneva had only recently emerged triumphant in a struggle to gain more ecclesiastical and political autonomy. The bishop of the city, a protégé of the duke of Savoy, had seen his power gradually dissipated by the champions of self-government. Joint military action by bishop and duke against Geneva was thwarted when, in 1526–1527, the city gained the support of Bern and Fribourg. The bishop fled the city, and in 1534 the elected magistrates, or syndics, declared the see vacant. Shortly thereafter, the bishop was forced to lift the siege of Geneva, while the victorious allies pressed on to attack Savoy. Geneva had gained political autonomy; the simultaneous rejection of her episcopal lord paved the way for reformation.

In 1533, Bern, now zealously Zwinglian, had sent William Farel to effect the reformation of Geneva. After numerous stormy confrontations with adherents of the traditional faith, including a lengthy public disputation between Catholic clergy and Protestant leaders in June, 1535,[4] Farel and his associates gained magisterial support. Churches, including the Cathedral of St. Pierre, experienced the onslaught of Protestantism and iconoclasm, and on August 10, 1535, the city council abolished celebration of the Mass. Catholicism had been officially abolished, but Protestantism was still disorganized. Neither Farel nor his colleague Pierre Viret had been able to bring order and effective direction to the fluid scene, despite the resolve of the citizenry, to live according to "this holy evangelical law and Word of God" and to reject "papal ceremonies and abuses."[5] The citizens also agreed to establish a school for their children, where attendance would be compulsory and, for the poor, free.[6] Geneva had pioneered in the field of compulsory public education.

In the following summer, Calvin, expecting to pass through the city, was implored by Farel to remain and guide the reform. Only when Farel warned him of divine punishment did Calvin overcome his hesitancy and accept the challenge of establishing the new church and reforming the life of the city. The two leaders

---

[4]B. J. Kidd, *Documents, Illustrative of the Continental Reformation* (Oxford: Clarendon), pp. 512–513.

[5]*Ibid.,* p. 519.

[6]W. F. Graham, *The Constructive Revolutionary John Calvin* (Richmond, Va.: John Knox Press, 1971), pp. 146, 147.

gained the support of the city fathers and formulated articles of faith for the city that would be the basis of a more elaborate statement on church discipline promulgated as law in 1537. Calvin envisioned a society where all members would adhere to his confession of faith, where only "worthy" members would be admitted to the Lord's Supper, and where the church would not be dominated by the magistracy. But the syndics, so recently freed from bishop and duke, had no intention of permitting a new ecclesiastical despotism. When the council later adopted the Bernese liturgy without consulting Calvin and insisted that the reform pastors did not have authority to excommunicate, the rift was complete. In 1538, both Calvin and Farel were expelled from the city. Farel returned to Neuchâtel, to remain there as a minister until his death in 1565. Calvin, determined to indulge his literary interests, went to Strasbourg, where he became a pastor to French exiles and a teacher in the school recently begun by the Lutheran educator Johann Sturm.

CALVIN IN STRASBOURG

In Strasbourg, Calvin collaborated closely with reformers such as Martin Bucer, Caspar Hedio, and Wolfgang Capito. Capito in particular had learned the lesson of gradual reform, so that under his influence Catholic bishop and Protestant council achieved some measure of cooperation. Even Anabaptists were permitted temporary asylum. Here Calvin found time to preach, teach, and write—and also to learn from other reformers. Largely influenced by Bucer, he wrote a liturgy that later became the standard form of Calvinist worship. His collaboration on the Psalter revealed his desire to incorporate congregational Psalm singing into the church service. On several occasions he attended Catholic-Lutheran colloquies in the Empire, thus forming a strong friendship with Melanchthon. In 1540, Calvin married Idelette de Bure, who bore him one son, but the child died in infancy. The marriage was a happy one, and when Idelette died in 1549, Calvin's writings bespoke a warmth and tenderness often belied by his austere demeanor.

With Calvin absent from Geneva, the exiled bishop hoped to return to St. Pierre. Cardinal Jacopo Sadoleto, a devout churchman and scholarly humanist, in 1539 wrote to the Genevans and urged their return to the Catholic faith. The letter was courteous and powerful, and no one in Geneva seemed competent to meet the intellectual challenge. Calvin now penned his conciliatory but firm *Reply to Sadoleto*.[7] The cardinal had admitted the pressing need for ecclesiastical reform; Calvin replied that the basic issue was not clerical abuse, but doctrine. Theological, not ethical, concerns were central. Calvin's efforts brought approbation from the Genevan magistrates, while Luther applauded the effort that would help to "finish the war against Antichrist."

[7]John C. Olin, ed., *A Reformation Debate. Sadoleto's Letter to the Genevans and Calvin's Reply* (New York: Harper & Row, A Harper Torchbook, 1966), pp. 53–90.

Reaction in Geneva to Calvin's letter was indicative of a changing mood. Leading opponents of the reformers had largely discredited themselves; several of them had been executed for crimes against the city. By 1541, the city council was ready to reverse its stand on Calvin. The sentence of banishment was annuled, and deputations sent to Calvin to urge his return. Despite protests that he would "submit to death a thousand times" rather than resume the difficult task he had faced in Geneva, he finally agreed to accept what he regarded as a divine call.

CALVIN'S TRIUMPHANT RETURN

In September, 1541, the former exile returned to a city that gave him a hero's welcome. He immediately embarked upon the work of reform that had been interrupted in 1538. Basic guidelines were outlined in the Ecclesiastical Ordinances,[8] approved by the magistrates and the general assembly (November, 1541). These ordinances, destined to become the basic pattern wherever Calvin's theology triumphed, established four orders of church offices: (1) pastors, to preach the word, administer the sacraments, and admonish the worshippers; (2) doctors, to instruct in "sound doctrine"; (3) elders, laymen chosen by the city's governing bodies, known as the Little Council, the Council of Sixty, and the Council of Two Hundred to "have oversight of the life of everyone" so that proper discipline might be exercised; and (4) deacons, also chosen by the magistracy, and responsible for the welfare of the poor and needy.

The Ordinances provided for an administrative body, the consistory, to enforce religious and social legislation. Composed of ministers and twelve elders, it often acted with a censoriousness and zeal that seemed to equate godliness with legalistic austerity. Although Calvin was highly regarded and profoundly influential, he was no dictator, for his requests were frequently denied, either by consistory or council.[9] One of the four syndics, not Calvin, presided at sessions of the consistory, and throughout his career in Geneva, there was firm magisterial opposition to the expansion of clerical influence. Marriage regulations, punishment of civil crime, and appointment of teachers remained the prerogative of the council, although Calvin's advice was respected and often accepted. The reformer was most deeply involved in educational affairs. He had been favorably impressed with Sturm's academy, and eventually, in 1559, he succeeded in establishing a counterpart in Geneva. The rector of this forerunner of the University of Geneva was Theodore Beza, one of a series of distinguished teachers who exemplified Calvin's relentless pursuit of academic excellence. Geneva became, in the opinion of John Knox, "the most perfect school of Christ," sending

---

[8]Phillip E. Hughes, ed. and trans., *The Register of the Company of Pastors of Geneva in the Time of Calvin* (Grand Rapids, Mich.: Eerdmans, 1966), pp. 35–49.

[9]See Hughes, *Register, passim.*

devout disciples of Calvin to various parts of Europe. Within a decade, 161 pastors had been sent to France, often to face martyrdom. Here was the Protestant counterpart to the zeal of the Jesuits.

CALVIN'S POLITICAL AND ECONOMIC VIEWS

Despite his ideal of a godly commonwealth in which the clergy should not hesitate to censure unacceptable acts by the magistrates, Calvin did not wish to minimize the significance of political office. He regarded government as a divine institution. Citizens were required to respect their rulers, and even to obey tyrants, provided that nothing contrary to God's law was required. Popular revolution he regarded with grave suspicion; if opposition to rulers became necessary, it should be expressed by the lesser magistrates. Calvin was less than enthusiastic about monarchy, for kings might be given some of the honor due God alone. He was equally hesitant about democracy, where the masses might lose respect for law. He believed that a combination of popular election and aristocratic government would best preserve responsible liberty. In short, he had no hesitation in suggesting the Genevan structure as a model worthy of emulation.

Calvin was also greatly concerned about the material well-being of his city-state. He stressed mutual responsibility rather than individual acquisitiveness. Geneva was to be a community of concern, where no one would hold his gifts for himself, or for his private use, but rather share them among his fellow members. The entire community bore responsibility for each of its members; begging was prohibited, and poor relief carefully and systematically administered. Excessive profiteers were punished. Although Calvin permitted five percent interest on loans, he urged that the poor be given loans without interest. At the same time, he encouraged the development of industry and commerce, and fostered cloth making and the production of silk. All citizens of Geneva were to have an opportunity to participate in the dignity of labor and productivity. Calvin believed that every man should honor God by diligent service in his particular "calling," or profession. Since God "called" man to a life of service, no profession should be regarded as being more noble than any other. The traditional distinction between religious and secular professions was removed. According to Calvin, the faithful peasant was performing a responsibility as noble as that of the dedicated minister, and physical labor could be as religious an act as formal worship. Furthermore, the divine "call" meant that all professions were open to the common people, in effect, equality of opportunity existed. This, coupled with Calvin's insistence that hard work and thrift were Christian obligations, could hardly fail to stimulate prosperity, which often found expression in capitalistic forms. Wealth and poverty should be used to honor God; yet wealth was by no means to be regarded as evidence of election and divine favor, nor was poverty an indication of God's displeasure.[10] Such claims would have sounded preposterous indeed to anyone familiar with the problems faced by many impoverished Calvinists. It must also be remembered that Calvin rejected selfish individualism and insisted that the state bear responsibility for public welfare. When persecuted French Protestants fled to Geneva, Calvin urged that they be given asylum and assistance. These refugees, for whom he secured citizenship, frequently became his staunchest supporters—to the chagrin of many proud Genevans.

THE STRUGGLE FOR RELIGIOUS CONFORMITY

The severest challenges to Calvin's authority centered on theological disputes. Since he identified his own cause with the divine will, the reformer had few qualms about demanding conformity or suppression. When the teacher Sebastian Castellio questioned some of Calvin's views on Scripture, he was expelled. This experience helped to make Castellio a champion of toleration, as expressed in his *Whether Heretics Should be Persecuted* (1554). Jerome Bolsec, a former monk, denounced Calvin's doctrine of predestination. Banished from the city in 1551, Bolsec subsequently converted back to Catholicism.

Not surprisingly, Calvin's insistence on rigid adherence to his moral standards alienated many of those who wanted a more relaxed attitude. On one occasion he found on his pulpit a placard denouncing him and threatening his life. A more serious challenge to Calvin's authority developed when he dared to reprimand some of Geneva's most prominent leaders for violation of the city's moral code. By 1549, his opponents had gained the dominant position in the city council. For the next few years, Calvin found himself hard-pressed to maintain his position.

Calvin was rescued from this precarious position when he defended orthodoxy against Michael Servetus (1511–1553). This versatile Spanish scholar, denounced by Catholic and Protestant for his rejection of the doctrine of the Trinity, had earlier written scurrilous attacks on Calvin, who had expressed his horror at the "ravings" of a heretic. Servetus was quickly arrested and, after a trial of more than two months, sentenced to death by burning. Other Protestant cantons were consulted; all agreed Servetus deserved death. Similar support came from Germany, and after the death of the heretic, Melanchthon declared that the church was indebted to Calvin for having rid the world of a "blasphemer." Although Calvin asked that the poor victim be granted a form of execution less excruciating than burning, he agreed that Servetus deserved death. Few religious leaders at that time shared Castellio's view that heresy should not be punishable by death; the man who had been tried and condemned by both Catholics and Protestants was sent to the stake.

This tragic but exemplary death extinguished the hopes of Calvin's enemies, for the reformer's prestige and influence now reached unprecedented heights. In

[10]Graham, *The Constructive Revolutionary*, pp. 66–76.

1555, some of the prominent citizens who had earlier challenged Calvin fled the city, while the city council became ever more responsive to the reformer's wishes. Until his death in 1564, Calvin dominated the city. His successor, Beza, carried on in a similar fashion. The power of Calvin's influence is suggested by the fact that for one and a half centuries, Geneva retained unaltered Calvin's principles and ordinances.

Calvin left Geneva the nerve center of Protestantism. With the death of Luther in 1546, and the defeat of the Schmalkaldic forces in 1547, Wittenberg lost its preeminence. Strasbourg, which in the more tolerant phase of its earlier reformation had exerted substantial influence, lost a good deal of its prestige when in 1548 it adopted a rigid Lutheran position. From various countries thousands of persecuted Protestants fled to Geneva and other Swiss centers, often to become passionate advocates of Calvinism. Both pope and Catholic prince rightly regarded Geneva as the most powerful threat to the old order.

THE QUEST FOR A UNITED PROTESTANT FRONT

During the second half of the sixteenth century, Calvinism gained a dominant role in several countries. Although it had neither the nationalistic fervor nor the princely support so often tied to the triumph of Lutheranism, the dynamism of the newer form of Protestantism threatened to carry everything before it. Buttressed by a conviction that God had willed their triumph, encouraged by a congregational structure that permitted the masses to participate in church government, stimulated by the fearless example of Calvin and the powerful missives that flowed from his pen, fired by a zeal that many had acquired while studying in the Genevan Academy, Calvinists confidently defied Catholic prince and bishop—as well as unsympathetic Lutheran prince and superintendent.

Well trained ministers carried Calvin's message to France, England, Scotland, Poland, Hungary, the Empire, and the Netherlands until this faith became truly international. Its champions confidently expected that through them God would create a new world order. When Calvin died, fifteen hundred students representing numerous countries, were enrolled in the Academy. Calvin and his successors agreed that education was the key to the success of the movement.

Like Zwingli and other reformers, Calvin hoped that he might unite the various forms of Protestantism. When Thomas Cranmer, archbishop of Canterbury, suggested that leaders of the Reformation meet for the purpose of "taking counsel together" and developing a united doctrinal position, Calvin enthusiastically endorsed the idea. For church unity, he declared himself ready to cross ten seas. Cranmer's project was cut short by his death, but Calvin continued to press for greater cooperation among various church bodies. His ecumenical spirit even allowed him to acknowledge that Catholics could be among the elect.

In Germany, this quest for unity met with strong opposition. No united front could be formed with Luther, for although the German reformer admired what had been done in Geneva, he could not accept Calvin's teaching on communion. Luther's death left the more conciliatory Melanchthon as the leading Lutheran spokesman, and Calvin long hoped that reform in Germany and Geneva might make common cause. Yet when Lutheranism split into the moderate Melanchthon group and the rigid, uncompromising supporters of Flacius, accommodation with Calvinism proved impossible. As Lutheranism became increasingly inflexible, tensions with Calvinism increased.

It was in Switzerland that the various forms of Protestantism finally found a common ground. In 1549, Calvin, Farel, and Bullinger outlined their shared beliefs in the Zurich Agreement, the *Consensus Tigurinus*. Elsewhere, too, Zwinglianism and Calvinism merged. Even Bern, at first strongly suspicious of Calvinism, adopted the *Consensus*. When in 1566 the Second Helvetic Confession was adopted by both Zwinglians and Calvinists, the union of the two branches was virtually complete. This movement, which resulted in the formation of the Reformed church, gained further momentum as Calvinist congregations in various countries adopted the Confession.

EXPANSION IN THE EMPIRE

Shortly before Melanchthon died in 1560, he noted with relief that in death he would be freed from ''the fury of theologians.'' A similar distaste for religious division was shared by Elector Frederick III (1559–1576) of the Palatinate, and in his quest for unity he prepared the way for the first major triumph of Calvinism in the Empire. In 1561 Protestant princes met at Naumburg to discuss religious unity, but the result was to divide Lutherans and Calvinists even more sharply. Frederick, a moderate Lutheran, was increasingly attracted to Calvinism and hoped that the views of Melanchthon and Calvin could be reconciled. The University of Heidelberg, as the dominant intellectual center in the state, seemed to be the logical place to undertake such an attempt. Elector Frederick appointed professors from both reform groups. Zacharias Ursinus (Baer) (1534–1583), a former student of Melanchthon, but ousted from his position as Lutheran minister in Breslau because of his moderate views, was invited to become a professor at Heidelberg (1561). His colleague Caspar Olevianus (1536–1587), had studied under Calvin and had become an eloquent champion of the Reformed position. In 1563, with the elector's vigorous encouragement, they completed the Heidelberg Catechism. This doctrinal statement, with its milder Calvinism, was adopted as the norm by Reformed churches in the Empire and in the Netherlands. Elsewhere, too, it gained approval. In the year following the publication of the Catechism, Frederick reorganized the church in his territory according to Calvinist patterns.

With the formal establishment of a Reformed church within the Empire,

Frederick challenged the Treaty of Augsburg on the grounds that it applied only to adherents of the Augsburg Confession and the "old religion." Lutheran princes urged Frederick to repudiate Calvinism, and Emperor Maximilian II issued a decree prohibiting religious innovation—specifically, the introduction of Calvinism. But the elector was not to be dissuaded. In 1566 he successfully defended his views before the diet, so that the imperial decree was withdrawn. Although Calvinism was not given official sanction, the inaction of the diet allowed the elector to continue his policy of supporting Calvinism.

Elector Frederick, while championing a Calvinist theology, was more attracted to the Zurich rather than the Genevan pattern of church-state relations. Regularly presiding at sessions of the consistory, which was composed of three ministers and three laymen, Frederick insisted that ultimate authority must rest with the state, not with the church. This view was vigorously supported by Thomas Erastus (c. 1524–1583), physician to the elector. While he did not condone the complete domination of church by state, as would be done by some later champions of "Erastianism," Erastus did oppose final ecclesiastical authority in disciplinary matters, especially in excommunication, since this would give the church too powerful a role in society. His *Seventy-five Theses on Excommunication*, published in 1589, outlined his views on checking excessive control by the church.

Frederick proved himself a zealous protagonist of Calvinism elsewhere as well. When the Dutch challenged the rule of Philip II, the elector sent money and troops; when Calvinists in France were hard-pressed, Frederick sent military support, then helped to gain a peace treaty that would be favorable to his co-religionists.

Ironically, when Frederick III died in 1576, his son Ludwig VI, the new elector, attempted to enforce a rigorously Lutheran position. Calvinist ministers and theologians fled the Palatinate, but when Ludwig died in 1583, his brother and successor, John Casimir, reversed the whole drama. Lutherans were now dismissed and Calvinists restored. The temporary expulsion of Calvinists, however, had helped to win other areas to the Reformed position. In Nassau, refugee Calvinists, together with moderate Lutherans expelled from Wittenberg, won adoption of the Heidelberg Catechism, while Olevianus helped to establish a Reformed university at Herborn. Elsewhere, as in Bremen and Wesel, reaction against rigid Lutheranism helped to give Calvinism a considerable following. By the end of the century, both Anhalt and Hesse had become largely Calvinistic.

Sometimes, however, official support of Calvinism aroused popular opposition. When John Sigismund, elector of Brandenburg, embraced Calvinism (1613), his attempts to replace Lutheranism with Calvinistic forms of worship were the occasion of riots and denunciation. Despite the elector's efforts, Brandenburg remained predominantly Lutheran. A change in the religion of a prince was no longer potent enough to change the religion of the state.

CALVINISM IN FRANCE

The Difficult Beginnings

During the first half of the sixteenth century, the Hapsburg-Valois rivalry was the overriding concern of the French monarchs. Although Francis I (1515–1547) and Henry II (1547–1559) sporadically attempted to exterminate Protestantism, their primary attention was devoted to consolidating the royal power and buttressing the political ambitions of France. The French king was prepared to cooperate with German Lutherans so that the emperor might be weakened. In 1535, King Francis invited such influential Protestant leaders as Melanchthon and Bucer to cooperate with him in bringing about a religious peace. The venture failed but it presaged an approach that would be frequently repeated. For Francis, as for Charles, political gain was well worth a religious loss.

Calvinism took full advantage of the royal quandary. Although both Francis and Henry made various efforts to speed the execution of the French Protestants, the vigorous propagation of the Geneva-based faith continued. Publication of the *Institutes*, training of Calvinist emissaries in Geneva, and encouragement by the indomitable Calvin himself all combined to fire advocates of the new religion with a zeal that established clandestine congregations throughout France. In 1545, the launching of what was proclaimed a "crusade against heresy" resulted in the massacre of several hundred Waldenses in Provence; it did not seriously jeopardize the expansion of Calvinism.

Shortly after Henry's accession to the throne, he set up an inquisitorial court, commonly known as the *chambre ardent* (burning chamber). By the Edict of Chateaubriand (1551) the king established procedures for expediting trial and execution of heretics. Literature from Geneva was barred. But when Henry attempted to introduce a Spanish type of inquisition, the *parlement* of Paris opposed this as being too sweeping a denial of human rights. Yet, the royal wrath, encouraged by the cardinal of Lorraine, Charles de Guise, did succeed in sending numerous Calvinists to the stake. Their plight was movingly portrayed in Jean Crespin's popular martyrology *Acts and Monuments*.

The reform movement gained a substantial following in several of the universities. Usually, converts came from the towns rather than the countryside, although a number of landed nobles also embraced Calvinism. When powerful nobles such as Gaspard de Coligny, Louis de Condé, and François d'Andelot gave their support, French Calvinists, known as Huguenots after the middle of the century, dared to hope for a Protestant France. Anthony, king of Navarre, father of the future Henry IV, temporarily adopted Protestantism in 1548. Some of the nobles who supported Calvinism hoped to use religion to further their political ambitions. The powerful, staunchly Catholic Guise faction had gained great influence at the court—and had also made determined enemies. Some Huguenots, such as the pamphleteer, François Hotman, hoped that German Protestants might give military assistance against the Guise ascendancy.

Early French Calvinism drew its support largely from town merchants and landed nobles. Often the position taken by local lords would determine the shape of the reform movement. If nobles sympathized with the movement, as in Navarre, Normandy, the Orleanais, Provence, or Dauphiné, congregations were able to organize openly. (Frequently, prominent nobles who championed the reformed cause manipulated congregations to further their own military and political ambitions.) In hostile areas, Huguenots met in secret; services were conducted in woods, in homes, or any convenient place. Much of the initiative and direction came from Geneva, and when the Huguenots held their first national synod in Paris in 1559, the ecclesiastical patterns they adopted reflected the image of Calvin. By 1561, Huguenot leaders estimated that their congregations totalled more than two thousand, many of them served by pastors from Switzerland. Not surprisingly, the French government requested Geneva to stop sending preachers who were disturbing the peace of the kingdom, but the clandestine infiltration continued.[11] Few concerns were as dear to the heart of Calvin as the progress of reform in France.

Calvinism as a National Force

Having been wounded in a tournament, Henry II died in July, 1559. The feeble Francis II ascended the throne at fifteen years of age, husband of Mary Queen of Scots. His reign ended abruptly in December, 1560, but even this short time witnessed important changes in the fortunes of the Huguenots. In some towns, Huguenots built their own churches; elsewhere, as in Rouen, they met openly in the city square; and in other centers, such as Valence, they simply seized churches and introduced Protestant worship. Religious and political factors became increasingly inseparable. Once again the conflict between the state and the individual conscience—or ambition—dogged the steps of the reformers. Calvin advised passive resistance, but this did not deter Condé in his Amboise conspiracy—that ill-fated attempt to seize King Francis, destroy the power of the Guises, and gain religious toleration for the Huguenots. The Guises discovered and were able to rout the scheme, but the incident demonstrated that the nation stood on the brink of disastrous conflict.

The sweeping ambitions of the Guise faction were now countered by the queen mother, Catherine de'Medici (1519–1589). She was determined to restore the royal power, if necessary by using the Protestants as a counterbalance against the dominant Guises. When Francis II died, to be succeeded by his sickly brother of nine, Charles IX, Catherine became regent. Determined not to let religion plunge the nation into war, she decreed that religious prisoners be freed and that prosecution for religious offenses cease. Then, hoping to bring Catholics and Protestants to a point where they might at least tolerate each other, she sum-

---

[11]For an analysis of the Genevan impact on Calvinism in France, see Robert M. Kingdon, *Geneva and the Coming of the Wars of Religion in France, 1555–63* (Geneva: Droz, 1956).

moned the Colloquy of Poissy (1561).[12] Here, before the king and the queen mother, Beza of Geneva, Peter Martyr of Zurich, together with leading French pastors, faced the Cardinal of Lorraine and an array of bishops and theologians. The cardinal, strongly supported by the Jesuit Diego Laynez, lost little time in denouncing the ''dogs of Geneva.'' No agreement could be reached, but the Huguenots gained a measure of toleration. The Edict of January 1562 prohibited Huguenot public worship within cities, but allowed them to gather outside the city walls. Chancellor Michel de l'Hôpital, largely responsible for the conciliatory tone of the edict, deplored the threat of coercion in matters of faith. His hope for a policy of mutual toleration was to be shattered; neither Huguenots nor Catholics were prepared to abandon force. Fanatical resort to violence on both sides pushed France into the cauldron of civil war. For the next three and one-half decades the grisly spectacle of war, plunder, assassination, and wholesale murder shaped the tragedy of the French Reformation.

CALVINISM IN SCOTLAND

A tangled web of diplomatic intrigue, political rivalry, dynastic alliance, and dogged resolution, coupled with a growing hostility toward the clergy, combined to bring triumph to Calvinism in Scotland. Although the uncompromising, intolerant, and often tactless John Knox eventually gained a resounding victory for his position, the uncertain forces of change had already undermined and shattered the old order before the irrepressible Scot came to direct his land relentlessly toward Calvinist doctrine and practice.

For centuries, Scotland had been fearful of her aggressive neighbor to the south; an alliance with France was the Scottish response to intermittent English invasion. In 1513, James IV turned the tables and invaded England. His temporary successes were halted on the battlefield at Flodden, where he and many of his earls and lords fell. Now temporarily ruled by a regent, Scotland hoped to bolster her own power by strengthening ties with France. Thus the new king, James V, was betrothed first to the daughter of Francis I, then, when she died, to Mary of the powerful French Guise family. James died in 1542, and the throne fell to his infant daughter Mary. Once again, there was a regent and once again France figured prominently in Scottish affairs—all the more so since the English king Henry VIII was determined to bring Scotland within his orbit. Close ties with France and fear of England profoundly influenced the Scottish Reformation. Also, mounting dissatisfaction with economic and social conditions prepared the way for revolution. The attack on Rome was combined with a nationalistic rejection of France and a repudiation of ecclesiastical privilege that had allowed

---

[12]Donald J. Ziegler, ed., *Great Debates of the Reformation* (New York: Random House, 1969), pp. 211–242.

church income to surpass ten-fold that of the crown (in 1560, churchmen could lay claim to about £ 400,000 whereas the crown had a yearly income of about £ 40,000).

EARLY SCOTTISH REFORMERS

Long before Knox thundered against "popery," Scottish humanists had criticized the church, while other reformers espoused continental views. In some areas, vestiges of Lollardy (a reform movement launched by John Wycliffe in the fourteenth century) felt the quickening pulse of reformation fervor, as when Tyndale's English version of the New Testament was introduced to Scotland (1526). As elsewhere, the church hierarchy was characterized by a great deal of diversity in religious practice. On the one hand, the eleven-year-old natural son of James IV was made archbishop of St. Andrews; in Aberdeen, by contrast, Bishop Dunbar called for sweeping reform, but not schism.

Among the early champions of reform was Patrick Hamilton, who had embraced Lutheranism while studying at Paris. He later studied at Marburg and openly espoused Lutheran doctrines. A zealous archbishop, James Beaton, had him apprehended and burned at the stake on February 27, 1528. But the martyrdom only intensified the determination of the zealots—as Beaton's supporters lamented, the smoke of Hamilton "infected all that it blew upon."[13] Commercial contacts with the continent facilitated the spread of Lutheran literature, despite King James V's resolve to "banish the foul Lutheran sect."[14] The popularity of numerous robust and often scurrilous ballads about corruption within the church indicated a climate favorable to change.

Beset by an impatient and often greedy nobility and threatened by the swell of popular agitation against Rome, the church was tragically entrusted to the care of leaders such as Cardinal David Beaton. In 1539 he had succeeded his uncle as archbishop of St. Andrews, and soon became papal legate. More concerned with eradicating heresy than with reforming his church, and determined to thwart English ambitions through ties with France, Beaton gave the Scottish reform movement an influential martyr—George Wishart. A student at both Wittenberg and Zurich, Wishart had embraced Zwinglian doctrines and published his English translation of the first Swiss Confession. Shortly after returning to Scotland, however, he was arrested by the Earl of Bothwell for seeking converts to his faith. The earl delivered Wishart to the cardinal, and on March 1, 1546, Wishart was burned at the stake. But his death only steeled the convictions of his friend

[13]Quoted in John T. McNeill, *The History and Character of Calvinism* (New York: Oxford University Press), 1954, p. 293.

[14]Gordon Donaldson, *Scotland: James V to James VII* (Edinburgh: Oliver and Boyd, 1965), p. 23; Kidd, *Documents,* p. 689.

and close associate, his former bodyguard and admirer, John Knox. Less than one month after the death of Wishart, a group of disgruntled nobles murdered the cardinal and hung his body from the foretower of the castle of St. Andrews. Knox, who hailed the deed as divine judgment, was undaunted by the fact that only one of the cardinal's assailants was a known Protestant.

JOHN KNOX

Until the death of Cardinal Beaton, Knox had lived in relative obscurity. Born probably in 1514, he gained a university education and became a devoted follower of Wishart. Soon after the cardinal was slain and his castle seized by attackers, Knox was urged to become preacher in the castle. His acceptance, expressed in a resolve to fight the pope, ''that man of sin,'' and his ''synagogue of Satan,''[15] presaged the tenor of religious struggle in Scotland. But Knox's hopes for an early victory for ''the true Kirk'' would be short-lived; in July, 1547, French ships launched a successful attack upon the castle. Knox was among the captives, and for nineteen months he served as a prisoner on a French galley. In 1549, he made his way to England where the Reformation policies of Edward VI and Archbishop Cranmer provided a ready opportunity for him. With the accession of Mary Tudor and the attempt to abolish anti-papal reforms, Knox fled to Frankfurt, but his intransigence on doctrinal matters, as well as his intemperate attacks on that ''Nero,'' Charles V, and ''Jezebel,'' Mary Tudor, made him a *persona non grata*. He was asked to leave the city, and then became minister to the English community in Geneva. He interrupted his work there to return briefly to England, where he married, and later went to Scotland, where he urged his countrymen to break their ties with Rome and France. He returned for a short time to Geneva once again, continued his battle with the pen. In 1556 he published his vitriolic *First Blast of the Trumpet Against the Monstrous Regiment of Women*. This diatribe, directed primarily against Mary Tudor, urged the English nobility to overthrow this ''monster'' whose rule violated the laws of nature. Knox regarded any monarchy ruled by a woman, as preposterous, especially since women were barred from virtually every political office. More important and compelling, however, was Mary's persecution of Protestants.

Events in Scotland, even with Knox absent, moved steadily in his favor. Lords and crown had become increasingly alienated. Mary of Guise, who had become regent when James V died in 1542, was determined to halt the spread of Protestantism and to thwart the ambitions of England; accordingly, she moved ever closer to the French. As French advisers displaced the resentful Scottish lords, anti-regent feeling gave rise to a powerful national pride. This sentiment was intensified in 1558, when, Mary Queen of Scots (daughter of James V and Mary of Guise), married Francis, the French dauphin; the French court felt that

[15]John Knox, *Works*, ed. David Laing, 6 vols. (Edinburgh: Bannatyne Club, 1846–64), I:189.

the marriage would save Scotland from being "wasted and ruined by the English."[16]

Spurred on by fear of French domination, and suspicious of the designs of the crown, a group of Protestant nobles, the "Lords of the Congregation," vowing their determination to "jeopard life and goods," in 1557 invited Knox to return to his homeland and continue his earlier work. Knox consulted Calvin who, perhaps recalling his own earlier experience, warned him that refusal would be "rebellious unto his God and unmerciful to his country."[17] But by now the reverberations of the "trumpet blast" had reached the ears of Elizabeth, who had just succeeded to the English throne. Knox was accordingly refused permission to travel through England, so he sailed directly from Dieppe to Leith. In spring of 1559, the formidable reformer launched a vigorous preaching campaign against the old religion. Reform proved inseparable from destruction. In Perth, Sterling, Linlithgow, and elsewhere, mobs destroyed statues, despoiled monasteries, and engaged in other acts of vandalism.[18]

Once again the regent sought military support from France. Mary Stuart (Queen of Scots) had just become queen of France, so the intensified involvement of French military power was not surprising, but it further antagonized the Scottish nobility. In desperation the Congregation turned to England, where Queen Elizabeth feared France more than she disliked Knox. English ships and soldiers now faced the French in Scotland. The Lords of the Congregation confidently demanded that ancient liberties be restored and that the French be sent home. The regent finally suggested that both French and English troops be withdrawn. When she died in June, 1560, her wish had gone far toward being fulfilled. By the terms of the Treaty of Edinburgh (July 6, 1560), French and English forces agreed to withdraw, thus creating a vacuum that Knox and the Congregation were determined to fill.

In accordance with the provisions of the treaty, the Scottish parliament met on August 1, 1560, and, without ascertaining the wishes of Mary Queen of Scots, now resident in France, proceeded to transform the realm. Lords and several bishops cooperated with Knox and other Protestant leaders in formally adopting reformation practices. The Calvinistic First Scottish Confession was approved by the parliament.[19] Papal authority was rejected, as was the Mass. A Book of Discipline, though not formally sanctioned by parliament, was approved by the Great Council and was widely adopted as a guide for church conduct. As in Geneva, church government was to be vested in both clergy and laity. A remarkable feature of the Book of Discipline was its emphasis upon compulsory education, undoubtedly a borrowing from the Genevan church.

The apparent triumph of the Reformation was soon confronted by a royal

---

[16]Antonia Fraser, *Mary Queen of Scots* (London: Weidenfeld and Nicolson, 1969), p. 69.
[17]Knox, *Works*, I:268.
[18]Knox disapproved of this wanton destruction by the "rascal multitude" (*Works*, I:322).
[19]Kidd, *Documents*, pp. 704–707.

ENGRAVED PORTRAIT: JOHN KNOX, by Hondius from the engraving in Beza's *Icones*, 1580

Eloquent, dynamic, and stubborn, Knox relentlessly fought for the triumph of Calvinism in Scotland. Uninhibited by fear of queen or noble, he championed the rights of parliament and gained substantial popular support.

British Museum

challenge, for in August, 1561, Mary returned to Scotland. Francis II had died the previous December, so she was now free to devote her attention to Scottish problems. When she proceeded to have the Mass celebrated, Knox used his pulpit in St. Giles Cathedral to denounce the practice. Mary attempted to be conciliatory in religious affairs, but Knox would have none of it, for, as he informed his queen, "conscience requireth knowledge . . . and I fear right knowledge ye have none.''[20] Queen and reformer had joined in a battle that would once again bring foreign intervention and tragedy.

Repeated meetings between Queen Mary and Knox brought no solution. When Mary reminded Knox of his duties as a subject of the queen, he defended his rights as a subject in the commonwealth. When the secretary of state questioned the right of the General Assembly to meet without royal approval, Knox retorted that a reformation faith required the ''liberty of assemblies.'' Despite Mary's exasperation with Knox and her attempt to follow a policy of moderation, the Scottish church became increasingly presbyterian in its policy. Synods and assemblies regulated the life of the church, watched its doctrine, and established use of Knox's liturgy.

During most of the 1560s, Mary attempted to conciliate the reformers. Her repeated refusals to support vigorous champions of the papal position might well have strengthened her position, but it was undermined by her unhappy marital connections. In 1565 she married Lord Darnley, but Mary found him incompetent and unreliable. The unstable consort, together with a band of disillusioned nobles, indulged his suspicions and frustrations by murdering David Riccio, the queen's secretary. This cruel act, carried out in Mary's presence on March 9, 1566, was followed in less than a year by the murder of Darnley. Mary, in the meantime, had grown increasingly fond of the Earl of Bothwell, whom she married in May, 1567. Knox and his supporters were quick once again to thunder against the queen, while the sordid and confused royal schemes alienated most of the sympathetic nobility. When the nobles rose against Mary and Bothwell, few lamented the defeat of the queen. In June, 1567, she was imprisoned and in the following month forced to abdicate. Five days later, her son, with Knox preaching the sermon, was crowned King James VI. When parliament assembled in December, it passed legislation requiring subsequent monarchs to swear to uphold the Protestant religion. At the same time, the General Assemblies were recognized as authoritative for the church. Scottish presbyterianism seemed firmly established when Knox died in 1572.

Yet the young king would soon challenge the independence of the church. James developed a strong addiction to the theory that kings rule by divine right—that all elements within the society, including the church, are subject to the monarch. Andrew Melville (1545–1622), educator and churchman, emerged as a leading opponent of the king's designs and bluntly informed James that he ''was not the head of the church.'' The king scored a hollow and temporary victory in 1584 with the passage of the ''Black Acts,'' which attacked presbyteries and asserted episcopal authority; the forces supporting Melville soon regained control. Throughout the rest of the century, James failed to break the power of presbyterianism. Although he was fully aware of the ''democratical

[20]Knox, *Works*, II:13.

designs'' of a system that he regarded as antithetical to kingship, he was not strong enough to prevent the enactment of a statute in 1592 establishing the presbyterian system. The hopes of John Knox had largely become reality.

Suggestions for Further Reading

Armstrong, Brian G. *Calvinism and the Amyraut Heresy.* Madison: University of Wisconsin Press, 1969.

Bainton, Roland. *Women of the Reformation in France and England.* Minneapolis: Augsburg, 1973.

Biéler, André. *The Social Humanism of Calvin.* Translated by Paul T. Fuhrmann. Richmond, Va.: John Knox Press, 1964.

Bratt, John H., ed. *The Rise and Development of Calvinism,* rev. ed. Grand Rapids, Mich.: Eerdmans, 1964.

*****Breen, Quirinus.** *John Calvin: A Study in French Humanism,* 2d ed. Hamden, Conn.: Archon Books, 1968.

Burleigh, John H. *A Church History of Scotland.* London: Oxford University Press, 1960.

Cadier, Jean. *The Man God Mastered: A Brief Biography of John Calvin.* Translated by O. R. Johnston. Grand Rapids, Mich.: Eerdmans, 1960.

Comite, Farel. *Guillaume Farel.* Neuchâtel: Delachaux et Niestle, 1930.

Davis, N. Z. *Society and Culture in Early Modern France.* Stanford: Stanford University Press, 1975.

Dickenson, W. Croft, ed. *John Knox's History of the Reformation in Scotland,* 2 vols. London: Nelson, 1949.

*****Dillenberger, John,** ed. *John Calvin: Selections from His Writings.* Garden City, N. Y.: Doubleday, 1971.

Donaldson, Gordon. *The Scottish Reformation.* London: Cambridge University Press, 1960.

Doumerge, Émile. *Jean Calvin, les hommes et les choses de son temps,* 7 vols. Lausanne: G. Bridel, 1899–1927.

Dowey, Edward A. *The Knowledge of God in Calvin's Theology.* New York: Columbia University Press, 1952.

Fortsman, H. Jackson. *Word and Spirit: Calvin's Doctrine of Biblical Authority.* Stanford: Stanford University Press, 1962.

Fraser, Antonia. *Mary, Queen of Scots.* New York: Dial Press, 1969.

Galpern, A. N. *The Religions of the People in Sixteenth-Century Champagne.* Cambridge, Mass.: Harvard University Press, 1976.

Harkness, Georgia. *John Calvin: The Man and His Ethics.* New York: Abingdon Press, 1958.

*****Higman, Francis M.** *The Style of John Calvin in His French Polemical Treatises.* London: Oxford University Press, 1967.

Hoogstra, Jacob T. *John Calvin, Contemporary Prophet.* Grand Rapids, Mich.: Eerdmans, 1959.

*Indicates paperback edition.

Hughes, Philip E. *The Register of the Company of Pastors of Geneva in the Time of Calvin.* Grand Rapids, Mich.: Eerdmans, 1966.

Hunt, G. L. *Calvinism and the Political Order.* Philadelphia: Westminister Press, 1965.

Imbart de la Tour, Pierre. *Les Origines de la Réforme,* 2 vols., 2d ed. Melun: Librairie d'argences, 1948.

Jansen, John F. *Calvin's Doctrine of the Work of Christ.* London: Clark, 1956.

Kingdon, Robert M. *Geneva and the Coming of the Wars of Religion in France, 1555–1563.* Geneva: Droz, 1956.

Lovy, René. *Les Origines de la Réforme française: Meaux, 1518–1546.* Paris: Librairie protestante, 1959.

MacGregor, Geddes. *The Thundering Scot, a Portrait of John Knox.* Philadelphia: Westminister Press, 1957.

Martin, A. L. *Henry III and the Jesuit Politicians.* Geneva: Droz, 1973.

McDonnell, Kilian. *John Calvin, the Church and the Eucharist.* Princeton: Princeton University Press, 1968.

McNeil, D. O. *Guillaume Budé and Humanism in the Reign of Francis I.* Geneva: Droz, 1973.

McNeill, John T. *The History and Character of Calvinism.* New York: Oxford University Press, 1954.

———. *On God and Political Duty.* Indianapolis: Bobbs-Merrill, 1956.

———, ed. *The Institutes of the Christian Religion.* Translated by Ford L. Battles. Philadelphia: Westminster Press, 1960.

Monter, E. W. *Calvin's Geneva.* New York: Wiley, 1967.

Mueller, William A. *Church and State in Luther and Calvin.* Nashville: Broadman, 1954.

Naef, Henri. *Les origines de la Réforme à Genève,* 2 vols. Geneva: Droz, 1968.

Niesel, Wilhelm. *The Theology of Calvin.* Translated by Harold Knight. Philadelphia: Westminister Press, 1956.

Nixon, Leroy. *John Calvin's Teachings on Human Reason.* New York: Exposition Press, 1963.

*****Olin, J. C.,** ed. *John Calvin and Jacopo Sadoleto; A Reformation Debate.* New York: Harper & Row, A Harper Torchbook, 1966.

Parker, T. H. L. *Portrait of Calvin.* Philadelphia: Westminster Press, 1954.

———. *Calvin's Doctrine of the Knowledge of God,* rev. ed. Grand Rapids, Mich.: Eerdmans, 1959.

Reid, W. S. *Trumpeter of God. A Biography of John Knox.* New York: Scribner's, 1974.

Ridley, Jasper G. *John Knox.* Oxford: Clarendon, 1968.

Shaw, Duncan, ed. *John Knox: A Quartercentenary Reappraisal.* Edinburgh: St. Andrew, 1975.

Shennan, J. H. *Government and Society in France, 1461–1661.* London: Allen and Unwin, 1969.

Stickelberger, Emanuel. *Calvin: A Life.* Translated by D. G. Gelzer. Richmond, Va.: John Knox Press, 1954.

Torrance, Thomas. *Calvin's Doctrine of Man.* Grand Rapids, Mich.: Eerdmans, 1940.

Wallace, Ronald S. *Calvin's Doctrine of Word and Sacrament.* Grand Rapids, Mich.: Eerdmans, 1957.

Walker, Williston. *John Calvin, the Organizer of Reformed Protestantism.* New York: Schocken Books, 1969.

Watt, Hugh. *John Knox in Controversy.* New York: Philosophical Society, 1950.

Wendel, François. *Calvin: The Origins and Development of His Religious Thought.* Translated by Philip Mairet. London: Collins, 1963.

Whitley, Elizabeth. *Plain Mr. Knox.* Richmond, Va.: John Knox Press, 1960.

Willis, Edward D. *Calvin's Catholic Christology.* Leiden: Brill, 1966.

8

The Reformation
in Scandinavia
and Eastern Europe

COLLAPSE OF THE UNION OF KALMAR

In few areas did Lutheranism score so complete a victory as in Scandinavia. Religious, political, economic, and dynastic factors combined to overthrow allegiance to the traditional faith.

Although the Union of Kalmar (1397) had brought Denmark, Norway, and Sweden together politically under a Danish crown, the bonds were only those of convenience and dynastic aspirations. The Danish kings exercised little power outside Denmark, Norway, and Iceland; in Sweden aristocratic elements in state and church dominated the government. In the absence of a succession law, the election of kings by nobles and higher clergy strongly intimidated any tendency toward royal absolutism. By 1500, fully half of Denmark belonged to the church, while the countryside was peopled with serfs and landless peasants. Commerce was largely dominated by the Hansa, which profited from a situation in which a weak king could not protect his realm from the intrigues of a league of trading centers. Throughout the Baltic region, the development of territorial states was resisted by the Hansa, for the emergence of strong central governments was inimical to the ambitions of an association that could flourish only if cities remained independent.

With the accession to the Danish throne of Christian II (1513–1523) an attempt was made to establish the monarch as more than a figurehead. Ambitious, resolute, and ruthless, he was determined to build a territorial state in which the aristocracy would be the servant of the king. Aided by the astute Sigbrit, mother of his mistress, Christian systematically enforced his will in Denmark. He skillfully posed as champion of townsmen and peasants, and used them against the nobility. By 1517, he felt ready to extend his triumph to Sweden, where a sharp division between native and pro-Danish elements provided the occasion for intervention. Sten Sture, the ambitious regent who had carefully courted Swedish support by exploiting anti-Danish sentiment, found his policies thwarted by Gustav Trolle, archbishop of Uppsala since 1514. Conflict resulted, with the Danish king sending military support to the archbishop. The effort failed, but in 1518, Christian II tried again to aid Trolle in his war with Sture. Christian gained papal support of his efforts so that in 1520, with Sture excommunicated and Sweden under an interdict, he once again pressed the attack. This time Sten Sture was defeated and fatally wounded. He died in February, 1520, leaving the anti-Danish element without effective leadership. The king and archbishop entered Stockholm in triumph. Gustav Trolle now brought charges of heresy against Sture and his associates. After a bizarre and highly irregular trial, the accused were condemned.[1] On November 8, 1520, more than eighty were beheaded; others were added to the list of victims in the next few days.

This "bloodbath of Stockholm" became an emotional rallying cry for those forces opposed to King Christian and Archbishop Trolle. Gustav Vasa, a prominent nobleman and son of one of the victims of the bloodbath, now emerged as the champion of Swedish interests; in April, 1521, he defeated the pro-Danish forces at Vaesteras and in May, captured Uppsala. His prospects improved considerably when the Hansa towns of Luebeck and Danzig came to his aid, thus depriving Christian of his control of Swedish waters.

The unhappy king now found himself plagued by revolt in Denmark. The nobility had become alienated by reforms that were designed to benefit peasants and burghers, while leading clergymen viewed with apprehension his apparent sympathy for Lutheran reforms. In March, 1523, the nobility elected Frederick of Holstein king. Christian fled, to spend the rest of his life in prison or exile.

Frederick soon turned his attention toward a resolution of the Swedish problem, but with Christian II plotting a return to his throne, and the forces of Vasa triumphant in Sweden, there was little that could be done to restore the Union. In June, 1523, Vasa accepted the crown of Sweden, thus asserting Swedish independence and signaling the end of a century and a quarter of the Union.

THE REFORMATION IN DENMARK

Prior to his deposition, Christian had launched Denmark on a course designed to strengthen royal power and bring religious reform. In his Secular and Ecclesiastical Code, promulgated in 1521–1522, he envisioned a state church independent of papal control. The law provided for sharp curtailment of clerical privileges: clergymen would have to be university trained and able to preach in Danish; no cleric was to possess land or property unless he married; no ecclesiastical court could try cases involving property; and in no circumstances could appeals be carried to Rome. Although the ousting of the king prevented immediate and complete application of his law, basic goals remained constant

[1]Michael Roberts, *The Early Vasas* (London: Cambridge University Press, 1968), p. 16.

among Christian's successors. Lutheran ideas found ready access in Denmark and other parts of Scandinavia, for commercial ties with Germany were strong. In addition, biblical humanism, as personified by the Carmelite Paul Helegesen (ca. 1485–1534), attacked the spiritual hierarchy for being too concerned with gaining wealth and power. Christian also encouraged Lutheran sympathizers to disseminate their views throughout the realm. Helegesen, now a supporter of Luther,[2] was appointed professor at the University of Copenhagen. The king also requested Elector Frederick to send Lutheran theologians to Denmark. Martin Reinhard came in 1520, soon to be followed by Luther's colleague Karlstadt. With the issuing of the Edict of Worms, however, Christian, afraid of antagonizing the emperor, abandoned his pro-Lutheran course.

Despite a coronation oath to fight heresy, Frederick of Holstein soon intensified pro-Lutheran efforts. Preachers such as the former monk Hans Tausen (1494–1561), who became the royal chaplain, freely spread Lutheran views. Polemical literature and translations of the Scriptures further speeded the Reformation. In 1524 the first Danish New Testament was printed, to be superseded in 1529 by the better translation of Christian Pedersen (1480–1554).

Economic and political aspirations of the aristocracy further weakened the position of the papacy. Church lands were ruthlessly seized by nobles and king. In 1526, Frederick disregarded the papal candidate and installed his own choice as archbishop of Lund, at the same time confiscating the customary fees. Episcopal pressure against this royal policy was effectively diverted at the session of the diet in Odense (1527), when Frederick further weakened the position of the traditional clergy by encouraging the seizure of ecclesiastical lands. Papal power was effectively negated when the diet decreed that henceforth bishops were to be confirmed not by the pope, but by the king.[3] The diet also took a remarkably tolerant stance and declared that ''everyman shall enjoy freedom of conscience.''[4] Christian II's ill-fated attempt to invade Denmark and regain the crown in 1531–1532 did not enhance the prospects of the bishops. Reform continued as traditional clergy were dispossessed, monastic orders dissolved, and Lutheran pastors and services established. In 1530, the Catholic bishops attempted once again to use the diet, in session at Copenhagen, to halt the new religion. Tausen, cheered by the populace, presented his Lutheran *Forty-Three Articles*, but they received little official support. The diet simply urged retention of the status quo but the dismemberment of the old church continued.

With the death of Frederick in 1533, the ensuing succession crisis presented a temporary opportunity for advocates of the old religious order to recoup their position. Although Frederick had been assured that his son Christian would be accepted as successor to the throne, the bishops exploited the situation, and for

---

[2]He broke with Luther when it became apparent that reform was leading to schism.

[3]B. J. Kidd, *Documents Illustrative of the Continental Reformation* (Oxford: Clarendon, 1911), p. 234.

[4]*Ibid.*

ENGRAVING: HANS TAUSEN

Sometimes called the "Danish Luther," his preaching and writing gave direction to the Danish Reformation.

Nationalhistoriske Museum, Frederiksborg

almost three years civil war ravaged the country. Bishops, townsmen, and peasants, now joined by Luebeck, gained control of Copenhagen for Catholicism. Only when the hard-pressed nobles received military assistance from the Swedish king were they able to triumph. Copenhagen was recaptured, and Frederick's son was proclaimed king as Christian III (1536–1559).

The new monarch lost no time in moving against those who had almost deprived him of his throne. All Catholic bishops in the realm were arrested, and church lands not yet seized by the nobles passed to the crown. In 1537, the Lutheran Bugenhagen came from Wittenberg to crown the king and queen, and to reorganize the Danish church according to Lutheran practices; episcopacy was simply abolished. Superintendents, later to be called bishops again, were appointed by the king to supervise ecclesiastical affairs. In 1539, a Church Order reflecting Luther's views was adopted as the basic constitution of the Danish church. The triumph of the Reformation established Lutheranism and greatly enhanced the power of the crown. The new church had been created by acts of state.

THE REFORMATION IN NORWAY

Christian III imposed a similar religious settlement upon Norway. Archbishop Olaf of Trondhjem had led Norway in supporting Luebeck against the king. With the victory of Christian, Norway was reduced to the status of a Danish province. Olaf and other bishops were replaced by Lutheran superintendents. By act of the crown, Norway officially became Lutheran. Numerous outbursts against this policy disrupted economic processes, but the king refused to modify his position.

THE REFORMATION IN SWEDEN:

The Attack on Papal Authority

Victory and coronation for Gustav Vasa signaled the end of civil war in Sweden, but the new monarch found his treasury depleted. With the country heavily indebted to an impatient Luebeck, and the peasantry unable to bear more taxes, the king turned upon the only convenient source of revenue—the church. Hereafter, increasingly anti-papal policies served as a pretext for confiscation of ecclesiastical property. Expansion of Lutheranism was the natural corollary.

Even before Vasa's triumph, Hanseatic ties had provided a convenient avenue for the introduction of Lutheran views. By 1523, reports of heresy moved Pope Adrian VI to send his legate, Johannes Magnus, to investigate. Magnus found that some clerics were profoundly alarmed by the spread of heresy. Hans Brask, bishop of Linkoeping, asked him to establish the Inquisition.

The new king had no desire to preserve papal influence. When Rome attempted to gain the restoration of Gustav Trolle, deposed by the diet as a traitor, Gustav Vasa declared he would have no foreigners ruling the Swedish church. He further demonstrated his independence by compelling the Swedish church to give him a loan. In 1524, Pope Clement abandoned his attempt to restore Trolle. Magnus, who had been chosen by the canons, was consecrated as archbishop of Uppsala. Clearly, Swedish insistence on self-determination in religion was placing pope and clergy in a difficult position.

Other forces were also undermining the old faith. Olav Petri (1493–1552), trained at Uppsala and Wittenberg, and appointed city clerk of Stockholm in 1524, became an ardent advocate of Lutheranism. His brother Lars (1499–1573) used his post as professor of theology at Uppsala to propagate Lutheran views. Then, as further demonstration of the royal will, Nicholas Stecker of Eisleben, a Lutheran, was appointed pastor of the Great Church in Stockholm. By 1524, Lars Andreae, the royal chancellor, was issuing pronouncements that sounded suspiciously Lutheran: The church was the whole community of the faithful; its resources belonged to the people. Gustav Vasa, though little concerned with theological issues, refused Bishop Brask's request to condemn Lutheran writings—there must first be a careful and impartial examination.

Gradually, Bishop Brask emerged as the champion of the opponents of Lutheranism and royal encroachment upon traditional church prerogatives. The bishop not only declared some of the chancellor's statements heretical, he also sought the support of the lay nobility and the peasantry, in combatting the king's despoliation of church property. Gustav Vasa systematically depicted the bishop and his fellow clerics as parasites of society. To the nobles, he offered the inducement of gain by plundering church properties, an example he himself set by divesting Brask of all his wealth.

The Diet of Vaesteras

Pressed by financial concerns, confronted by a rebellion in Dalarna, his realm divided in religion, the king summoned the Estates to meet in Vaesteras (1527). To them he presented a lengthy report on the problems of the country, contending that only the church could supply the needed revenues. In conclusion, he announced his intention to abdicate the throne of an ungrateful nation. A sharply divided diet debated the king's proposal. Bishop Brask, outnumbered but indomitable, fought to save the church from spoliation, but his situation was hopeless. Eventually the diet issued its Recess of Vaesteras: If the king would remain on the throne, he was promised full support; "superfluous" church property—as defined by Gustav—would go to the monarchy; and all lands donated to the church since 1454 were to revert to the donor's family or, if the family had ceased to exist to the king. Then, far from condemning Lutheranism, the Estates, having dutifully conducted a disputation between Olav Petri and Peder Galle—the latter an ardent opponent of Luther—declared that the reformers had been vindicated. King Gustav was urged to insure that "God's Word may be purely preached everywhere in the realm."

Gustav Vasa moved swiftly to consolidate his victory. The Ordinance of Vaesteras,[5] quickly approved by the diet, implemented the Recess, and effectively brought the church under the crown. No higher clergy were to be appointed without royal assent; most church property was confiscated; legal privileges of

[5]*Ibid.,* pp. 234–236.

the clergy were eliminated; mendicant orders, permitted to beg only ten weeks in a year, were virtually condemned to extinction. The church was at the mercy of a king who contended that "useless priests" were an unnecessary economic burden. Chancellor Lars Andreae, resolutely anti-papal, used every opportunity to weaken the old church and strengthen Lutheranism. Although there had been no official repudiation of traditional doctrine or papal authority, Bishop Brask, his position made increasingly intolerable, left Sweden, eventually to die in exile in a Polish monastery.

Relentless pressure against the higher clergy, coupled with dissatisfaction on the part of some of the nobility, led to an insurrection in 1529. Gustav Vasa, after granting concessions to the rebels, was soon in a position to make the insurgents regret their attempt to enthrone Maens Bryntesson as new king of Sweden. When the revolt collapsed, some of the leaders fled. Others, including Maens, were executed.

The Triumph of Lutheranism

Meanwhile, the expansion of Lutheranism continued. In 1528, Olav Petri published *A Little Book of the Sacraments*, which recognized as sacraments only baptism and the Eucharist, provided for communion in two kinds, and rejected the doctrine of purgatory. His *Swedish Handbook* (1529) provided for church services in the vernacular. A hymn book published in the following year and the *Swedish Mass* (1531) expressed a newly found pride in the language of a young nation. Olav Petri successfully defended his contention that "God does not despise our speech beyond the speech of others." Emotional appeals to nationalistic pride were successfully used against advocates of the old Latin mass.

Lutheranism was further strengthened when King Gustav in 1531 summoned more than a hundred clergy to elect a new archbishop of Uppsala. Archbishop Johannes Magnus had fled to Poland, thus leaving the see, from the king's standpoint, vacant. Lars Petri, recently returned from Wittenberg, was elected. Consecrated without papal sanction, he now became the principal architect of the Swedish Lutheran Church. As sees became vacant, they were filled with Lutherans. Protestant literature flooded the country, and Luther's *Shorter Catechism*, translated into Swedish, became a most powerful means of spreading the new teachings. The first complete Swedish translation of the Bible, largely the work of Lars Petri, appeared in 1541.

The new archbishop had no intention of simply surrendering all church possessions to the crown; rather, revenues taken from the church were to be used for charitable and educational purposes. Similarly, Olav Petri and Lars Andreae urged the king to halt the decay of learning. By 1539, king and archbishop clashed decisively, for Gustav Vasa was determined to rule the church, and to regulate its affairs as a department of state. In that year, the king brought charges of high treason against Lars Andreae and Olav Petri, while the archbishop was compelled to serve as one of ten judges. Both reformers were condemned to death; the king, having demonstrated his supremacy, commuted both sentences to fines. Lars Andreae retired to Straengnaes, but Olav Petri continued as a vigorous champion of the Reformation. In 1543 he became pastor of the Great Church of Stockholm, there to continue his preaching and writing. Clearly, reformer and monarch had reached a stalemate in their relationship.

Still suspicious of the energetic reformers, King Gustav relied increasingly on two Germans, recently imported into the kingdom. Conrad von Pyhy, made chancellor in 1538, shaped the crown-church relationships according to the king's designs, while George Norman, appointed superintendent of the church in 1540, initiated a rigorous program of visitation and confiscation that removed clergymen deemed unworthy—and simultaneously stripped churches of "superfluous" plate and vestments. Even ecclesiastical libraries did not escape plunder.

The Revolt of Nils Dacke

In 1542, the smoldering discontent, fed by the continuing confiscation of church property as well as the king's determination to intensify control of trade and to raise taxes, erupted in the revolt of Nils Dacke.[6] This peasant leader scored some remarkable military successes, even though support from the nobility was small. Gustav found himself obliged to negotiate a truce, while numerous rivals and aspirants attempted to take advantage of the situation by forming an alliance with the rebels. Early in 1543, the king, his position now strengthened, denounced the truce and launched an attack on Dacke's forces. This time the peasant forces were defeated. In July, 1543, the rebellion collapsed, and Dacke was killed. Gustav had triumphed, but he also recognized that Pyhy and Norman were following a dangerous policy. Pyhy, a convenient scapegoat, was imprisoned, there to remain until his death in 1553. Norman was more fortunate, although he too was discretely moved into the background.

The Final Triumph of Gustav Vasa

But Gustav had no intention of surrendering one iota of royal authority. At the Diet of Vaesteras (1544) the king laid before the Estates a comprehensive national program. Since German mercenaries had proved ineffective in the revolt, provision was made for a permanent native army, the first in Europe.[7] Other actions by the diet included the prohibition of "popish practices" and the acceptance of the Succession Pact, a document that established a hereditary monarchy vested in the house of Vasa. No king had ever before stood so tall in the Swedish realm.

[6]Roberts, *The Early Vasas*, pp. 132–143.
[7]*Ibid.*, p. 139.

In economic affairs, foreign and domestic, the king pursued an equally energetic program. He was determined to free his commerce from Hanseatic control, and so encouraged trade with western Europe. Internal trade was regulated by the crown, as were prices and marketing. The iron industry, under royal supervision, flourished as never before. Through it all, the royal purse was steadily fattened, so that the throne could be made more secure by the building of new castles and a navy. When Gustav Vasa died in 1560, he left an indelible impress on his country: Firmly centered around the crown, the nation had achieved a unity once thought impossible, and, hand in hand with political unity, went a Lutheranism so strongly entrenched that successive monarchs could not restore the old faith.

THE EASTERN KINGDOMS

As the Protestant Reformation established itself in northern Europe, it inevitably influenced developments on the eastern European frontier of Catholicism. Most of the territory lying between the Baltic Sea and the Ottoman Empire comprised the kingdoms of Hungary, Bohemia, and Poland, with each of the monarchies consisting of several semiautonomous states. Polish kings were also grand dukes of Lithuania, and thus ruled over a territory so vast that they could confidently lay claim to great power status. Kings of Bohemia included Moravia and several smaller territories in their realm, while the crown of Hungary also ruled the kingdom of Croatia.

The Background of Eastern Europe

During the sixteenth century, these kingdoms experienced economic and political developments that were markedly different from those of Western Europe. Whereas numerous countries in the West were experiencing both a rapid expansion of commercial interests and a more central political structure, the kingdoms on the fringes of Latin civilization found themselves ever more under the power of the landed nobility whose chief interest was to expand agricultural production. Here the vast plains of superb arable land presented a compelling enticement to large-scale agricultural production, more lucrative now that Western Europe was becoming urbanized. With political power safely in their hands, nobles systematically reduced peasants to serfdom, and eastern monarchs were in no position to challenge the nobles' bid for power. Indeed, since the nobility provided the king with his military forces, cooperation between king and nobles was a royal necessity.

Nobles dominated the sessions of the various eastern European diets. All three kingdoms had, in addition to their general diets, provincial assemblies that were fiercely jealous of their privileges. Only in Bohemia were the burgesses recognized as an estate, and even here the vast preponderance of influence rested with

The Reformation in Eastern Europe

Moscow

Oka R.

RUSSIA

Baltic Sea

W. Dvina R.

EAST PRUSSIA

LITHUANIA

Warsaw

POLAND

SILESIA

Vistula R.

Krakow

MORAVIA

Kiev

UKRAINE

KHANATE

Dnieper R.

OF THE

Dniester R.

Vienna

TRANSYLVANIA

MOLDAVIA

CRIMEA

Buda

Debrecen

HUNGARY

Torda

Mohács

Don R.

Belgrade

WALLACHIA

Black Sea

Danube R.

O T T O M A N

MONTE-NEGRO

Adriatic Sea

Constantinople

E M P I R E

the nobility. No royal policy could hope to succeed without aristocratic support. Such a determined adherence to local political independence could be used to permit a large measure of liberty—or it could be used effectively to thwart the development of a strong central government so necessary to combat both foreign foe and internal dissent. In Poland, the nobility throughout the sixteenth century successfully defended its independent position, and simply added self-determination in religion to the sweeping political and economic "liberties." In Hungary, the pressure from the Turks largely absorbed the energies of king and nobles, but did little to weaken the traditional power structure. Instead lords situated along the Turkish frontier often became virtually autonomous and were fully prepared to play off Hapsburg against Ottoman. A somewhat different situation emerged in Bohemia, for here some of the Bohemian nobles and towns made common cause with the German Lutherans. With the imperial defeat of the Schmalkaldic League in 1547, Ferdinand, King of Bohemia, was in a position to strengthen his hand. Towns were deprived of their traditional liberties, yet nobles suffered little loss of independence.

Church and State in Poland, Hungary, and Bohemia

At the beginning of the sixteenth century, the financial resources of the church in Poland far exceeded those of the crown. Possessions of individual bishops, abbots, and cathedral chapters compared favorably with those of the great nobles, and prelates such as the archbishop of Gniezno, primate of Poland, or the bishop of Krakow, held estates far superior to those of any Polish nobleman. With this impressive economic power, the higher clergy were often more concerned about maintenance of their power and influence than about spiritual conditions in the church. Simony was common, and the bishop of Krakow let it be known that he placed more emphasis upon payment of tithes than upon believing right doctrine.

Members of the nobility often attempted to curb clerical power. Thus, for example, already by the early 1500s the nobility had successfully established the principle that appointees to high ecclesiastical office must be members of the nobility. And whenever the king requested greater financial support, the nobility suggested the church as a ready reserve. In session after session, the diet adopted legislation designed to restrict the church's influence and decrease its wealth. Simultaneously, the landed aristocracy saw to it that peasants were stripped of all legal rights and compelled to labor for their lords as serfs.

In Hungary, the church, dominated by king and nobles, functioned as a department of state, with the king nominating appointees to important clerical offices. Indeed, tradition held that the Hungarian kings possessed both apostolic and legatine authority. When the throne was held by a weak king, ambitious nobles filled the vacuum. Papal authority had little impact here. Also, in the eastern part of the kingdom, Transylvania had a large number of adherents to the Orthodox faith. Thus, in a land where Catholicism and Orthodoxy regularly felt the pressure of Islam, the papacy could play only a minor role.

In sixteenth-century Bohemia the church had already suffered a series of setbacks that undermined papal power. The bitter Hussite wars of the fifteenth century had firmly established Utraquism as the religion of the vast majority of the people, with the practice of communion in both kinds. The king adhered to the Catholic faith, but the estates of the realm were overwhelmingly Utraquist. Although Pope Pius II had pronounced Utraquism heretical in 1462, its practitioners insisted that neither papal nor conciliar decree could supersede the Scriptures. Yet the Hussites were still far from being a truly Protestant sect. They maintained many Catholic practices and beliefs, including the seven sacraments, emphasis upon good works, and clerical celibacy. In addition to the dominant national church, a smaller, more radical body, the Bohemian Brethren, continued to influence the religious life of the nation. This movement, characterized by insistence on Scriptural authority and the piety and autonomy of local congregations, contributed substantially to the Bohemian Reformation movement. At the same time, Bohemian nationalism had long resented incursions from Germany, so that there was little inclination to supplement, let alone supplant, a Hus with a Luther.

One of the major factors that prepared the way for the reception of Reformation ideas was humanism. Hungary, preserving some of the glories of Matthias Corvinus,[8] continued to encourage humanistic endeavor, and also welcomed the ideas of Erasmus and various German humanists. Close contacts with German humanists facilitated the dissemination of Lutheran writings, even though as early as 1524 a Lutheran bookseller was burned at the stake. In the previous year the king had asked the diet to "proceed against all Lutherans and their supporters by capital punishment and forfeiture of all their goods," but the request went largely unheeded. In Poland, many of the bishops and nobles were ardent admirers of Erasmus, while the University of Krakow became a lively center of humanism. In addition, Polish nobles often sent their sons to study abroad. Krakow was also an important printing center, with a wide market that included most of eastern Europe. Books published here in the 1520s and 1530s included works of various reformers. By 1520, Luther's writings were sold and debated in Krakow.

THE COMING OF LUTHERANISM
TO EASTERN EUROPE

In both Hungary and Poland, the spread of Lutheran ideas was sometimes associated with social struggle. Thus, in 1524, Danzig was disturbed by a wave of political unrest and by popular demands for economic changes. This state of turmoil provided a setting conducive to the spread of revolutionary religious ideas. The townsmen installed a new council, sympathetic to their demands, and proceeded to abolish church privilege. Iconoclasm rocked the city, while church property was seized and Lutherans were installed as pastors. The challenge to the old order became even more critical when East Prussia adopted Lutheranism in 1525. Only when King Sigismund and an army of Polish nobles seized the city in April, 1526, could the Lutheran and social revolt be halted.

By the late 1520s, Lutheranism had gained a limited but significant entrance to the eastern kingdoms. When Livonia became Lutheran in the 1520s, and then when Albert of Hohenzollern established Lutheranism in Prussia, a natural inroad to the neighboring Polish kingdom had been provided. Albert's capital,

---

[8]This king, who ruled Hungary from 1458–1490, transformed Buda into one of Europe's most brilliant centers of art and learning.

Koenigsberg, served as a printing center for Lutheran literature in both German and Polish. Here Luther's *Shorter Catechism* appeared in Polish in 1530. In 1544, a Lutheran university was founded in the city. On the whole, however, the Polish nobles showed little enthusiasm for Lutheranism with its German flavor, and its emphasis on obedience to the ruling prince.

In Hungary and Bohemia the impact of the Reformation teaching was profoundly affected by the disaster of Mohacs. Sultan Suleiman's victory here on August 29, 1526, weakened the Catholic church and crippled the monarchy. The death of Louis II led to a bitter civil war in which Ferdinand, claimant to the throne of Hungary and Bohemia, faced John Zapolya, the former *Voivode* (governor), who received substantial aid from the Turks and Hungarian nobles. During most of the rest of the century, even though the actors changed, the tragedy of civil conflict beclouded Hungarian history. The western part of Hungary was held by the Hapsburgs, while the center, "Turkish Hungary," was incorporated into the Ottoman Empire. The eastern part, Transylvania, successfully defended its independence from Ferdinand, at least until Zapolya's death in 1540. A secret arrangement between Ferdinand and Zapolya provided that at the latter's death, Transylvania would accept Hapsburg rule. Instead the Transylvanian estates chose Zapolya's son, John Sigismund, as their new king and appealed to the sultan for support. Ferdinand's attempts to gain control over all Hungary failed so completely that by 1547 he was prepared to accept a peace which required him to pay tribute to the sultan. Transylvania remained virtually independent, although under Turkish protection.

Mohacs had an equally debilitating effect on the established church. Seven of the country's sixteen prelates died on the battlefield. Many of the sees remained vacant, for the unsettled political situation led to rival nominees. Often the papacy responded by confirming none. In areas held or dominated by the Turks, Protestant ministers were given a relatively free hand, for the Sultan was prepared to tolerate those who opposed the papacy and its allies. The cause of Lutheranism was substantially strengthened when a number of bishops, such as Ferenc Thurzó of Nitra and András Sbardellati, adopted this faith. Gradually, most of the Germans of Transylvania embraced the Reformation. In this they followed the example of their chief magistrate, Mark Pemfflinger. The Magyar parts of Hungary were slower to change, but nonetheless the work of a former student at Wittenberg, Matyas Devai Bíró and his associate, Stephen Magyari Kis of Szegedi, gained broad acceptance of the new faith. Secular lords, quick to take advantage of the religious changes, often seized property and patronage belonging to the traditional faith and subsequently installed Lutheran pastors. Similarly, numerous town councils, responding to popular pressure, appointed Lutheran preachers.

Bohemia remained outside the orbit of Turkish power, but a long tradition of religious nonconformity prevented King Ferdinand from realizing his goal of a uniform faith in the realm. The Utraquists were too strongly entrenched to be overawed by the royal will, but Ferdinand hoped that he could prevent the spread of both the Bohemian Brethren and the new threat of Lutheranism. The German-speaking parts of Bohemia showed considerable receptivity for the theology of Wittenberg, and a number of town councils, as in Pilsen, Asch, and Joachimsthal, appointed Lutheran pastors. Royal objections had little effect. Luther himself paid tribute to the work of Hus, and hoped that closer ties could be formed between the German and Bohemian movements. The Bohemian Brethren in particular welcomed cooperation with Luther, but no formal union resulted.

CALVINISM CHALLENGES CATHOLICISM

Soon after the middle of the sixteenth century, Calvinism began to develop as a potent challenge to Catholicism in Poland and Hungary, and rapidly became the dominant Protestant faith in these kingdoms. Here the nobility, jealous of ecclesiastical wealth and privileges, proved highly receptive to a religion that rejected a ruling church hierarchy. Furthermore Calvinism was not German, nor did it stress subordination to the sovereign as much as did Lutheranism. Equally attractive was its presbyterian form of church government. Lay participation at all levels of church life seemed a logical corollary to a political situation where lords participated fully in shaping secular policies of the realm. When the rich Lithuanian magnate, Prince Nicholas Radziwill, embraced Calvinism, the reform movement gained a powerful voice both in the diet and at the royal court. For a time, Protestant nobles formed a majority in the diet, and only a determined coalition of king and bishops was able finally to hold them in check.

Radziwill, the most powerful secular lord in Lithuania, vigorously propagated Calvinism throughout his territories. In Brest he established a printing press which issued the ''Brest Bible'' (1563) as well as an assortment of Calvinistic literature. The tolerant king, Sigismund II, declared that ''I am not king of the consciences of my subjects,''[9] and continued his cordial relations with those lords who had adopted Protestantism. From 1552 to 1565, the marshals of the Polish diet were Protestants.

The leading intellectual figure of Polish Calvinism was Jan Laski (1499–1560). A nephew of the primate of the same name, he became an enthusiastic humanist and later embraced the Reformation. As a student in western Europe, he won the friendship of Erasmus and other humanists. Although he was a Catholic priest, his support of Protestant doctrines brought him excommunication in 1544. He left Poland and organized Protestant congregations in Germany, Denmark, the Netherlands, and England. At first a Lutheran, he moved gradually to Calvinism. In 1556, the Calvinistic churches in Poland asked him to return so that he might establish a national and unified synod. His efforts culminated in the formation of united Calvinistic bodies in Lithuania, Little Poland, and Great Poland. Then, encouraged and assisted by Lord Radziwill and the court preacher,

[9]Bernhard Stasiewski, *Reformation und Gegenreformation in Polen* (Muenster: Aschendorf, 1960), p. 45.

ENGRAVING: NICHOLAS RADZIWILL, by Dominicus Custos

Powerful and rich, his voice for moderation in the religious arena helped to alleviate tensions created by the rival claims of Catholic, Protestant, and Orthodox religious leaders.
Kunstsammlung der Veste Coburg

Francis Lismanini, Laski worked to form a Polish National church which would unite Lutherans, Calvinists, and Bohemian Brethren, but the effort failed. This inability of Protestant movements to reach a common ground of belief would eventually prove fatal to their existence in Poland.

Around the middle of the century, Hungary also became the scene of a thriving Calvinism which soon displaced Lutheranism as the dominant Protestant faith. Here also the lords welcomed a non-German religion that provided for extensive lay involvement in the ecclesiastical structure. Under the influence of the reformer Matyas Devai Biró, who himself had made the transition from Lutheranism to Calvinism, Debrecen became the "Hungarian Geneva." Its

173

PORTRAIT: JAN LASKI

A strong supporter of Calvinism in Poland, he deplored the intolerance so often demonstrated by his co-religionists elsewhere. The failure of his attempts to unify Polish Protestantism signaled the end of effective opposition to Catholic attempts to reassert the traditional faith as dominant in the land.

Courtesy Lutherhalle, Wittenberg

bishop, Peter Melius Juhász, organized Calvinists in northeastern Hungary and gave them the Calvinist *Confessio Catholica* (1561). For twenty-five years Juhász served as bishop in Debrecen, and during that time he published numerous works, including partial translations of the Scriptures, a hymn book, and various polemical writings designed to strengthen Calvinism. Although doctrine closely paralleled that of John Calvin, church government, with retention of bishops, corresponded in that respect to Lutheranism. With secularization of church lands approved by the diet of 1557, the Transylvanian nobles also embraced Calvinism. In 1563, they adopted their own confessional statement; and in 1564, the diet approved local religious autonomy for both Calvinist and Lutheran towns, thus establishing Transylvania, like Poland, as a haven for religious nonconformists.

THE GROWTH OF ANTI-TRINITARIANISM

It was in this atmosphere of relative toleration, created largely by the inability of any one faith to gain the ascendancy, and conditioned by the ever present threat of Islam, that anti-trinitariansim flourished. This movement with its rejection of rigid dogma, stressed right actions rather than right belief. In 1562 anti-trinitarians set up their own church, the "Lesser Community." While some of the lords joined the movement, most members were drawn from the lower classes. Frequently, these radicals criticized social injustice and urged all people to be productive members of society. Converts to the movement were especially numerous in Poland and parts of Hungary. John Sigismund, prince of Transylvania, as well as Ferenc David, the leader of the Calvinists in that principality, joined the anti-trinitarians. Late in the sixteenth century, Fausto Sozzini (1539–1604) became the dominant figure among the anti-trinitarians, later to be known as Socinians. He prepared the Krakow catechism, which was published in 1605 and outlined the principles of this religion.

MOVEMENTS TOWARD TOLERATION

In the latter decades of the sixteenth century, some measure of unity was achieved among the various Protestant faiths in eastern Europe. In Bohemia, the *Confessio Bohemica* expressed the joint faith of Utraquists, Lutherans, and Bohemian Brethren. Its appearance in 1575 did not reflect a united Bohemian church, but rather an attempt to present a common front against Catholicism. In Poland, Calvinists and Bohemian Brethren gradually developed a working relationship, but Lutherans were more reluctant to enter into close association with other religious groups. Eventually, however, recognizing the political advantages to be gained through consolidated efforts, Lutherans, Calvinists, and Bohemian Brethren in Poland adopted the Consensus of Sandomir (1570). This agreement, while it did not establish a united Protestant church in Poland, did provide for united political action and occasional synods of the three bodies. The expected confessional cooperation remained largely a dead letter, for Polish Lutheranism, like its German counterpart, became increasingly uncompromising in the later 1570s.

With the death of Sigismund II, the Polish crown was offered to Henry of Anjou—but not before the diet had adopted the Confederation of Warsaw (1573), affirming religious liberty for everyone. This remarkable agreement declared that "as there is great discord in this kingdom touching the Christian religion, we promise, in order to avoid sedition such as has come to other kingdoms . . . that all of us of differing religions will keep the peace between ourselves and shed no blood."[10] The new king had to swear to uphold this charter of liberties, but scarcely had he done so when the vacancy on the French throne induced him to return to Paris. His successor, Stephen Bathory (1575—1586), upheld the Confederation and denounced efforts to extend a religion by means of "force, fire or sword." Rather than squander the nation's resources in internal strife, Bathory resolved to expand Polish frontiers. He forced Russia, then led by Ivan the

[10]Quoted in J. H. Elliott, *Europe Divided, 1559–1598* (New York: Harper & Row, A Harper Torchbook, 1968), p. 234.

Terrible, to cede large parts of Livonia to Poland. With the Muscovite danger removed, the king now made grandiose plans for a crusade against the Turks, but his death in 1586 ended this quest for Polish grandeur.

In Hungary the reign of Maximilian II (1564–1576) was characterized by a large measure of religious toleration. Since most Protestants adhered to the Heidelberg Catechism of 1563, they enjoyed a brief period of harmony. With the accession of Rudolf II, however, Protestantism was confronted with a vigorous Catholic champion. Throughout the rest of the century, Hungarian Protestants found themselves on the defensive.

Suggestions for Further Reading

Bergendoff, Conrad. *Olavus Petri and the Ecclesiastical Transformation of Sweden.* New York: Macmillan, 1928.

Dunkley, E. H. *The Reformation in Denmark.* London: S.P.C.K., 1948.

Fox, Paul. *The Reformation in Poland.* Baltimore: Johns Hopkins, 1924.

Garstein, Oscar. *Rome and the Counter Reformation in Scandinavia.* New York Oxford University Press, 1963.

Halecki, Oskar. *A History of Poland*, rev. ed. London: Dent, 1956.

———. *From Florence to Brèst.* Hamden, Conn: Archon Books, 1968.

Hoffmann, J. G. H. *La Réforme en Suède.* Paris: Delachaux et Niestlé, 1945.

Kot, Stanislaw. *Socinianism in Poland.* Translated by E. M. Wilbur. Boston: Starr King, 1957.

Larsen, Laren. *A History of Norway.* Princeton: Princeton University Press for the American-Scandinavian Foundation, 1948.

Mecenseffy, Grete. *Geschichte des Protestantismus in Oesterreich.* Graz: H. Boehlaus Nachf., 1956.

Murray, Robert. *Olavus Petri.* Stockholm: Svenska kyrkans diakonistyreleses bokfoerlag, 1952.

Reinerth, Karl. *Die Reformation der siebenbuergisch-saechsichen Kirche.* Guetersloh: Verein fuer Reformationsgeschichte, 1956.

Roberts, Michael. *The Early Vasas.* London: Cambridge University Press, 1968.

Schramm, Gottfried. *Der polnische Adel und die Reformation.* Wiesbaden: F. Steiner, 1965.

Szabo, J. S. *Der Protestantismus in Ungarn.* Translated by B. von Horvath. Berlin: Verlag des evangelischen Bundes, 1927.

Teutsch, F. *Geschichte der evangelischen Kirche in Siebenbuergen*, 2 vols. Hermannstadt: W. Krafft, 1921–22.

Waddams, H. M. *The Swedish Church.* London: S.P.C.K., 1946.

Yelverton, E. E. *The Manual of Olavus Petri.* London: S.P.C.K., 1953.

———. *An Archbishop of the Reformation, Laurentius Petri.* Minneapolis: Augsburg, 1959.

9

The Reformation in England

For England, the sixteenth century was characterized by dynamic tensions and creative outpourings of energy. It was a time of building, of accelerated growth, of exploring new dimensions. As the century dawned, the nation was still binding up the wounds of the Wars of the Roses; by the time the last of the Tudors had passed from the scene, however, the English, now passionately devoted to their queen, viewed the future with a confidence and pride born of the successes with which the nation had met both the internal and external challenges of the century. Despite religious turmoil and economic unrest (such as that occasioned by the enclosures), the era was characterized by confidence and optimism. The old aristocracy had met the buoyant, new commercial interests and there emerged a people who had all the marks of future greatness.

EARLY REFORM MOVEMENTS

Long before Henry VIII's break with the papacy, various elements in England threatened allegiance to Rome. Religious, economic, and intellectual factors were awaiting fortuitous political developments.

At the beginning of the sixteenth century, although Wycliffe had been dead for well over a century, his followers, the persecuted Lollards, persisted. Wycliffe had attacked the papacy, the wealth of the church, and a variety of abuses in the church. Powerful nobles protected him from angered ecclesiastical leaders. By 1500, the Lollards' numerical strength was uncertain; while the Reformation martyrologist John Foxe was probably overly optimistic when he spoke of the "secret multitude," Lollardy continued in a number of organized congregations and remained strong enough to be a concern of religious and civil leaders. Lollards were especially numerous in Buckinghamshire, but frequently heresy trials in London, Kent, Essex, Berkshire, and many other areas showed that dissent was not confined to any particular area. Though the movement had become largely amorphous and no longer possessed a uniform body of doctrine, its adherents retained their emphasis on the Scriptures and their determined anti-clericalism. Lollardy or a similar movement was certain to continue in a land where many believed that church privileges were excessive, ecclesiastical jurisdiction overbearing and preemptive, monetary obligations to the church unwarranted, and the lives of the overwhelming majority of clerics less than exemplary.

Discontent with the traditional religion drew much of its support from the craftsmen and town-laborers. It was augmented by the increasingly influential merchant class, which resented not only the wealth of the church, but also the church's otherworldly stance on such issues as commercial enterprise per se, the taking of interest, and the exalted status of vocations not concerned with material acquisition. Lutheranism arose, and England's geographical proximity to the continent brought about a natural mingling of Lollard and Lutheran views. Although England's thriving trade with the continent was centered in London, other towns such as Cambridge also served as terminal ports for the Hansa trade. Repeatedly, as Bishop Tunstall lamented in 1523, Lutheranism was adding "new arms"[1] to Lollardy.

By 1519 Lutheran literature had achieved a sizable audience throughout England, and in 1521 Thomas Wolsey, cardinal, papal legate, Archbishop of York, and Chancellor of the Realm ordered his bishops to confiscate Lutheran books. Meanwhile, a group of Cambridge humanists met regularly in the White Horse Tavern, soon dubbed "Little Germany," to discuss Lutheran teachings. In 1525 one of the members, Robert Barnes, prior of the Augustinians at Cambridge, preached a sermon that brought about charges of heresy. After trial and imprisonment, he fled to the continent. In all likelihood, the circle also included William Tyndale, who translated the New Testament into English; Hugh Latimer, later a Protestant bishop; and John Frith. Ironically, the latter was appointed to teach at Oxford, in Wolsey's college. When, in 1528, the cardinal learned that his foundation was being used to disseminate Lutheran views, Frith and his associates were arrested and imprisoned. Wolsey permitted Frith to go into exile on the continent. From here he continued his literary attack on English opponents of Luther and his defense of Protestant views.

No member of the Cambridge or Oxford Protestant groups would be more influential in the early English Reformation than William Tyndale.[2] After studies at both Oxford and Cambridge, he attempted unsuccessfully to enlist the support of Cuthbert Tunstall, bishop of London, in preparing a vernacular translation of the Scriptures. The bishop, like many other reform-minded humanists, looked askance at an act that might play into the hands of the Lollards. Disappointed,

---

[1] Quoted in A. G. Dickens, *The English Reformation* (New York: Schocken, 1964), p. 37.

[2] For an analysis of the impact of Tyndale and his associates, see William A. Clebsch, *England's Earliest Protestants, 1520–1535* (New Haven: Yale University Press, 1964).

Tyndale left for Wittenberg in 1524. Two years later, in Worms, he published the first printed English translation of the New Testament, a work that was smuggled into England and widely distributed. In the following years, Tyndale collaborated with Miles Coverdale in translating parts of the Old Testament. In 1536, his literary production, which included unsolicited advice to King Henry and an exposition of his contract theory of government, came to an abrupt end. The long arm of Sir Thomas More, spanning the channel, had secured his execution in the Netherlands as a heretic.

Long before the death of Tyndale, however, steps had been taken to halt the spread of Lutheranism in England. In 1526 some merchants in the Hansa district of London were tried for propagating the continental heresy. Prohibitions, trials, and Wolsey's public burning of Luther's writings followed, all to no effect. An increasing number of authorities shared the alarm of William Warham, archbishop of Canterbury, that parts of the realm were "infected with Lutheranism."

ENGLISH HUMANISTS

The reform movement in England, as on the continent, received support from numerous humanists. Among the distinguished array of scholars who vigorously denounced corruption in the church were Thomas More, John Colet, Reginald Pole, and Bishop Tunstall. Like Erasmus, they championed the new learning and welcomed the emphasis on biblical and patristic studies, but they had no desire to challenge Catholic dogma. Thus when Luther issued his program for reform of the church, they held that the cure was worse than the disease. And later, when Bugenhagen addressed an appeal to Englishmen to join the Reformation (1525), More ridiculed the suggestion—the continental reformers had only degraded that which was holy and had themselves become corrupt and degenerate.

More's confidence in the loyalty of his countrymen to the one true church was dealt a shattering blow by the king himself. The uncompromising champion of Catholicism saw Christian principles yield to expediency as Henry's matrimonial problems led to his repudiation of papal authority. A bitterly disappointed More found that his former royal patron was now his—and his church's—most deadly foe.

THE YOUNG HENRY

King Henry VIII (1509–1547) had earlier provided a receptive atmosphere for humanist endeavor within the framework of traditional loyalty to church and pope. When Luther attacked various sacraments, Henry responded with his "Defense of the Seven Sacraments"—an effort the pope rewarded by bestowing on him the title, "Defender of the Faith." However, the king was soon to find that his chief problems did not stem from the theology of Wittenberg.

Henry's early career illustrates his love of power and popularity. Shortly after

PORTRAIT: HENRY VIII, after Holbein

The historian Bishop William Stubbs described Henry as "a man of unbounded selfishness." Various contemporaries, however, while noting that the king was adequately endowed with egotism, applauded his determination to unify the realm and remove all foreign control.

National Portrait Gallery

ascending the throne he invited complaints from all who believed themselves to have been subjected to extortion in the previous reign. Subsequently two of the King's counselors were sent to the scaffold, although they had been no more than efficient royal servants. The new monarch also resolved to stand high in the councils of nations. In 1511, he indulged his desire for glory by joining the papacy, Spain, and Naples in their Holy League against France. Early English failures drove Henry personally to lead his troops in the invasion of France.

Here, in 1513, he won the "Battle of the Spurs," and gained several noted prisoners as well as several towns. At the same time, England met and defeated the Scots at Flodden Field, leaving ten thousand Scots, including James IV (1488–1513), dead on the battle ground. The Scottish threat had been removed for the greater part of Henry's reign. In negotiations after the French defeat (1514), Henry demonstrated that he had quickly become a master of treacherous diplomacy: He gained Tournai, wrested an increased annual subsidy from France, and married his sister Mary to King Louis XII. Henry's allies, who had tried to make peace behind his back, found that their partner was well able to safeguard his own interests.

The French war also produced an astonishingly adroit and successful royal minister, Thomas Wolsey, who from 1515 to 1529 dominated English affairs. In addition to holding the highest office under the crown, Wolsey also filled the second highest ecclesiastical post, and was cardinal and papal legate. Significantly, all these powers were the direct result of royal favor, so when that essential element was withdrawn, the cardinal, in Shakespeare's graphic phrase, was left "naked to [his] enemies."

During the period of his ascendancy, Wolsey was plagued by financial worries. His personal interests, including the construction of Hampton Court Palace and the establishment of a college at Oxford, required strong financial support, yet he found that heavy financial exactions stimulated anti-clericalism and fed the flames of religious revolt.

In 1519 he brought England into the Hapsburg-Valois rivalry. In supporting Charles in his attempt to become emperor, Wolsey hoped that a grateful Hapsburg would aid him in his papal aspirations—but these hopes were repeatedly disappointed. An attempt at better relations between France and England led to the lavish pageantry of the "Field of the Cloth of Gold," where Henry and Francis engaged in good-natured joustings. In 1521, however, the first Hapsburg-Valois conflict disrupted Wolsey's hope for peaceful manipulation of the respective rulers. England, as an ally of the Empire, became embroiled in a futile struggle. Hard pressed to finance English forces in the attack upon France, Wolsey attempted to override Parliament's denial of funds and to levy his own tribute, but armed resistance compelled him to abandon such a policy. The imperial victory at Pavia (1525) left Francis a prisoner but gave Wolsey nothing. The cardinal concluded his own peace with France, and gained increased subsidies for himself and the king.

In 1526, the versatile Wolsey turned the tables and forged an alliance with France in the Treaty of Cognac. He was apparently well aware of the danger of allowing one ruler to dominate the continent, but uppermost in his mind was the attempt to gain papal favor. The league proved to be a dismal failure, and in 1527, a mutinous imperial army assailed Rome. Pope Clement VII was at the mercy of the emperor. Wolsey's policy of vacillating between emperor and pope

PORTRAIT: THOMAS WOLSEY

Able, ambitious, and arrogant, Wolsey met with almost uninterrupted personal success until he failed to gain papal approval for the dissolution of his king's marriage. His tragedy is not inaccurately reflected in his words in Shakespeare's *Henry VIII:*

Had I but serv'd my God with half the zeal
I serv'd my king, he would not in mine age
Have left me naked to mine enemies.

National Portrait Gallery

had failed to fulfill the cardinal's ambitions. And by 1527 Wolsey, because of "the king's great matter," desperately needed the support of both the pope and emperor.

With the pope a virtual prisoner of the emperor, Wolsey attempted to establish himself as a deputy pope, until Clement should be free. Only four cardinals indicated support of the desperate gesture. The complete triumph of Charles was apparent when he and Francis signed the peace of Cambrai in August, 1529. Wolsey, ally of Francis, was not even consulted. Wolsey's pursuit of glory abroad had ended in failure; two months later, he had fallen from power, unable to satisfy the king's demands for an annulment of his marriage to Catherine of Aragon.

HENRY'S MARITAL DILEMMA

The king's determination to end his marriage with Catherine stemmed from a series of events and expectations. Henry had long wanted a male heir, and had even considered special action to legitimize his natural son the Duke of Richmond. Queen Catherine had borne Henry a number of children, but only Mary lived beyond infancy. Henry, convinced that a nation so recently involved in the Wars of the Roses needed a strong male heir, hoped to resolve the problem by marrying Anne Boleyn, with whom he had fallen passionately in love. Also, Henry contended that his failure to obtain a male heir proved divine displeasure with a marriage that had been contrary to canon law, for Catherine had, a year prior to her marriage to Henry, been the wife of the King's older brother, Arthur. A special papal dispensation of 1503 allowed her to become the wife of Henry. Increasingly convinced that Catherine had never really been his wife, Henry charged Wolsey with the responsibility of obtaining such a declaration from the pope.

But Pope Clement was in no position to grant the king's wish. To do so would be to invalidate the act of an earlier pope. Furthermore, Charles V now dominant in Italy, staunchly supported his aunt, Queen Catherine. Clement, hard pressed from all sides, bargained for time. He sent Cardinal Campeggio and his legate to assist Wolsey in examining the case, hoping that Catherine might resolve the problem by entering a monastery, or that Henry might be persuaded to change his position. But the efforts were futile, and Clement ordered the case transferred to Rome. The failure of Wolsey to execute the king's wish presented the occasion for destroying the great cardinal's power. No doubt Henry had for some time looked askance at his too powerful chancellor who spoke of ''I and my king,'' and who was popularly regarded as the real ruler of the realm. In October, 1529, Wolsey was dismissed and indicted for having abused his legatine powers. A year later he was arrested and charged with high treason for having attempted to involve the king of France in Henry's troubles. Enroute to his trial, the disgraced and broken cardinal died.

Even before his repudiation of Wolsey, Henry had more than once intimated that he might find it necessary to adopt some of the anti-papal procedures of continental Lutheran rulers. He now resolved to champion strong sentiments of anti-clericalism and opposition to foreign interference. Henry found that his anti-papal posture was widely acclaimed, and that forces of opposition were weak and disorganized.

Henry's chosen vehicle of action was Parliament. When it met in November, 1529, no one could foresee the revolution which this "Reformation Parliament" would carry out within the next six years. Inexorably, under the skillful leadership of the king and his astute ministers, Parliament moved to assert royal supremacy in the church.

REFORMATION BY LEGISLATION

The Reformation Parliament was ushered in by a vigorous attack upon Wolsey by the new chancellor, Sir Thomas More. This outcry paved the way for a crescendo of often vituperative outbursts against the clergy that, from the first session, intimidated the bishops and abbots who consitutued half the membership of the Lords. Henry reasoned that pressure on the clergy would induce the pope to change his mind, but to no avail. The king then tried to gain added support by seeking the opinions of numerous foreign universities, but such tactics proved of little consequence, for even Wittenberg refused to support Henry; other tactics would have to be used.

In 1530, Henry launched a frontal assault on the English clergy via the medieval Statute of Praemunire. This act, designed to protect the rights of English bishops from excessive papal claims, was subsequently expanded by the courts until, as the imperial ambassador noted, its interpretation lay "solely in the king's head." Now, this flexible weapon was directed against the English clergy because they had aided Wolsey's illegal actions by contributing financially to him as legate. The clergy, meeting in Convocation, secured the king's pardon only after paying heavy subsidies (£100,000 was contributed by the Convocation of Canterbury and £18,840 by the Convocation of York), and recognizing Henry as "protector, single and supreme lord, and, as far as the law of Christ allows, even Supreme Head" of the English church.

Having successfully manipulated English national pride and anti-clericalism for his own use, Henry now sought an able, ambitious, and unscrupulous architect to provide the legal framework for a state church. These qualities he found in Thomas Cromwell, a protégé of Wolsey who demonstrated a resourcefulness that would have done credit to his former master. As one of the "new men" of the Tudor era, Cromwell had served in several capacities under Wolsey. When the cardinal fell, Cromwell adroitly shifted his allegiance, retained the royal favor, and entered the Commons. By 1531, he was a member of the king's council, soon to become chancellor of the exchequer and principal secretary, in addition to acquiring various other positions.

In 1532, Cromwell, directing the royal attack on the legislative independence of the church, drafted a document entitled the "Supplication of the Commons against the Ordinaries,''[3] which charged the clergy with a wide range of offenses against the people of England. Church officials were accused of nepotism, of undermining the royal prerogative, of imposing excessive fees, and of abusing the power of excommunication, among other things. In the ensuing deliberations, the king urged that ecclesiastical law be brought into harmony with royal law, and that no new church ordinances be issued without royal assent. The King achieved his ends on May 15, when English ecclesiastics laid before him a statement, the Submission of the Clergy,[4] in which Archbishop Warham also acquiesced. The king was now the supreme legislator of the English church, but he had lost the services of one of his most competent ministers—on May 16, Thomas More had resigned as chancellor. Henry kept pressure on the papacy, and early in 1533 the pope agreed to accept Henry's nominee, Thomas Cranmer, as archbishop of Canterbury, even though Cranmer was already married.

With the English clergy thoroughly subdued, Henry, in 1533, launched a direct attack on the papacy when Parliament passed the Act in Restraint of Appeals.[5] The crown, not the pope, was empowered to render final judgment in ecclesiastical matters. Archbishop Cranmer set up his own court to rule on the king's marriage and promptly annulled it. Anne Boleyn, whom Henry had married in January, 1533, was now crowned queen. Then, with the passage in 1534 of the Act in Restraint of Annates,[6] Henry seized the chief source of papal revenue in the kingdom. He further consolidated his position with the passage of two acts that year, one to deprive the pope of legal rights in England, the other—the Act of Supremacy[7]—to reassert more emphatically Henry's position as head of the church. The First Succession Act,[8] with implicit rejection of papal supremacy, declared it treason to reject the validity of Henry's second marriage. Sir Thomas More, denouncing the act as ''repugnant to the laws of God and his holy church,''[9] refused to take an oath supporting the act; he and John Fisher, the erudite bishop of Rochester, were executed. Others, including a number of Carthusians, were also sent to the gallows, but the vast majority of clergymen submitted. When the newly elected Pope Paul III excommunicated Henry (1534), the king reflected a widely shared confidence when he declared he would not care if the pope issued ten thousand excommunications. Erastian principles had triumphed completely; the English church was now at the mercy of the state. Both spiritual and temporal authority rested ultimately with the monarch, while the definition of treason was repeatedly expanded to include a wide range of

[3]Henry Gee and William J. Hardy, eds., *Documents Illustrative of English Church History* (London: Macmillan, 1910), pp. 145–153.

[4]*Ibid.*, pp. 176–178.

[5]A. G. Dickens and Dorothy Carr, *The Reformation in England* (New York: St. Martin's, 1968), pp. 55–57.

[6]An annate is a payment owed the pope upon the appointment of a bishop to his see.

[7]Gee and Hardy, *Documents,* pp. 243–244.

[8]*Ibid.*, pp. 232–243.

[9]Dickens and Carr, *Reformation in England,* p. 71.

offenses against either the state or the church.[10] Equally important, the king had ministers who knew how to make practical use of the royal supremacy.

THE ATTACK ON THE MONASTERIES

By the mid-1530s, Thomas Cromwell was ready to move against the monasteries. Here was an obvious source of wealth for the depleted royal purse. The monasteries had offered little firm resistance to royal supremacy—Carthusians and the strict Franciscans were the exception—but their cooperative attitude did not deter Cromwell from pursuing easy prey. By now, most monastic estates had been leased to members of the gentry. Only in some parts of northern England did houses still significantly function as necessary centers of hospitality and poor relief. Elsewhere, they often served as comfortable inns where the influential could be entertained. To a highly practical man such as Cromwell, the monasteries no longer presented a serious challenge to the king's anti-papal program— for the monks had submitted easily enough; rather they were an untapped source of royal income. England's defenses badly needed strengthening against a threat from Spain; the French pension had been discontinued and troubles in Ireland further depleted the treasury. The king's chief minister shrewdly concluded that it would be easier to confiscate monastic properties than to persuade Parliament to vote for higher taxes.

Pretexts for dissolution were easily found. Earlier, ardent foes of clerical privilege had launched vigorous attacks upon those whom the pamphleteer Simon Fish described as "ravenous wolves" who were "devouring the flock." His *Supplication for the Beggars*[11] accused the "holy idle thieves" of having acquired the choicest parts of the realm, of deliberately suppressing knowledge of the Scriptures, and of perverting justice by abusing clerical influence. The expression of such sentiments was now officially encouraged by the king's ministers. Examiners were sent to monasteries and returned with reports of scandal and corruption that only corroborated the observations of earlier visitors. But this time the accounts of lecherous monks and corrupt practices were designed not to reform abuses, but to destroy the houses. Selective dissolution had occurred earlier, as when Wolsey dissolved several monasteries; now systematic confiscation was envisioned.

In 1536, Parliament was informed of the monastic "enormities," and used this pretext to justify swift action. One act provided for the dissolution of the

---

[10]Something of the bewildering nature of the redefinitions of treason is suggested by the fact that the First Succession Act (1534) declared it treason to question the validity of Henry's marriage to Anne Boleyn, but the Second Succession Act (1536) asserted that to recognize the Boleyn marriage as lawful would now be regarded as treason (J. R. Tanner, *Tudor Constitutional Documents* [London: Cambridge University Press, 1951], pp. 378–395).

[11]Lewis W. Spitz, ed., *The Protestant Reformation* (Englewood Cliffs, N.J.: Prentice-Hall, 1966), pp. 148–151.

more than 300 houses with annual incomes of less than £ 200.[12] Why only the smaller houses deserved extinction remained unclear. Another act established a Court of Augmentations to transfer properties to the crown. Monks were moved to other houses or given pensions or benefices.

DISSOLUTION AND REBELLION

During the process of monastic dissolution, Cromwell's policies were challenged by a series of revolts known collectively as the "Pilgrimage of Grace." The latter part of 1536 saw rebellion in Lincolnshire, Yorkshire, Lancashire, and several other counties. Inspired in part by religious uncertainty, wild rumors, and fear of Cromwell's policies, the uprisings drew powerful stimuli from economic distress. Robert Aske, a principal leader of the insurgents, expressed fears of economic deprivation should monastic lands revert to absentee landlords, while other rebels denounced some of Cromwell's judicial processes and his extension of monarchial supremacy. Having made various promises to the insurgents, King Henry persuaded the largest contingent to disperse. Subsequently, the king's lieutenants systematically executed more than two hundred participants, including Aske. The safety of the realm was apparently a more compelling factor than a solemn promise to disloyal subjects.

The Pilgrimage served only to delay, not to halt, Cromwell's work. Since no significant support for the revolt had come from the populous and powerful south of England, the king proceeded to reinforce his authority more directly in the north. Finally, in 1539, Parliament provided for the dissolution of the remaining monasteries. Frequently, the seizure of these properties was accompanied by pillage of shrines, such as that of Becket at Canterbury, or by destruction of libraries and works of art.

The sweeping secularization of monastic properties profoundly affected the social structure of the kingdom. Most of the confiscated wealth flowed into the king's treasury, which was augmented by more than £ 100,000 annually, a sum that was approximately equal to total crown revenue when Cromwell began his ministry. Other new found monies were used to endow six new sees and to establish or expand numerous grammar and cathedral schools, as well as to found Trinity College at Cambridge and to complete Christchurch at Oxford. At both universities five Regius professorships were established. Much of the seized property was sold or given to members of the nobility and gentry, thus further strengthening the position of the crown. The exclusion of abbots from the House of Lords dealt a strong blow to clerical influence in politics.

Suppression of the monasteries only temporarily alleviated royal economic pressures. As elsewhere in Europe, England was feeling the impact of substantial inflation. Problems of population growth, accentuated by largely static produc-

[12]*Ibid.*, pp. 98–102.

tion and coupled with the influx of precious metals from the New World, occasioned a great deal of agrarian and urban discontent. Also, the continued demand for wool encouraged enclosures and added to rural depopulation, dislocation, and distress. Other measures, such as rack-renting and increasing competition among tenant farmers brought about by higher farm prices did not help to alleviate the situation. Occasionally, from 1526 until 1551, the government attempted to increase its income by debasing the currency. Devaluation, however, raised prices disastrously and worked great hardships on the whole realm. Belatedly, such measures came to be recognized as nonproductive and self-defeating. Much of the support gained by the Pilgrimage was directly related to these economic pressures, which, coupled with religious fervor and uncertainty, were quite enough to create upheaval.

THE UNCERTAIN REFORMATION

During the last decade of Henry's reign, England witnessed an intense struggle between those who wished to make the nation more thoroughly Protestant and those who wished to retain Catholic doctrine, even without papal supremacy. This conflict was complicated by the ever present threat of foreign intervention. Henry himself was deeply suspicious of doctrinal change, and repeatedly asserted his adherence to the traditional faith. Archbishop Cranmer, much more inclined toward Lutheranism, was caught in the uncomfortable and perilous middle, as was Thomas Cromwell. Opposed to them was a powerful group of conservative officials and courtiers led by the Duke of Norfolk and Stephen Gardiner, Bishop of Winchester. The issue was not one of recognition of royal supremacy—that had been accepted by both groups—rather it was the shape reform doctrines were to assume, as well as conflicting personal ambition, that locked the antagonists in mortal combat.

In 1540, Norfolk and Gardiner gained a significant victory when they destroyed Cromwell. The fall of this unquestioningly loyal minister was intricately associated with foreign policy. When, in 1533, an alliance between Francis I and Charles V appeared likely, Cromwell sought to ensure England's position through an alliance with the League of Schmalkald. But the price demanded by the German Lutheran princes—financial support and adherence to the Augsburg Confession—proved too high. The king was determined to control his own reformation. His opposition to Lutheran doctrine was expressed in the Six Articles Act,[13] written in part by Henry himself and passed by Parliament in 1539. It reaffirmed basic Catholic beliefs such as transubstantiation, communion in one kind, clerical celibacy, and auricular confession. Severe penalties were provided for violators, for the king was resolved to crush nonconformity. Some bishops resigned their sees in protest, while Cranmer returned his wife to her family in

[13]Gee and Hardy, *Documents,* pp. 303–319.

Germany. Norfolk and Gardiner had scored a resounding triumph. Cromwell, still convinced that alliances with continental powers were essential, now urged upon Henry marriage with Anne of Cleves. The king, who in part had been deceived by a flattering portrait painted by Holbein, was thoroughly disillusioned when he first met the "Flemish mare." Within a few months, Henry proceeded to have the marriage annulled. Simultaneously, the Duke of Norfolk interested the king in Catherine Howard. Both she and the late Anne Boleyn were Norfolk's nieces; Anne had been beheaded and Catherine would suffer a similar fate in little more than a year. In the meantime, however, Norfolk and Gardiner had succeeded in their mission. Easily persuaded, Henry listened to charges of heresy and treason against the loyal Cromwell and without a trial, executed him by act of attainder. The conservative faction gained little by the event, but the king had lost his most industrious and capable servant.

Despite the sacrifice of Cromwell, Henry had no intention of allowing the conservatives to dominate his policies. With serene impartiality the king sent to the block those who seemed to tend too strongly toward either Catholicism or continental Protestantism. With the execution of Queen Catherine, Norfolk found his own influence sharply reduced. His pitiful attempt to retain royal favor by joining in the condemnation of his niece failed to convince Henry. Clearly, the king would remain undaunted in his attempt to lead his nation along a *via media*.

Throughout the latter part of Henry's reign, Archbishop Cranmer remained the most influential of the reformers. In Convocation, he found himself decidedly in a minority, but the royal favor provided a more than adequate counterbalance. When Cranmer was charged with heresy the king jestingly informed the archbishop that he had discovered "the greatest heretic in Kent" and placed him in charge of the investigation.

Among the more noteworthy of the archbishop's achievements was his distribution of the Bible in English translation. Commonly called the Great Bible, it was a revision by Miles Coverdale of the earlier version largely prepared by Tyndale. In the preface, Cranmer asserted that "it is convenient and good [for] the Scripture to be read [by] all sorts and kinds of people, and in the vulgar tongue."[14] The king ordered a copy placed in each parish church (1541). A few years later the archbishop prepared an English litany, which Henry ordered used throughout the kingdom. Later, this would form part of the *Book of Common Prayer*, a work that was virtually complete when Henry, with his trusted archbishop at his side, died in 1547. The king's confidence in Cranmer, however, was not to be viewed as a repudiation of traditional belief. The crafty monarch was taking no chances—his will provided for the saying of masses for his soul "for ever perpetually."[15]

[14]Quoted in Spitz, *The Protestant Reformation,* p. 167.
[15]Quoted in Lacey B. Smith, *Henry VIII, the Mask of Royalty* (Boston: Houghton Mifflin, 1971), p. 268.

EDWARD VI: REFORMATION THROUGH
PROTECTOR AND ARCHBISHOP

Henry left the crown of a mourning nation to his nine-year-old son Edward and to a Council of Regency he had appointed a month before his death. Remarkably, ardent champions of the conservative position, such as Bishop Gardiner, were excluded. Real power was quickly grasped by the Earl of Hertford, soon to be made Duke of Somerset. As Protector and advocate of Protestantism, he had Parliament enact legislation that removed numerous restrictions on Reformation practices. The harsh features Henry had incorporated in the Treasons Act were abolished, as was the statute *De Haeretico Comburendo*, which provided for the burning of heretics. Further parliamentary action voided both the Six Articles Act and restrictions on printing and teaching the Scriptures. Communion in both kinds was declared the law of the land. England temporarily became a sanctuary of persecuted continental Protestants.

Somerset proceeded vigorously to increase his power by further secularizing church properties. A Chantries Act of 1545 had provided for royal seizure of the chantries—endowments that provided for masses for the dead. This act was expanded in 1547[16] and enforced throughout the realm. Dispossessed chantry priests were awarded pensions, but most of the wealth went to support education. Thomas Becon, one of the reformers involved in the confiscation, became the first Englishman to press for the founding of schools for girls.

In such an atmosphere, Cranmer was able to pursue his reformation of the English church. The first prayer book, enforced by the Act of Uniformity of 1549,[17] became the only accepted form of worship. Cranmer deliberately avoided sharp attacks on Catholic doctrine to facilitate its acceptance by most Englishmen. Designed to preserve old practices which Cranmer did not regard as contrary to Scripture, the liturgy was the reformer's attempt to avoid the bitter doctrinal controversies even then plaguing the continent. At the same time, numerous Protestant pamphleteers and propagandists seized the opportunity provided by the tolerant attitude of Somerset. Raucous drama, poetry, and diatribe ridiculed the Catholic doctrines. Writers such as Thomas Becon produced works that gained wide popularity. Hugh Latimer, leader of the "Commonwealth Men," combined fervent defense of Protestantism with scathing denunciation of social injustice, as graphically recorded in his "Sermon of the Plowers"[18] (1548).

While Somerset was busily engaged in advancing Cranmer's reformation ideals, serious peasant uprisings in 1549 threatened the tranquility of the realm. A rebellion in Devon and Cornwall was crushed by German mercenaries. More

---

[16]Dickens and Carr, *Reformation in England*, pp. 127–130.

[17]*Ibid.*, pp. 132–135.

[18]Allan G. Chester, ed., *Selected Sermons of Hugh Latimer* (Charlottesville: University of Virginia Press, 1968), pp. 28–49.

PORTRAIT: HUGH LATIMER, by unknown artist

A fervent champion of religious and social reform, Latimer refused to accommodate himself to every whim of Henry VIII. He was imprisoned when he refused to support the Six Articles, but was released upon the accession of Edward VI. He remained a prominent and eloquent spokesman for reform until he was again imprisoned in the reign of Mary.

National Portrait Gallery

serious was the revolt in Norfolk, led by Thomas Kett. The rebels were inspired by economic grievances, especially the pressures of enclosures. Eloquent preachers, such as Matthew Parker, the later archbishop, gained rousing support for demands that "all bondmen may be made free," and that privileges of the clergy be restricted.

With Kett's forces approaching 12,000, it became apparent that Somerset would have to act. Although the insurgents professed their allegiance to the Reformation—they used the new prayer book and assembled under the "Oak of

Reformation''—they were nonetheless rebels. Ironically, Somerset had all along been a champion of the lower classes, having fought for tenants' rights and the regulation of enclosures, both before Parliament and by means of commissions to protect tenants' rights. But now, with rebellion in the land, the man who had antagonized many powerful nobles through these actions was compelled to use force to crush Kett and his supporters.

The whole affair was enough to discredit Somerset. In 1549 he was removed from power, and the earl of Warwick, soon to be duke of Northumberland, ascended the treacherous summit of power. Popular support for the fallen Somerset convinced Northumberland that his predecessor would have to be eliminated. A charge of treason served as a pretext for the execution of an enigmatic duke whose championing of the poor and powerless had alienated those who held real power.

During the ascendancy of Northumberland, the drive toward Protestantism was intensified. Cranmer strengthened his ties with continental reformers, especially those of Zurich, Geneva, and Strasbourg, and invited many to come to England in hopes of developing a form of Protestantism that would be acceptable to the various branches. From Italy came Peter Martyr Vermigli, who was appointed professor at Oxford, and Bernardino Ochino, once leader of the Capuchins and chaplain to Charles V, now recipient of a prebend at Canterbury. Martin Bucer, whose position had been made untenable by the emperor's defeat of the Protestants, came from Strasbourg to teach at Cambridge. Another reformer to transfer his activities to England was John Knox. In keeping with his penchant for impulsive and fearless pronouncements, he did not hesitate to denounce the execution of Somerset. Northumberland decided, however, not to accept the challenge of the thundering Scot.

Some of the immigrants directly assisted Cranmer in shaping the beliefs and practices of the English church. Their influence was apparent in the 1552 revision of the prayer book, in the second Edwardian Act of Uniformity (which made weekly church attendance obligatory), and in the Forty-Two Articles (1553). This confession of faith, not only outlined the basic tenets of acceptable belief, but contained numerous attacks on Catholicism and Anabaptism. The articles asserted such common Protestant doctrines as justification by faith and the authority of Scriptures; they rejected purgatory, the invocation of saints, and transubstantiation, and generally followed a conciliatory policy where Lutheranism and Calvinism differed.

THE RESTORATION OF PAPAL AUTHORITY

On July 6, 1553, King Edward died, leaving Northumberland in a precarious position. The duke's late drive to strip churches of their movable wealth, such as plate and vestments, had enraged many moderates. Then, his futile attempt to retain power by securing the succession of Lady Jane Grey rather than Princess

Mary antagonized most Englishmen. Popular support for the daughter of Henry VIII proved stronger than any reservations because of religion. Mary was duly proclaimed queen, while Northumberland, together with others of his coterie, was sent to the tower.

For five troubled years, Mary attempted a restoration of the faith to which she had passionately clung throughout her life. Protestant leaders, including Cranmer, Ridley, and Latimer, were imprisoned and burned, and an Act of Repeal[19] voided the religious policies enacted under Edward VI. In enforcing the act, Mary found that she was able to restore Catholic bishops to their posts. However, when it came to restoring church lands, religious fancy might be indulged, but not at the expense of recently acquired possessions. Similarly, Parliament refused at this juncture to grant Mary's request that royal supremacy be rescinded.

Domestic religious problems were soon complicated by foreign issues. When the queen indicated her desire to marry Philip II of Spain, Parliament—and many other Englishmen—expressed strong apprehension about such an alliance. Even ardent supporters of Mary's religious policy, such as Chancellor Gardiner, vigorously opposed the venture. But to no avail—Mary was resolved to have her marriage. The specter of Spanish domination, coupled with a dislike of the queen's religious policies, and secret encouragement by the French ambassador Noailles, was enough to arouse rebellion. Early in 1554, Sir Thomas Wyatt, with 4,000 supporters from Kent, marched on London. When members of the London militia joined the rebels, the queen's position was imperiled. But she was a woman of resolution. Supported largely by those who had held power under Northumberland, the queen was rescued and the rebels dispersed. Wyatt, with perhaps a hundred of his followers, was executed.

The queen's victory enhanced her position and gave her increased popular sympathy. The unfortunate Lady Jane Grey was now executed and Princess Elizabeth sent to the Tower. In July, 1554, Philip II arrived to celebrate his marriage with the queen. Then, in November, Reginald Pole, cardinal and papal legate, and Cranmer's successor as Archbishop of Canterbury, returned to England. Parliament, professing its contrition, was granted absolution. England and Rome were reconciled. Parliament now proceeded to repeal the Henrician anti-papal statutes,[20] although it was understood that confiscated lands would not be restored. Laws against heresy and treason were restored and expanded, and by February, 1555, the long procession to the stake began.

During the next three and one half years, almost three hundred people were burned for heresy. Among them were Bishops Cranmer, Latimer, Ridley, Hooper, and Ferrar. Most of the victims were from the working classes of society; many of the more prosperous heretics could emigrate. The pathetic

---

[19]Dickens and Carr, *Reformation in England*, pp. 143–144.
[20]*Ibid.*, pp. 149–154.

ENGRAVING: THE BURNING OF CRANMER, from John Foxe, *Book of Martyrs*

Tried and condemned to death in the church of St. Mary the Virgin in Oxford, he recanted, then repudiated his recantation. He vowed that, since his right hand had "offended, writing contrary to my heart, . . . it shall be first burned." The martyrologist Foxe reported that the archbishop kept his word.

Courtesy Rare Books Department, University of California Library, Los Angeles

spectacle of the burnings aroused widespread sympathy, for while the holocaust was nothing unusual when compared to contemporary events on the continent, it was unprecedented in English history. Expressions of popular revulsion forced the government to make demonstrations of sympathy a capital offense. Despite warnings of serious alienation as a result of the executions, Cardinal Pole and the queen, seconded by Chancellor Gardiner and Bishop Bonner, resolved to purge the realm. But a policy designed to eradicate the last vestiges of Protestantism simply intensified Englishmen's devotion to it. Many who had viewed the Reformation with indifference now became its champions. And in the minds of the people ecclesiastical tyranny and the papacy became inseparable. When at last the fires of Smithfield were extinguished, they left a legacy of fanatical antipathy toward the papacy.

Mary's last years were times of unmitigated frustration and disillusionment. Her husband quarreled with Pope Paul IV. Cardinal Pole, despite his furious drive to root out Protestantism, found himself summoned to Rome to answer charges of heresy.[21] England was dragged into the war between France and Spain. Calais, last stronghold of England's medieval French empire, fell in 1558. Although the queen bitterly mourned the loss, the nation blamed Mary and her Spanish advisers. By the time of her death in November, 1558, the queen had effectively destroyed allegiance to herself, her religion, and her alliance. A relieved nation learned of her death and waited expectantly for the reign of Elizabeth.

THE ELIZABETHAN SETTLEMENT

When the last of the Tudors ascended the throne in 1558, the pattern of future English Reformation history was far from clear. Numerous variables, both internal and external, precluded any simple prediction of the new monarch's course. Just across the channel, Spanish armies were demonstrating ever greater determination to carry out Philip's resolve to banish heresy. With the treaty of Cateau-Cambrésis in 1559, both France and Spain were at last free to shore up defense of the old faith, and Philip lost little time in attempting to strengthen his hold over the Netherlands. To the north, Elizabeth confronted an unsettled political situation. Mary Queen of Scots was regarded by many as the rightful successor to Mary Tudor, while an ambitious French court used her marriage to lay claim to the English throne. In her own realm Elizabeth faced an uneasy situation in which only a minority of her subjects shared her faith.

The new queen lost little time in reversing her late sister's policies. When Philip II proposed marriage, the queen not only declined; she also declared that she did not adhere to his faith. Even before Parliament acted she expressed disapproval of what she regarded as Roman religious practices, and did not hesitate to leave in the middle of a church service to emphasize her disapprobation. Elizabeth soon gathered Protestant advisers about her and began anew the quest for a *via media*. One of the new ministers, William Cecil, later Lord Burghley (1520–1598), proved admirably suited to the task of satisfying the queen's vanity and giving the nation wise and successful guidance. Few servants of the crown ever did more to bring prosperity and tranquillity to the realm.

Parliament began its deliberations on January 25, 1559. In two weeks, the Commons was aggressively expanding a government bill to ''restore the supremacy of the Church of England to the Crown of the realm.'' A more reluctant House of Lords attempted to tone down the Protestant emendations of the bill. Eventually the Commons agreed to the more moderate version; even so the Act of Supremacy (1559)[22] once again ended papal jurisdiction in England. Later in

---

[21] At Mary's insistence, he remained in England.
[22] Spitz, *The Protestant Reformation,* pp. 172–174.

PORTRAIT: QUEEN ELIZABETH I, attributed to M. Gheeraedts

Seldom in English history have the aspirations of sovereign and subject so nearly coincided as in the reign of Elizabeth. Spanish armada and papal excommunication and deposition served only to strengthen allegiance to the "phoenix of the world."

National Portrait Gallery

the same year, Parliament passed another supremacy bill in which the queen substituted the title "Supreme Governor" for that of "Supreme Head." The revision was designed to make the bill more palatable to English Catholics. This third supremacy bill also abolished the Marian heresy laws and revived various Henrician statutes, such as those of Annates and Appeals. Clergymen and offi-

196

cials of state were required to take an oath recognizing the queen's supremacy in church and state.

By the Act of Uniformity (1559)[23] a revised form of the Edwardian prayer book was restored as the only permissible form of worship. The act, in its retention of vestments, crucifixes, and various other Catholic practices, disappointed many of the more avid champions of a drastic reformation. Many Protestant leaders, in exile during Mary's reign, had imbibed deeply at Calvinistic springs on the continent; they were now determined to rid the church of "Romish" elements. With strong representation in the Commons, they began to press for more sweeping reform. A bitter Vestiarian Controversy developed and split English Protestants. The event was an ominous portent of the growing cleavage that would, in the following century, plunge the nation into civil war. For the "Puritans," nothing less than abolition of everything that smacked of "popery" could be acceptable.

The queen continued her policy of moderation by appointing her former tutor, Matthew Parker, archbishop of Canterbury. When Marian bishops refused to consecrate the candidate, four men who had held bishoprics under Henry or Edward performed the act. Despite papal objections, the English claim to apostolic succession had been preserved. Parker's close associate, John Jewel, the bishop of Salisbury, presented a vigorous defense of the Elizabethan Settlement in his learned *Apologia Ecclesiae Anglicanae* (1562). In the following year the Edwardian Forty-two Articles were revised and issued as the Thirty-nine Articles, the definitive doctrinal statement of the Church of England. Also in 1563 there appeared the popular and propagandistic martyrology by John Foxe, *Acts and Monuments*. With its accounts of the heroism of Protestant martyrs and depiction of the papacy as an institution of cruelty and death, this work long nourished anti-papal sentiment.

The English quickly adjusted to the far-reaching Elizabethan Settlement. Long before Richard Hooker's *Laws of Ecclesiastical Polity* (1597) gave classical expression to the rationale of the middle way, most people had made their peace with a religious policy broad enough to embrace most of Protestantism. While fifteen of seventeen Marian bishops refused to accept the new Act of Supremacy, all but a small fraction of the parish priests took the oath of supremacy and thus retained their posts.

Catholics who wished to remain loyal to the pope were in a difficult position. Private Catholic worship, while contrary to law, was nonetheless often tolerated, for it posed no real threat. A more acute problem was presented in 1570 when the papal bull *Regnans in Excelsis* declared Elizabeth excommunicated and urged all faithful Catholics to disobey and depose the queen. Some Catholics, faced with a

<hr/>

[23] Spitz, *The Protestant Reformation*, pp. 174–176.

choice between pope and state, chose loyalty to the pope and were executed for treason. Most English Catholics, however, refused to take the bull seriously. They were Englishmen first. Not until the latter part of the century, with the coming of numerous determined Catholic missionaries from the continent, did the old faith regain some measure of its former power.

At the other end of the spectrum, the increasingly vocal Puritans demanded more sweeping repudiation of "popery." At Cambridge, Thomas Cartwright called for an end to episcopacy and the introduction of the Genevan model. He was soon relieved of his professorial post and, like many Puritan dissidents, went into exile. But the drive for change continued, whether by Parliament or Convocation, and as the 1580s brought an intensified Spanish and papal threat to England, Puritanism and patriotism became virtually synonymous—at least in the opinion of the Puritans. Convinced that they were the divinely chosen bearers of history, they had little difficulty identifying the cause of the Almighty with their own.

Thus faced with challenges from right and left, the *via media* of Anglicanism owed its success in no small measure to the queen herself. Skillfully resisting parliamentary maneuvers for religious change, Elizabeth forged an alliance of ecclesiastical and political leaders thoroughly devoted to her policies. Even so inveterate a foe as Pope Sixtus V was forced to admit, "She is a great woman; and were she only Catholic, she would be without her match."[24]

Suggestions for Further Reading

Bindoff, S. T. *Ket's Rebellion, 1549.* London: The Historical Association, 1949.

*———. *Tudor England.* Baltimore: Penguin Books, 1950.

Black, J. B. *The Reign of Elizabeth.* Oxford: Clarendon, 1959.

Booty, John E. *John Jewel as Apologist of the Church of England.* London: S.P.C.K., 1963.

Brett, Sidney R. *The Tudor Century, 1485–1603.* London: Harrap, 1962.

Bromiley, G. W. *Thomas Cranmer, Theologian.* London: Oxford University Press, 1956.

Brook, V. J. K. *Whitgift and the English Church.* New York: Macmillan, 1957.

———. *A Life of Archbishop Parker.* Oxford: Clarendon, 1962.

Caspari, F. *Humanism and the Social Order in Tudor England.* Chicago: University of Chicago Press, 1954.

Chester, Allan G. *Hugh Latimer, Apostle to the English.* Philadelphia: University of Pennsylvania Press, 1954.

Chidsey, Donald Barr. *Elizabeth I.* New York: Knopf, 1955.

Child, G. W. *Church and State Under the Tudors.* London: Longmans, Green, 1950.

*Indicates paperback edition.

[24] A. L. Rouse, *The England of Elizabeth* (New York: Collier Books, 1950), p. 14.

Clebsch, William A. *England's Earliest Protestants, 1520–1535.* Nev University Press, 1964.

Collinson, Patrick. *The Elizabethan Puritan Movement.* London: Jonath

*****Creighton, Mandell.** *Queen Elizabeth.* New York: Crowell Collier anu ₁ᵥᵢ.. 1966.

Cremeans, Charles. *The Reception of Calvinist Thought in England.* Urbana: University of Illinois Press, 1949.

Cross, Claire. *The Royal Supremacy in the Elizabethan Church.* New York: Barnes and Noble, 1969.

Davies, E. T. *Episcopacy and Royal Supremacy in the Church of England in the XVIth Century.* Oxford: Blackwell, 1950.

Dawley, Powel M. *John Whitgift and the English Reformation.* New York: Scribner's, 1954.

Dickens, A. G. *Lollards and Protestants in the Diocese of York, 1509–1558.* London: Published for the University of Hull by the Oxford University Press, 1959.

———. *The English Reformation.* London: Batsford, 1964.

Doernberg, Erwin. *Henry VIII and Luther.* Stanford: Stanford University Press, 1961.

Duffield, G. E., ed. *The Work of William Tyndale.* Philadelphia: Fortress Press, 1965.

Elton, G. R. *England under the Tudors.* London: Methuen, 1957.

———. *The Tudor Constitution, Documents and Commentary.* London: Cambridge University Press, 1960.

———. *The Tudor Revolution in Government: Administrative Changes in the Reign of Henry VIII.* London: Cambridge University Press, 1962.

Fairfield, L. P. *John Bale, Mythmaker for the English Reformation.* Lafayette, Ind.: Purdue University Press, 1976.

Gairdner, James. *Lollardy and the Reformation in England,* 4 vols. London: Macmillan, 1908–1913.

Garret, Christina H. *The Marian Exiles.* London: Cambridge University Press, 1938.

Gee, H., and W. J. Hardy. *Documents Illustrative of English Church History.* London: Macmillan, 1914.

George, Charles H., and Katherine George. *The Protestant Mind of the English Reformation.* Princeton: Princeton University Press, 1961.

Haller, William. *The Rise of Puritanism.* New York: Columbia University Press, 1938.

———. *Elizabeth I and the Puritans.* Ithica, N.Y.: Cornell University Press, 1938.

Harbison, E. Harris. *Rival Ambassadors at the Court of Queen Mary.* Princeton: Princeton University Press, 1940.

Harrison, David. *Tudor England,* 2 vols. London: Cassell, 1953.

Haugaard, William P. *Elizabeth and the English Reformation.* London: Cambridge University Press, 1968.

Hoak, D. E. *The King's Council in the Reign of Edward VI.* Cambridge, Mass.: Harvard University Press, 1976.

Hughes, Philip. *The Reformation in England,* 3 vols. London: Hollis & Carter, 1950–54.

Hurstfield, Joel. *Elizabeth I and the Unity of England*. London: English Universities Press, 1960.

*Hutchinson, F. E. *Cranmer and the English Reformation*. New York: Collier Books, 1962.

Jones, Whitney R. D. *The Tudor Commonwealth, 1529–1559*. London: University of London, Athlone Press, 1970.

Jordan, W. K. *Edward VI*, 2 vols. Cambridge, Mass.: Harvard University Press, 1968.

*Knappen, M. M. *Tudor Puritanism*. Chicago: University of Chicago Press, 1939.

Knowles, Dom David. *The Religious Orders in England*, 3 vols. London: Cambridge University Press, 1948–59.

Lemberg, S. E. *The Reformation Parliament, 1529–1536*. London: Cambridge University Press, 1970.

Loane, Marcus. *Masters of the English Reformation*. London: Church Book Room Press, 1954.

Mackie, J. D. *The Earlier Tudors, 1485–1558*. Oxford: Clarendon, 1952.

*Mattingly, Garrett. *Catherine of Aragon*. New York: Vintage Books, 1941.

*————. *The Armada*. Boston: Houghton Mifflin, 1962.

Maynard, Theodore. *The Life of Thomas Cranmer*. Chicago: Henry Regnery, 1956.

McConica, James K. *English Humanists and Reformation Politics under Henry VIII and Edward VI*. Oxford: Clarendon, 1965.

McGrath, Patrick. *Papists and Puritans Under Elizabeth I*. London: Blanford, 1967.

Meyer, Carl S., *Elizabeth I and the Religious Settlement of 1559*. St. Louis: Concordia, 1960.

————, ed. *Cranmer's Selected Writings*. London: S.P.C.K., 1961.

Morris, Christopher. *Political Thought in England: Tyndale to Hooker*. London: Oxford University Press, 1953.

*Neale, John E. *Elizabeth I and Her Parliaments*, 2 vols. London: Jonathan Cape, 1953–57.

*————. *The Elizabethan House of Commons*. London: Jonathan Cape, 1961.

New, John. *Anglican and Puritan*. Stanford: Stanford University Press, 1964.

Oxley, James. *The Reformation in Essex to the Death of Mary*. Manchester, England: Manchester University Press, 1965.

Parker, T. H. *English Reformers*. Philadelphia: Westminster Press, 1965.

Parker, T. M. *The English Reformation to 1588*. London: Oxford University Press, 1950.

Paul, John E. *Catherine of Aragon and Her Friends*. New York: Fordham University Press, 1971.

*Pollard, A. F. *Henry VIII* New York: Harper & Row, A Harper Torchbook, 1966.

*————. *Wolsey*. New York: Harper & Row, A Harper Torchbook, 1966.

Pollard, Arthur. *Richard Hooker*. London: Longmans, 1966.

Porter, H. C. *Reformation and Reaction in Tudor Cambridge*. London: Cambridge University Press, 1958.

*Powicke, F. M. *The Reformation in England*. London: Oxford Paperbacks, 1961.

Prescott, Hilda F. M. *Mary Tudor*. New York: Macmillan, 1953.

Prothero, G. W. ed. *Select Statutes and Other Constitutional Documents Illustrative of the Reigns of Elizabeth and James I.* Oxford: Clarendon, 1949.

Read, Conyers. *The Tudors.* New York: Holt, 1936.

———. *Mr. Secretary Cecil and Queen Elizabeth.* London: Jonathan Cape, 1955.

———. *Lord Burghley and Queen Elizabeth.* New York: Knopf, 1960.

Richardson, W. C. *Mary Tudor: The White Queen.* Seattle: University of Washington Press 1970.

Ridley, Jasper. *Thomas Cranmer.* Oxford: Clarendon, 1962.

*Rowse, A. L.** *The England of Elizabeth.* London: Macmillan, 1950.

Rupp, E. Gordon. *The English Protestant Tradition.* London: Cambridge University Press, 1947.

———. *Six Makers of English Religion, 1500–1700.* London: Hodder and Stoughton, 1957.

*Scarisbrick, J. J.** *Henry VIII.* Berkeley: University of California Press, 1968.

Schenk, Wilhelm. *Reginald Pole, Cardinal of England.* London: Longmans, Green, 1950.

Smith, Herbert M. *Henry VIII and the Reformation.* London: Macmillan, 1948.

Smith, Lacey Baldwin. *Tudor Prelates and Politics.* Princeton: Princeton University Press, 1953.

Southgate, W. M. *John Jewel and the Problem of Doctrinal Authority.* Cambridge, Mass.: Harvard University Press, 1962.

Steuart, A. F., ed. *The Trial of Mary, Queen of Scots.* London: Hodge, 1951.

*Thompson, C. R.** *The English Church in the Sixteenth Century.* Washington: Folger Shakespeare Library, 1958.

Tjernagel, N. S. *Henry VIII and the Lutherans.* St. Louis: Concordia, 1965.

Trimble, William. *The Catholic Laity in Elizabethan England, 1558–1603.* Cambridge, Mass.: Harvard University Press, 1964.

Trinterud, Leonard J., ed. *Elizabethan Puritanism.* New York: Oxford University Press, 1971.

Walzer, Michael. *The Revolution of the Saints: A Study in the Origins of Radical Politics.* Cambridge, Mass.: Harvard University Press, 1965.

Williams, Neville. *Elizabeth the First, Queen of England.* New York: Dutton, 1968.

Woodhouse, H. F. *The Doctrine of the Church in Anglican Theology, 1547–1603.* London: S.P.C.K., 1954.

Woodward, George. *Reformation and Resurgence, 1485–1603.* London: Blandford, 1963.

Wright, Louis B. *Religion and Empire: The Alliance Between Piety and Commerce in English Expansion, 1558–1625.* Chapel Hill: University of North Carolina Press, 1943.

10

Catholic Reform
and Resurgence

REFORM THROUGH MONASTICISM

For centuries, medieval Catholicism had found renewal through the founding of new orders or the revitalization of the old. The sixteenth century was no exception, as a series of new movements reinvigorated Catholicism. Sometimes, in keeping with the recommendations of bodies such as the "commission of reform" (Concilium) of 1537, old orders were required to institute reform measures. Benefices were to be distributed only to the deserving; religious houses were expected to move firmly against lax discipline. The proposals also called for an end to nonresidency of bishops and parish priests, and frankly admitted that popes themselves had been "the origin of these evils"; an unsparing analysis of "diseases and their remedies"[1] showed that reform was to be taken seriously.

Widespread resolve to cope with the threat of stagnation expressed itself in the rise of numerous reform movements. One of the more influential institutions formed at this time was the Oratory of Divine Love.[2] Founded in 1497 in Genoa, it spread to other cities, and shortly before 1517 was established in Rome. It drew its impetus from men who believed that examples of individual piety might stimulate a reformation. In the 1520s, the Roman fraternity numbered about sixty, and included several adherents who later became very prominent in Catholic reform: Gaetano da Thiene, Gian Pietro Carafa, and Reginald Pole. Although the Oratory remained small, few movements contributed such an array of architects of Catholic reform. The quest for renewal attracted ever more supporters. In Rome, Philip Neri (1515–1595), respected, popular advocate of

[1] J. C. Olin, ed., *The Catholic Reformation: Savonarola to Ignatius Loyola* (New York: Harper & Row, 1969), p. 187.
[2] See the rule of the Genoese Oratory in Olin, *ibid.*, pp. 18–26.

personal piety, gained broad influence at all levels of society. His emulation of a happy but devout religious life inspired widespread imitation, and the oratory he founded, with its emphasis on prayer, singing, and acts of mercy served as a model in Italy and beyond.[3]

Devotion to the church and the passion for renewal brought a mushrooming of new orders. The Camaldolese, refounded in 1522, embraced both hermits and cenobites, and soon spread throughout Italy, France, Poland, Germany, and Austria. This order emphasized the ascetic, contemplative life in which the participant withdrew from the world. Led by devout and austere men such as Paolo Giustiniani (d. 1528), close friend of several popes and prominent clerics, the order served as a model and inspiration for many who recognized the need for reform.

A strong impetus for renewal came with the founding in 1524 of the Theatines. Cooperative efforts by Gaetano da Thiene (1480–1547) and Gian Pietro Carafa (1476–1559), who later became Pope Paul IV, produced an order that was determined both to live in poverty and to assist the secular clergy in its mission of service to the lay community. Through its efforts to rout out various abuses in the ranks of the secular clergy, it served to groom many future bishops and noted preachers. Membership in the order remained small, for the houses were designed to be not "seminaries for priests" but rather "seminaries for bishops."[4]

Among the more successful attempts to reform an order was the founding of the Capuchins by Matteo da Bascio (1495–1552). This Franciscan resolved to restore the simplicity and austerity of Francis of Assisi, and to observe literally the rigid demands of his last will. The Franciscans had already split into two factions—the Observants and the Conventuals. But the Capuchins—so called because of the square brown hoods they wore—were apparently unconvinced of the Observants' sincerity in following the saint's injunctions. In 1528 the group was recognized by the pope. The Capuchins lived in strictest poverty and carried on extensive works of mercy for the sick and the poor, but they were especially noted for their emphasis on preaching. Members were expected to be "evangelical preachers"[5] and thorough scholars of the Scriptures. Catholicism had found an order that was fully prepared to use the pulpit to confront Protestantism. The movement suffered a severe setback when the fourth vicar general, Bernardino Ochino, renowned for his preaching oratory that could "move stones," as a contemporary Italian reported, joined the Protestants (1542). Despite demands that the order be suppressed, the pope allowed it to continue. In the second half

[3]Meriol Trevor, *Apostle of Rome: Philip Neri, 1515–1595* (London: Macmillan, 1967).

[4]Pierre Janelle, *The Catholic Reformation* (Milwaukee: Bruce, 1963), p. 97. The rule of the Theatines is printed in Olin, *The Catholic Reformation*, pp. 130–132.

[5]Olin, *The Catholic Reformation*, p. 174.

of the century, the Capuchin movement grew rapidly and became one of the most powerful forces in combating Protestantism.

THE JESUITS

None of the new orders, however, would prove as effective and influential in strengthening Catholicism and halting the spread of Protestantism as the Jesuits. This order, founded by Ignatius of Loyola (1491–1556),[6] would justly be referred to as "the shock troops of the Counter Reformation." Ignatius, son of a Basque nobleman, experienced a rather adventurous youth, even serving for a while as page to King Ferdinand. In 1521, while defending Pamplona against French invaders, he received a fractured leg. A long illness ensued, and the leg never healed properly. While recuperating, he read devotional works and resolved to use his energies in the service of his church. In 1522, he made a pilgrimage to the shrine of the Virgin Mary in Montserrat. Here, in a night-long vigil, he determined to embrace a spiritual knighthood.

Resolutely committed to this new life, Ignatius decided to undertake a pilgrimage to Jerusalem. A plague in Barcelona delayed him, so he spent almost a year in Manresa. During this period, he devoted himself to a rigorous discipline of prayer, fasting, self-flagellation, and begging. His quest for peace of conscience ended with complete submission of his will to that of the church. What faith meant for Luther, obedience meant for Loyola. He needed no new theology, only unswerving adherence to the old.

While at Manresa, Loyola wrote the broad outlines of his *Spiritual Exercises*. The final form would not be completed until 1541. The work was designed to be a manual for prayer and meditation, a guide whereby the faithful might conquer their will. When completed, the *Exercises* fell into four parts. The first section, the "Annotations," summarized Ignatius's view of the Christian life. In section two, the "Exercises," the author prescribed in minute detail preparatory activities to occupy one month's time: meditation on man's wickedness and the terrors of hell, and on the mercies of Christ and his Mother. Through contemplation, the participant was to be led to an act of will—an unquestioning dedication to the teachings and commands of the church. In the third part of the *Exercises*, Ignatius outlined procedures to be followed in meditating on the life of Christ, and in the final section he listed rules to be observed in such matters as almsgiving and "thinking with the church." It was in this section that Ignatius made his sweeping demand that "we ought always to be ready to believe that what seems to us white is black if the hierarchical church so defines it."[7] Here was a book, not to be read, but to be lived, a book to steel the will in its devotion to the

---

[6]Early development of the order is examined in Michael Foss, *The Founding of the Jesuits* (New York: Weybright and Talley, 1969).

[7]Quoted in Edward M. Burns, *The Counter Reformation* (Princeton, N.J.: Van Nostrand, 1964), p. 127.

PORTRAIT: IGNATIUS LOYOLA, by Juan de Roelas

No man so profoundly influenced the Catholic Reformation as did Ignatius Loyola. The order he founded spearheaded Catholic renewal and resurgence.

Museo Provincial de Bellas Artes, Sevilla

church. Although Ignatius stated that there could be no salvation without predestination, he de-emphasized this view; rather he insisted that good works were essential to salvation. Man must cooperate with God.

Early in 1523, Ignatius left Manresa and embarked on his pilgrimage to Palestine. Here he soon abandoned his earlier hope of converting the believers of Islam, and returned to Spain. His brief visit had convinced him that before he could hope to be effective, he would have to acquire an education. Although he was already over thirty years of age, he began a program of studies that would occupy almost a decade. At the universities of Barcelona and Alcalá, he indulged his voracious appetite for knowledge. At Alcalá, he gained four ardent supporters who became his inseparable companions. Ignatius's zeal in propagating his views aroused suspicion, so that the ecclesiastical authorities had him arrested and imprisoned for forty days. Then, when he continued his studies at Salamanca, the Dominicans brought him before the Inquisition. Again he was released, but now he decided to continue his studies in Paris. Here, too, he aroused the suspicions of the inquisitors, but nothing could deter the indomitable Basque.

Inspired by Ignatius's example and leadership, a devoted group of followers joined him in a brotherhood. Drawn from various sections of society, they became some of the most effective and celebrated leaders in a resurgent Catholicism: Pierre Favre, son of a Savoy peasant; Francis Xavier, an aristocrat from Navarre, later to become the renowned missionary to the Far East; Diego Laynez, son of a merchant, successor to Ignatius as leader of the Jesuits; Nicholas Bobadilla, whose indomitable will later helped to prevent Catholic princes from adopting the compromises of the Augsburg Interim; Alfonso Salmeron, like Laynez, vigorous champion of papal interests at Trent; and Simon Rodriquez, who became an influential adviser to King John III of Portugal (1521–1557).

On August 15, 1534, Ignatius and his six followers gathered in a chapel on Montmartre and vowed to devote themselves to the work of the church. Favre celebrated Mass and the group took a triple vow to observe poverty and chastity and to go to the Holy Land as missionaries. Should the latter prove unfeasible, they would offer their services to the pope. Soon three others joined the group. By 1537, they were in Venice, ready to go to Palestine. Here Ignatius and the five of his companions who were not yet priests were ordained. War between Venice and the Turks dashed hopes of sailing to the East, and so the group offered its services to the pope. On September 27, 1540, the bull *Regimini militantis ecclesiae*[8] established the company as the Society of Jesus, but well before that time, Ignatius and his followers had become some of the most trusted emissaries of the pope. In 1541, Ignatius was unanimously elected head of the new order.

The Jesuits were soon engaged in a wide range of activities. Education, preaching, poor relief, and various other avenues were used to propagate and defend the faith, and to assist those in need. Members of the order established orphanages, workhouses, and centers for rehabilitating social outcasts. On April 7, 1541, Francis Xavier and three companions set sail for the East Indies, thus initiating a missionary program that would profoundly affect the Far East and the Americas.

Nowhere would the Jesuits exert so profound an influence as in education. The order began by teaching destitute children on the streets of Rome; soon it was teaching at the most influential and prestigious universities. In those areas

[8]Olin, *The Catholic Reformation,* pp. 203–208.

PETRVS CANISIVS SOCIETAISIESV.

Hunc habuit Petrum felix Germania, Patrem,
Quem stupuére olim Curia, Templa Scholæ ·
Nunc stulpta térre quidem fas est hâc ora tueri ·
Illius at vita est suspicienda magis ·   C. Grinerfiet.

ENGRAVING: ST. PETER CANISIUS

His untiring efforts resulted in the founding of numerous Jesuit colleges throughout the empire. At the conclusion of more than thirty years work in Germany, he left well over one thousand Jesuits in that land. In many areas, their role would be decisive in shaping the future of religion.

Courtesy Lutherhalle, Wittenberg

where the order met with opposition from established academicians, it established its own schools, which were increasingly in demand by the nobility. In Portugal, King John welcomed Jesuits to his new university at Coimbra and simultaneously dismissed humanist teachers. In Spain, Francis Borgia, Duke of Gandia and Viceroy of Catalonia, placed his university in Jesuit hands and joined the order. Eventually he would become the third general. In France, opposition at the Sorbonne closed that door, but the Jesuits established their own schools at Douai, St. Omer, and Rheims.

The Catholic Reformation gained one of its greatest triumphs when Favre won over the German Peter Canisius (1521–1596) to the movement. Canisius, gifted writer, influential educator, and distinguished scholar, rallied the disorganized Catholic forces in Germany and Austria, and tried to regain those whom he called the "separated brethren."[9] In Bavaria, Canisius persuaded Duke Albert V to launch a vigorous campaign to reform Catholicism and root out Protestantism. Convinced that education was the key to the renewal of Catholicism, Canisius helped to reform existing schools and establish many new ones. His educational efforts at the University of Cologne proved especially effective, for when the archbishop, Elector Hermann von Wied, attempted to introduce the Reformation, Canisius successfully organized the opposition. Later, he went to Vienna and became confessor to Emperor Ferdinand. Here, and elsewhere, as at Ingolstadt, the Jesuit colleges he founded became highly influential centers in training people in the propagation and defense of Catholicism. Canisius had taken to heart the conclusion of Favre: The inadequacies of the priests, not the attractiveness of Lutheranism, were responsible for the loss of large sections of Germany. Catholicism in the Empire found its greatest intellectual and theological champion in Canisius. His *Summary of Christian Doctrine*, published in 1555 and designed to counteract Luther's *Large Catechism*, was repeatedly reissued and translated. Throughout the Empire, it became the most widely used Catholic statement of doctrine. As in many other instances, a Jesuit had played a decisive role in preserving the old faith.

The Society expanded rapidly, so that by the time of the death of its founder in 1556, there were one thousand members. By the end of the century, the number was in excess of ten thousand. Jesuits exerted a strong influence at the Council of Trent and at the imperial court. In numerous cities, they proved the decisive factor in halting and reversing the spread of Protestantism. Laynez was especially successful in crushing nascent Protestantism in Venice, Padua, and Brescia. Salmeron restored virtually complete adherence to Catholicism in Modena. Other Jesuits crushed the Protestantism that Renée, Duchess of Ferrara, was encouraging in that city. Throughout much of the Empire, Jesuits were in the vanguard against Lutheranism. They gained the support of William, Duke of Bavaria, and persuaded him to oppose the 1548 Interim. In Austria, Emperor Ferdinand allowed Canisius to plan strategy for eradicating Protestantism. Those suspected of leaning toward Lutheranism, whether counselor, magistrate, professor, or preacher, were to be deprived of office. Heretical books were ordered burned; Germany had found a second Boniface.

In France, however, the Society was long regarded with deep mistrust, for the French viewed the movement as essentially Spanish, and the long tradition of strife between Spain and France had left a legacy of suspicion and fear. Furthermore, both Parlement and the Sorbonne determined to safeguard the liberties of the Gallican church and to oppose the intrusion of an order that seemed to have

---

[9]Canisius appears to have coined this phrase which gained such wide currency with the Second Vatican Council. This according to Henri Daniel-Rops, *The Catholic Reformation* (New York: Image Books, 1964), I:89.

excessive privileges. Despite these obstacles, the Jesuits gradually established schools in numerous cities. Well before the end of the century, Huguenot influence had been checked. Under the powerful patronage of the cardinal of Lorraine and the bishop of Clermont, Jesuits occupied ever more prominent roles in French life. Numerous colleges were established, although hostility toward the Jesuits brought about their eviction in 1594 from all towns where they had schools. The act was revoked in 1603, but tensions between Jesuits and advocates of ecclesiastical Gallicanism remained.

REFORM THROUGH THE PAPACY

Events early in the sixteenth century demonstrated that Catholic reform could be successful only with papal support. Similarly, papal disappointment such as that experienced by Adrian VI emphatically repudiated the notion that reform would come as soon as the pope willed it. Cooperation among pope, curia, and bishops was clearly imperative to the success of any reform movement. Numerous half-hearted efforts never got beyond the stage of pious intentions because pope or curia in particular refused to give highest priority to spiritual matters.

During the early stages of the Reformation, papal inaction facilitated the spread of the new faith. When staunch champions of the church warned Leo that to delay reform would be perilous, he chose rather to occupy himself with maintenance of a resplendent Renaissance court. An avid devotee of humanism and the arts, he surrounded himself with musicians, actors, poets, and artists. Religious turmoil in Germany, Franco-imperial rivalry, Turkish threats, and innumerable pleas for reform did not deter Leo from enjoying the splendor of a court ever alive with glittering carnivals, elaborate pageantry, and irrepressible artistic endeavor. Nonetheless, he was not altogether impervious to the demands for ecclesiastical reform. When the fifth Lateran Council (1512–1517), attended almost exclusively by Italian bishops,[10] made a series of proposals to correct such abuses as episcopal nonresidence, simony, and nepotism, Leo tacitly approved. However, several papal bulls issued to implement the suggestions remained largely a dead letter. Entrenched interests found that there was little papal pressure to enforce the bulls—indeed Leo's example was hardly one to encourage serious observance of the council's reform decrees.[11] For the pope, to enjoy the Rome of Michelangelo, Raphael, and Bramante, was more rewarding than to reform the church.

Under Leo's successor, Adrian VI (1522–1523), reform efforts were sharply accelerated. Immediately upon his coronation, he launched a vigorous program

[10]Hubert Jedin, *A History of the Council of Trent,* trans. Ernest Graf (London: Thomas Nelson, 1957), I:128.

[11]See Ludwig Pastor, *The History of the Popes from the Close of the Middle Ages,* trans. F. I. Antrobus, R. F. Kerr, et al., 40 vols. (London: Kegan Paul, Trench, Trubner and Co., 1891–1953), VIII:410–412.

of rigid austerity and strict observance of the church's ecclesiastical standards. Convinced that earlier popes had ignored religion for the arts, he reversed the emphases. Beautiful ancient sculpture, collected by his predecessors, he denounced as barbaric idolatry. Corruption and extravagance were attacked wherever the pope thought he saw them; and he confidently announced that he would ''expend every effort to reform first this Curia,'' for ''the illness has spread from the head to the members.''[12] This frontal assault on clerical abuses aroused determined curial and episcopal opposition, so that virtually the entire Roman hierarchy was up in arms against papal policies. When the frustrated pope died in 1523, it was apparent that papal zeal alone, especially if devoid of diplomacy and cultural awareness, could never reform the church.

With Clement VII (1523–1534), reform again receded into the background. Struggling desperately to preserve papal independence from French and imperial ambitions, and also determined to continue patronage of the arts, the pope paid only scant attention to abuses that were calling forth an ever greater chorus of dissent.

Family interests and Italian politics so absorbed his energies that reform attempts, such as Clement's appointing of a commission of cardinals to recommend corrective actions, remained little more than a gesture. Despite papal inaction, pressures for decisive reform mounted. Calls for a general church council, from the emperor and other rulers, finally forced Clement to agree to summon such a body. Various delaying tactics only made Clement's position more difficult, especially in light of the independent actions taken by reform-minded Theatines and Capuchins.

Finally, during the reign of Paul III (1534–1549), reform became possible because ''head and members'' agreed that corrective measures were imperative. Appointees to the College of Cardinals were now drawn from the ranks of the reform movement. A special commission, appointed by the pope, examined the whole ecclesiastical establishment and issued a scathing list of indictments. Paul recognized the validity of these findings and ordered remedial action. Then, hoping to heal the schism in the Empire, he sent nuncios to negotiate with the Protestant princes and theologians. Cardinal Contarini achieved a measure of understanding with Melanchthon and Bucer, but some papal advisers insisted that the conciliatory cardinal had granted too much. Paul also feared that the price of reunion might be too high. Rather than make concessions, he intensified his efforts to purify and invigorate Catholicism. In 1542, he reestablished the Roman Inquisition. Soon thereafter, the Index was compiled to halt the spread of dangerous ideas. Then, when he summoned the Council of Trent, Paul clearly served notice that reform would be taken in earnest. Everyone knew that it was late for conciliar action; no one could know that it was too late. Like his contemporaries, Paul hoped that Trent might provide the answer to the tragedy of delay,

[12]Olin, *The Catholic Reformation*, p. 125.

division, and defeat. A new era had dawned. A reform papacy stood in the vanguard of the forces of change and consolidation.

IN QUEST OF A COUNCIL

Amidst the rubble of an already fractured Christendom, religious and secular leaders increasingly staked their hopes on a general council of the church. Luther and Calvin, Emperor Charles V and princes of the Empire, like various leaders in the Catholic church, clung tenaciously to the belief that a council would bring reform and reform would bring unity. The precise locus of authority in any proposed council was not, however, at all clear. Papal supporters viewed such a council as an agency to be used by the pope for reforming the church. Protestant conciliarists repudiated any suggestion of papal control of the council. On the contrary, Luther viewed such an assembly as a tool for implementing his views of biblical Christianity, a task in which the papacy as then constituted could not participate.

Ranged against Catholics and Protestants who urged the calling of a council were those champions of papal supremacy who feared that any council might develop into an attack on papal authority. The curia had not forgotten that the Councils of Constance (1414–1418) and Basel (1431–1449) had mounted powerful and partially successful assaults upon papal supremacy. Such attacks were reinforced when territorial princes took ecclesiastical matters into their own hands. In the Pragmatic Sanction of Bourges (1438) France served notice that popes must be regarded as subordinate to councils. The "Gallican liberties" were vigorously affirmed: clerical appointments were removed from papal control; payment of annates to Rome was abolished; appeals to the Roman Curia from French courts were, with a few exceptions, prohibited. In addition, the royal ordinance called for the implementation of reform measures within the French church. In view of these setbacks in fifteenth-century France, many supporters of the papal position were convinced that further councils could only bring renewed erosion of the papal prerogative. But the suspicions of those opposed to conciliar action could not stem the flood of insistent demands that a council be convened.

Some of the champions of conciliar action, including Luther and the diet, urged that a "free Christian council" be held in the Empire, to assure its independence from papal control. When the Diet met at Worms in 1521, the view that "a council alone . . . is in a position to ascertain whether Dr. Martinus has written against the faith" was no longer an isolated sentiment.[13] Even prominent Catholic leaders, such as Albert of Mainz, urged that a council be called, and that it be held in Germany. For the archbishop, there was no necessary incompatibility between a national council and papal authority. His view, however, met

[13]Jedin, *Council of Trent,* I:201.

strong opposition. Both emperor and pope opposed a German council on the grounds that it might well become an instrument of divisive nationalism. Throughout the tortuous negotiations that finally led to the calling of a council, it became increasingly apparent that papal authority and claims to universalism, on the one hand, were ranged against insistence on independence of the national church and rejection of papal supremacy, on the other. Conciliar optimists hoped that these differences might be bridged, but the attempts at reconciliation were destined to fail.

Charles V was among those whose hopes for a church council were most sanguine. At the Diet of Nuremberg in 1523, the emperor supported the demands of the estates that a council be called within the Empire. Pope Adrian had earlier supported the summoning of a general council; now he concluded that a council held in Germany might accentuate division. When he died in 1523, the council was as remote as ever. The new pope, Clement VII, emphatically resisted the notion that religious peril could be met in a national council, and only slowly did he come to admit that a general council might help to heal the schism. By November, 1527, a reluctant Clement VII, his city ravaged by the recent sack, agreed to summon a general council at the earliest opportunity. The emperor hoped that he would be able to pressure Clement into calling a council without delay, but the pope was not at all convinced that what he called a "corpse in shreds"[14] could best be revived by a program dominated by the emperor. Clement was well aware of the councils of the previous century, and the desperate struggle to reassert papal supremacy. Renewed war between Charles and Francis, as well as a fresh attack by the Turks, helped briefly to divert imperial attention from a prospective council, but whenever the military threat subsided, the demand for a council was intensified. The Diet of Speyer (1529) urged the emperor to press for a general council, and at the Diet of Augsburg, Charles received provisional papal assurance that a council would be summoned. Once again, however, no council was convened, for the Protestants refused to abandon their position and permit enforcement of the Edict of Worms. In 1532 the demand for a council was intensified, as the Diet of Nuremberg declared its determination to call a national council. Neither pope nor emperor was prepared to condone such schismatic action. In 1533, Pope Clement reluctantly agreed to call a council. This time, the League of Schmalkald demurred; a council would be acceptable only if the final authority of the Scriptures, rather than pope or council, were recognized. For the Lutheran estates, their demand for a "free Christian council" could be met only by recognition of the principle of *sola Scriptura*. The breach was widening.

When Clement died in 1534, the issue of a council was still unresolved. His successor, Pope Paul III (1534–1549), was determined to seize the initiative, however. Resolute, shrewd, and diplomatic, he was determined to enhance the stature of his office and his church. When Henry VIII proved intractable, he was

---

[14]Daniel-Rops, *The Catholic Reformation,* I:101.

excommunicated and England placed under an interdict. Pope Paul urged continental rulers to take military action against the schismatic, but neither Charles nor Francis cooperated. Paul further urged Francis to exercise the utmost severity against French Protestants, and Catholic princes in Germany were advised to defeat the League of Schmalkald.

In Rome, the pope appointed champions of reform to high office. A "commission of reform," given sweeping powers of examination, presented its report in 1537. This document was a scathing indictment of practices throughout the church, even in the papal household. The pope was urged to wipe out simony, corruption in the curia and in monastic houses, ordination of unworthy priests, and numerous other abuses, many of them previously castigated by Catholic and Protestant reformers. Less positive, however, was the recommendation to curtail intellectual freedom through censorship and restriction of the use of Erasmus's *Colloquia* in schools. By and large, the commissioners assumed that correction of abuses would end schism. For the more basic doctrinal issues raised by Luther and the reformers, there was little understanding. Pope Paul welcomed the report and attempted to follow its guidelines. Lutheran propagandists, however, saw in the report a verification of their charges against the papacy.

THE UNCERTAIN BEGINNINGS

The pope agreed to summon a council to study further the problems confronting the church. After several abortive attempts to call a council to meet in Mantua (1537), then in Vicenza (1538), Trent was finally agreed upon as the meeting place. Pope Paul had hoped that the council would begin its sessions in 1543 but once again war between France and the Empire preempted center stage; not until December, 1545, did the deliberations begin. At Trent, an Italian city just inside the imperial borders, action was to be taken that would reinvigorate Catholicism and present a determined front against Protestantism.

Throughout the summer of 1545, prelates straggled into the city. Many mistrustful princes were less than enthusiastic about permitting bishops to attend the deliberations. Francis I added to the uncertainty by recalling some of his emissaries. Yet, despite suspicion and sparse representation, the discussions began.

Three papal legates were appointed to preside over the council: Cardinals del Monte (later Pope Julius III); Cervini (later Marcellus II); and Reginald Pole of England. As the sessions opened, another cardinal, four archbishops, twenty-one bishops (mostly Italian), five generals of orders, and some fifty canonists and theologians were present. Most German prelates were ominously absent. In its procedural deliberations, the council first recognized papal supremacy; then it decided to restrict voting to bishops, heads of religious orders, and representatives of monastic congregations, rather than to permit voting by nations, as had been the policy at Constance and Basel. A third and crucial decision was to disallow proxy voting by absent bishops, a step that assured Italian and papal domination.

Political considerations soon intruded upon the council. Charles, hoping to conciliate the German Protestants, supported German bishops who declared that only reform could save the church and that correction of abuses be given highest priority, but the pope insisted that dogma be defined first. The council then agreed to examine doctrine and reform simultaneously. Among the more important actions taken was the definition of authority in the church. Scripture and tradition were declared to be of equal authority; the Protestant insistence on *sola Scriptura* was rejected. Some of the conciliatory bishops suggested that the Scriptures contained all that was necessary to salvation; Cardinal Pole, however, insisted that beliefs and worship "depend upon tradition."[15] The cardinal carried the day, thus solidifying a position he knew would effectively bar Protestant participation. The council went on to assert that the Vulgate translation was authoritative, and to define original sin and justification in terms sharply differing from Luther.[16]

Meanwhile, the emperor was defeating the League of Schmalkald. After Muehlberg (1547), Charles seemed to be in a position of unprecedented strength. Still hoping to reach an accommodation with the Protestants, he issued the Interim (May 15, 1548), which allowed communion in both kinds and permitted clerical marriage. Once again, the pope feared imperial intrusion and proceeded to form a Holy League to check Charles. In the midst of these deliberations, Paul died (November, 1549). In the previous year, the pope had transferred the council to Bologna. Charles, who knew that Germany would not accept decrees from a city in the papal states, ordered his prelates to remain in Trent. The council was accordingly suspended at the very moment when the imperial military triumph offered the papacy a remarkable opportunity to restore the old religion. Once again, animosity between pope and emperor prevented the development of a unified, effective policy. Suspicion and distrust played no small part in preserving Protestantism.

In 1550 Cardinal del Monte was chosen as pope and took the name Julius III. The new pope was more amenable to the wishes of the emperor. He agreed to reconvene the council, to reexamine the decrees of the first session and to invite the Lutherans. The council reassembled in May, 1551, but immediately encountered difficulties. Once again, events in the political arena stayed effective action. A dispute over Parma brought war between the pope and Ottavio Farnese. Henry II of France, a supporter of Farnese, denounced the council and refused to permit his prelates to attend. By 1552, however, Julius III, resenting the emperor's influence and his insistence that Protestants be heard at the council, reversed his position and formed an alliance with Henry. The French king was also allied to Maurice of Saxony and other German princes.

[15]B. J. Kidd, *The Counter-Reformation* (London: S.P.C.K., 1963), p. 60.
[16]Jedin, *Council of Trent*, II:149–162 and 307–309; John H. Leith, ed., *Creeds of the Churches* (Chicago: Aldine, 1963), pp. 404–424.

THE FAILURE OF CONCILIATION

Amidst these bewildering political developments, the sparsely attended sessions at Trent continued. Protestant delegates were present from January to March, 1552, and presented their doctrinal statements. For a moment, the prospect of reunion appeared on the horizon. German prelates supported the Lutheran demand that communion in both kinds be permitted, but the council rejected this position. This action, as well as the previous decision to accept as binding the work of the earlier assembly, demonstrated the vastness of the chasm between the two faiths. The council, at the urging of the influential Jesuits, Alfonso Salmeron and Diego Laynez, also adopted traditional statements on the Eucharist, penance, and extreme unction.

In April, 1552, the council was again suspended, for a victorious Protestant army, led by Maurice, was in pursuit of the emperor. Charles barely escaped capture at Innsbruck, while Maurice was rumored to be preparing to march on Trent. In the ensuing confusion, the council agreed to suspend deliberations for at least two years. The sessions would not be resumed until 1562.

During this intervening decade, momentous events changed the face of Europe. In 1555, the Peace of Augsburg recognized the religious division of the Empire, and a bitterly disillusioned emperor soon abdicated. From 1555 to 1559, Cardinal Carafa, resolute defender of traditionalism, reigned as Paul IV. In his grim determination to defend his church, he did not hesitate to move ruthlessly against any suggested accommodation with Protestants. Cardinal Morone was imprisoned for taking a too conciliatory position toward Protestantism. Cardinal Pole, on similar charges, was ordered to appear in Rome, but Queen Mary blocked such action. Inquisition and Index were used to the fullest extent as the pope, under the prodding and influence of the Jesuits, determined to crush liberal Catholicism and all forms of heresy. Clerical morals and the administration of ecclesiastical affairs came under sharp scrutiny. When the pope learned that his nephews had been among the principal offenders, he expelled them from Rome and deprived them of their offices. Pope Paul agreed that reform was necessary—but he was firmly convinced that he could carry out such a task more effectively than any council.[17]

When Paul died, the city which had felt his heavy hand for four years burst into rioting. Offices of the Inquisition were sacked and heretic prisoners freed. When the cardinals met to choose a successor, they agreed that the new pope should be less harsh and authoritarian. After more than three months of deliberation, they chose a lawyer-diplomat, Pius IV (1559–1565). The new pope, while thoroughly committed to the maintenance of the power of his office and the reform program of Paul IV, even to the extent of hanging a cardinal, generally

[17]Marvin R. O'Connell, *The Counter Reformation* (New York: Harper & Row, 1974), p. 91.

MONUMENT: POPE PAUL IV, by Pirro Ligorio

Passionately devoted to what he believed to be the best interests of the church, he regarded no one as being above rigorous scrutiny and correction. Even the proud republic of Venice bowed to his demands that suspects accused of heresy be delivered to Rome.

in S. Maria sopra Minerva, Rome; Alinari

proved more lenient and flexible. By a papal order, the council once again resumed its deliberations (January, 1562). Now that Charles V had been succeeded by his brother, the shadow of imperial threat was substantially reduced. Emperor Ferdinand still hoped to reach an understanding with the Protestants, and accordingly urged the council to accept such compromise measures as communion in two kinds, marriage of the clergy, and reduction of papal authority. His program was supported by most of the German bishops, but they were only a small minority at Trent. French bishops, headed by the Cardinal of Lorraine, supported some of the German demands, but the Spanish bishops resolutely opposed any doctrinal revision. Even without Spanish support, the Italians always had a voting majority.

THE PAPACY TRIUMPHANT

Pope Pius understood well the necessity of close cooperation with the temporal powers, and so, while the council deliberated, he negotiated with the emperor and the kings of Spain and France. Skillful diplomacy enabled the pope to ally himself with both temporal rulers and thus to avoid many of the problems that had confronted his predecessors. A particularly urgent issue for the imperial and French representatives was the question of giving the chalice to the laity. Pope Pius indicated some sympathy with these requests, but champions of a rigid position, led by Laynez, eventually persuaded the pope and council to oppose such a concession. French insistence was gradually dissipated, for the outbreak of war with the Huguenots convinced the king that he needed full papal support. And Ferdinand, having listened to the skillful and persuasive arguments of the Jesuit Peter Canisius, also modified his position. The cause of reform, Ferdinand agreed, would be best served by close collaboration between pope and emperor, especially since the pope seemed more conciliatory than the curia.

The task of wooing the emperor was carried on by Cardinal Morone, papal legate at Trent. After lengthy discussion with the emperor—and numerous concessions, among them papal support for Ferdinand's son Maximilian as emperor designate and a promise that communion in both kinds would be permitted— Morone convinced his imperial host that further objections would be inadvisable. French demands for reform had been championed by the Cardinal of Lorraine, but his position was jeopardized when his brother, the Duke of Guise, was murdered and the king was forced to make concessions to the Protestants. The cardinal was also becoming aware of his need for papal support. Then, when Pius offered him the office of apostolic legate in France, the cardinal decided to make his peace with the pope. As the council held its last session in 1562 and 1563, papal interests emerged triumphant. Cardinal Morone closed the council on December 4, 1563, and on January 26, 1564, Pope Pius gave his approval to its decrees and canons. The bull *Benedictus Deus* published on June 30, 1564 approved all decrees without modification. Papal authority had been vigorously asserted and defended—a Jesuit had even attempted to include a statement on papal infallibility, but that would not become recognized doctrine until the First Vatican Council of 1870. The ranks of the Catholic church, largely united in doctrinal issues, were drawn up in battle array; Protestantism was now confronted by a rigidly defined faith which demanded uncompromising adherence. The disarray, uncertainty, and attempts at reconciliation which had enormously contributed to the early Protestant successes were now over.[18]

[18]To assert that reconciliation had become impossible, as some historians have done— for example, Norman Sikes, *The Crisis of the Reformation* (New York: Norton, 1967), p. 99—however, seems too harsh a judgment.

THE IMPACT OF THE COUNCIL

Responding vigorously to the challenge of Protestantism, the council defined Catholic dogma in terms that clearly set it apart from the beliefs of its opponents. Because of persistent division some issues were left unresolved at Trent, most notably the question of the nature of the church itself—a question Protestant reformers had regarded as crucial.

Trent did, however, establish a doctrinal stance that would determine the position of the Catholic church in modern times. In addition to adopting statements that rejected the Protestant emphasis on *sola Scriptura* and *sola fide*, the council imposed obligatory residence on bishops and priests, defined the sacraments and insisted that all seven were valid, ordered that seminaries be established to train priests, and approved the use of indulgences, invocation of saints, and veneration of relics. Abuses had been boldly attacked. Simony, plural benefices, lack of adequate training for priests—all came under severest censure. Specific, high standards were set for the clergy. The well trained, carefully disciplined, elevated priest was one of Trent's most consequential legacies.[19]

Of approximately 250 signatories, more than two-thirds were Italian. Attempts to gain approval by secular authorities were successful in Italy and Poland, but not in the Empire, where the diet withheld its approval, despite the fact that a number of territorial princes vigorously enforced the decisions of Trent. And in France, attachment to old Gallican and conciliar views, as well as a reticence to accentuate divisions between Calvinists and Catholics, prevented official French confirmation of the disciplinary decrees, although the dogmatic statements were accepted. Spain, with obvious determination to safeguard royal power, granted approval insofar as the decrees were "without prejudice to the rights of the king." Although Pius IV objected to Philip's determination "to be pope as well as king," the monarch refused to surrender any of his prerogatives. Even in strictly religious matters, the king, not the pope, determined Spanish policy. Altogether, the council and pope could only define religious practices; observance depended upon support from secular authorities. Thus when temporal authorities, especially in the strongly centralized states, found papal support superfluous, they once again reverted to national self-interest.

Suggestions for Further Reading

Boehmer, Heinrich. *Ignatius von Loyola*. Stuttgart: Koehler, 1951.

Broderick, James. *The Origin of the Jesuits*. London: Longmans, Green, 1940.

———. *The Progress of the Jesuits*. London: Longmans, Green, 1947.

———. *Saint Francis Xavier*. London: Burns & Oates, 1952.

*Indicates paperback edition.

[19]O'Connell, *The Counter Reformation*, p. 102.

———. *St. Ignatius Loyola: The Pilgrim Years.* New York: Farrar, Straus and Cudahy, 1956.

Brown, G. K. *Italy and the Reformation to 1550.* Oxford: Blackwell, 1933.

*****Burns, Edward M.** *The Counter-Reformation.* Princeton, N.J.: Van Nostrand Reinhold, 1964.

Church, F. C. *The Italian Reformers.* New York: Columbia University Press, 1932.

*****Cohen, J. M.**, ed. *The Life of St. Teresa of Avila.* Baltimore: Penguin Books, 1957.

Cristiani, L. *L'Eglise à l'époque du Concile de Trente.* Paris: Bloud et Gay, 1948.

*****Daniel-Rops, H.** *The Catholic Reformation.* Translated by J. Warrington, New York: Dutton, 1962.

*****Dickens, A. G.** *The Counter Reformation.* New York: Harcourt, Brace & World, 1969.

Douglas, Richard M. *Jacopo Sadoleto, 1477–1547: Humanist and Reformer.* Cambridge, Mass.: Harvard University Press, 1959.

Dudon, Paul. *St. Ignatius of Loyola.* Translated by W. J. Young. Milwaukee: Bruce, 1949.

Dunn, Richard. *The Age of Religious Wars, 1559–1689.* New York: Norton, 1970.

Evennett, H. O. *The Cardinal of Lorraine and the Council of Trent.* London: Cambridge University Press, 1940.

———. *The Spirit of the Counter-Reformation,* edited by John Bossy. London: Cambridge University Press, 1968.

Fenlon, Dermot. *Heresy and Obedience in Tridentine Italy.* London: Cambridge University Press, 1972.

Garstein, Oskar. *Rome and the Counter-Reformation in Scandinavia.* Oslo: Universitetsforlaget, 1963.

Harney, M. P. *The Jesuits in History.* New York: American Press, 1941.

Hughes, Philip. *Rome and the Counter-Reformation.* London: Burns & Oates, 1942.

Janelle, Pierre. *The Catholic Reformation.* Milwaukee: Bruce, 1949.

Jedin, Hubert. *A History of the Council of Trent,* 2 vols. Translated by E. Graf. St. Louis: Herder, 1957, 1961.

Kidd, B. J. *The Counter-Reformation.* London: S.P.C.K., 1933.

McNally, Robert E. *Reform of the Church.* New York: Herder and Herder, 1963.

———. *The Unreformed Church.* New York: Sheed & Ward, 1965.

*———. *The Council of Trent, the ''Spiritual Exercises'' and the Catholic Reform.* Philadelphia: Fortress Press, 1970.

McNair, Philip. *Peter Martyr in Italy.* Oxford: Clarendon, 1967.

*****O'Connell, Marvin R.** *The Counter Reformation.* New York: Harper & Row, 1974.

Olin, J. C. ed. *The Catholic Reformation: Savonarola to Ignatius Loyola.* New York: Harper & Row, 1969.

Rahner, Hugo. *Ignatius von Loyola.* Freiburg: Herder, 1964.

Richter, Friedrich. *Martin Luther and Ignatius Loyola.* Translated by L. F. Zwinger. Westminister, Md.: Newman Press, 1960.

Searle, G. W. *The Counter Reformation.* Totowa, N. J.: Rowman and Littlefield, 1974.

Tedeschi, John A. *Italian Reformation Studies in Honor of Laelius Socinus.* Florence: LeMonnier, 1965.

Tuechle, Hermann, et al. *Réforme et Contre-Réforme.* Paris: Editions du Seuil, 1968.

***Von Matt, Leonard, and Hugo Rahner.** *St. Ignatius of Loyola.* Maryknoll, N.Y.: Orbis Books, 1963.

Willaert, Léopold. *Après le Concile de Trente: La Restauration catholique, 1563– 1648.* Paris: Bloud et Gay, 1960.

Young, W. J., ed. and trans. *Letters of St. Ignatius Loyola.* Chicago: Loyola University Press, 1959.

***Zeeden, E. W.** *Das Zeitalter der Gegenreformation.* Freiburg: Herder, 1967.

11

Inquisition,
Index,
and Intolerance

As the struggle for the religious allegiance of Europe's citizens became more bitter, both sides adopted desperate measures to gain control over the minds of the people. Participants in the conflict regarded the issue as one of the highest priority. Hopes for reconciliation seemed increasingly remote, so that rival camps came to view their own survival as dependent upon the destruction of their opponent.

The tone for the increasingly bitter confrontation was quickly set by pen and burin. Intensely emotional appeals confronted the masses as the reason and moderation of the humanists receded into the background. Scurrilous attacks by the various antagonists became commonplace. A flood of pamphlets, broadsides, cartoons, and other propaganda devices poured from the presses. In the spring of 1521, *The Passional of Christ and Antichrist* appeared and set the tone for much subsequent anti-papal caricature. The *Passional*, composed of twenty-six woodcuts, attempted to discredit the papacy by depicting the pope as always doing the opposite of what the Scriptures taught, and eventually consigned to eternal damnation. Similar themes appeared in *The Papacy Painted and Described by its Members*. Caricatures of various ecclesiastics, accompanied by vitriolic verse from the pen of Hans Sachs, depicted popes, cardinals, bishops, and priests as a blight on society. The book gained great popularity and was frequently reprinted.

Cartoons and broadsides carried the message to the illiterate, as vendors sold their wares throughout the countryside. A favorite target of cartoon was the pope, who was often depicted as a donkey, an extortioner, a lecher, or worse. Often he was shown as either coming from, or descending into hell. Catholic caricaturists responded by portraying Luther as the devil or a fool. Neither side felt bound by the restraints of propriety or decency.

Early in the Lutheran Reformation, the pamphlet came to be an especially effective means for influencing the masses. Usually composed of not more than

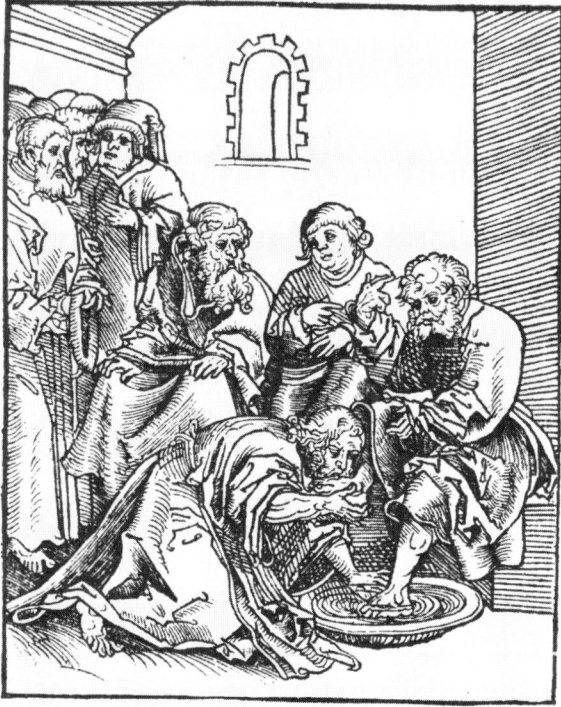

Paſſional Chriſti und

WOODCUTS: FROM THE PASSIONAL CHRISTI UND ANTICHRISTI
by Lucas Cranach the Elder

In a series of woodcuts, the pope was depicted as the antithesis of everything Christian. The theme of the pope as Antichrist is found repeatedly in late-medieval anticlerical literature, such as that of John Wycliffe. Here the artist depicts the humility of Christ as he washed the feet of the disciples. The other shows the pope being devoured by hell. Everyone could understand the savagery of such vituperation.

three or four printed sheets and adorned with a woodcut, the pamphlet became probably Luther's most effective instrument of mass indoctrination. Opponents of Luther, quick to realize the effectiveness of this device, were soon excelling in their own use of vitriolic prose. The technique spread rapidly, so that wherever Catholicism and Protestantism stood in opposition, pamphlets inundated the scene.

Drama and music were similarly forged into weapons of war, both on the continent and in England and Scotland. Anti-Lutheran plays were performed in England in the 1520s; soon thereafter, however, roles were reversed as playwrights such as John Bale (1495–1563) championed the Lutheran cause.[1] Bibli-

[1]See Rainer Pineas, *Tudor and Early Stuart Anti-Catholic Drama* (Nieuwkoop: de Graaf, 1972), p. 5.

Antichristi.

cal and historical events were cast into a simple mold of good versus evil, in which vices were inevitably portrayed as Catholic. The pope was represented as the devil, while Christ and the saints took on Protestant form. In music, the contrast between good and evil was equally stark and simple. Luther early recognized the power of music in shaping his movement, and the singing congregation became characteristic of Protestantism. At the same time, the less sophisticated recognized the power of music as a weapon to attack, castigate, or ridicule. As popular ballads were transformed into expressions of scurrilous denunciation, artistic endeavor began to resemble a propaganda campaign.

THE INQUISITION

In this atmosphere of enmity and suspicion, systematic attempts were made to crush the opposition. Of all the weapons forged to fight Protestantism, few would prove as effective and ruthless as the Inquisition. This institution had been used to combat heresy in the Middle Ages. Under the Dominicans and Franciscans, it became a terrifying weapon for depriving heretics of their possessions, their civil rights, even their lives. The inquisitorial courts themselves did not inflict the death penalty; this was carried out by the state. The Inquisition, expressing Pope Innocent III's insistence that it was "infinitely more serious to offend against the Divine Majesty than to injure human majesty"[2] hunted heretics as kings hunted traitors. The extinction of the Cathari and the decimation of the Waldenses owed much to the zeal of inquisitors.[3]

In the later Middle Ages, the Inquisition had fallen into disuse throughout most of Europe. Only in Spain, with the drive for national consolidation, had the institution been reinstituted by Papal bull (1478). Here the Inquisition, dominated by Ferdinand and Isabella, became a powerful weapon of secular authority. Under the Inquisitor-General Tomás de Torquemada, Spain witnessed a holocaust that claimed hundreds of victims. At least 2,000 people were burned at the stake between 1480 and 1498, and thousands more languished in prisons. Most of these early victims were Jews or Moors, regarded as potential threats to the unity of the realm. Later, with the rise of Protestantism, this instrument was used to purge the realm of heretics.

The Spanish Inquisition, having demonstrated its effectiveness in creating uniformity, greatly impressed Cardinal Carafa, papal nuncio in Spain. When he returned to Rome, Carafa convinced Pope Paul III that the Spanish device might well be adapted by the papacy. According to Carafa, the Lutheran heresy had gained widespread support in Italy, among both statesmen and ecclesiastics. In reality, however, this report had been blown all out of proportion. At any rate, Ignatius of Loyola warmly endorsed the proposal, and on July 21, 1542, the papal bull *Licit ab initio* established the congregation of the Holy Office, the Roman Inquisition. Six cardinals, among them Carafa, were appointed Inquisitors-General, each of whom was authorized to try cases of heresy, to imprison suspects, to impose penalties, and to call for support from secular authorities.

The zeal of the Inquisitors augured well for their success. Even before he was given papal funding, Carafa bought a house in Rome and equipped it with trial chambers, prison cells, and instruments of torture. His zeal, expressed in his command to his inquisitors not to show "toleration towards any sort of heretic,"[4] made the Inquisition a terrifying device. Cardinal Seripando noted that from no other courts were "more horrible and fearful sentences to be expected."[5] Carafa realized that heresy would be exterminated only if its leaders were destroyed. Throughout the Italian peninsula, he now launched a vigorous campaign not only against heretics but also against all advocates of liberal reforms. There could be

[2]B. J. Kidd, *The Counter-Reformation* (London: S.P.C.K., 1963), p. 40.

[3]The Cathari denouncing the material world as evil, rejected beliefs in the Incarnation and the sacraments, while the Waldenses denounced ecclesiastical wealth and power and emphasized preaching and scriptural authority. They also rejected participation in war and demanded that the Sermon on the Mount serve as a guide to human conduct.

[4]Owen Chadwick, *The Reformation* (Baltimore: Penguin Books, 1964), p. 270.

[5]Ludwig Pastor, *The History of the Popes* (London: Kegan Paul, Trench Trubner & Co., 1938), XII:508.

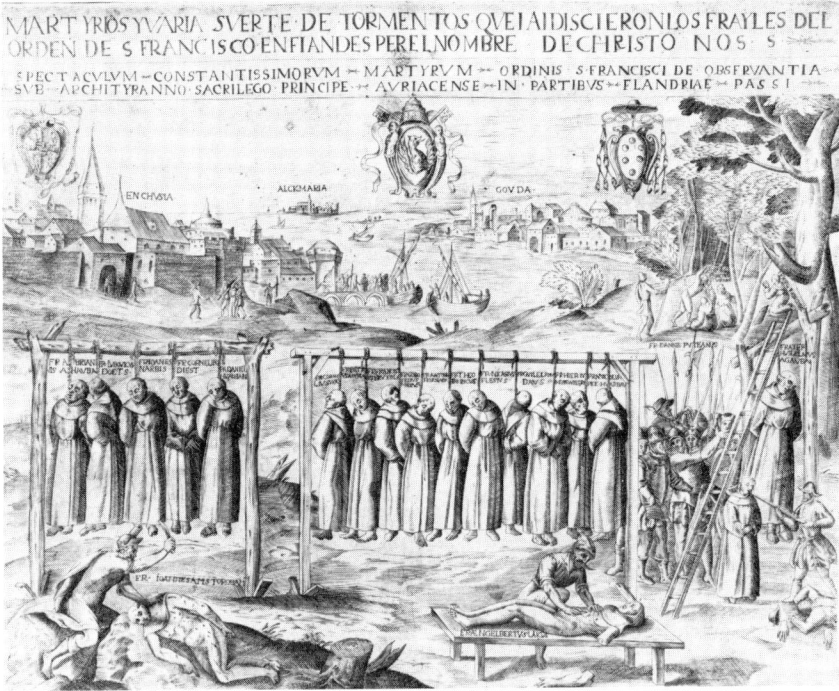

ENGRAVING: MASSACRE OF OBSERVANTINE FRIARS

No side had a monopoly on religious intolerance and persecution. In 1580, fanatic Dutch Protestants barbarously massacred these Observantines.

British Museum

no compromise with the errors of heretics—nor with those who, though orthodox in faith, still called for leniency toward Protestants. Outside the borders of Italy, sovereigns were largely able to resist this new system of papal courts, but within the peninsula even such fiercely independent states as Venice bowed to the indomitable will of Carafa and his associates. Moderate Catholic leaders were powerless to assert their will.

Inquisitors soon found that it was not always easy to differentiate between nascent Protestantism and liberal reform. In such cases, suspects, were seldom given the benefit of the doubt: better to imprison an innocent suspect than to run the risk of spreading heresy. As the Inquisition expanded its operations, many suspects sought refuge in flight; some were fortunate enough to be protected by powerful friends. When Bernardino Ochino was summoned to Rome in 1542, he fled to Geneva and openly embraced Protestantism. This event merely confirmed Carafa's suspicions that the Italian situation was critical; methods that were already rigorous would have to be intensified. The Blessed Fellowship—the circle of Juan de Valdés in Naples—found that their advocacy of reform had given rise to grave suspicions and indeed some adherents of the group later embraced Protestantism. Pietro Carnesecchi, one of the Valdesiani,[6] formerly apostolic protonotary at the court of Clement VII, survived a trial in 1545. In 1559 he was summoned to appear before the Inquisition, but he fled to Geneva and was condemned *in absentia*. In 1562, his friend Cosimo de'Medici obtained a reversal of the sentence and Carnesecchi retired to Florence—only to fall victim to relentless papal and inquisitorial pressure that eventually resulted in condemnation and death. Another member of the Valdesiani, Peter Martyr Vermigli, former prior of the Augustinians at Naples and later at Lucca, fled from the threat of the Inquisition. He later became a professor at Oxford and defended with Beza the views of French Calvinists in the Poissy Colloquy. The Bishop of Bergamo, also a member of Blessed Fellowship, was imprisoned for two years, then temporarily freed, only to be arrested again and dismissed from his office (1558). Other prominent critics of ecclesiastical abuses similarly found their position untenable. Pietro Paolo Vergerio, several times papal nuncio in Germany, and bishop of Capo d'Istria from 1536 to 1549, was tried and deposed. He fled to Wuerttemberg and became a leader of Italian Lutherans there. Some centers of learning, such as the academies of Modena and Naples, found the inquisitorial atmosphere so oppressive that the faculties disbanded.

Carafa's iron resolve to free the Catholic church of any trace of heresy often brought suffering to the innocent. When Cardinal Contarini died in 1542, he was under a heavy cloud of suspicion as a heretic. Cardinal Morone, bishop of Modena, was arrested and kept in prison from 1557 until Carafa, now Pope Paul IV, died in 1559. A similar fate would have befallen Cardinal Pole, but he was then safely in England, attempting to root out Protestantism there. Any sign of a predilection toward reform was enough to render a clergyman suspect.

Relentlessly, the Inquisition burned out traces of Protestantism throughout Italy. Even cities with a long tradition of fierce independence gradually succumbed to the demands of the Inquisitors, and towns that contained groups of organized Protestants—such as Casalmaggiore, Mantua, and Lucca—witnessed intensive efforts to drive out heresy. Renée, duchess of Ferrara and friend of Calvin, was eventually driven from her country, only to continue her involvement with Protestants in France. In Venice, Protestants felt strong enough to urge the senate to grant them religious toleration; yet city government proved no match for inquisitorial zeal, as authorities succumbed to Pope Paul IV and sent several heretics to their death at the stake in Rome. Nothing was to be permitted to obstruct "truth": "Even if my own father were a heretic," vowed the pope, "I would gather the wood to burn him."[7] Such rigorous repression was bound to arouse opposition, and when Pope Paul died, the Roman populace sacked the buildings of the Holy Office, burned the records of the dreaded proceedings, and

---

[6]The Valdesiani, followers of Juan de Valdès, are to be distinguished from the Valdesi (Waldenses), disciples of the medieval reformer, Peter Waldo.

[7]Pastor, *The History of the Popes,* XIV:300.

demolished the statue that had been erected to the pope. Destruction of a few symbols of the Inquisition, however, had little permanent effect. Throughout the rest of the century—and beyond—the Holy Office continued its dreaded operations.

THE *INDEX*

Rome also attempted to combat heresy through preventive measures—by attempting to control literature to which the unlearned might be exposed. In 1559 the pope issued the first official Roman *Index* of prohibited books. This *Index librorum prohibitorum* had been preceded by earlier attempts to restrict printing, as well as by frequent denunciations of heretical books. Local indexes had been issued in Paris, Louvain, Milan, and elsewhere. Now the pope's official list of "dangerous" books divided all such works into three categories: (1) all works by authors who were guilty or suspected of heresy, even though individual volumes might be inoffensive (all works of Erasmus were included in this category); (2) selected works of otherwise orthodox authors, since these specific books might undermine the faith of some; and (3) various books which contained heretical teachings, many of them of anonymous authorship. The *Index* also prohibited the reading of vernacular translations of the New Testament. All publications coming from some sixty-one presses were condemned. Included in the sweeping prohibitions were all the writings of Machiavelli, Rabelais, Peter Abelard, and numerous others. Various ecclesiastical leaders, including the influential Jesuit Canisius, protested that the Index was too severe, but the pope insisted that the gravity of the threat to Christendom demanded such sweeping measures.

The *Index* received scant attention in most countries, but in Italy it occasioned widespread bookburning. One bonfire in Venice disposed of more than ten thousand books, while Sixtus of Siena congratulated himself for having disposed of twelve thousand books in Cremona. Included in this destruction were all available copies of the condemned Talmud. The harsh Roman *Index* was modified in 1564, but even the more moderate version made pursuit of the liberal arts difficult. It was not a time for free inquiry and expression, for in this battle for the minds of men, every method seemed justified. By the middle of the century, the last vestiges of the earlier tolerance so characteristic of the humanistic movement seemed obliterated.

THE TRIUMPH OF INTOLERANCE

If intolerance had become a dominant characteristic of the papacy, it had also become a distinctive characteristic of most of Protestantism. Religious liberty and freedom of expression were denounced by Catholic and Protestant alike. While nothing in Protestant Europe ever equalled the Inquisition in scope and efficiency, Protestant theologians and princes had their own means for eradicating unorthodox views.

Sometimes, the Protestant response to doctrinal deviation was hesitant and spasmodic. As a young reformer, Luther had called for rejection of physical coercion in matters of faith. False doctrine should be overcome by biblical teaching, not the sword. When the bull *Exsurge domine* was issued, Luther contended that to burn heretics was contrary to the teachings of Christ. Faith could not be produced by compulsion. In 1523, Luther, in his *Concerning Secular Authority*, insisted that no one should be forced to believe; heresy could not be effectively countered by sword, fire, or water. Secular rulers had no jurisdiction in spiritual affairs and thus had no right to deprive anyone of the right to believe as he wished.

Already under the threat of the Peasants' War, however, Luther began to modify his view of the state's role in combatting religious error. Soon he was prepared to admit that secular authorities should use their power to compel all citizens to hear the truth and to prevent heretics from disseminating their doctrines. In 1526 Luther expressed a view that would eventually be confirmed in the Peace of Augsburg: A prince had the right to permit only one religion— otherwise civil order would yield to division and turmoil. In the following year, Luther's visitation program in Saxony imposed a uniform worship service. Uneasy about the use of secular power to enforce his religious views, Luther now explained his actions by noting that no force was being used to compel belief, only outward conformity. Conscience, he declared, was still free but civil disorder was being prevented. Luther agreed, however, that those who refused to attend Lutheran church services should be expelled from the land.

Eventually, Luther moved beyond recommending enforced exile to a limited support of the death penalty. In 1528, he still opposed capital punishment even for those who denied the Trinity, but some of his associates deplored his hesitancy. Melanchthon, despite his conciliatory efforts, in 1530 wrote that those who openly championed blasphemous views should be executed, even if such beliefs were not seditious. A year later, when Elector John Frederick asked if Anabaptists should be put to death, Melanchthon wrote the response. Capital punishment, even for peaceful Anabaptists, was warranted. Luther's footnote to the document revealed once again the anguish he felt over this problem; nonetheless, he gave it his reluctant approval.[8] The reformer who had once insisted that it was wrong to burn heretics now condoned death for wrong belief, an opinion he would subsequently reiterate. Although Luther had no desire to instigate procedures that would ferret out all those who disagreed with his teachings and Saxony never suffered any large-scale execution of Catholics and non-Lutheran Protestants, earlier hopes of religious toleration in Lutheran states had been shattered. Ironically, the ardently Lutheran Philip of Hesse disagreed with such stringent policies, and refused to execute anyone because of his belief, but his position was emulated by few.

[8]*Corpus Reformatorum*, IV:740.

In Switzerland, meanwhile, Zwingli demonstrated that he was less reluctant than Luther to use coercion in matters of faith. By 1526, he was prepared to condone capital punishment for serious religious deviation. In 1527, he approved the drowning of an Anabaptist and subsequently urged secular authorities to prevent the spread of unapproved doctrine. Furthermore, citizens of Zurich were compelled to attend the Zwinglian church services, under penalty of expulsion. With unembarrassed inconsistency, Zwingli urged authorities in Catholic cantons to permit the free preaching of the gospel, yet once Zwinglianism had become dominant, he quickly prohibited voluntary observance of traditional practices. Celebrating the Mass, or attending such celebrations, became a crime to be suppressed by civil authorities.

It was in Strasbourg, the thriving commercial center, that religious toleration temporarily gained considerable support.[9] As Zwinglianism and Lutheranism both attempted to displace the old faith, nonconformist elements such as the Anabaptists were briefly permitted broad liberties by a city council that was more concerned about prosperity and tranquillity than about doctrinal nuances. Yet, as leaders such as Capito and Bucer gradually emerged as dominant religious figures, they persuaded the civil authorities that to permit religious diversity would be to destroy the city. In 1533, Bucer lamented that the church in Strasbourg had been ruined by the tragedy of tolerating various religious movements. Only vigorous and drastic action could save the true faith. As a result of continued pressure from the leading reformers in the city, the government embarked upon a program of rigorous suppression of religious deviation. A brief experiment in partial toleration had been effectively crushed by the zealous efforts of Bucer and his associates. Intolerance had found its strongest champions, not in the ranks of the magistracy, but among the clergy.[10]

Like Luther, Zwingli, and Bucer, Calvin insisted that the power of the state be used to safeguard truth and suppress error. In Geneva adherence to the reformed faith was mandatory, and serious deviation could bring death. The burning of Servetus was only one of numerous executions in Geneva because of unorthodox beliefs. Throughout Catholic and Protestant cantons of Switzerland, to deny the Trinity or to reject infant baptism was to invite death. Calvin, unlike Luther, had no hesitancy in using force to destroy unacceptable belief. Convinced of the absolute validity of his views, he resolutely denounced toleration in matters as important as religion. Beza, echoing Calvin's sentiments, contended that anyone who opposed suppression of heresy by the magistrates was "despising the Word of God." Such views did not prevent either Calvin or Beza from carrying on

[9] See Miriam Chrisman, *Strasbourg and the Reform* (New Haven: Yale University Press, 1967).

[10] For a convincing refutation of the widely held view that Bucer championed religious toleration, see Henry G. Krahn, *An Analysis of the Conflict Between the Clergy . . . and the Leaders of the Anabaptist Movement* (Unpub. Ph.D. dissertation, University of Washington, 1969).

extensive correspondence with Catholics or non-Calvinistic Protestants. Thus, when the Jesuit Lucas Pinelli visited Geneva in 1580, Beza received him courteously and had an amiable discussion with him—but there was no thought of allowing Jesuits free rein in the city of Calvin.

Toleration was no better known under English Erastianism. As Henry VIII broke with Rome, he emphatically condemned any religious deviation from the position approved by the crown. Catholics who, as a matter of conscience, could not accept the Henrician reforms, were executed at Smithfield—along with Protestants who carried their reformation further than the king desired. England was to have no religion save that of Henry. Lutherans, Zwinglians, and especially Anabaptists were hounded because of unacceptable beliefs. Under Edward VI, Cranmer intensified his warm relationship with continental reformers, and the range of permissible religious views was expanded, although Anabaptists were still burned at the stake. Cranmer had no hesitancy in using the power of the state to enforce religious uniformity. An even more intensive policy of repression characterized Mary's reign, only this time the official religion was Catholic. Then, during the long reign of Elizabeth, when broadly inclusive Anglicanism became the legal religion, unacceptable dissent continued to be harshly repressed. The queen agreed with her secretary of state, William Cecil, that "the State could never be in Safety, where there was a Tolleration of two religions."[11] Nonetheless, although toleration was not an official policy, quiet Recusants—Catholics who refused to embrace the state religion—were usually not harassed. Some were even permitted to hold positions at court.[12]

THE QUEST FOR RELIGIOUS FREEDOM

Despite the overwhelming spectacle of religious intolerance in virtually all Catholic and Protestant states, voices clamoring for liberty in matters of faith continued to be heard. Economic, philosophical, and humanitarian motives constantly gave rise to pleas for freedom.

In the early stages of the Reformation, some of the humanists urged that matters of faith be settled through discussion, not coercion. Erasmus, with his frequent denunciations of war and violence, deplored the burning of heretics, but even this most liberal of humanists agreed that in extreme cases heretics should be sent to the stake. In 1526 he suggested that tolerance of Lutheranism until a general council could be called might be better than forcible suppression. However, permanent toleration of differing religions, he contended, could only engender dissension and strife.

It was within the ranks of Anabaptism that religious freedom found some of its earliest champions in the Reformation era. Balthasar Hubmaier's *Concerning*

---

[11]Joseph Lecler, *Toleration and the Reformation*, 2 vols., trans. T. L. Westow. (New York: Association Press, 1960), II:355.

[12]A. L. Rowse, *The England of Elizabeth* (New York: Collier Books, 1966), p. 390.

Heretics and Those Who Burn Them (1524) forcefully argued that to burn heretics was contrary to the teaching and example of Christ. False teaching should be confronted by right doctrine and godly living, never by physical coercion. To burn a heretic was worse than being a heretic. Subsequently, Hubmaier expanded on the theme of religious toleration and urged a separation of church and state. Churches should be characterized by voluntary membership, with no state enforcement of any matters of belief or religious practice. Attendance at church services should be voluntary, with everyone granted complete freedom of conscience.

Other Anabaptist leaders maintained similar positions. In 1524, when disquieting news concerning Thomas Muentzer's militancy reached Switzerland, a group of Zurich Anabaptists, including their leader Conrad Grebel, warned Muentzer that the sword ought not to be used either to protect or propagate religious belief. In matters of faith, coercion must be rejected. Muentzer's frightening assertion that "a godless person has no right to live if he hinders the Gospel"[13] was in total contradiction with the position of most Anabaptists. Again, in 1527, the Anabaptist leader Hans Denck contended that belief should be "free, voluntary and uncompelled." A Moravian Anabaptist urged the Strasbourg authorities to permit complete religious toleration, even for Jews and Turks, while Zurich Anabaptists protested to an unresponsive city council that it had no right to control and persecute the conscience. Similarly, Menno Simons, who had been appalled at the recourse to violence in Muenster, repeatedly decried any attempt to use the power of the magistracy to compel religious conformity. To the Anabaptists, it seemed self-evident that, since faith was a gift of God—as Luther, Calvin, and other reformers also maintained—then it was absurd to use coercion to compel belief.

A number of mystic spiritualists also vigorously championed religious toleration. In conformity with their basic thesis that faith was a highly personal and individualistic phenomenon—even to the extent that many of them rejected any formal church organization or sacraments—they opposed any attempt to use coercion and violence in the arena of religion. Sebastian Franck, deploring the religious confusion about him, and rejecting the insistence on various external religious forms, insisted that without free human response there could be no genuine divine-human relationship. Physical coercion was incompatible with the essence of faith. Far ahead of prevailing sentiments of his day, he declared that a papist, a Lutheran, a Zwinglian, an Anabaptist, yes, even a Turk "was a brother."[14] His numerous writings gained him a wide audience, as well as a notable array of opponents, including Luther and Erasmus.

Another mystic spiritualist, Caspar Schwenckfeld, devoted much of his energy to the defense of religious liberty. His voluminous writing and frequent

[13] George H. Williams, *Spiritual and Anabaptist Writers* (Philadelphia: Westminister Press, 1957).
[14] Lecler, *Toleration*, I:265.

wandering led to the establishment of a number of loosely organized groups of followers, who also championed the notion that faith was an inner and individual matter. Coercion in matters of conscience was foreign to Christianity, Schwenckfeld wrote, adding that intolerance could only hinder belief. He contended that the state should not be involved in the affairs of the church; the coercive nature of the state he regarded as antithetical to religion. For him, freedom of conscience and freedom of choice were essential elements of religion. Secular authorities should take care of secular concerns and not attempt to regulate spiritual affairs. In religious matters, every man should be free to follow his conscience.

Of all champions of toleration in the Reformation, few were as thorough in their analysis of intolerance as Sebastian Castellio. Reared in the traditions of French humanism, he fled Lyons when the oppressive policies of Cardinal de Tournon left no room for anything but strict conformity. Castellio came to Strasbourg in 1540, when the city still enjoyed a large measure of toleration. In the following year he went to Geneva to head Calvin's new academy, but by 1543 he found the rigid doctrinal position of that city too uninviting. He withdrew to Basel, there to continue his studies and eventually become professor at the university. When news of the burning of Servetus reached Castellio, he penned his *Concerning Heretics, Whether They are to be Persecuted.* The work appeared under a pseudonym, but Castellio was quickly suspected. Both Calvin and Beza responded to the diabolical challenge presented by the notion of religious liberty. To permit religious toleration, Beza commented, was simply to allow everyone "to go to hell in his own way."[15] In *Concerning Heretics*, Castellio insisted that man must be free to follow his conscience, and that reason must prevail in the establishment of societal norms. Creeds must be authenticated by quality of life, and Castellio could not accept dogmas that left no room for human dignity and freedom of choice. For Castellio, religion could never be removed from the subjective and volitional; to coerce belief was simply to encourage hypocrisy. Neither political nor religious leaders were ready for such radicalism. Castellio was eventually brought to trial, but his death in 1563 cut the trial short.

Other champions of toleration included Bernardino Ochino, the renowned Capuchin leader whose sermons had drawn kings and throngs to hear him. When religious intolerance in Venice brought a thunderous denunciation from Ochino, the pope intervened and summoned the friar to Rome. Ochino suspected the worst and fled to Switzerland. In 1542 he came to Geneva and became a pastor to the Italian refugees. Three years later, he moved on to Augsburg, but the Schmalkaldic war made him a refugee. Eventually he came to Zurich, and here in 1563 he published his *Dialogues*.

In one of the dialogues he denounced the attempts to curb heresy by use of the sword. To kill a person because he believed error was tyranny of the worst sort.

[15] Roland Bainton, *The Travail of Religious Liberty* (New York: Harper & Row, A Harper Torchbook, 1958), p. 114.

Ochino insisted that harsh Old Testament injunctions against heresy had been superseded by the teachings and examples of Christ. Heresy, he declared, was a spiritual problem and should not be combatted by temporal weapons. The appeal for toleration elicited swift response: A few weeks after the publication appeared, the Zurich city council encouraged by Bullinger, expelled him from the city. Despite his seventy-six years, the widowed reformer and his four children were driven out into the December cold. When he sought asylum in Basel, he was refused. After a brief respite in Poland, he was again forced to resume his wanderings. Eventually, in 1565, he found refuge among Moravian Anabaptists, where he died in the same year. All but one of his children had perished in the miseries of flight and plague.

In 1565, another Italian refugee in Switzerland, Jacob Acontius, published a strong defense of toleration, *Satanae Strategemata*. Here the author contended that persecution because of unacceptable belief was actually a service to the devil rather than to God. He urged that everyone be permitted to exercise religious freedom, and optimistically concluded that, when differing views were freely permitted to confront each other, truth would prevail.

EXPERIMENTS IN TOLERATION

Political events in Eastern Europe sometimes helped to create a greater measure of toleration than was to be found in the West. In Poland, the insistence on local autonomy, the weakness of the central diet, and the proliferation of a wide variety of beliefs often resulted in a princely decision not to press for religious uniformity. On occasion, arrangements were made which provided for mutual toleration of Catholics and Protestants. Not surprisingly, this relative freedom attracted so many refugees that Cardinal Hosius lamented that Poland had become an "asylum for heretics." Conditions were similar in Moravia, where powerful lords frequently tolerated Protestantism, even though the king tried repeatedly to curb heresy. Again, a weak diet permitted a large measure of local determination of religious policies.

In the principality of Transylvania, religious toleration gained a remarkable degree of support as the diet repeatedly liberalized its stance. Priot to 1574, more than twenty acts were passed specifically to broaden the range of permitted religious opinions. An act adopted in 1557 by a predominantly Protestant diet declared that everyone was free to "maintain whatever faith he wishes, with old or new rituals, . . . just so long, however, as they bring no harm to bear on anyone else."[16] This document, the *Supplicatio*, also called for the holding of a national synod so that religious differences might be resolved. Transylvania thus became the first continental state to adopt so sweeping a declaration of religious toleration. This stand was again reinforced in the Toleration Act of 1568 when the diet, meeting in Torda, adopted legislation stipulating that congregations

[16] M. E. Osterhaven, *Transylvania*, occasional paper by *The Reformed Review* (1968), p. 22.

PAINTING: PROCLAMATION OF RELIGIOUS LIBERTY, DIET OF TORDA by Aladár
Körösföy-Kriesch

In 1568 the Transylvanian Diet, meeting in Torda, proclaimed religious liberty. The elected
king, John Sigismund, is seated on the throne as he listens to Francis David present an
eloquent defense of freedom of conscience.

Courtesy of the Hungarian Historical Society

should be free to "keep the preachers whose doctrines they approve."[17] The
elected Transylvanian king, John Sigismund, ardently championed freedom of
religion; his views, however, were shared by few of his ruling contemporaries.

Suggestions for Further Reading

Amphoux, Henri, *Michel de L'Hôpital.* Paris: Fischbacher, 1900.

Bainton, Roland. *Bernardino Ochino.* Florence: Sansoni, 1941.

——. *The Travail of Religious Liberty.* Philadelphia: Westminister Press, 1951.

*——. *Hunted Heretic. The Life and Death of Servetus.* Boston: Beacon Press,
   1960.

*Indicates paperback edition.

[17]*Ibid.*, p. 23.

*Bender, Harold. The Anabaptists and Religious Liberty in the Sixteenth Century. Philadelphia: Fortress Press, 1970.

Berthoud, Gabrielle, et al. *Aspects de la Propagande Religieuse.* Geneva: Droz, 1957.

Buisson, A. *Michel de L'Hôpital.* Paris: Hachette, 1950.

Burke, R. *What is the Index?* Milwaukee: Bruce, 1952.

Hassinger, Erich. *Religioese Toleranz im 16. Jahrhundert.* Basel: Helbing und Lichtenhahn, 1966.

Hermelink, H. *Der Toleranzbegriff im Reformationszeitalter.* Leipzig: Verein fuer Reformationsgeschichte, 1908.

Jordan, W. K. *The Development of Religious Toleration in England,* 4 vols. Cambridge, Mass.: Harvard University Press, 1932–40.

*Kamen, H. A. *The Rise of Toleration.* New York: McGraw-Hill, 1967.

Klein, A. J. *Intolerance in the Reign of Elizabeth.* Boston: Houghton Mifflin, 1917.

Lecler, Joseph. *Toleration and the Reformation,* 2 vols. Translated by T. L. Westow. New York: Association Press, 1960.

Littell, F. H. *Landgraf Philipp und die Toleranz.* Bad Nauheim: Christian-Verlag, 1957.

Longhurst, J. E. *Erasmus and the Spanish Inquisition: The Case of Juan de Valdès.* Albuquerque: University of New Mexico Press, 1950.

———. *Luther and the Spanish Inquisition: The Case of Diego de Uceda.* Albuquerque: University of New Mexico Press, 1953.

Smithson, R. J. *The Anabaptists: Their Contribution to our Protestant Heritage.* London: Clarke, 1935.

Tavard, G. H. *Holy Writ or Holy Church: The Crisis of the Protestant Reformation.* New York: Harper & Row, 1959.

12

Calvinism
Confronts
Catholicism

Soon after the Peace of Augsburg proclaimed that Catholic and Lutheran would attempt to live peacefully in the Empire, the confrontation of Rome and Geneva assumed massive military dimensions. In France and the Netherlands especially, a long series of campaigns, intrigues, and ghastly massacres shocked even the sixteenth-century conscience. The stakes were high, and the methods correspondingly desperate. With a ferocity that approved assassinations and torture, antagonists attempted to establish truth by drowning error in a sea of blood.[1] Voices of toleration and moderation were few, and seldom did they prevail.

FRENCH CALVINISM AT MID-CENTURY

When finally, in 1559, the Treaty of Cateau-Cambrésis brought an end to the long wars between France and Spain, the French king had good reason to be alarmed about the growth of heresy in his realm. The constant wars had brought great financial distress to the kingdom; they had also witnessed the steady expansion of Calvinism. Now King Henry II seemed in a position to concentrate his efforts on domestic problems. Yet he died in that same year, leaving the crown to his 15-year-old son Francis II. The powerful Guises now emerged as the dominant force in government. Their ranks included such influential figures as Charles, Cardinal of Lorraine, and Francis, duke of Guise. Once again, rigorous measures were adopted to achieve religious uniformity in France. Houses where Huguenots met were to be destroyed, and organizers of such meetings executed. When Huguenots requested Calvin's support in staging an armed insurrection, he strongly opposed the proposal, apparently because it did not have appropriate

[1]For an analysis of this violent age, see Natalie Zemon Davis, *Society and Culture in Early Modern France* (Stanford, Calif.: Stanford University Press, 1975), pp. 152–187.

leadership.[2] Nonetheless, plans were readied for the Conspiracy of Amboise (March, 1560), according to which the king was to be captured, the Guises arrested, and a pro-Huguenot government established. Instead the abortive scheme brought death to many Huguenots and prison to Louis, prince of Condé. The sickly Francis died in 1560, to be succeeded by his ten-year-old brother, Charles IX. By astute diplomacy, Catherine de'Medici, the queen mother, became regent. She was determined to end the internecine religious clashes and to initiate a policy of conciliation. Condé was released, and France's liberal chancellor, Michel de l'Hôpital, aided the regent in efforts to bring Catholics and Huguenots together.

The Poissy Colloquy

In 1561, under the prodding of Catherine, Protestant and Catholic theologians met at Poissy to seek a *modus vivendi*. The sessions began ominously as the cardinal of Tournon expressed his sentiments about the "Genevan dogs." Beza and the Italian Peter Martyr Vermigli (see p. 150) faced various French prelates and later the Jesuit theologian Laynez. When Beza outlined the Calvinist view of the Eucharist, he was denounced for blasphemy. The Cardinal of Lorraine, after making an eloquent plea for reunion, defended the Catholic view of the sacrament. The exchanges became more bitter and vituperative as Laynez, who had arrived late, condemned attempts at reconciliation with "wild beasts."[3] Despite continued efforts by Catherine, the lines of division hardened. No compromise was in sight as the colloquy ended. France had been robbed of an opportunity to prevent thirty years of violence and bloodshed.

EXPERIMENTS IN TOLERATION

Tensions continued to mount, and in various parts of the kingdom, militias were being organized. Catherine, hoping to calm the situation, issued the Edict of St. Germain in January, 1562. This gave legal recognition to Huguenots and permitted them to worship privately in their own homes and publicly outside town walls. Less than two months later, however, Huguenots meeting in a barn in Vassy were surprised by the Guises and their retinue. The ensuing massacre was the signal for war. The Guises and the Constable de Montmorency led their forces against those of Louis, Prince de Condé, and admiral Gaspard de Coligny; the ghastly specter of civil war would haunt France for the next three decades. In 1563, Condé agreed to the Pacification of Amboise, but the settlement provided

[2]See Robert M. Kingdon, *Geneva and the Coming of the Wars of Religion, 1555–1563* (Geneva: Droz, 1956), p. 69.
[3]Donald Ziegler, ed., *Great Debates of the Reformation* (New York: Random House, 1969), p. 242.

only a limited religious liberty, and chiefly for the nobility. Both Calvin and Admiral Gaspard de Coligny accused the prince of having betrayed the Huguenot masses. During the war, the duke of Guise had been assassinated by a Calvinist,[4] while both Condé and the constable had been captured, so that Catherine's position was stronger than ever.

For five years, the uneasy, armed truce continued, to be broken when the Huguenots attempted unsuccessfully to kidnap the king. This time the Catholics were assisted by troops from the Duke of Alva's army in the Netherlands, while the Protestants received assistance from John Casimir, son of Elector Frederick of the Palatinate. This episode ended with the Treaty of Longjumeau (March 23, 1568) which reasserted the terms of the Edict of Amboise.

Increasingly, the intervals of armed peace were being used to prepare for a more decisive confrontation. Intrigue and intensive propaganda were used by both sides as the conflict came to embrace an ever greater part of the populace. Jesuits spearheaded a drive designed to warn the masses of the Huguenot danger as well as to arouse popular support. Huguenots, at first divided on the issue of armed resistance, gradually overcame their reticence. From Geneva, Beza now exerted a powerful influence that gained increasing support for military action. When the cautious Frederick, the Elector Palatine, averred that prayer might be the best weapon for the Huguenots, Beza convinced him to fight as well as pray. Beza also helped ro raise a number of loans to finance Huguenot military operations. Relationships between the Huguenot military organization, headed by Condé and Coligny, and the Huguenot churches were increasingly solidified, so that eventually the Calvinist churches functioned as an arm of the military operations. Ministers urged their parishioners to join the Huguenot forces, and as the soldiers marched into battle, they confidently sang Psalms translated by Beza and the poet, Clément Marot. Nonetheless, contemporaries noted that this identification of Calvinism with militarism helped to check popular support for the reform. The Venetian ambassador observed that the change from "words to weapons" brought widespread disillusionment.

In September, 1568, the smoldering fires of war erupted again. This time, Huguenots suffered severe defeats in the battles of Jarnac and Montcontour (1569). When Condé died at Jarnac, many expected the Huguenots to succumb. At this juncture, however, Jeanne d' Albret, queen of Navarre, astonished Europe with her efficient administration and skillful diplomacy. A few years earlier she had resolutely established Calvinism in her land; now she became a powerful force in providing financial and military support for her embattled cause.[5] The war continued and Coligny moved skillfully to recoup his position. Finally, both parties, weary of the long drawn conflict, agreed to the Peace of St.

---

[4]See the contemporary account in *The Huguenot Wars*, ed. Julien Coudy (New York: Chilton, 1969), pp. 145ff.

[5]Nancy Lymon Roelker, *Queen of Navarre, Jeanne d'Albret* (Cambridge, Mass.: Harvard University Press, 1968), pp. 310–314.

Huguenot Centers

Fortified towns as provided
by the Edict of Nantes

FRANCE

Atlantic Ocean

Beauvoir

Saumur

Loire R.

Jargeau

Thouars

Louduon

Marans Chatellerault

Maillezais

La Rochelle Niort S. Maixent

La Charite

S. Jean-d'Angely

Cognac

Pons

Bordeaux

Castillon

Bergerac

Dordogne R.

Casteljaloux

Monflauquin

Tartes Mont-de Marsan

Figeac

Capdenac

Lectoure

Eauze

Marvejols

Grenoble

Meuvezin

Montauban

Livron

Die

Verdun

Montelimar

L'isle-Jourdain

Garonne R.

Castres

Serres Gap Embrun

Uzes

Sommieres Nimes Tallard

Clermont-l'Herault Gignac

Montpellier Lunel

Aigues Mortes

Marseilles

0   50   100 km

Rhône R.

Seine R.

Germain (August, 1570). This time, the Huguenots gained substantial concessions in the four fortified towns they were able to hold as security: La Rochelle,
Montauban, La Charité, and Cognac. Limited freedom of public worship was
reasserted.

Many hoped that they had seen the last of civil strife. Gaspard de Coligny was
invited to join the royal court, where he became an influential member of the
king's council. In his pursuit of a united French policy against Spain, he stressed
that internal dissension might be forgotten if Protestant and Catholic faced a
common foe. Accordingly, the admiral attempted to gain support for his scheme
of invading the Spanish Netherlands—and also helping William of Orange in his

struggle with Alva. Catherine and the Guises strongly opposed such a policy, which would necessarily also be anti-Catholic, but Coligny pressed on.

In the midst of these maneuvers to develop a foreign policy toward Spain, Henry, King of Navarre, married Catherine's daughter Marguerite. The queen mother hoped this would ensure peace. Huguenot and Catholic nobles were in Paris for the occasion. After the wedding on August 18, 1572, the continuing festivities were interrupted on August 22 when a would-be assassin wounded Coligny. The Guises, who had often proclaimed their determination to have the admiral killed, were immediately suspect, as was Catherine. On August 23, the queen mother and the Guises resolved to dispose of the Huguenot leaders. The reluctant king, persuaded that the Huguenots were planning a coup, finally gave his approval. Secret preparations were made to carry out the deed on the morning of August 24. Coligny, together with the most prominent Huguenot leaders except Henry of Navarre and the prince of Condé, was killed. In Paris, an aroused mob carried on a massacre so that "blood flowed through the streets as though it had rained."[6] The frenzy rapidly engulfed the provinces and left death in its wake. Neither the queen mother nor her advisers had wanted such a bloodbath. Their goal had been to eliminate the Protestant leaders, but the mobs soon took matters into their own hands and committed the most terrible crime "ever perpetrated in the name of Faith."[7]

The gory spectacle shocked many and delighted others. Philip II sent his congratulations, as did Pope Gregory XIII. The pope had a commemorative medal struck to celebrate the victory, while the Venetian senate decided to hold a triumphal procession. Many of the Huguenot aristocrats, convinced that their cause was lost, reverted to Catholicism, so that local pastors once again assumed the task of directing Calvinist congregations. French Protestantism seemed to have returned to its old course when popular support, rather than aristocratic power, had been its chief strength. There were sporadic clashes throughout various parts of the kingdom, and although an uneasy peace returned in 1573, the division between Huguenots and the royal court hardened. Protestants were busily engaged in preparing for further military action.

HUGUENOT AND *POLITIQUE*

In anticipation of further hostilities, Huguenots, especially in the south of France, set up their own local governments. A standing army was maintained, and citizens in the area, whether Protestant or Catholic, were required to pay taxes to this "state within the state." Ecclesiastical revenues were often seized. Philosophically and theologically, too, the Huguenots were girding for war. Until the Massacre of St. Bartholomew, French Protestants had generally insisted

---

[6]Contemporary account quoted in Coudy, *Huguenot Wars*, p. 204.
[7]Henri Daniel-Rops, *The Catholic Reformation*, trans. J. Warrington (New York: Dutton, 1962), I:239.

PAINTING: THE MASSACRE OF ST. BARTHOLOMEW by François Dubois d'Amiens

This massacre, the bloodiest spectacle in the savage French wars of religion, demonstrated the intensity of beliefs and passions that divided a nation.

Musée Cantonal des Beaux-Arts, Lausanne

that their chief opponent was not the king, but the Guises, who were destroying the realm. After the massacre, this fiction became absurd—there could be no escape from the fact that Huguenots were resisting the crown.

Numerous treatises defending resistance to tyrants now appeared. Calvin, always cautious about attacking secular authority, had insisted that tyrants could be deposed only in accordance with specific laws and constitutional practices. In 1573, his successor Beza wrote a treatise on *The Rights of Magistrates over their Subjects*. Here he contended that magistrates were the guardians of the rights of the people; if a king abused his subjects, magistrates had the right to depose him. This "aristocratic" theory of revolution was also defended in Francis Hotman's *Franco-Gallia* (1573). The author, a French jurist, insisted that French history demonstrated that the estates, not the king, held final authority. Monarchs who failed to meet their obligations could be deposed by representatives of the people. The right to exercise authority derived from a contractual relationship between the king and the people and implied mutual responsibilities. The social contract theory of government, later to be popularized by John Locke and other political philosophers, was already being vigorously championed.

During the latter part of the sixteenth century, Huguenots increasingly jus-

241

tified their revolutionary actions by drawing parallels with Calvin's covenant theology. Calvin taught that God had made a covenant with man: God provided salvation, and man was expected to respond with obedience. This convenantal relationship was vigorously championed as a pattern for political and social structures. In *Vindiciae contra Tyrannos* (1579), Philippe Du Plessis-Mornay (1549–1623) argued that just as there was a covenant between God and man, so too there was a covenant (contract) between a king and his people. The king's exercise of power was conditional upon exercising justice. A monarch did not make the law—which was the expression of the collective wisdom of the people—rather it was his responsibility to enforce the law and to act as its guardian. Should a king become a tyrant, magistrates, as guardians of the covenant and as representatives of the community, could act to depose him. Such action, however, the *Vindiciae* stipulated could be undertaken only by those holding public office, not by private citizens.

Although these views were actually advanced to combat anarchy, Calvinist towns turned them to their own advantage in defending their right to resist a royal tyrant. In 1574 the councils of several Huguenot cities presented a series of demands to the king, including religious toleration for Huguenots throughout France, the maintenance of Huguenot garrisons, and royal condemnation of those responsible for the massacre. Numerous other stipulations, even more humiliating to the crown, served notice that the Huguenots were far from ready to surrender.

As the tensions mounted, voices of moderation urged that if religious strife were not quickly halted, it would bring ruin upon the kingdom. Gradually, there emerged a loosely organized body of *politiques* who contended that the pursuit of religious unity should be abandoned in the interest of political survival. Moderate Catholic nobles, bankers, and merchants who were suffering economically, opponents of the Guises, and others who viewed the civil war with horror joined together to save France. Civil order and political unity must be preserved, even if this meant opposing the king's religious policy. Francis, duke of Alençon, Catherine's youngest son, readily agreed to be a leader of the *politiques*, while another influential Catholic, Montmorency-Damville, son of the Constable Montmorency, used his office as governor of Languedoc to advance *politique* goals. A Huguenot-*politique* alliance gradually emerged, and in 1574, the two groups met at Nîmes and agreed to establish a virtually autonomous state in southern France. Here there would be religious toleration and peace.

When Charles IX died in 1574, the kingdom was in turmoil. His successor, Henry III (1574–1589) finally agreed to abandon the attempt to crush the Huguenots and therefore concluded a peace with them. In 1576 the Peace of Monsieur (named after the king's brother, the duke of Alençon), gave the Huguenots eight places of security within the realm, admission to various civil offices, and religious liberty everywhere except in Paris.

Such sweeping concessions appeared to the Guises a betrayal of the traditional religion, so they proceeded to form a Catholic League or "Holy Union." The young Henry, duke of Guise, whose father had been killed in 1563, emerged as leader of the movement. Indicating its determination to create a second "state within a state" if the king should oppose its designs, the League demanded that the Estates-General be summoned. Members of this body, largely the product of League-manipulated elections, met in Blois in 1576. Huguenots and *politiques* boycotted the sessions, but the king correctly concluded that the power of the League was too formidable to be overlooked. He announced that he would lead the League in its determination to restore religious uniformity and political unity. Many of the concessions granted earlier that year to the Huguenots were withdrawn, and once again civil war erupted.

In October, 1577, hostilities were temporarily halted with the royal Edict of Poitiers. All leagues were declared dissolved, and the Huguenots were once again granted limited religious toleration. The aged queen mother worked tirelessly to maintain the tense peace, but the prospects for an amicable settlement seemed remote. The royal secretary Villeroy expressed the frustration of a nation: "We cannot either make peace or war."[8]

In 1584, the Catholic League expanded its activities. In that year, the death of Francis, duke of Anjou, left Henry of Navarre, professed Huguenot and leader of his co-religionists, the immediate heir to the throne. The Guises now supported the candidacy of the cardinal of Bourbon against Henry of Navarre, while Philip II of Spain concluded the Treaty of Joinville with the League in December, 1584. In return for Spanish support of the League and its candidate, Philip was promised French Navarre, Cambrai, and some other towns. Henry III, aware that he was losing control of French affairs, agreed to abolish all concessions granted the Huguenots. The Treaty of Nemours (1585), concluded between Catherine and the duke of Guise, prohibited Huguenot worship, declared Henry of Navarre incapable of succeeding to the throne, and gave Huguenots six months to renounce their heresy. Failure to do so was to be punished with exile. Confronted with the threat of extinction, the Huguenots again took up arms. During the course of the war, which was complicated by foreign entanglements, the king was brought increasingly under the domination of Guise and the League. In May, 1588, the Guises defied the king and marched into Paris—in order to ensure French benevolent neutrality while Philip II launched his attack on England. In return, the Spanish king was to recognize Guise and the League as masters of France. Realizing that he was totally unable to control Guise, the unhappy king finally fled Paris. An uneasy alliance between king and duke was maintained, but before the end of the year, Henry had both the duke and his brother, the Cardinal of Lorraine, assassinated.[9]

[8]Quoted in J. H. Elliott, *Europe Divided, 1559–1598* (New York: Harper & Row, A. Harper Torchbook, 1968), p. 255.

[9]Contemporary accounts of this bloody episode may be found in Coudy, *Huguenot Wars*, pp. 292–305.

Reaction against the king was swift. The Sorbonne denounced Henry as a tyrant unworthy of obedience. Many cities, including Paris, renounced all allegiance to the "assassin," while the League assumed an openly revolutionary policy and set up a *de facto* government. Deserted and devoid of strong influence, Henry III allied himself with Henry of Navarre and besieged Paris. While thus engaged in trying to reclaim the capital, the king was assassinated by a monk resolved to avenge the murder of the Catholic leaders.

THE TRIUMPH OF NAVARRE

At once a crisis of succession gripped the nation. Henry of Navarre, as next in line, claimed the throne as Henry IV, but he was rejected by the League in favor of the Cardinal of Bourbon, now Navarre's prisoner. Henry IV made a bold bid for support by declaring that Catholicism would remain the official religion, that religious toleration would be granted to the Huguenots, and that he would accept instruction in the Catholic faith. Such pronouncements, however, were inadequate, and the war continued.

In 1590, Henry IV seemed to have victory almost within his grasp. League forces were defeated at Ivry, and Paris was again besieged. Then, with the capital on the verge of surrender because of massive starvation, aid came from Philip II. Alexander Farnese, the Spanish commander in the Netherlands, invaded France with a substantial army and forced Henry to abandon the siege. Spain had saved the day for the League. Other attacks broadened what had been basically a civil war. A Spanish force landed in Brittany, another garrisoned Paris; Charles-Emmanuel of Savoy seized a main port in Provence. In 1593, Philip II even urged the Estates-General to accept the Infanta as queen, but this was too much for the delegates. Finally, in July, 1593, in a bid for peace and *politique* support, Henry renounced his Huguenot faith and became a Catholic. The bleak prospects of curbing the power of the League and its allies had convinced him to subordinate religion to patriotism and ambition. Even now, some members of the League remained adamant, but gradually Henry consolidated his position and emerged undisputed victor. In February, 1594, amidst the acclaim of his people, and despite the continued opposition of a wary pope, Henry was crowned in Chartres. A young Jesuit student, encouraged by the pope's hesitancy to grant absolution to the king, attempted to assassinate Henry IV. This event was used as a pretext to expel the Order from France, but the basic reason was French fear that the Jesuits might threaten traditional "Gallican liberties" of the church.

A remarkable phenomenon coincided with the improvement of the king's fortunes—a massive peasant uprising against the League and anti-royalist nobles. Driven to sheer desperation by the ravages of war and incessant oppression by the nobles, the peasants wildly acclaimed the king as their protector. From 1593 to 1595, bands of peasants, known as the *croquants*, waged a determined struggle against the nobility. Calling for an end to the wars of religion and espousing the cause of religious toleration, the *croquants* attempted to combine economic reform with religious freedom. In the end, this challenge to economic privilege had little effect; the peasants' plight remained desperate.

With this chapter in French history to all intents closed with Henry's accession in 1594, the monarch could well afford to be magnanimous in victory. Those who had once been his strongest opponents became his staunch supporters, and the *politique* demand that the needs of the state take precedence over those of religion was finally fulfilled. Henry brought further unity to France when he declared war on Spain in 1595. As an ally of the Calvinist United Provinces (the Netherlands), Catholic France resolved to check the expansion of Spanish power. Clearly, Henry felt that alliance with heretics was preferable to loss of national independence. When a number of French towns, including Calais, fell to the Spaniards, England determined that the time had come to ally herself with France and the United Provinces (1596). Philip was given a grim warning when in the spring of 1596 an English expedition sailed against Cádiz and for two weeks devastated Spanish territory. Philip's attempt to send another armada against England failed dismally. In France, too, the war was going badly for Spain. On May 1, 1598, the exhausted countries concluded the Peace of Vervins and returned basically to the conditions of Cateau-Cambrésis. Both England and the United Provinces, however, continued the struggle as a reluctant Philip gradually was forced to retreat from northern Europe.

The Edict of Nantes

Just a few days before making peace with Spain, Henry had issued the Edict of Nantes for the "union, concord and tranquillity" of the realm. The edict was a compromise measure, but the king was strong enough to enforce it. Pope Clement VIII denounced it as "the worst edict that can possibly be imagined" for it "permits liberty of conscience, the worst thing in the world."[10] A nation that had stood for centuries as a proud defender of the Catholic faith had now officially permitted heresy within its borders.

Both sides were disappointed in the restrictions which the edict contained. The Huguenots were granted full civil rights, which were to be enforced by joint Catholic-Huguenot courts. Catholic worship was to be permitted everywhere, while Protestant worship could be conducted only where it had been customary before, and was prohibited altogether in Paris. All public offices were to be open to Huguenots, and they were permitted to fortify, at royal expense, more than a hundred places of security, in effect, constituting a state within a state. Despite its limitations, the edict's recognition of minority religious rights within a unified political entity was a revolutionary concept. Most ecclesiastical and political leaders throughout Europe still insisted that religious and political unity were

[10]Quoted in Elliott, *Europe Divided,* pp. 364, 365.

inseparable, and the cruel fate of Huguenots in later years lent credence to that assumption.

CALVINISM AND THE STRUGGLE FOR INDEPENDENCE IN THE NETHERLANDS

While France was torn and battered by civil war, an equally desperate struggle was being waged in the Netherlands. Here, economic, political, diplomatic, and linguistic factors, all profoundly affected by religious movements, eventually created a new nation.[11]

By the middle of the century, the Netherlands had become one of the most prosperous and progressive areas of Europe. Ports bustled with trade, towns became increasingly mercantile, burghers prided themselves on their advanced education and cosmopolitanism. The country that had showered honors on Erasmus boasted vigorous intellectual activity and constant artistic creativity. Antwerp, Europe's greatest commercial city, as well as numerous other ports, served as natural centers for artistic and intellectual exchange. The prosperous burghers had little desire to become involved in the military ambitions of the Hapsburg rulers. They wanted peace and—above all—the right to determine their own economic and political policies. Any ruler who would challenge a fierce tradition of independence was certain to meet with opposition.

Charles and Centralization

During much of the first half of the sixteenth century, Charles attempted to consolidate and unite the Low Countries. Each of the provinces, however, with its own governor and estates, vigorously attempted to maintain its ancient liberties, especially its control over taxation. It was here and in the towns that the real power lay, not in the States General, which functioned merely as a consultative body. When Charles found that his proposals were often blocked by artisans from these provincial governing bodies, he attempted to exclude guilds from government bodies. Occasionally, as in Brussels (1528), such efforts succeeded, but the imperial anti-democratic policies served only to strengthen the determination to gain broader autonomy.

The problems of political decentralization were further complicated by the fact that the Netherlands, forming only a relatively small part of Charles's multi-national empire, were all too often the victim of policies that reflected the sweeping ambition of Europe's most powerful ruler. The interests of the Nether-

[11]A colorful, lively, but thoroughly biased account is given in J. L. Motley, *The Rise of The Dutch Republic,* 3 vols. (New York: 1883). A more balanced analysis is presented in Pieter Geyl, *The Revolt of the Netherlands 1555–1609* (London: E. Benn, 1958).

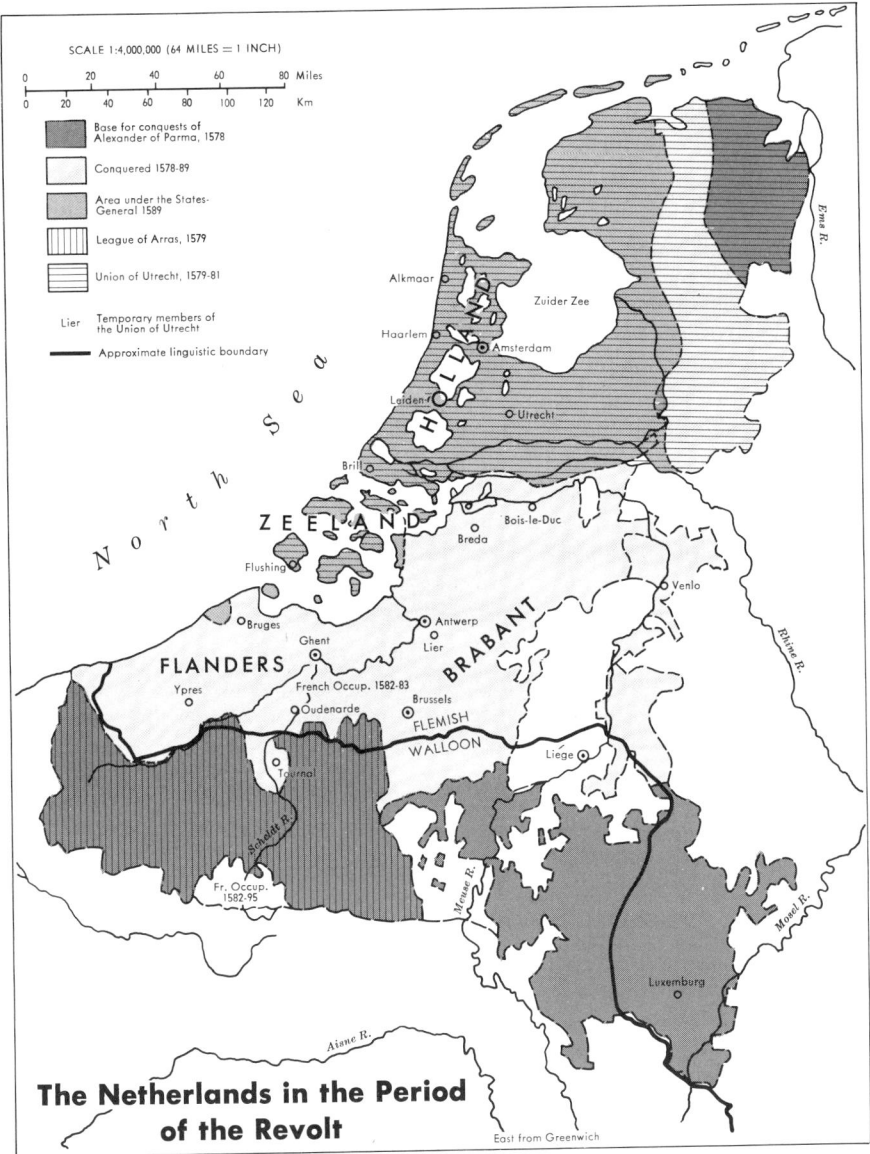

The Netherlands in the Period of the Revolt

lands repeatedly clashed with Charles's policies, and divisions hardened until a complete rupture occurred. Although a semblance of unity was maintained throughout the reign of Charles, long before he abdicated he had charted a course that would bring disaster to his successor in the Netherlands.

When Charles ascended the throne, he proceeded to add to his realm those provinces that did not yet owe him direct allegiance. The "Seventeen Provinces" were gradually brought under unified rule when Charles acquired Tournai (1521), Friesland (1523), Overijssel and Utrecht (1528), Groningen (1536), and Guelders (1543). But the unity they acquired was little more than nominal, for the provincial estates thwarted attempts at royal absolutism. In addition, linguistic divisions furthered the spirit of provincial autonomy. Seven northern provinces, largely sea-faring, spoke Flemish-Dutch, while the ten more agricultural southern provinces spoke French. Yet the increasing prominence of the Netherlands as a prosperous hub of trade gave the provinces a measure of economic unity, while their resistance to imperial encroachment gave them a common concern.

Early Reformation Attempts

In this proud, prosperous, and staunchly independent land, the Reformation made its appearance in the 1520s. Charles responded in 1521 by issuing "placards" prohibiting the printing or reading of Lutheran works. In the same year he pressed for the enforcement of the Edict of Worms throughout the provinces, and by July, 1523, two Augustinian friars had been executed in Brussels because of their Lutheran views. Thus began a long procession to the stake. Gentler souls such as Erasmus, fled the country. But the fires of persecution did not eradicate Luther's ideas; the reformer's writings and translation of the New Testament were widely circulated. Ardent champions appeared in Antwerp, the Hague, Dortrecht, Utrecht, Ghent, and elsewhere.

Then, after 1530, Anabaptism gained numerous adherents in the Netherlands, and, for a short period, became the largest Protestant movement in many provinces. It should be noted that Dutch Anabaptism was not a revolt of impoverished workers; instead followers included wealthy merchants, prominent scholars, and noblemen, as well as artisans and laborers of every trade. Charles responded to the threat of Anabaptism by issuing a series of edicts that prescribed death even for reading the Scriptures, and also by appointing judges to carry out the Inquisition. Public burnings of heretics and their writings, sentences of death even for failure to report Anabaptist suspects, economic reprisals, and other repressive measures eventually drove some of the Anabaptists to take desperate measures. In the Netherlands a number of small-scale incidents occurred patterned after the fiasco of Muenster. One group of Anabaptists seized and fortified a monastery in Friesland, only to be slaughtered. Another group gained brief control of the city hall of Amsterdam; its leaders were subjected to barbarous mutilation and eventually to death. Both peaceful and revolutionary Anabaptists were marked for death. Some were saved by friends, some hid, and others fled. The number of deaths can only be estimated. The Venetian ambassador reported that Charles's wrath had brought death to 30,000 heretics, mostly Anabaptists. Such a figure, while greatly exaggerated, illustrates a contemporary's impression of the holocaust. By 1563, under the title of *Het Offer des Heeren* (The Sacrifice of the Lord), the Anabaptists had published a collection of accounts of numerous martyrdoms. Early in the seventeenth century *Het Offer* was substantially enlarged and published as *Het Bloedigh Tooneel* (the Bloody Theater), a work much read by succeeding generations under the title, the *Martyrs' Mirror*.

PHILIP AND THE NETHERLANDS

Tensions which plagued the rule of Charles became even more acute under his son and successor, Philip II. In 1555, Charles, disillusioned by failure in the Empire, summoned a meeting of the States General to abdicate his throne. As he entered the tapestried hall in Brussels, leaning on the arm of William, Prince of Orange, none could know the role this prince would eventually play in ending the religious and political unity of the Netherlands, and in thwarting the hopes of the new king. Philip, duly installed as ruler, swore to uphold the ancient liberties of the provinces; however, he would never gain the loyalty earned by his father. In the Netherlands he was viewed as a foreigner, a sentiment that gained further credence during his residence there from 1555 to 1559, as all efforts to strengthen royal authority failed.

When Philip left the Netherlands, government was entrusted to a Council of State and the regent, Margaret of Parma. Prominent members of the council included the prince of Orange, the count of Egmont, and Antoine Perrenot, bishop of Arras, soon to be Cardinal Granvelle (1561). The council confronted major problems immediately: factional struggles among the nobility; the growth of heresy; hostility to the presence of Spanish soldiers; and mounting royal pressure for increased taxation. Antagonism toward what was regarded as a foreign regime became vocal in 1561 when Philip announced his determination to implement radical ecclesiastical reorganization. In accordance with a bull published in 1561, the Netherlands would no longer form part of the archiepiscopal provinces of Cologne and Rheims, but was to be divided into three provinces—Cambrai, Malines, and Utrecht. In addition, fourteen new dioceses were to be added to the existing four, while bishops were to be chosen by Philip. The scheme was designed to bring efficiency to the ecclesiastical system, so that heresy might be more effectively checked and royal power extended. Simultaneously, Granvelle attempted to centralize the government according to the Spanish pattern. The program, eminently rational, and designed to harmonize national religious and political interests, was viewed as a dangerous attempt to strengthen Philip's direct rule. Resentment against the absentee king expressed itself in

TITLE PAGE: THE MARTYRS' MIRROR, by Thieleman van Braght

In the Netherlands, as elsewhere, religious dissent was met by barbarous cruelty. This martyrology recorded the death of more than 800 Anabaptists.

denunciation and vilification of Granvelle, who functioned as Philip's chief minister. Led by William of Orange, leading nobles banded together and demanded that Granvelle be dismissed. When Philip refused, the prince and Egmont withdrew from the Council of State (1563). Mounting pressure convinced Philip to reverse his position; apparently the estates and the great nobles had triumphed. Orange and Egmont returned to the council.

Numerous basic issues remained unresolved. Victorious nobles were still reluctant to vote taxes. Philip's rigorous treatment of heretics aroused resentment, while his trading quarrels with England cut off imports and created unemployment. The ensuing social distress, political agitation, and religious confusion proved fertile soil for the growth of anti-Spanish sentiment. Frequently, rejection of a foreign king involved repudiation of the religion he so vigorously defended.

INCREASING OPPOSITION TO ROYALIST POLICIES

Popular agitation and social distress facilitated the emergence of an ever more aggressive Calvinism. Ministers of this religion urged repudiation of the placards and opposition to the Inquisition. As sentiment increasingly favored such action, the Council of State had to choose between pleasing the king or the masses. Philip for his part showed no signs of compromise; instead in 1564 he published the decrees of Trent and demanded their enforcement. Again the council was caught in the middle. It wished to pose as the champion of the interests of the Netherlands, not as an agent of an absentee and foreign king—nor as a supporter of aggressive Calvinism. Philip did little to solve the council's dilemma; when it warned that enforcement of the Tridentine decrees would violate ancient liberties of the provinces, the king refused to acquiesce. Orange and his supporters, drawing upon a comparatively liberal, humanistic tradition, issued pamphlets and petitions designed to swell popular support. Calvinist preachers exploited the rising tide of resentment against Spanish rulers and the Inquisition, while Marranos—Iberian Jews who had adopted Christianity and fled Spain—warned of the terrors of the Inquisition. The shape of things to come was indicated in December, 1565, when a group of nobles—Catholic as well as Protestant—formed a compromise, or league, and demanded an end to religious persecution and inquisitorial practices. While the nobles professed allegiance to Philip, they warned him that they were prepared to resist violation of traditional rights.

The rift widened in April, 1566, when a group of nobles presented a petition to Margaret and urged that the Inquisition be abolished, the decrees of Trent disregarded, and the States General summoned. One of the regent's counselors urged her to disregard these beggars—"*ces gueux.*" The epithet quickly became the rallying cry of the anti-royalist forces. The lines of division were hardening, but they did not necessarily coincide with religious configurations.

PORTRAIT: WILLIAM OF ORANGE, after Antonio Moro

In his devotion to the principles of freedom and toleration, William was well ahead of his time. After his death, the Estates accurately reflected the mood of a grateful people when they ordered the following inscription placed on his tomb: "To the Glory of God and to the everlasting memory of William of Nassau, Father of the Fatherland, who valued the fortunes of the Netherlands above his own."

Prinsenhof, Delft; A. Dingjan

The Upsurge of a Militant Calvinism

In this volatile situation, enthusiastic Calvinist preachers increasingly identified Spanish tyranny with the old religion. In the summer of 1566, iconoclastic mobs, their ranks swelled by refugees and unemployed laborers, stormed through the streets of towns, smashing images and windows, destroying paintings, frescoes, and manuscripts. While many Calvinist ministers deplored this vandalism, there was little they could do to halt the pillage. Catholic and Lutheran nobles, as well as a paralyzed magistracy, were shocked and angered by the fury of the mob. Regent Margaret, without substantial military support at her disposal, promised leaders of the Compromise that religious persecution would cease if Catholic worship were left undisturbed and peace restored.

William of Orange was quick to see that this wanton destruction might jeopardize his hopes of ending Spanish control. He worked feverishly to unite Catholics, Lutherans, and Calvinists in the struggle for self-determination, but mutual suspicions increasingly divided the factions. The prince of Orange hoped to gain support from German Lutheran princes, but few of them wished to endanger the Augsburg arrangement. Continuing rebel action made the prince's conciliatory policy virtually impossible. When, in 1567, insurgents appeared at the gates of Antwerp, William barricaded the city and awaited their defeat outside Antwerp by united Catholic and Lutheran forces. Valenciennes, a town where rebel forces had established control, was captured and its rebel captain, Guy de Brès, hanged. In this desperate hour, William could support neither side. He now withdrew to his German estate in Dillenberg, there to await events and

ENGRAVING: SYMBOLS OF THE BEGGARS

The beggar's jug, sack, and bowl are used here as symbols of the united champions of independence from Spain. The practice of drinking toasts from the beggar's bowl became a popular act of defiance. Confidence in divine support of the struggle is indicated both by the Hebrew inscription Jahweh and the poem, the second line of which is reminiscent of Luther's "A Mighty Fortress Is Our God."

The Rijksmuseum

ENGRAVING: ICONOCLASM IN THE NETHERLANDS, by Franz Hogenberg

Enthusiastic supporters of early Calvinism in the Netherlands engaged in widespread destruction of "idols" in the churches. Excesses of this sort by "robbers of the churches" alienated many who were sympathetic to attempts to gain independence for the Netherlands.
The British Museum

lay plans for further action against Spain. Meanwhile, the insurgents were everywhere defeated. Many were apprehended, others fled. At least for the time being, the revolt had collapsed.

Alva and the "Council of Blood"

For the Spanish king, the mere fact that the rebellion had been quelled was inadequate. The rebels would have to be rooted out, lest the Netherlands become another France. To carry out this task, Philip dispatched the Duke of Alva to lead ten thousand veterans from Milan to the Low Countries, there to burn out every trace of heresy or rebellion.

In the ensuing reign of terror, Alva aroused such bitter animosity that Catholics, Lutherans, and Calvinists once again took up a common cause against the dreaded foe. Philip's rigor revived an almost inert nationalist cause. Pope Pius V had urged Philip to punish only leaders of the revolt, but the king would have no half-hearted measures. His coffers replenished with a record shipment of silver from the New World, Philip resolved to spare no effort in eradicating threats to his rule and his religion.

On August 22, 1567, Alva entered Brussels. To the distress of Margaret, he initiated a policy that allowed for no conciliation. A new tribunal, the "Council of Troubles," soon known as the "Council of Blood," ferreted out those suspected of heresy or treason. Thousands were tried, and hundreds executed. Among the victims were moderates such as the counts of Egmont and Horn, whose public execution made them national heroes. But mere antipathy toward Alva could not defeat his armies, and by the spring of 1569, the duke could congratulate himself on having vanquished his foes, while William of Orange could be dismissed as a "dead man."[12]

Military triumph encouraged Alva to seek administrative and fiscal control as well. Increased taxation brought widespread economic stagnation and indignant protest. Some towns, such as Amsterdam, successfully rejected the duke's demands, but Alva's power remained largely unchallenged. Military efforts by both William and his brother Louis of Nassau proved futile—until aid came from an unlikely source, the remarkable "Sea Beggars."

The "Sea Beggars"

This motley array of privateers, composed of such diverse elements as remnants of Louis of Nassau's defeated forces, Calvinist nobles and exiles, and unemployed workers and fishermen, gradually developed a naval force that could not be ignored. At first simply a menace to channel shipping, the Beggars gained a semblance of legality when William of Orange, in 1570, granted them letters of marque. Spanish ships bore the brunt of the assault, though the absence of any effective control over the Sea Beggars created hazardous shipping conditions for all nations trading in the area. An exasperated Elizabeth, who earlier had recognized the letters of marque, in 1572 ordered "all freebooters of any nation" to leave English ports.

Expelled from England, the fleet sailed for the Netherlands. Brill, left virtually undefended by the Spaniards, was quickly seized. Flushing and other ports followed in rapid succession, with the enactment of a regular scenario: expulsion of royalists from city councils and the forcible establishment of Calvinism as the official religion. Largely through the conquests of the Sea Beggars, the provinces of Holland and Zeeland were almost completely brought under the flag of William. Meanwhile, the prince, encouraged by Louis of Nassau's recruitment of Huguenots to invade the Netherlands, was himself raising forces in Germany. Even the French king, persuaded by Coligny that Spanish designs must be thwarted, wrote William that a force of 15,000 would be sent to help him. At that juncture, William felt he had reason to expect a triumphant march through Flanders. His hopes were dealt a stunning blow when the Massacre of St. Bar-

---

[12] Alva to Philip, quoted in Roger Lockyer, *Hapsburg and Bourbon Europe* (London: Longmans, Green, 1974), p. 242.

tholomew destroyed the prospect of French military support and removed his staunch ally Admiral Coligny.

The massacre saved the day for Alva, for William had correctly analyzed the situation as largely dependent upon France. Without the expected aid, the forces of both Orange and Nassau retreated before Alva's veterans. Town after town was captured and sacked, the inhabitants often put to the sword. Desperate attempts to halt Alva's troops by opening the dikes, as at Alkmaar, brought occasional relief against the Spaniards, and the Beggars still retained naval supremacy. More importantly, anti-Spanish sentiment reached a new high, as the savage reconquest, often coupled with the ruin of commerce, now alienated those who had remained loyal to Philip. By the end of 1573, it was apparent that Alva's policy had failed abysmally. He was succeeded by Don Luis de Requesens, who attempted to conciliate the rebels by granting limited amnesty and reduced taxation concessions that were too few and too late. William, supported by the States General, demanded withdrawal of Spanish troops, restoration of ancient liberties, and freedom of conscience. Philip, who declared he would rather lose the Netherlands than rule over heretics, again resorted to force of arms. Throughout the summer of 1574, Spanish efforts centered on an attempt to seize Leyden. Finally, William and the estates of Holland decided to open the dikes. As barges brought relief to the starved city, the Spaniards were forced to retreat. A thankful city and prince commemorated the rescue by establishing the University of Leyden.

GROWING RELIGIOUS DIVISION

Other factors were complicating the struggle. Militant Calvinists were pressing for repudiation of Catholicism, thereby jeopardizing William's policy of uniting both Catholics and Protestants against Spain. At a general synod held at Dort in 1574, plans were made to establish a Calvinist church in every town. Zealous Calvinists carefully aligned their faith with the national cause; some even clamored for the exclusion of all other faiths.

Amid these religious developments, Requesens died in 1576. With the Council of State unable to govern effectively and the army mutinous, William decided to make his move for control. In September he arrested unsympathetic members of the Council and, in his determination to gain a united front, formed a new Council that forthwith summoned the States General. Anti-Spanish sentiment was now intensified by the tragic massacre and sack of Antwerp. For eleven days, unpaid Spanish soldiers pillaged the city they were supposed to protect, and several thousand inhabitants perished. This "Spanish fury" was enough to convince north and south that there must be a united effort against Philip. On November 8, thirteen provinces, by the Pacification of Ghent,[13] declared their

[13]The name was derived from a formal conclusion of war between Holland and Zeeland, and the other provinces.

resolve to drive out the Spanish forces. Limited religious toleration was pro-claimed, and edicts against heresy were declared suspended. Two months later the other four provinces announced their acceptance of the Pacification.

Thus, when Don Juan of Austria, hero of Lepanto, arrived to assert Philip's interests in the Netherlands, he met a solid front of opposition. Accordingly, he began negotiations and agreed to withdraw his troops. Catholic leaders now felt that the major objective had been achieved; but Calvinists were determined to press their own religious interests. William urged the factions to cooperate, but this voice was drowned in a sea of intractable Calvinists who accused him of denying his faith. Despite the fact that William was enthusiastically welcomed by the predominantly Catholic population of Brussels in 1577, and was also made *stadholder* of Brabant by the States General, it was clear that the uneasy union was falling apart. Religious tensions flared up in the open as a series of anti-Catholic riots plagued the country. In a number of towns, Calvinist rebels ousted Catholic magistrates and attempted to halt Catholic worship. Especially in Flanders and Brabant, where the guilds were an integral part of city government, religious division was often tied to social and political protest. Magistrates who had collaborated with the Spanish governors were attacked. In numerous towns, guilds served as the vehicle for expressing popular animosity toward the aristocratic Catholic councils. Spurred on by fiery Calvinist preachers, iconoclastic mobs often forced the old councils to abandon their position. New governments, responsive to the revolutionary populace and the intransigent Calvinists, adopted policies that were both anti-royalist and anti-Catholic. When William urged his co-religionists to be more moderate, he was vilified and opposed.

William's mediating position was made even more difficult when Philip sent the outstanding military commander, Alexander Farnese, to assist Don Juan in ending the rebellion. The illustrious and popular Farnese,[14] son of Margaret of Parma, soon added to his earlier victories. Defeat of William's forces was facilitated by factional rivalry. In desperation, William and other leaders, eventually supported by the States General, invited Duke Francis of Anjou, brother to the French king, to become "defender of the liberties of the Low Countries against the tyranny of the Spaniards." Rigid Calvinists opposed this appeal to a Catholic and instead invited John Casimir of the Palatinate to aid them. Catholic and Calvinist seemed ready to destroy each other as preparations were made for civil war.

The skillful Farnese proved more than a match for William's diplomacy. Ever since the death of Don Juan in 1578, the duke had zealously pursued the goal of a Catholic union. In January, 1579, the formation of the Union of Arras signified a division in the ranks of the insurgents. The southern provinces agreed to adopt a conciliatory policy toward their king, and to adhere to the traditional faith. In return, their ancient liberties would be recognized. The north responded with the

---

[14]Marvin R. O'Connell, *The Counter Reformation* (New York: Harper & Row, 1974), p. 259.

Union of Utrecht, which asserted the necessity of recognizing religious freedom. Once again, differences in religion had proved a vital factor in shaping political events. The outlines of two future states had been drawn. William still hoped that the differences could be bridged, but he was becoming ever more clearly identified with the Calvinist cause.

THE DECLARATION OF INDEPENDENCE

Philip moved to take full advantage of anti-Calvinist sentiment in the south and throughout his realm. In 1580, he proclaimed William an outlaw and placed a price on the head of "the chief disturber of the whole state of Christendom." The Spanish king had hoped that mass desertions from Orange would ensue; instead the prince became an ever more popular hero in the north. At the sessions of the States General in Delft in 1580, William presented his vindication. This *Apology*, presented with an explanatory letter, savagely denounced Philip as a tyrant who delighted in the death of "good and virtuous people," who by "deception and treason" had subjected the country and robbed it of its ancient liberties. The long catalog of vices ascribed to Philip demonstrated the depth of passion that years of oppression had stirred. In sharp contrast, William depicted his own cause as that of freedom of conscience and preservation of traditional rights.

William's repudiation of Philip was given formal sanction when the States General of those provinces comprising the Union of Utrecht met in The Hague in 1581 and issued a Declaration of Independence. An Edict of Abjuration declared allegiance to Philip ended. This declaration, a graphic expression of the theories developed by the Frenchman Du Plessis-Mornay in his *Vindiciae contra Tyrannos* (see p. 242) declared that Philip as a tyrant had forfeited his right to allegiance. "God did not create the people slaves to their prince to obey his commands, whether right or wrong, but rather the prince for the sake of the subjects."[15] When a king violated his God-given trust, faithful subjects were morally bound to dethrone him. The document also appealed to "laws of nature" and enjoined that all necessary methods be used to restore "ancient liberties and privileges."[16]

William, convinced that assistance from foreign powers was essential for the success of his cause, persuaded the rebel estates to ask Anjou to become the new sovereign. This duke, as a Catholic and brother of the French king, would add respectability to the rebellion, contribute military support, and possibly bring unity to all the provinces. Anjou eagerly accepted the opportunity—and promptly resolved to expand his power. In 1583, with William recovering from an assassination attempt, Anjou attempted to seize Antwerp and gain control of the rebel

---

[15]Quoted in F. G. Eyck, *The Benelux Countries* (Princeton, N.J.: D. Van Nostrand, Anvil Books, 1959), p. 130.

[16]*Ibid.*, p. 134.

government. In that city, Catholic and Calvinist united to oppose this "French Fury," so that the treachery ended in ignominy. Despite personal betrayal, William still defended Anjou, in the hope that through him the Netherlands might be saved. But even the prince could no longer allay the resentment against the incompetent foreigner. Discredited and largely powerless, the duke returned to France, there to die in June, 1584.

THE STRUGGLE FOR SURVIVAL

Exactly one month after the death of Anjou, Orange was shot by an assassin. A horrified States General eulogized him as the "father of his country"—a nation whose future was still far from secure. With their greatest leader slain, and with Farnese steadily consolidating his position in the south, members of the States General asked Henry III to become their ruler. When the king refused, the rebel provinces turned to England and received limited aid in troops and money. Elizabeth and her ministers had decided to challenge Spanish hegemony. Five thousand soldiers, led by the earl of Leicester, came none too soon, for already Spanish troops had taken numerous cities in Flanders and Brabant. Brussels fell in February, 1585, and six months later, after a long and bitter siege, the great port of Antwerp fell to Farnese's forces. Only four provinces—Holland, Zeeland, Utrecht, and Friesland, plus a part of Gelderland—stood between Farnese and total victory. The brilliant soldier and strategist had good reason to expect an early and triumphant end to his campaign, and was thus doubly infuriated by English intervention.

The rebel provinces quickly learned to their dismay that Leicester's offer was not based on altruistic motives. The earl's attempt to exercise arbitrary power and dismiss claims to local rights met with stiff opposition, and his intervention in trade between Spain and the Netherlands proved ruinous to merchants who provided much of the financial support for the war. In addition, his rigid Protestantism further alienated the Catholics. Disillusioned he left the Netherlands in 1587. His departure marked the end of the quest for a foreign prince. Borne along on a wave of anti-monarchial propaganda, the States General asserted its sovereignty. No further symbol of legitimate authority was needed.

By this time, the mantle of revolutionary leadership had fallen on Jan van Oldenbarneveldt (1547–1619), advocate of Holland, and on William's remarkable son, Maurice of Nassau (1567–1625). These two skillful warriors soon began to gain a series of victories that by 1593 had driven the Spanish forces from the northern provinces. The success of the campaigns had been profoundly influenced by King Philip's determination to fulfill "God's obvious design" and bring England under his rule. When "the enterprise of England," the Spanish Armada, foundered in the Channel, it deprived Farnese of substantial military support (since 1586, he had been duke of Parma), further weakened Spanish naval power, and fortified the resolve of the Netherlands. In addition, a frustrated

PORTRAITS: OLDENBARNEVELDT AND MAURICE

These two leaders successfully carried on the struggle for the independence of the Netherlands. Tragically, once this freedom had been gained, the dominant Calvinists became rigidly
intolerant of religious dissent. When Oldenbarneveldt championed toleration, he was denounced as a traitor. Despite his earlier heroic leadership against Spain, he was executed as an
enemy of the people he had liberated. Maurice, hoping to strengthen his own position, condoned the execrable deed.

Parma was forced to dispatch many of his troops to aid Spain in its renewed
conflict with France. Thus handicapped on every side, not even the greatest
military strategist of the day could hope to succeed. Alexander Farnese, perhaps
the greatest military captain of the era, died in undeserved disgrace in 1592.

THE TRIUMPH OF THE UNITED PROVINCES

The death of Parma signalled the end of hopes for a Spanish victory in the
Netherlands. A series of successful military campaigns by Maurice of Nassau
convinced both France and England that a new European power had arisen. In
1596, both countries made an alliance with the northern states, thus giving
formal recognition to the United Provinces. Philip, still determined to regain

260

control of the northern provinces, gave the Netherlands to the Austrian archduke Albert, soon to be married to the Infanta Isabella. At Philip's death in 1598, the United Provinces although nominally under Hapsburg control, had successfully asserted their independence. The south accepted the rule of Archduke Albert. Finally, in 1609, the Twelve Years' Truce gave virtual recognition to the independence of the United Provinces.

After decades of bitter war, after countless marauding expeditions, after a series of sieges and massacres, a nation had been born. An aroused people, determined to resist Philip's attempts to increase his administrative control, impose higher taxation, and reduce traditional liberties, had successfully rallied against an "alien" king. The hope of forming a unified nation, however, composed of the whole Netherlands, had been dissipated in the bitterness of religious division. During the long war, religious differences had been accentuated. William's lofty vision of a united society unmarred by religious persecution had not been achieved. After 1609, Protestantism was systematically eliminated in the south; the northern state, now free of external control, reasserted some of William's ideals and proclaimed religious toleration. The ravages of war exacted a high toll in the once prosperous Flanders and Brabant. Before the wars were

261

concluded, economic leadership had passed to the commercial and maritime north. The launching of the Dutch East India Company in 1601 was proof that, despite the interminable war, the United Provinces were showing remarkable economic expansion. After a generation of war, a new state was ready to enter its golden century.

Suggestions for Further Reading

Baumgartner, F. J. *Radical Reactionaries. The Political Thought of the French Catholic League.* Geneva: Droz, 1976.

Bietenholz, Peter G. *Basel and France in the Sixteenth Century.* Toronto: Toronto University Press, 1970.

*****Cadoux, C. J.** *Philip of Spain and the Netherlands.* Hamden, Conn.: Archon Books, 1969.

Coudy, Julien. *The Huguenot Wars.* Translated by J. Kerman. New York: Chilton, 1969.

*****Dillenberger, John,** ed. *John Calvin: Selections from His Writings.* Garden City, N.Y.: Doubleday, Anchor Press, 1970.

*****Elliot, J. H.** *Europe Divided, 1559–1598.* New York: Harper & Row, 1968.

Erlanger, Philippe. *St. Bartholomew's Night.* Translated by P. O'Brien. London: Weidenfeld and Nicholson, 1960.

Febvre, Lucien. *Au Coeur Religieux du XVIe Siècle.* Paris: Sevpen, 1957.

Geyl, Pieter. *The Revolt of the Netherlands, 1555–1609.* London: E. Benn, 1958.

Grierson, Edward. *The Fatal Inheritance: Philip II and the Spanish Netherlands.* New York: Doubleday, 1969.

Jensen, De Lamar. *Diplomacy and Dogmatism: Bernardino de Mendoza and the French Catholic League.* Cambridge, Mass.: Harvard University Press, 1964.

Kingdon, Robert M. *Geneva and the Coming of the Wars of Religion in France.* Geneva: Droz, 1956.

*———. *Geneva and the Consolidation of the French Protestant Movement, 1564–1572.* Madison: University of Wisconsin Press, 1967.

*****Kingdon, Robert M., and Robert D. Linder,** eds. *Calvin and Calvinism: Sources of Democracy?* Boston: D. C. Heath, 1970.

Kossman, E. H., and A. F. Mellink. *Texts Concerning the Revolt of the Netherlands.* London: Cambridge University Press, 1974.

Linder, Robert. *The Political Ideas of Pierre Viret.* Geneva: Droz, 1964.

*****Neale, J. E.** *The Age of Catherine de Medici.* New York: Harper & Row, A Harper Torchbook, 1962.

Nogueres, Henri. *The Massacre of St. Bartholomew.* Translated by C. E. Engel. London: Allen & Unwin, 1959.

Nugent, Donald. *Ecumenism in the Age of the Reformation: The Colloquy of Poissy.* Cambridge, Mass.: Harvard University Press, 1974.

*Indicates paperback edition.

*Roeder, Ralph. *Catherine de Medici and the Lost Revolution*. New York: Vintage Books, 1964.

Roelker, Nancy, ed. *The Paris of Henry of Navarre*. Cambridge, Mass.: Harvard University Press, 1958.

———. *Queen of Navarre Jeanne d'Albret, 1528–1572*. Cambridge, Mass.: Harvard University Press, 1968.

*Salmon, J. H. M., ed. *The French Wars of Religion*. Boston: D. C. Heath, 1967.

———. *Society in Crisis: France in the Sixteenth Century*. New York: St. Martin's, 1975.

*Sutherland, N. M. *Catherine de Medici and the Ancien Régime*. London: Historical Association, 1966.

Wedgwood, Cecily V. *William the Silent*. New Haven: Yale University Press, 1944.

Williams, Roger. *The Actions of the Low Countries*, edited by D. W. Davies. Ithaca, N.Y.: Cornell University Press, 1964.

Wilson, C. H. *Queen Elizabeth and the Revolt of the Netherlands*. Berkeley: University of California Press, 1970.

13

A Divided Christendom Confronts Islam

THE HEGEMONY OF SPAIN

Throughout the latter half of the sixteenth century, the task of preserving the interests of the Catholic church rested to a very large extent on Philip II. Seldom have needs of church and state so nearly coincided. Repeatedly, whether combating Islam in the Mediterranean or Calvinism in the Netherlands and France, or rooting out the remnants of heresy in Spain, the king found that his enemies were also those of the pope. Philip was profoundly gratified to know that in defending his crown, he was defending his church. When his father abdicated at Brussels, the son had sworn to "preserve the Catholic faith in all its purity." Later, Philip solemnly declared that he would rather lose his kingdom and his life than rule over heretics. He rightly fancied himself as the great defender of the faith, and in the resolute devotion to what he believed to be his divine mission, he was prepared to demand any sacrifice, both of his country and himself.

The Quest for Uniformity

Scarcely had Philip assumed his royal duties in 1556 when he learned that pockets of Protestantism had been discovered in Spain. The movement received only scant support, but this was no comfort to a king who had seen heresy grow from small beginnings elsewhere. With passionate fervor he urged on the inquisitors. A series of great autos-da-fé in 1559 and 1560 virtually eliminated Protestantism in the Iberian peninsula. As the king purified his realm, Catholic reformers such as Erasmians and Illuminists often found themselves innocent victims of the purges.

Philip found the Inquisition a ready and effective tool for the eradication of unorthodox ideas. Resolutely, the king increased the influence and power of the

ENGRAVING: PHILIP II, by Hieronymous Wierx

During his long reign, Spain stood at the height of her glory. It was an age of prodigious and magnificient literary and artistic creativity, as well as of imperial expansion. In Philip's view, however, his greatest achievement was that he had preserved the realm from heresy, while religious leaders such as St. Teresa and St. John of the Cross had given a renewed fervency to the Spanish church.

The Rijksmuseum

institution, for thereby he was not only combating heresy but also enhancing royal authority. In 1558 censorship of the press was entrusted to the Inquisition, a move that anticipated by several years the establishment of the papal *Index*. The Spanish censors were, however, more liberal than their papal counterparts in that they made provision for expurgation of parts of censured works. But in any event, there could be no deviation from approved religious and intellectual positions.

Revolt of the Moriscos

Atlantic Ocean

Burgos •

Ebro R.

SPAIN

PORTUGAL

Madrid •

Tagus R.

Valencia•

Lisbon

Guadalquivir R.

Granada

• Seville

Cadiar •

•Almeria

Málaga •

▨ Area of revolt

Mediterranean Sea

The Attack on the Moriscos

It was this passionate pursuit of conformity that eventually also led to a clash between Philip and the Moriscos. These converted Moors conformed outwardly to Catholic practices but more often than not retained their Moorish culture and religion. The king, obsessed by the fear that the true faith was in dire peril because of the joint threat of Protestantism and Islam, often saw enemies where none existed. He was understandably alarmed by the growing Islamic presence in the Mediterranean. Conceivably, the Moriscos might aid the advancing Turks; on some occasions, Barbary pirates had indeed received support from a few Moriscos. Encouraged by the pope and the archbishop of Granada, Philip determined to root out those vestiges of Moorish culture which had survived the repressive policies of his predecessor. In 1525, Charles V had issued an edict for the eradication of Moorish customs, but the Moriscos had successfully offered

80,000 ducats for revocation of the edict. This time there would be no reprieve, for Philip's convictions were not for sale. In the *pragmatica* (decree) of 1566–67, the king attempted to destroy Moorish culture. The use of Arabic was prohibited; Moorish dress and observances were forbidden under threat of stringent penalties. Desperate pleas by a Morisco delegation failed to move the king. Despite warnings by his counselors that, with Alva's forces engaged in combating the revolt in the Netherlands, Spain could not risk another uprising, Philip remained adamant. Triumphant in North Africa, the crescent was rising ever higher in the Mediterranean—soon the Moors of Spain might openly flock to this standard.

Faced with the choice between submission or rebellion, the Moriscos determined to preserve their heritage. In December, 1568, Granada erupted. From the first, barbarous cruelty marked the conflict. Massacres, women and children being sold as slaves to Barbary corsairs, and wholesale plundering brought

FRESCO: WAR IN GRANADA

When the Morisco rebellion broke out in 1568, Spain was in a peculiarly vulnerable position, for the *tercios* were in other lands. Defense thus depended largely upon levies from the towns and the nobility. The ensuing savagery in the war reflected the desperation sensed by both sides. This fresco, from the Hall of Battles of the Monastery of El Escorial, depicts the battle of the Higueruela in the struggle with the Moriscos.

El Patrimonio Nacional

desolation to the area. Commanders such as the Marquis de los Veles, the "iron-headed devil," insisted that even peaceful Moriscos must be annihilated. The hard pressed Moriscos did receive some support from the Viceroy of Algiers (about 800 soldiers), but promised aid from the Turkish fleet, occupied with an attack on Cyprus, was not forthcoming. As the struggle dragged on, Philip placed the royal forces under the command of his half-brother, Don Juan of Austria. Late in 1570, the revolt was brought under control. Moriscos were now deported from Granada to other parts of Spain, while settlers from various provinces were brought in to repopulate the desert that had once been one of Spain's most flourishing provinces. Philip had his victory, but it had been bought at a terrible price in lives, relationships, and property. Besides, the Morisco danger had been only temporarily removed; it would appear again on the stage of Spanish history.

THE TURKISH THREAT

For Philip, the suppression of the revolt in Granada represented a significant triumph of Christendom in its long struggle with Islam. Both before and after the defeat of the Moriscos, Spain stood as the great opponent of Islamic expansion in the Mediterranean. Despite the efforts of Charles V, during the latter part of his reign, the Mediterranean was in danger of becoming a Turkish lake. By the middle of the century, Spanish strongholds on the North African coast included only Oran and Mers-el-Kebir. Pirates raided Italy and Spain, as well as the islands in the western Mediterranean. When Philip sent 12,000 soldiers to seize the island of Djerba in preparation for the recapture of Tripoli, the expedition ended disastrously (1560). The struggle between Philip and Suleiman the Magnificent (1520–1566) reached a climax in the dramatic siege of Malta throughout the summer of 1565. Under the skillful leadership of Jean de la Valette, the Knights of St. John, to whom Charles V had entrusted the island, survived until a Spanish fleet brought relief.

This Turkish defeat gave Spain scarcely a breathing space. Under a new sultan, Selim II (1566–1574), the Turks, determined to deprive Christendom of its easternmost Mediterranean outpost, launched an invasion of Cyprus. At the urging of Pope Pius V, Philip decided to overlook his traditional rivalry with Venice and join that republic, together with the papacy, in a Holy League (May, 1571). A combined fleet was entrusted to the command of Don Juan, but by the time the ships sailed, Famagusta, the last Venetian fortress in Cyprus, had fallen (August, 1571).

On October 7, Don Juan's forces—more than 200 vessels and 28,000 soldiers—sighted the Turkish fleet of perhaps 300 vessels and 25,000 soldiers. Battle was joined at once, and when the smoke from the firing of the Spanish arquebuses had cleared, Don Juan had gained the greatest naval triumph of the century. Virtually the whole Ottoman fleet had been destroyed. News of the

Battle of Lepanto, "the noblest occasion that past or present ages have seen,"[1] brought wild enthusiasm to Europe and adulation to Don Juan. Turkish control of the Mediterranean was ended and, while Cyprus remained under the suzerainty of the sultan, Philip now proceeded to strengthen his position in the west. In 1573, Spanish rule was again established in Tunis. The western Mediterranean clearly seemed to be Philip's private preserve.

Despite the hopes of the king and the illustrious feats of Don Juan, the promise of Lepanto remained largely unfulfilled. Tunis fell again in 1574—although Turkish fleets never again threatened Spanish coasts—and too many other pressures were bearing in upon the king. Continued revolt in the Netherlands gave the king ominous portents of the growing threat in the north. And, although imports of bullion from America continued to flow into the royal treasury, Philip's income was not equal to the growing cost of ruling his realm. In 1575, with his credit exhausted and a staggering debt of 37,000,000 ducats accumulated, Philip suspended payments to his creditors. Commerce in parts of the kingdom was paralyzed; failure to pay the troops in the Netherlands precipitated the tragic "Spanish fury"; trading centers throughout Europe felt the economic squeeze; the two largest banks in Seville failed to meet their obligations. Only gradually did the situation improve. Reduction in interest rates, sale of some church lands, imposition of a variety of taxes, and substantial silver shipments from the New World once again gave the king some freedom to maneuver.

FOR THE GREATER GLORY OF SPAIN

Philip promptly took advantage of the improvement in his fortunes. The 1580s and 1590s were devoted to ambitious, even spectacular, imperial enterprises. When an ill-fated expedition in Africa robbed Portugal of its king in 1578, Philip quickly recognized the opportunity to unify the entire peninsula. After a short war, the duke of Alva seized Lisbon and gave Philip his wish. The two largest colonial empires in the world were now united under one crown. Almost equally significant was the Spanish acquisition of the five Portuguese harbors on the Atlantic, as well as a large and well manned fleet. When France, alarmed at Spanish expansion, sent a fleet to seize the Azores before Spain could do so, Philip dispatched his trusted admiral, the Marquis of Santa Cruz, who destroyed the French ships (1582). The legend of Spanish invincibility was gaining strength. The victorious admiral now confidently urged Philip to send an armada against England—only by crushing English power could Philip hope to end the costly revolt in the Netherlands.

By this time, Philip had reason to consider vigorous action against Elizabeth. Despite his efforts on her behalf, the queen was showing scant gratitude. Philip

---

[1]Miguel de Cervantes in the preface to *Don Quixote,* part II.

had earlier persuaded Mary Tudor to treat Elizabeth with consideration; at the time of Cateau-Cambrésis, he had tried to regain Calais for England; he had even offered marriage to Elizabeth—all this, yet England was aiding the rebels in the Netherlands and robbing Spanish ships engaged in American trade.

Philip had long been in a dilemma. During the early years of his reign, he realized that to aid movements designed to overthrow Elizabeth and place Mary Queen of Scots on the throne would only strengthen the position of France, and allow the Duke of Guise to dominate not only France, but also England, Scotland, and Ireland. Throughout the 1560s, Philip did his best to save Elizabeth, and the long delayed bull of excommunication against her was evidence of Philip's influence at the papal court.

During the 1570s, however, the scene was altered. The Huguenots, who had seemed ready to plunge France into war with Spain by aiding the revolt of the Netherlands, suddenly found themselves leaderless and in disarray after St. Bartholomew's Massacre. As the struggle in France assumed the dimensions of a crusade against heresy, leaders of the Guise faction moved closer to Philip. By 1577, the Duke of Guise was sending troops to aid Don Juan against the Prince of Orange. The Pyrenees no longer separated implacable foes. In 1584, when the Duke of Anjou died, the Protestant Henry of Navarre became heir to the French throne. Should Henry III die—and three of his brothers were already dead—a Protestant might claim the throne. To prevent such a calamity, Philip and the Guises signed the Treaty of Joinville (1584), by which they agreed to eradicate French heresy and to prevent Henry of Navarre from gaining the throne. For his efforts, Philip was promised Navarre and Béarn. With France and Spain thus temporarily in league, the English government became increasingly nervous about the imprisoned Mary Stuart. Her supporters might now expect help from both Spain and France. At last, convinced by the arguments of her counselors, Elizabeth agreed to the death of her cousin, and on February 18, 1587, the unhappy Mary was executed in Fotheringay prison.

With the French threat removed, Philip turned his attention to England. Santa Cruz, the honored admiral, recommended that top priority be given to the destruction of the English fleet. Then an invasion would establish Spanish control. Philip vetoed the proposal as too costly. Instead he decided to use the Spanish ships simply to transport Farnese's reinforced army from the Netherlands to England. Preparations for the assault upon England moved slowly, for Philip could not afford to withdraw his Mediterranean fleet nor those ships plying the Atlantic. Then, in 1587, Francis Drake carried out a disastrous raid on the ports of Cadiz and Lisbon. The death of Santa Cruz early in 1588 robbed Philip of a skill and competence that was far from replaced when the Duke of Medina Sidonia was appointed to direct the expedition.

Finally in May, 1588, Philip launched a venture that a contemporary Jesuit described as "the most important undertaken by God's Church for many hun-

PAINTING: DESTRUCTION OF THE ARMADA

As the Spanish fleet sailed for England, one of the Armada's officers expressed his fear that "unless God helps us by a miracle," disaster would result. After the battle a jubilant victor exclaimed, "God breathed and they were scattered."

St. Faith's Church, Gaywood, King's Lynn, Norfolk

dreds of years."[2] Some 130 ships and 30,000 men began their voyage to the straits of Dover. As the Armada sailed up the channel, English rearguard attacks took their toll; yet, after anchoring at Calais, the fleet seemed ready to transport troops across the channel. However, Farnese's troops were blockaded by a Dutch fleet off Dunkirk and Nieuport and were thus unable to put out to sea. When the English sent fire ships among the Spanish vessels, Medina Sidonia was forced

[2]Pedro de Ribadeneyra, quoted in J. H. Elliott, *Imperial Spain, 1469–1716* (New York: Mentor Books, 1966), p. 284.

271

out into open waters, where English and Dutch ships continued the attack and drove the enemy into the North Sea. Superior fire power and better ships decided the issue, so that the expedition ended in failure. After a difficult voyage around Scotland and past the Irish coast, a badly mauled fleet, having lost more than 60 ships, straggled home. But the psychological blow to Spain was even greater than the losses at sea. Europe's greatest power had proved to be vulnerable. The completely imperturbable Philip, however, declared his gratitude that the "wind and waves of God"[3] had not destroyed more of his fleet.

Protestants throughout northern Europe agreed with the Huguenot commander Francis de la Noue that in saving herself, England had saved Protestantism.[4] The measure of English optimism was indicated when in 1589 Elizabeth sent 20,000 men to invade Portugal and thus further plague Philip. The expedition failed to rouse strong Portuguese support against the Spanish and ended in failure. Nonetheless, brazen defiance of Philip continued and reached a height in 1596 when the Earl of Essex entered Cadiz harbor and sacked the city. The scepter of power was slowly slipping from Philip's grasp.

PHILIP'S THWARTED *WELTPOLITIK*

In France, Spanish hopes were similarly eclipsed. When Henry III was assassinated in 1589, Philip seemed to be on the verge of gaining the French crown either for himself or for his protégé, but Henry of Navarre demonstrated unexpected resourcefulness. A large part of the French nobility, as well as a growing body of *politiques*, refused to consider a Spanish monarch. When Philip ordered Farnese to bring his troops into France, Navarre found himself temporarily hard pressed, but the rebels in the Netherlands quickly took advantage of the diminished Spanish presence. Clearly, Philip was attempting more than his resources would permit. Then, with Henry's acceptance of Catholicism in 1593, Philip found himself at war not with a mere French faction as before, but with an increasingly united nation. The French War, complicated by the continuing Spanish struggle with England and the Netherlands, helped to convince Philip to attempt to pursue peace.

Added to his military and political difficulties was a desperate financial burden. In 1596 Philip again suspended payment on his debts. Now hoping to destroy Dutch shipping, the King tried to bar Netherlands ships from peninsular trade, but the Dutch proceeded to establish footholds in Spanish America. Combined English and Dutch inroads on the Spanish monopoly resulted in a dwindling colonial income for Spain.

The king's resolve to end his wars led to the Treaty of Vervins (May, 1598).

[3]Garrett Mattingly, *The Armada* (Boston: Houghton Mifflin, 1959.) p. 390.
[4]Quoted in J. H. Elliott, *Imperial Spain*, p. 285.

ENGRAVING: THE ESCORIAL

Philip instructed Juan Herrera, the builder of the Escorial, to create a monument that would have "simplicity of form, severity in the whole, nobility without arrogance, majesty without ostentation." The king had good reason to be pleased with the structure that became his residence and his tomb.

Real Monasterio, El Escorial

By its terms, France and Spain ended their long struggle. Except for Cambrai, Spain returned all the possessions she had gained from France in the war. In the Netherlands, despite Philip's diplomatic efforts, the revolt dragged on, for the northern provinces would settle for nothing less than independence. Similarly, the Spanish war with England persisted until 1604.

In September, 1598, stoically bearing the excruciating pains of a lengthy illness, the old king died. From his beloved palace, the Escorial, he had witnessed the failure of his most passionate desires. He had been unable to establish Spanish control in northern Europe; heresy was still rampant; his successor faced a staggering debt of some 100,000,000 ducats. Even so, Philip might have congratulated himself, for he had checked Protestant expansion. Had it not been for Philip, France could have lost its Catholicism. Similarly, the southern Netherlands were solidly Catholic. In Spain, the old faith had triumphed completely, and the church had proved to be an effective instrument in strengthening the government. Not the least of Philip's triumphs was the decisive blow he had dealt Islamic westward expansion. Only a monarch as demanding as Philip would have been unsatisfied with such a record.

ISLAM AND THE WEST

Throughout the sixteenth century, the persistent specter of Islam haunted much of Europe. Repeatedly, western Europe was unable to resolve internal difficulties because of threats from the East. Popes and emperors still talked of Crusades; would-be bearers of the imperial crown promised the early conquest of Constantinople, should their ambition be realized. And Europe had good reason to be concerned, for when the Turks triumphed in the great battle of Mohacs in 1526, they stood as conquerors of the Balkans, with the Aegean and most of Hungary in their grasp. Earlier, the capture of Rhodes (1522) had served notice to Mediterranean powers that the crescent was a power to be reckoned with on the high seas. The flood of anti-Turkish pamphlets in the 1520s graphically testified to Europe's consternation at the threat now being pressed by land and sea.

The persistent pressure from the southeast profoundly influenced the shape of European events. As we have seen, imperial efforts to crush Protestantism were repeatedly thwarted by the onslaught of the Turks. Then, too, the aid of territorial princes was generally contingent on their maintaining territorial autonomy. Turkish ambitions also figured prominently in Hapsburg-Valois rivalry, for the ''most Christian king'' did not hesitate to welcome the sultan as ally in his struggle with the emperor. Then, at the height of Spanish power, Philip II found his efforts against Protestantism in the north jeopardized by the Islamic advance in the Mediterranean. A Europe divided against herself frequently provided opportunity for Turkish expansion.

The Advance of Suleiman the Great

Seldom have powerful military conquerors terrified so much of Europe for so long a period as Suleiman the Magnificent (1520–1566). When Suleiman ascended the throne, he had at his disposal an army that his father Selim I had been readying for conquest. The son wasted no time in advancing into the Balkans. By 1521, Belgrade was in his hands, and in the following year the Knights of St. John, long predators on Muslim commerce, were evicted from their fortress on Rhodes. The mighty sultan briefly consolidated his conquests, then resumed the march on Europe. He found the Hungarian monarchy in disarray and division, totally unable to stem the Turkish advance. After the smashing victory at Mohacs, he marched on to Buda and crossed the Danube. His troops freely pillaged the towns, which gave up all resistance. Then, when news of serious unrest in other parts of his empire reached the great warrior, he was forced to abandon many of his conquests.

This respite proved of little advantage to shattered Hungary, for with the death of King Louis II on the Mohacs battlefield, the illustrious Jagiellon dynasty had come to an end. Rival claimants to the throne—the ambitious Ferdinand, archduke of Austria, and John Zapolya, prince of Transylvania—now plunged the unhappy land into civil war. Ferdinand, hoping to build a bulwark against the Turks by uniting Hungary to his Austrian and Bohemian territories, emerged as victor. In desperation, Zapolya requested Turkish support. Suleiman quickly responded declaring himself ready to defend his protégé, the "king of Hungary." Ferdinand refused to recognize the Turkish right to intercede, so the Hapsburg-Turkish struggle continued. By September 27, 1529, Suleiman stood before the gates of Vienna. Despite repeated assaults, the city withstood the siege. However, Suleiman's retreat in mid-October did not signify that the Turks had abandoned Hungary. In Buda, Zapolya seemed firmly established. Clearly, any significant Hapsburg action would have to be based upon imperial support. Emperor Charles analyzed the situation correctly; if he wished to give aid to his brother Ferdinand, the Protestant princes of the Empire would have to be placated.

The drama was repeated in 1532. In that year, a large Turkish army again invaded Hapsburg lands, but a stubborn defense of the small town of Gulns prevented the sultan from advancing to Vienna. Nonetheless, Charles, Ferdinand, and the German princes had readied themselves for the attack on Suleiman—and with Protestant aid came at least temporary toleration of the Reformation within the Empire. The sultan was proving to be one of Lutheranism's greatest benefactors.

During the rest of the decade, Suleiman devoted little attention to his Austrian rival. In 1533, the two rulers concluded a peace that recognized the right of "the king of Vienna" to that part of Hungary which Suleiman had not conquered. It was also tacitly understood that any agreement between Ferdinand and Zapolya would have to be given prior approval by the sultan. Thus released from major wars in the Balkans, Suleiman turned his attention to problems on his eastern borders. By 1536, he had inflicted notable defeats on Persia, and was again free to look westward.

Meanwhile, the Mediterranean was becoming an ever more active theater of Hapsburg-Turkish confrontation. Charles V was vigorously pressing his desire to gain control of North Africa, whether by treaty or direct conquest. The Knights of St. John, with imperial support, had established themselves at Tripoli and Malta, while the great Genoese admiral Andrea Doria had successfully launched an invasion of the Morea by seizing Coron (1532). Two years later, the Ottoman troops recaptured the town.

Suleiman, shrewd diplomat that he was, resolved to exploit the rivalry between Hapsburg and Valois by giving France special trading rights. By 1536, Francis I was again at war with Charles. Then, in 1537, the notorious Barbary corsair leader, Khair ad-Din "Barbarossa," attacked Hapsburg possessions in Italy by pillaging the region near Otranto. In the following year, this vassal of the sultan defeated a joint Venetian and papal fleet. Ottoman power was clearly moving westward in the Mediterranean. In 1540 Venice, facing commercial ruin, bought peace by ceding to the sultan her last Aegean and Morean possessions.

Stalemate in Hungary

By now, events in the divided kingdom of Hungary were demanding the sultan's attention. Conflict between Zapolya and Ferdinand had been temporarily suspended by a treaty in 1538. Each claimant was to retain the title of king, but in the event of Zapolya's death, his lands would revert to Ferdinand. However, upon Zapolya's death in 1540, a strong group of Hungarian nobles refused to recognize Ferdinand's claims. Zapolya's infant son, John Sigismund, was declared rightful heir to the throne. Ferdinand set out to enforce his claims to the throne, only to encounter the resolute opposition of the sultan.

By the summer of 1541, the Ottoman armies had again advanced to Buda, and in the following years penetrated ever more deeply into Hapsburg lands. Ferdinand and his German allies were hard pressed and gained a truce in 1545. Two years later, the Austrian archduke made peace. He retained only the western and northern fringes of the kingdom and agreed to pay the sultan 30,000 Hungarian ducats annually. Central and southern Hungary were now provinces of the sultan, while Transylvania in the east was a vassal state. In the bitter Ottoman-Hapsburg struggle, the tide was continuing to favor the designs of Suleiman. Despite renewed military efforts by Ferdinand in 1549, and intermittent war until 1562, the forces of the sultan could not be dislodged. Ottoman power seemed firmly entrenched in most of the Balkan peninsula. Indeed, when death came to the indomitable sultan in 1566, he was once again engaged in a military foray into Hungary. The new sultan, Selim II, made peace in 1568, but only after the new emperor, Maximilian II, had agreed to continue the annual tribute of 30,000 ducats. This continuation of the status quo ante bellum indicated that the Balkan struggle between Islam and Christendom had reached a stalemate on the battlefield. Ironically, the advance of Islam spurred calls for easing religious burdens, for example, church taxes on the peasants, for significant numbers were embracing the less restrictive Muslim faith.[5]

The Struggle for the Mediterranean

In the Mediterranean, however, the confrontation was soon resumed. Here, as had been demonstrated in the unsuccessful Turkish assault on Malta in 1565, the only power that could hope to check Islamic advance was Spain. When Pius V ascended the papal throne in 1566, he attempted to unite Spain, France, Venice, and various Italian states in a great crusade against the Turk, but national rivalries

---

[5]Carl M. Kortepeter, *Ottoman Imperialism During the Reformation* (New York: New York University Press, 1972), p. 152.

thwarted his efforts. In addition, problems within Philip II's empire jeopardized his effort to hold the sultan in check. In 1568 the revolt of the Moriscos further complicated a situation already problematic because of the rebellion in the Netherlands.

Turkish ambitions in the Mediterranean became painfully apparent when in 1570 Constantinople dispatched an envoy to Venice and demanded the cession of Cyprus. After protracted debate in the senate, Venice refused the ultimatum to surrender her vital Levantine commercial center. War—and the long delayed formation of the Holy League—were the result. Turkish forces invaded Cyprus in July, 1570, and a year later, with the capture of the fortress of Famagusta, completed the conquest of this island. Then came Lepanto.

Although the victory could be described as nothing other than resounding, Venice proceeded to buy peace at a price so high that Lepanto might never have been fought. The republic, seeing its trade being ruined, abandoned claims to Cyprus and possessions along the Dalmatian coast. In addition, Venice contributed 30,000 ducats to the sultan's coffers. The Holy League had disintegrated.

Spain now withdrew from the eastern Mediterranean and concentrated on eliminating Ottoman influence in the west. Tunis was seized by Don Juan in 1573, but in the following year the Turks regained it. The Turks had no intention of abandoning their positions in North Africa. Eventually both Turk and Spaniard agreed to accept the stalemate. In 1578, both powers signed a truce so that they could devote their energies to other urgent matters. The sultan wished to take advantage of confusion in the Persian empire, while Philip was anxious to end the revolt in the Netherlands. By turning his back upon Europe, the sultan permitted the Mediterranean to remain divided into two spheres of influence. North Africa, however, had been brought firmly under Ottoman rule. There the intermittent Spanish attempts to establish control and check Islam had ended in failure.

RELIGIONS IN CONFLICT

Throughout the long conflict between the Ottoman empire and western Christendom, the military and political issues were regularly compounded by further religious division. Eastern Orthodoxy, Catholicism, Protestantism, and Islam all played their role in attempting to gain the allegiance of the minds of men. The long tension between Orthodoxy and Catholicism in the Balkans and eastern Europe was now complicated by the intrusion of two aggressive and dynamic faiths. Even in the face of determined Islamic advance, the three branches of Christendom cooperated only with greatest reluctance.

In the early stages of the rise of Protestantism, some of its protagonists had hoped to gain close ties with Orthodoxy. Luther, in his debate with Eck at Leipzig, cited the Orthodox churches as evidence that Christians did not have to be submissive to the pope. On other occasions, he recognized as his brothers those Christians suffering under Islamic rule. For Luther, the Turk vied with the pope as the incarnation of the Antichrist. In some of his later writings, however, Luther expressed a growing disenchantment over Orthodoxy's refusal to embrace the Reformation, and in one of his characteristically unrestrained comments he declared that the devil had devoured both the church of Rome and the church of Constantinople.[6]

Some Lutheran theologians were more optimistic. In 1559, the Augsburg Confession was translated into Greek and sent, together with a warm letter from Melanchthon, to the patriarch of Constantinople. Despite Greek aloofness, Lutheran efforts continued. At Tuebingen, the theologian Martin Kraus warmly espoused a union of Lutheran and Orthodox churches, a position he fostered by inviting Greek students to study under him and at other Lutheran universities.

An added impetus came when David von Ungnad, the imperial ambassador at Constantinople, and a Lutheran, attempted to gain the favor of Patriarch Jeremias II. In 1574 Ungnad presented to the patriarch a Greek translation of the Augsburg Confession. Lutheran theologians now urged Jeremias to support their position, but he countered with the suggestion that Lutherans join the Orthodox church instead. When the Lutherans persisted, Jeremias broke off the correspondence. For the greater part, the hierarchy of the Eastern churches was unenthusiastic about the rise of Protestantism, and tended to view it as further evidence of the West's tendency to be obsessed with innovation. A mutual hostility toward the papacy was not a sufficiently compelling motive for unity.

Farther to the north, Orthodoxy proved no more receptive to the Protestant faith. Religious leaders in the emerging Russian state claimed a spiritual superiority and exclusiveness that showed little inclination to tolerate other faiths. Early in the sixteenth century an Orthodox monk expressed a widely held and court-supported sentiment when he wrote to his Tsar: "Two Romes have now fallen, and the third one, our Moscow, still stands. A fourth one there shall never be. . . . In all the world you alone are the Christian Tsar." As Russian leaders such as Ivan III and Ivan IV expanded westward into Lithuania and Livonia, they vigorously supported the parallel growth of Orthodoxy. In 1577, when Ivan IV encountered a Lutheran pastor in a Livonian town he had just captured, he burst out, "To the devil with you and your Luther." Moscow, the mighty "third Rome," would tolerate no upstart schismatics. Yet, well before the creation of the patriarchate of Moscow in 1589, a Lutheran congregation had been established in the city.

Islam and Orthodoxy

The Turkish conquest of territories strongly Orthodox gradually sapped the vitality and energy of the Eastern church. Frequently, confiscation of wealth and harassment of the clergy, coupled with the flight of many scholars, left Orthodox

[6]*Werke, W.A.* L:579.

civilization only a shadow of its former illustrious past. Sons of the impoverished and heavily taxed peasants were often sent away to become janissaries and to be reared under Islam. Decayed and abandoned churches dotted the austere countryside.

Typical of the weakened state of the Eastern church was the subordination of the patriarch of Constantinople to the sultan. Naturally, it was to the sultan's advantage to strengthen the patriarch's control over other bishops. The patriarch held office only at the pleasure of the sultan, and he was continually at the mercy of the sultan and subject to constant pressures for money or other favors. Other factors added to the distress of Orthodoxy. As Turkish troops conquered new areas, usually at least one church in a town would be changed into a mosque, and often other churches were preserved only because of the payment of substantial tribute. Sometimes the adherents of Orthodoxy were expelled from specific regions, with little provision made for their livelihood. Yet despite the heavy hand of the victor, the masses in Islamic Europe remained faithful to the Eastern church.

Nonetheless, the ever present threat of persecution did nothing to soften Orthodoxy's traditional hostility toward Rome, nor did it stimulate strong movements toward Protestantism. Orthodoxy kept its faith, its liturgy, and its proud traditions. When, in the latter part of the sixteenth century, Jesuits in Ottoman Europe tried to strengthen relations between Rome and Constantinople, they met only scant success. In 1572, Patriarch Metriphanes, suspected of favoring reunion, was summarily excommunicated and deposed by Orthodox leaders. But the papacy persisted. Pope Gregory XIII in 1577 founded the College of St. Anthanasius in Rome for the training of Greek boys. Other schools were established by Jesuits within Ottoman territory. Such efforts, however, were largely unsuccessful, for the overwhelming majority of Orthodox adherents remained staunchly committed to its heritage.

Suggestions for Further Reading

Benz, Ernst. *Wittenberg und Byzanz.* Marburg: Elwert-Graefe und Unzer, 1949.

Bohnstedt, John. *The Infidel Scourge of God.* Philadelphia: American Philosophical Society, 1968.

Braudel, Fernand, *The Mediterranean and the Mediterranean World in the Age of Philip II,* Vol. 1. Translated by Sian Braudel. New York: Harper & Row, 1973.

Coles, Paul. *The Ottoman Impact on Europe.* London: Thames and Hudson, 1968.

Davies, R. T. *The Golden Century of Spain, 1501–1621.* New York: Harper & Row, A Harper Torchbook, 1965.

Elliott, J. H. *Imperial Spain, 1469–1716.* New York: Mentor Books, 1963.

*Indicates paperback edition.

Hauser, Henri. *La prépondérance espagnole.* Paris: Presses universitaires, 1948.

Lewis, Michael. *The Spanish Armada.* London: Pan, 1966.

Loomie, A. J. *The Spanish Elizabethans.* New York: Fordham University Press, 1971.

Lynch, John. *Spain under the Hapsburgs.* London: Oxford University Press, 1964.

***Mattingly, Garrett.** *The Armada.* Boston: Houghton Mifflin, 1962.

Merriman, R. B. *Suleiman the Magnificent, 1520–1566.* Cambridge, Mass.: Harvard University Press, 1948.

Nagy, Barnabas, ed. *Heinrich Bullingers Sendschreiben an die ungarischen Kirchen und Pastoren.* Budapest: Synodalkanzlei der Reformierten Kirchen, 1968.

Petri, Sir Charles. *Philip II of Spain.* New York: Norton, 1963.

Pierson, Peter. *Philip II of Spain.* Levittown, N. Y.: Transatlantic Arts, 1975.

Rouillard, C. D. *The Turk in French History, Thought, and Literature, 1520–1600.* Paris: Boivin, 1941.

***Rule, John C., and John J. TePaske.** *The Character of Philip II: The Problem of Moral Judgments in History.* Boston: D. C. Heath, 1963.

14

Europe After
a Century of
Religious Turmoil

As the century of the Reformation drew to a close, Europe concluded one of its most volatile and violent eras. A continent had been reshaped so drastically as to be scarcely recognizable. Religious, political, economic, and social structures had undergone changes so basic as to suggest that a new world had been forged.

In few areas was change so pronounced as in religion. Early in the century a lethargic papacy, more concerned about the arts and politics than about religion, had witnessed the rending of a religiously unified Western Europe; in the latter part of the century, a reinvigorated, resolute papacy demonstrated a martial vigor that not only stopped its opponents, but regained substantial territories. Repeatedly, the course of religious history had been inextricably intertwined with political vicissitudes, although political factors were not necessarily decisive in shaping religious settlements. Frequently, an aroused populace forced political and ecclesiastical establishments to conform to the popular will. Often individuals found it impossible to accommodate their consciences to the whims of princes and were thus compelled to form part of the long procession to the stake or executioner's block. For this was an age of robust if not always discriminating faith. Men lived, killed, and died for values that transcended temporal considerations. Catholics and Protestants championed their positions with a passion and zeal born of earnest conviction and unfaltering certainty. Many political as well as religious leaders shared Luther's sentiments that the well-being of a country did not depend upon its economic resources or its military might but upon its citizens of ''education, enlightenment, and character.'' The participant in the Reformation often demonstrated his conviction that he was helping to build God's kingdom upon earth; as such, he was the bearer of history. In this confidence he found meaning for his life, and dedication to what he regarded as a divinely entrusted responsibility. This belief in divine approval often strengthened national resolve, and accounts at least in part for the tenacity with

Europe in the Reformation

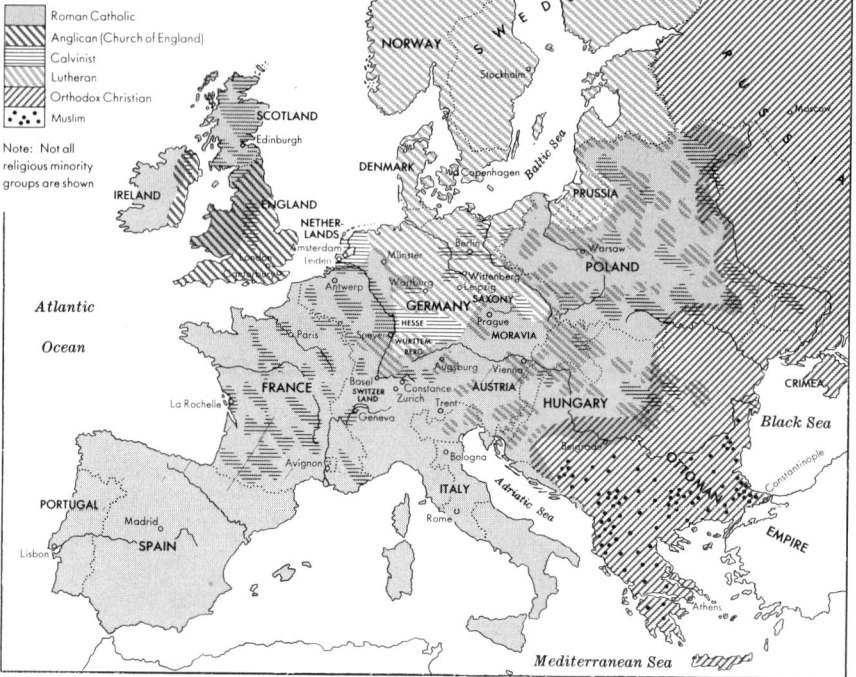

Legend:
- Roman Catholic
- Anglican (Church of England)
- Calvinist
- Lutheran
- Orthodox Christian
- Muslim

Note: Not all religious minority groups are shown

Map labels: NORWAY, Stockholm, SCOTLAND, Edinburgh, DENMARK, Copenhagen, IRELAND, ENGLAND, NETHERLANDS, Amsterdam, Leiden, Berlin, Münster, Warsaw, PRUSSIA, POLAND, Antwerp, Wittenberg, Leipzig, GERMANY, SAXONY, HESSE, Prague, MORAVIA, Paris, Speyer, WURTEM-BERG, Augsburg, Vienna, Basel, SWITZER-LAND, Constance, AUSTRIA, La Rochelle, Zurich, Trent, HUNGARY, CRIMEA, Geneva, Black Sea, Avignon, Bologna, OTTOMAN EMPIRE, Constantinople, PORTUGAL, Madrid, ITALY, Rome, Adriatic Sea, Lisbon, SPAIN, Athens, *Atlantic Ocean*, *Mediterranean Sea*

which some rulers sought their goals. Thus, political leaders such as Charles V, John Frederick, and Philip II, certain that God was on their side, were keenly disappointed when their relentlessly pursued objectives remained elusive.

The century of vigorous faith and debilitating confessional strife also witnessed profound changes in the political and economic arenas, for the centers of decisive power shifted to northern Europe. By the end of the century, Europe was markedly affected by the gradual retreat of Spanish power, as France, England, and the United Provinces loomed ever larger on the political horizon. As Philip II lay dying in the Escorial, the failure of his northern policy was becoming apparent. The goal of a unified Netherlands, subordinated to the Spanish crown, had proved to be unattainable, while the Peace of Vervins served notice that France would play an ever greater role in the coming era. At long last, a continental power had arisen to counterbalance Spanish influence. For the papacy, for the Italian states, for the Empire, the emergence of a united France, led by a vigorous Catholic king, was an event that was bound to shape European history. Finally, the papacy, freed from the overwhelming influence of Spain, was free to resume

282

its traditional role in striving to keep a balance of power that would assure maximal papal freedom.

LUTHERANISM: FROM DIVISION TO ERASTIAN UNITY

In the Empire political particularism had become all the more firmly entrenched by the religious divisions. Ferdinand I (1556–1564), determined to live in peace with the Protestant princes, declined to move as vigorously against Lutheranism as the papacy wished. He was more concerned about his Hapsburg lands than about eradication of heresy. His son and successor, Maximilian II (1564–1576), similarly showed a greater concern for dynastic than for Catholic interests. He tolerated Lutheranism in the hereditary Hapsburg lands, and attempted to strengthen his bonds with Lutheran princes. Only during the reign of Rudolph II (1576–1612) did the emperor embark upon a vigorous anti-Protestant program. Jesuits were now invited to rid the land of unacceptable religious practices.

Following the Peace of Augsburg, when Lutheranism enjoyed a large measure of toleration, it showed a strong tendency toward self-destruction. With the patriarchal figure of Luther gone, Melanchthon's supporters, commonly called "Philippists," championed a rather tolerant attitude toward other Protestants, while the rigid "Gnesiolutherans" became more Lutheran than Luther, and fought bitterly against any collaboration with the Calvinists. The two emphases within Lutheranism tended to be centered in the universities of Wittenberg and Jena, respectively. When the indomitable Flacius Illyricus attempted to mold Jena into an ever more intransigent bastion of extreme Lutheranism, Duke John Frederick finally deposed him together with a group of supporters, and assumed a greater measure of control of religious affairs. The duke now established a consistory to regulate excommunication. Religious strife was providing the opportunity for the expansion of Erastian policies.

Various Lutheran leaders, deeply disturbed by the continuing divisions and bitterness, attempted to effect a reconciliation. Again, political leaders provided much of the initiative. Duke Christopher of Wuerttemberg encouraged Jacob Andreae, chancellor of the University of Tuebingen, to pursue efforts to bring unity. Secular rulers such as Julius of Brunswick and Elector Augustus of Saxony, took similar action. By 1580, conferences and discussions had made possible the publication of the *Formula of Concord*. This massive document, largely the work of Martin Chemnitz, contained several Lutheran creedal statements including the Augsburg Confession of 1530, and further presented a candid analysis of differences among Lutherans together with conciliatory amplifications of doctrine. It was eventually adopted throughout most of Lutheran Germany and Scandinavia. Lutheranism had substantially recovered its earlier unity; significantly, however, theological problems had been resolved in large part because of intervention by secular authorities. Church and state had been drawn ever more closely together, a development not at all unwelcome to Lutheran theologians. Protected in this manner, Lutheranism had successfully maintained its identity and had resisted efforts to align itself with either Calvinism or Catholicism.

CATHOLIC RESURGENCE

The consolidation of Lutheranism was paralleled by a growing Catholic determination to take decisive measures against Protestantism in all of its forms. Throughout the latter part of the century, Philip of Spain attempted with only limited success to persuade the emperor to take stronger measures against non-Catholics. Diplomats such as Guillen de San Clemente, Spanish ambassador to Prague in the 1580s and 1590s, systematically organized aristocratic support for stronger policies against the Protestants. Many members of the nobility were prepared to live with increased Spanish influence at the court if the only alternative was the continued advance of heresy.

In Poland, the end of the century saw a significant resurgence of Catholic influence. In 1575, after Henry of Anjou returned to France to claim his throne, Stephen Bathory was elected Polish king. Since 1571, he had been prince of Transylvania; now he moved into a larger arena. As a Catholic king, he urged reform in accordance with the decrees of Trent, but at the same time he refused to use coercion to eradicate Protestantism. In accepting the Confederation of Warsaw, he agreed that Catholicism should be extended only "by instruction and good example." Meanwhile he pursued a vigorous policy against Russia that, after seven years of warfare, resulted in the cession by Tsar Ivan IV of large sections of Livonia (1582). By the time Stephen Bathory died in 1586, he had substantially expanded both Polish boundaries and Catholic influence. Under his successor, Sigismund III, Jesuits were encouraged to continue their program of expansion; they could already boast of having founded a dozen colleges. Then, with the death of the Swedish king John III in 1592, Sigismund became heir to that throne. When he attempted to restore Catholicism in Sweden, the estates resisted and eventually deposed him (1599). Scandinavia would remain staunchly Lutheran.

Throughout much of western and northern Europe, the religious scene was a mixture of Catholic stalemate and success. France was safely Catholic, although the Calvinists there enjoyed an unusually large measure of freedom. The southern part of the Netherlands was solidly Catholic, while the north, the United Provinces, had become officially Protestant. In Germany, disputes within Lutheranism, coupled with inroads by Calvinism, kept Protestantism divided. Bavaria, like the Hapsburg possessions, was characterized by a repressive Catholicism that gradually choked out Protestant elements. A resurgent Catholicism was also forcing Protestantism to retreat in Hungary. Protestantism remained firmly dominant in England, Scotland, and substantial sections of Switzerland; In addition, it retained some measure of influence in large parts of Bohemia and Transylvania.

THE ECONOMIC SCENE

Especially during the latter part of the sixteenth century, economic expansion proceeded more rapidly in northern Europe than in the Mediterranean states. The Spanish bankruptcies of 1557, 1575, and 1597 dramatically demonstrated that Philip's political and military ambitions were beyond his economic resources. Despite steadily rising profits from overseas trade, Spain's colonial undertakings did not prove sufficient to finance protracted military campaigns in the Mediterranean, in the Netherlands, and against England. Simultaneously, other powers were rising to challenge the maritime supremacy of Spain. The northern European states were not only making even deeper inroads into formerly Spanish trading lanes—they were also developing new trade routes across the Atlantic. When the century opened, probably the only European cities with a population of more than 100,000 were Constantinople, Paris, Naples, Milan, and Venice. By 1600, London, Lisbon, Seville, Palermo, Antwerp, and Amsterdam had joined the list. Significantly, most of these cities were ports and five of the new metropolises were centers of Atlantic trade. Here was a striking indication that commerce, influence, and power were moving northward. This development could not be discounted, especially in light of the fact that the stronghold of Protestantism was also in the north.

Everywhere the growth of cities reflected both increasing population pressure and changing economic patterns. In most areas of Europe, population growth exceeded productivity increases, so that inflation became a common problem. The rise in prices, as in Spain and France, was often accompanied by the stress of war. Sometimes, as in the French civil wars, peasants were glad to flee the countryside in the hope of finding a more secure place in the city. Enclosure movements, resulting from increased demands for wool, also decreased the need for peasant labor, thus again adding to population pressures in the towns. More often than not, the urban centers were unable to provide adequate employment for the dislocated population. Numerous revolts during the century demonstrated that existing institutions were finding it very difficult to cope with changing social pressures. The *Germania*[1] in Valencia, the Peasants' War in Germany, Kett's Rebellion in England, the *croquants* in France, all were expressions of seething discontent that could be expected to erupt at any time.

The social ferment among the peasants and urban workers was closely related

---

[1]The Germania (brotherhood) was a violently revolutionary urban movement (1519–1522) in which artisans and town laborers rose against the nobility. The city of Valencia was temporarily seized and nearby estates of the nobles devastated.

to tensions among the upper classes. Power struggles between king and nobility were common. In the Empire, the nobles successfully resisted attempts to enhance imperial control. In Spain, the power of the crown increased as monarchs effectively and vigorously championed the authority of the central government. In France, a bitter struggle among factions of the nobility lent credence to Jean Bodin's plea for a strong king who would be able to hold the nation together and save it from destruction by an enraged aristocracy. By the end of the century, the house of Bourbon was well on its way toward an ever stronger, centralized monarchy, and the French nobility as well as local self-government, were suffering a marked decline in influence. In England, the decline of the aristocracy did not result in a corresponding increase in the power of the monarch, for the House of Commons, largely through its control over taxation, strengthened the posture of Parliament. Some contemporaries charged that the monarch was deliberately aiding the middle class in an effort to weaken the aristocracy. Be that as it may, by the end of the century, the House of Lords was less powerful than it had been in 1500. And other factors, such as the elimination of abbots from the upper house and the creation by the crown of new peers, further weakened the old aristocracy.

THE WORLD OF LEARNING

The religious controversies of the sixteenth century had a marked impact on learning and educational patterns. Both Catholic and Protestant leaders quickly concluded that education would be a deciding factor in shaping the new society. Men such as Luther, Melanchthon, Calvin, Loyola, and Canisius were convinced that the struggle for the minds of men must be waged and won in the institutions of learning. Not surprisingly, the second half of the century saw the establishment of numerous schools and universities. Since the motivating force was largely religion, theology came to occupy a prominent place alongside law and medicine in the curriculum. At the same time, the emphasis upon biblical study stimulated the study of Greek and Hebrew, as well as the publication of numerous translations of the Scriptures. Although Luther's work in this area was of paramount significance, other noted efforts in the vernacular exerted a profound influence. Various English translations of the Bible—the Geneva (1560), the Bishops' (1568), and the Rheims (1582) versions—reflected Calvinist, Anglican, and Catholic tendencies. Scholars such as Lefèvre d'Etaples and Pierre-Robert Olivétan endeavored to introduce French translations. Similar efforts were made for their respective languages by Danish, Swedish, Magyar, Bohemian, Polish, and other scholars. Theological study and controversy were increasingly conducted in the vernacular.

Neither did the reformer or Catholic resurgent overlook the importance of a good grammar school education. Johann Sturm's famous academy at Strasbourg inspired numerous imitations. Although Sturm's school had attempted to adapt humanist ideals to religious goals, other schools, including those at Lausanne and

Geneva, determined to use Sturm's pedagogy to produce zealous Protestants. Jesuit teachers used similar techniques to train effective champions of their faith. However, all of these grammar schools had in common an emphasis on the study of Latin and rhetoric and a desire to inculcate religious zeal.

Since education was increasingly viewed as didactic, the earlier cosmopolitanism of university towns tended to disappear. Professors were expected to propound only accepted views; increasingly, universities became centers serving the interest of the local prince and the territorial church. Similarly, self-respecting princes felt it necessary to have at least one university under their domination.

Advocates of various religious persuasions also used disciplines other than theology to lend credence to their views. Thus, in the *Magdeburg Centuries* (1559–1574) history was the vehicle used to demonstrate the corruption of the papacy and the Catholic church. A similarly biased history was the basis of Cardinal Caesar Baronius' reply, the *Annales Ecclesiastici* (1588–1607). Similarly partisan preconceptions characterized the historical works of writers such as John Knox and John Foxe. Political beliefs also colored historical analysis, as when the staunchly pro-Venetian Pietro Paolo Sarpi (1552–1623), although a Catholic, published a vigorously anti-papal *History of the Council of Trent* (1619). Such literary propagandistic efforts were an expression of nationalist and religious fervor, and were not directly related to university education, for history was not included in the curriculum.

As the century drew to a close, there was at least a semblance of peace over the continent. The death of Philip II presaged an end to the war in the Netherlands. In France, the bloody civil strife had ended, and a Catholic king had granted toleration to Protestants. Across the channel, a revered queen ruled over a kingdom more interested in burgeoning commerce than in continental religious rivalries. In the Empire, an ominous quiet prevailed over kingdom and duchy, as prince and elector viewed each other with a suspicion unmitigated by temporary truce.

Europe in 1600 was a society characterized by competing ideas and diverse faiths. The continent was far from homogeneous in any respect, and the successful challenge to a traditional religious system accelerated the quest for new approaches to problems in all facets of life. Some leaders were coming to recognize that such a quest presupposed at least a measure of personal liberty and freedom of conscience. Thus, paradoxically, while some voices insisted that the ills of a divided continent could be resolved only through the greater exercise of power, others confidently asserted their faith in the worth of the individual, and his right to make decisions in an ever widening arena. At the beginning of the seventeenth century, the outcome of the clash between these views was far from certain. What was apparent, however, was that the past one hundred years had left a legacy of vitality and dynamism that perhaps outweighed the bitterness and frustration. Continuing, if unpredictable, change was ensured in a vibrant society.

Suggestions for Further Reading

Chaplin, F. K. *The Effects of the Reformation on Ideals of Life and Conduct*. Cambridge: Heffer and Sons, 1927.

Dawson, Christopher. *The Dividing of Christendom*. New York: Sheed & Ward, 1965.

Forell, George W., et al. *Luther and Culture*. Decorah, Ia.: Luther College, 1960.

Green, R. W., ed. *Protestantism and Capitalism*. Boston: D. C. Heath, 1959.

*Holl, Karl. *The Cutural Significance of the Reformation*. Translated by Karl and Barbara Hertz and John Lichtblau. New York: Meridian Books, 1966.

*Kitch, M. J. *Capitalism and the Reformation*. London: Longmans, Green, 1967.

Lortz, Joseph. *The Reformation: A Problem for Today*. Translated by J. C. Dwyer. Westminister, Md.: Newman, 1964.

Murray, R. H. *The Political Consequences of the Reformation*. New York: Russell and Russell, 1960.

Nickerson, Hoffman. *The Loss of Unity*. London: Sidgwick and Jackson, 1961.

O'Brien, G. A. *An Essay on the Economic Effects of the Reformation*. New York: Kelley, 1970.

Pauck, Wilhelm. *The Heritage of the Reformation*. Glencoe, Ill.: Free Press, 1961.

Pelikan, Jaroslav. *Obedient Rebels: Catholic Substance and Protestant Principle in Luther's Reformation*. New York: Harper & Row, 1964.

*Troeltsch, Ernst. *Protestantism and Progress*. Translated by W. Montgomery. Boston: Beacon Press, 1958.

*Indicates paperback edition.

CHRONOLOGY OF SIGNIFICANT EVENTS
IN REFORMATION EUROPE

1483	Birth of Martin Luther at Eisleben
1484	Birth of Huldrych Zwingli at Wildhaus
1491	Birth of Ignatius Loyola
1498	Burning of Savonarola
1500	Birth of Charles, future emperor, at Ghent
1506	Beginning of reconstruction of St. Peter's Rome
1509	Accession of Henry VIII
	Erasmus writes his *In Priase of Folly*
1512	Fifth Lateran Council begins
1513	Leo X elected pope
1515	Charles declared of age in the Netherlands
	Accession of Francis I of France
1516	Charles proclaimed sovereign of Spain
	Publication of Thomas More's *Utopia*
	Publication of Erasmus's Greek New Testament
1517	Charles lands in Spain; death of Cardinal Jimenes
	Conclusion of Fifth Lateran Council
	Publication of Luther's Ninety-five Theses
1519	Charles V elected emperor
	Leipzig debate between Luther and Eck
1520	*Exsurge domine* threatens Luther with excommunication
	"Bloodbath of Stockholm"; Gustav Vasa leads Swedish rebellion against Christian II
	Revolt of Spanish *communeros*
1521	Diet of Worms; Charles issues edict against Luther
	Beginning of war between Charles V and Francis I
	Turks under Suleiman I conquer Belgrade
	Death of Leo X
1522	Adrian VI elected pope
	Treaty of Windsor between Charles V and Henry VIII
	Publication of Luther's New Testament
1523	Death of Adrian VI; election of Clement VII
	Defeat of Sickingen's forces in Knights' War
	First Lutherans to be burned as heretics die in Brussels
	Christian II driven from Denmark
	Gustav Vasa proclaimed Swedish king
	Reformation and disputations in Zurich
1524	Peasants' Revolt in Germany
	Francis I conquers Milan

1525   First Anabaptist congregation formed in Zollikon
         Imperial forces defeat France at Pavia
         Peasants defeated; Muentzer executed
         Albert of Hohenzollern adopts Lutheranism and secularizes
            lands of Teutonic Knights
1526   Peace of Madrid between Charles V and Francis I
         Battle of Mohacs, with death of Louis II of Hungary;
         John Zapolya and Ferdinand of Austria claim Hungarian
            throne
         Diet of Speyer leaves regulation of religious matters
            in hands of princes, pending a general council
         Zurich decrees death for Anabaptists
1527   Imperial army sacks Rome
         Diet of Vaesteras introduces Reformation into Sweden
1528   Basel and Bern introduce Reformation
         Capuchin Order founded
         Strasbourg introduces Reformation
1529   Diet of Speyer issues warning against Lutherans;
         Lutheran princes "protest"
         Marburg Colloquy between Luther and Zwingli
         Wolsey fails to secure papal divorce for Henry VIII
            and is disgraced
         Beginning of Reformation Parliament in England
         Turks under Suleiman II besiege Vienna
1530   Clement VII crowns Charles at Bologna
         Diet of Augsburg; reading of Augsburg Confession; Charles urges
         Clement to call a general council
         Protestants form League of Schmalkald
1531   Ferdinand elected king of the Romans
         Parliament recognizes Henry as "supreme head" of the
            church in England
         Zwingli dies on the battlefield at Cappel
1532   Imperial Diet offers temporary concessions to the Protestants
         Submission of the English clergy
1533   Henry VIII marries Anne Boleyn; Parliament passes Act of Appeals
1534   Anabaptists gain control in Muenster
         Death of Clement VII; election of Paul III
         Loyola founds the Society of Jesus
         Act of Supremacy declares Henry head of the English church
         Luebeck aids Sweden in war with Denmark
         French "placards" denouncing Catholic faith bring swift royal
            retaliation
1535   Charles V conquers Tunis
         Fall of the Muenster "kingdom"; Anabaptists massacred

1536   Francis I and Suleiman II form alliance; renewed war between Charles
        and Francis
        The "Pilgrimage of Grace"
1536   Paul III summons general council to meet in Mantua; Protestants call for
        council in Germany
        Publication of John Calvin's *Institutes*
        Death of Erasmus
1537   Paul III calls for general council to meet in Vicenza
        but receives little support
1538   Reformation established in Geneva; Calvin and Farel
        expelled
1540   Edict of Fontainebleau serves notice that heresy in
        France will be systematically attacked
        Paul III gives official sanction to Society of Jesus
1541   Diet of Regensburg fails to provide religious compromise
        Calvin returns in triumph to Geneva; *Ecclesiastical
        Ordinances* are issued
        Publication of Loyola's *Spiritual Exercises*
1542   Renewed war between Charles V and Francis I
        Paul III issues call for general council
1543   Charles defeats duke of Cleves, adds duchy to Hapsburg possessions
1544   Diet of Speyer agrees to help Charles against French
        and Turks; princes to determine religious policies until
        general council held
        Peace of Crépy between Charles and Francis
1545   Council of Trent begins
1546   Death of Luther
        Schmalkaldic War begins
1547   Death of Henry VIII; accesssion of Edward VI
        Pope transfers council from Trent to Bologna
        Death of Francis I; accession of Henry II
        Charles crushes Schmalkaldic League
1548   The Augsburg Interim attempts to impose religious
        compromise on Empire
1549   Kett's Rebellion in England
        First English Book of Common Prayer
        Death of Paul III; election of Julius III
1550   Duke of Northumberland wrests regency from duke of Somerset
1551   Second session of Trent begins
        Charles V and Henry II resume war
1552   Henry II, in alliance with German Protestants, gains
        bishoprics of Metz, Toul, and Verdun
        Charles is forced to flee from Innsbruck
        Second session of Trent ends

	Treaty of Passau recognizes Lutheranism
1553	Mary Tudor succeeds Edward VI; reintroduces Catholicism
1554	Wyatt's Rebellion
	Philip, son of Charles V, marries Mary Tudor, but Parliament refuses to recognize him as king
1555	Paul IV elected pope
	Peace of Augsburg brings recognition of *cuius regio eius religio* principle
	Charles abdicates sovereignty of Netherlands
1556	Charles abdicates sovereignty of Spain and Empire; Ferdinand becomes emperor; Philip II becomes ruler of Spain, Netherlands, Naples, and overseas empire
	Death of Loyola
1557	Scottish "Covenanters" revolt; support Reformation
1558	Turkish fleet sails freely in western Mediterranean; attacks Naples and Minorca
	Charles dies in monastery at Yuste
	Elizabeth succeeds to English throne
1559	Papal *Index* established
	Peace of Cateau-Cambrésis between Spain and France
	Parliament passes Act of Uniformity
1560	Royal edicts establish temporary partial religious toleration in France
	Scottish Parliament establishes Reformation
	Turks defeat Spanish-Italian fleet off Tunisian coast
1561	Colloquy of Poissy fails to bring religious harmony to France
1562	First French War of religion begins
	Third session of Trent opens
1563	Peace of Amboise brings truce in French religious war
	Council of Trent concludes its sessions
	Publication of the Thirty-nine Articles
1564	Death of Calvin
	Cardinal Granvelle dismissed from Netherlands Council of State
	Benedictus Deus gives papal sanction to Tridentine decrees
1566	Netherlands rebellion begins
	Suleiman conducts last campaign in Hungary
1567	Duke of Alva sets up Council of Troubles in Netherlands
	French religious war is renewed
1568	Egmont and Hoorn executed
	Morisco revolt in Granada
	Mary Queen of Scots flees to England
	Diet of Torda proclaims religious liberty in Transylvania

1570   Peace of St. Germain gives limited toleration and fortified cities
       to Huguenots
       Elizabeth excommunicated by Pius V
       Turks attack Cyprus
1571   Turks capture Cyprus
       Don Juan annihilates Turkish fleet at Lepanto
1572   Sea Beggars capture Brill
       St. Bartholomew's Massacre
1573   Requesens succeeds Alva in Netherlands
       Venice surrenders Cyprus to Turks
       Confederation of Warsaw affirms religious liberty
1574   Henry of Anjou, king of Poland, succeeds to French throne
1575   Stephen Bathory elected king of Poland
1576   Pacification of Ghent repudiates Spanish control
       French Catholic League formed to fight Huguenots
1578   Alexander Farnese appointed governor in Netherlands
1579   Netherlands divided: Catholic Union of Arras against
       Protestant Union of Utrecht
       Publication of *Vindiciae contra Tyrannos*
1580   Philip II conquers Portugal
       William of Orange proclaimed outlaw
       Formula of Concord published
1581   Declaration of Independence in Netherlands
1584   Assassination of William of Orange
1585   Philip II forms alliance with French Catholic League
1587   Mary Queen of Scots executed
1588   Catholic League gains control of Paris; Henry III flees
       Spanish Armada is defeated
       Duke of Guise is murdered
1589   Henry III is assassinated; Henry of Navarre fights for
       throne
1590   Spanish forces invade France
1593   Henry IV adopts Catholic faith
1594   Henry IV gains Paris
1596   United Provinces gain formal recognition from France
       and England
1597   Publication of Hooker's *Laws of Ecclesiastical Polity*
1598   Edict of Nantes establishes religious toleration in France
       Peace of Vervins ends war between France and Spain
       Death of Philip II
1603   Death of Elizabeth

RULERS OF REFORMATION EUROPE

I. The Holy Roman Empire
Maximilian I
(1493–1519)
Charles V (1519–1556)
Ferdinand I (1556–1564)
Maximilian II
(1564–1576)
Rudolph II (1576–1612)

II. The Ottoman Empire
Bayazid II (1481–1512)
Selim I (1512–1520)
Suleiman II (1520–1566)
Selim II (1566–1574)
Murad III (1574–1595)
Mohammed III
(1595–1603)

III. England
Henry VII (1485–1509)
Henry VIII (1509–1547)
Edward VI (1547–1553)
Mary I (1553–1558)
Elizabeth I (1558–1603)

IV. France
Charles VIII (1483–1498)
Louis XII (1498–1515)
Francis I (1515–1547)
Henry II (1547–1559)
Francis II (1559–1560)
Charles IX (1560–1574)
Henry III (1574–1589)
Henry IV (1589–1610)

V. Spain
Ferdinand (1479–1516)
and Isabella
(1474–1504)
Charles I (V) (1516–1556)
and Joanna
(1504–1555)

Philip II (1556–1598)
Philip III (1598–1621)

VI. The Papacy
Alexander VI (Borgia)
(1492–1503)
Pius III (Todeschini-
Piccolomini) (1503)
Julius II (della Rovere)
(1503–1513)
Leo X (Medici)
(1513–1521)
Adrian VI (Dedel)
(1522–1523)
Clement VII (Medici)
(1523–1534)
Paul III (Farnese)
(1534–1549)
Julius III (del Monte)
(1550–1555)
Marcellus II (Cervini)
(1555)
Paul IV (Carafa)
(1555–1559)
Pius IV (Medici)
(1559–1564)
Pius V (Ghisleri)
(1566–1572)
Gregory XIII
(Buoncompagni)
(1572–1585)
Sixtus V (Peretti)
(1585–1590)

Urban VII (Castagna) (1590)
Gregory XIV (Sfondrati)
(1590–1591)
Innocent IX (Facchinetti)
(1591)
Clement VIII
(Aldobrandini)
(1592–1605)

Index

Dacke, Nils, revolt of, 166
Dalarna, rebellion in, 164
Darnley, Lord, 155
Debrecen, 173–74
Denck, Hans, 121
Denmark, Reformation in, 160–63
Dérogeance, 5
Devai, Matyas. *See* Biró, Matyas
Devotio Moderna, 11–12
Discourse on Free Will, 77
Dominican order, 17, 33, 206
Doria, Andrea, admiral, 82, 275
Drake, Francis, 270
Dürer, Albrecht, 7, 19, 71
Dutch East India Company, 262

Ecclesiastical Ordinances (of Calvin), 142
Eck, Johann, 38–39, 42, 105
Eckhart, Johann (Meister), 29
Edinburgh, Treaty of, 153
Education, public, 140
Edward VI, king of England, 152, 190
Egmont, count of, 249, 255
Einsiedeln, 100
Eisenach, 25, 50
Eisleben, 24, 86
Elizabeth I, queen of England, 153, 195–98, 255
Enchiridion militis Christiani, 20
Enclosures, 4, 15
England: early reform movements in, 177–79; Reformation in, 177–98
Erasmus, Desiderius, 12, 15, 18–22, 39, 41, 48, 77, 100, 103, 106, 230, 248
Erastianism, 147, 230
Erastus, Thomas, 147
Erfurt, University of, 25–26, 39
Escorial, 273, 282
Estates, General, 134
Exsurge Domine, papal bull, 42, 228

Faber, Johann, 102
Farel, William, 140–41
Farnese, Alexander, 244, 257, 259
Farnese, family, 86
Farnese, Pier Luigi, 89
Favre, Pierre, 206, 208
Feltre, Vittorina da, 11
Ferdinand I, Holy Roman emperor, 64–66, 79, 81–82, 84–85, 90, 92–93, 123, 171, 217, 275, 283
Ferdinand, king of Spain, 47
Ficino, Marsilio, 11, 14
First Blast of the Trumpet, 152
Fish, Simon, 186
Fisher, John, bishop, 185
Flacius, Matthias, 90, 146, 283
Flodden Field, battle of, 150, 181
Formula of Concord, 283
Forty-three Articles, of Denmark, 161
Forty-two Articles, (1553), 192; of peasants, 58
Foundation of Christian Doctrine, 128
Foxe, John, 287
Francis, duke of Anjou, 242, 257–59
Francis, king of France, 16, 36, 48, 66, 77–78, 80, 82–83, 85, 89, 100, 135, 150
Francis II, king of France, 149, 152, 154, 236
Francis, duke of Guise, 152
Francis, bishop of Muenster, 86
Franciscan order, 17, 203
Franck, Sebastian, 129–30, 231
Franco-Gallia, 241
Franconia, 59, 92
Frankenhausen, 59
Frankfurt-am-Main, 58
Frankfurt Interim, 84
Frederick I, king of Denmark, 160–61
Frederick II, elector of the Palatinate, 86
Frederick III, elector of the Palatinate, 146–47
Frederick the Wise, elector of Saxony, 28, 32–33, 36–38, 42, 48, 50–51, 53, 60, 161
Freedom of the Christian Man, 41
Froschauer, Christopher, 101
Fuggers, 4, 33, 48

Gaismaier, Michael, 60
Gallicanism, 135, 209, 211, 218
Gallicius, Philip, 108
Gardiner, Stephen, bishop, 188, 190, 193
Geiler of Kaisersberg, Johann, 10
Gelassenheit, 123

Geneva, Academy of, 145, 232
Geneva, reformation in, 140–43
George, duke of Saxony, 38–39, 59, 66, 72, 82
Germania, 12, 285
Geyer, Florian, 59
Ghent, Pacification of, 256–57
Glarus, 98–99, 112
Gnesio-Lutherans, 90
Goetz von Berlichingen, 57, 59
Granvelle, Antoine, cardinal, 249–51
Great Schism, 9
Grebel, Conrad, 103, 117–18, 123, 231
Gregory XIII, pope, 240, 279
Grey, Lady Jane, 192–93
Grocyn, William, 14
Groote, Gerard, 11
Guilds, 70, 98, 106, 125
Gustav Vasa, king of Sweden, 160, 163–67

Haetzer, Ludwig, 117, 121
Haller, Berchtold, 105–6
Hamilton, Patrick, 151
Hanseatic League, 4, 159, 163, 178
Hapsburg-Valois rivalry, 77–79, 85
Hedio, Caspar, 141
Heidelberg, University of, 146
Heidelberg, Catechism, 146–47
Held, Matthew, 83
Helegesen, Paul, 161
Helvetic Confession, second, 113, 146
Henry, duke of Brunswick-Wolfenbuettel, 85
Henry VIII: attack on Luther, 41; foreign relations, 78, 83–85; king of England, 48, 128, 150, 179–89, 230; reformation under, 184–89
Henry II, king of France, 80, 92, 148–49, 214, 236
Henry III, king of France, 242, 244, 259, 270, 272
Henry IV, king of France, 148, 240, 243–46, 272
Henry, duke of Saxony, 82
Heptameron, 16
Het Offer des Heeren, 249
Hofmann, Melchior, 125
Hofmeister, Sebastian, 108
Holbein, Hans, the Younger, 11
Holy League, 277
Hooker, Richard, 197
Horn, count of, 255
Hôpital, Michel de l', 150, 237
Hotman, François, 148
Hubmaier, Balthasar, 103, 117, 121, 123, 230–31
Hugo, bishop of Constance, 101
Huguenots, 140, 148–49, 209, 217, 236–46, 255, 270
Humanism, 11–22; English, 14–15; French, 16–17; German, 12–14; Spanish, 17, 18; and reformation, 76–77
Hungary, reformation in, 169–75
Hus, Jan, 35, 39
Hussites, 40
Hut, Hans, 121
Hutten, Ulrich von, 14, 55–56, 103
Hutter, Jacob, 123

Idelette de Bure, 141
Imperial Cameral Tribunal (*Reichskammergericht*), 47, 82, 89
Imperial Governing Council (*Reichsregiment*), 47
Index of Prohibited Books, 227, 265
Indulgences, papal, 31–35
Ingolstadt, University of, 38
Innocent III, pope, 224
Inns of Court, 15
Inquisition: Roman, 223–27; Spanish, 224, 251
Institutes of the Christian Religion, 138–39, 148
Isabella, queen of Spain, 17, 47
Islam, and Christianity, 274–79
Ivan IV, tsar, 175–76, 278, 284

James IV, king of Scotland, 150, 181
James V, king of Scotland, 150–51
James VI, king of Scotland, 155
Jeanne d'Albret, 238
Jeremias II, patriarch, 278
Jesuit order, 204–9
Jimenes de Cisneros, 17–18
Joachim I, elector of Brandenburg, 32
Joachim II, elector of Brandenburg, 85
John, elector of Saxony, 66–67, 72
John Frederick, elector of Saxony, 58, 85, 87–88, 92, 228
John Sigismund, elector of Brandenburg, 147, 276
John Sigismund, king of Hungary, 85, 234
Joinville, Treaty of, 243
Juan of Austria, Don, 257, 268–70